Vol. 5
The Slashers

Story and Art by **Norihiro Yagi**

D054356?

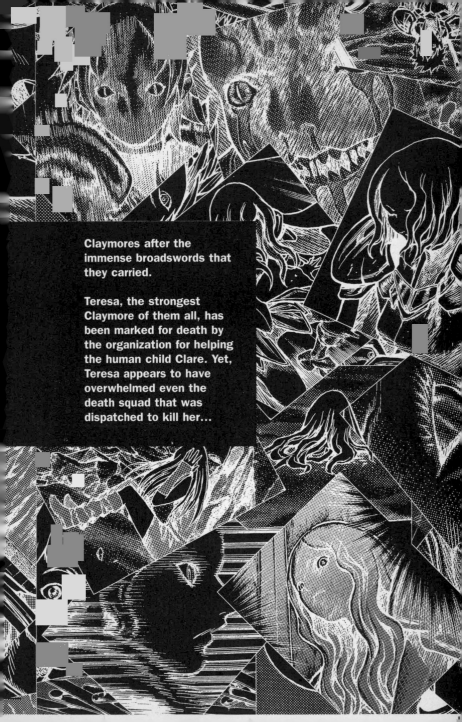

Claymores after the immense broadswords that they carried.

Teresa, the strongest Claymore of them all, has been marked for death by the organization for helping the human child Clare. Yet, Teresa appears to have overwhelmed even the death squad that was dispatched to kill her...

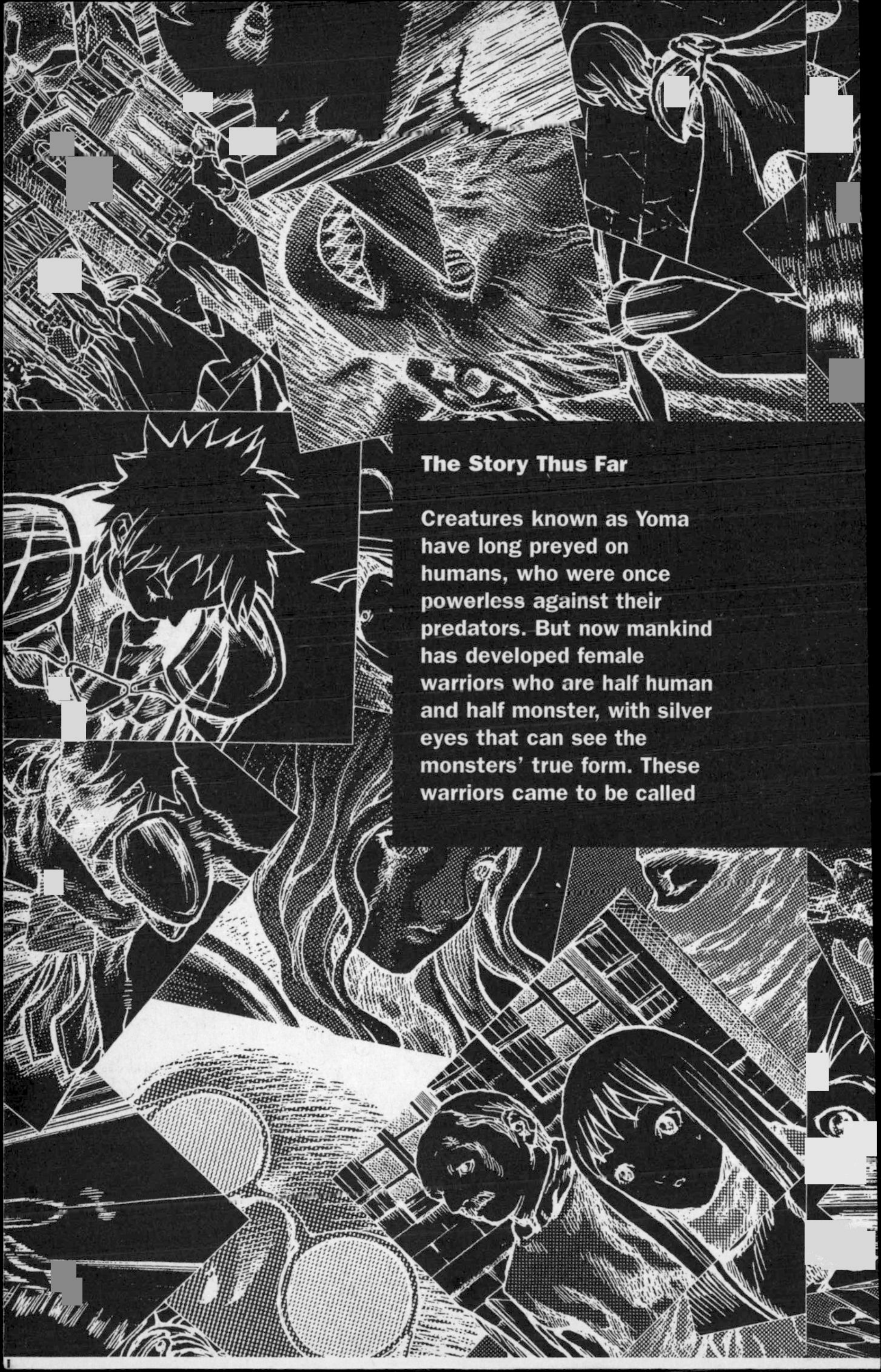

The Story Thus Far

Creatures known as Yoma have long preyed on humans, who were once powerless against their predators. But now mankind has developed female warriors who are half human and half monster, with silver eyes that can see the monsters' true form. These warriors came to be called

Claymore

クレイモア

Vol. 5

CONTENTS

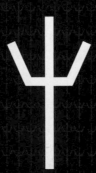

Scene 22: Marked for Death, Part 5

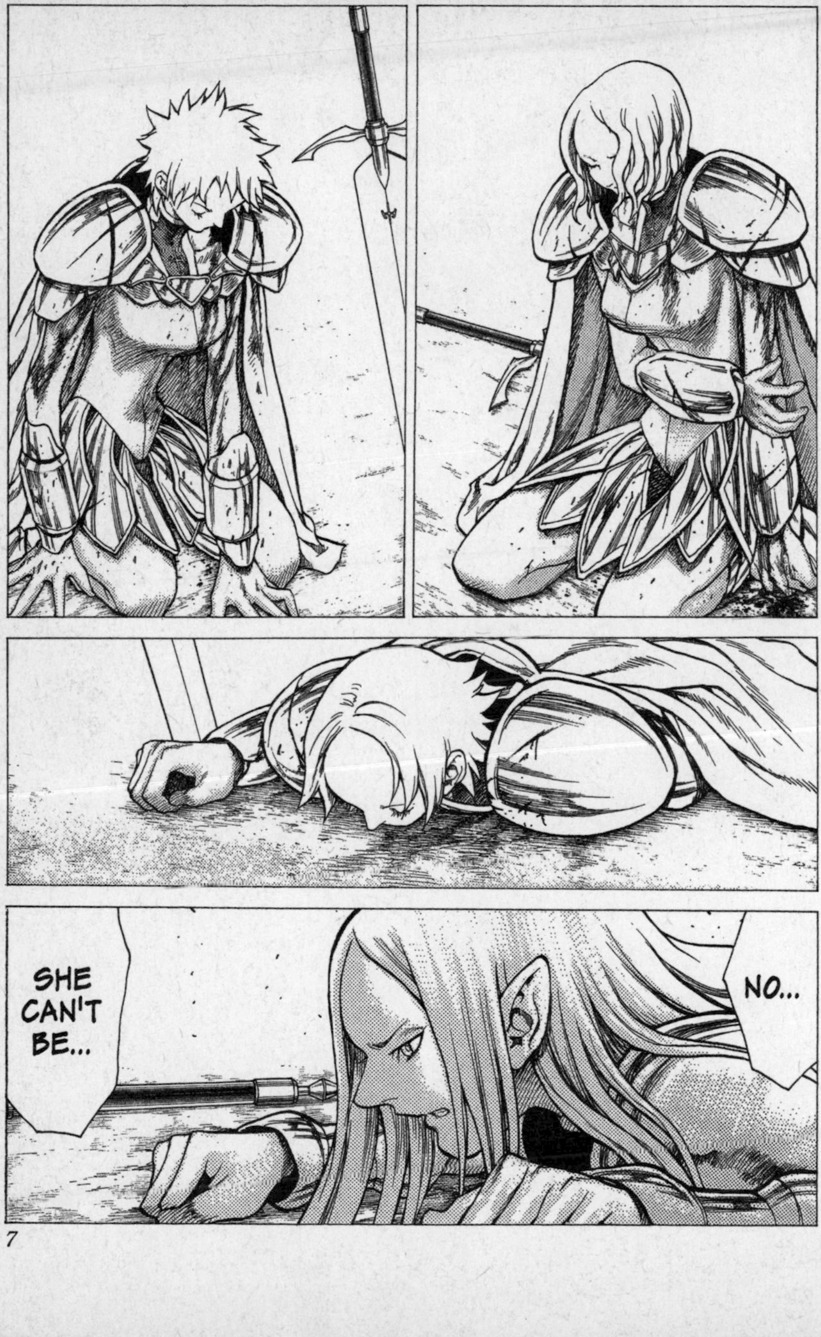
NO...
SHE CAN'T BE...

SCENE 22: MARKED FOR DEATH, PART 5

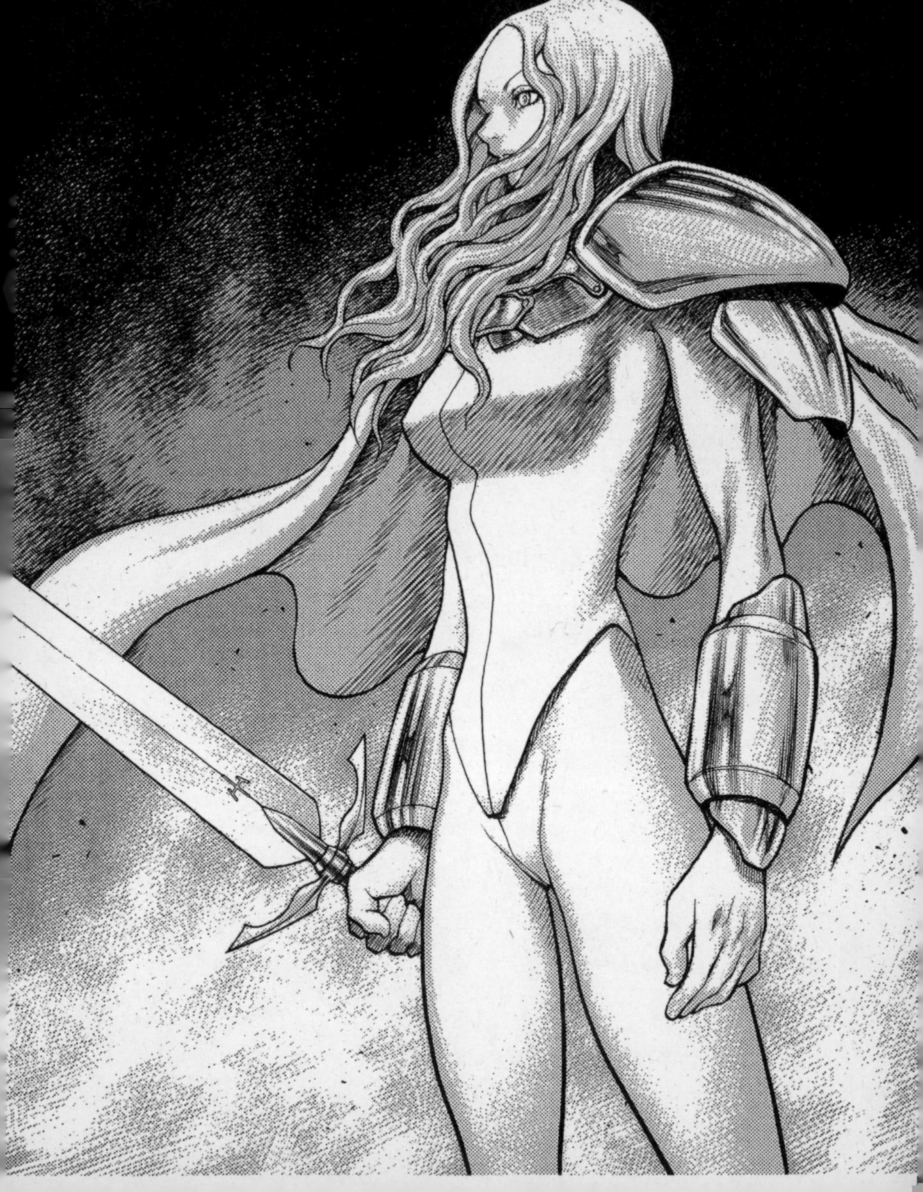

READ THIS WAY

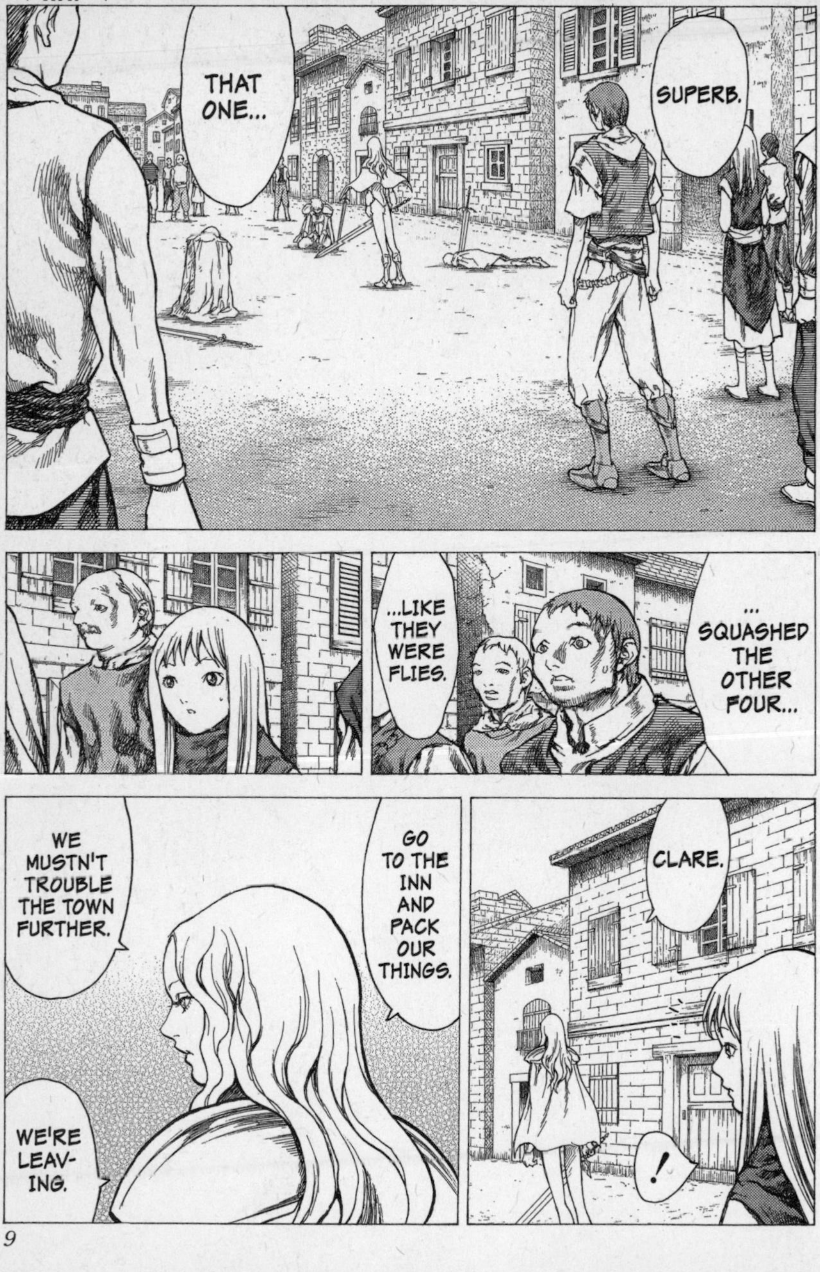
SUPERB.
THAT ONE...
... SQUASHED THE OTHER FOUR...
...LIKE THEY WERE FLIES.
CLARE.
!
GO TO THE INN AND PACK OUR THINGS.
WE MUSTN'T TROUBLE THE TOWN FURTHER.
WE'RE LEAVING.

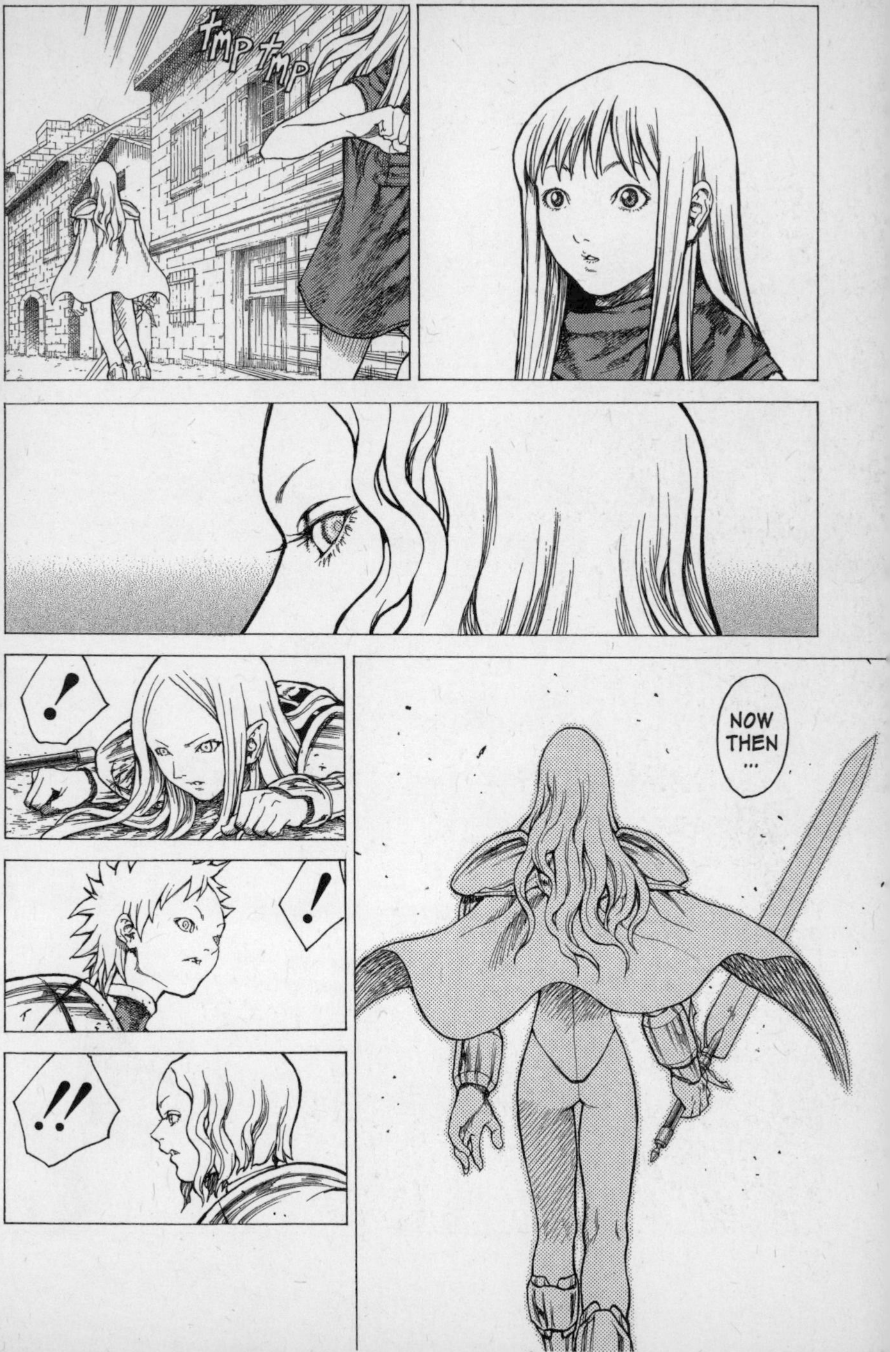
tmp tmp
NOW THEN ...
!
!
!!

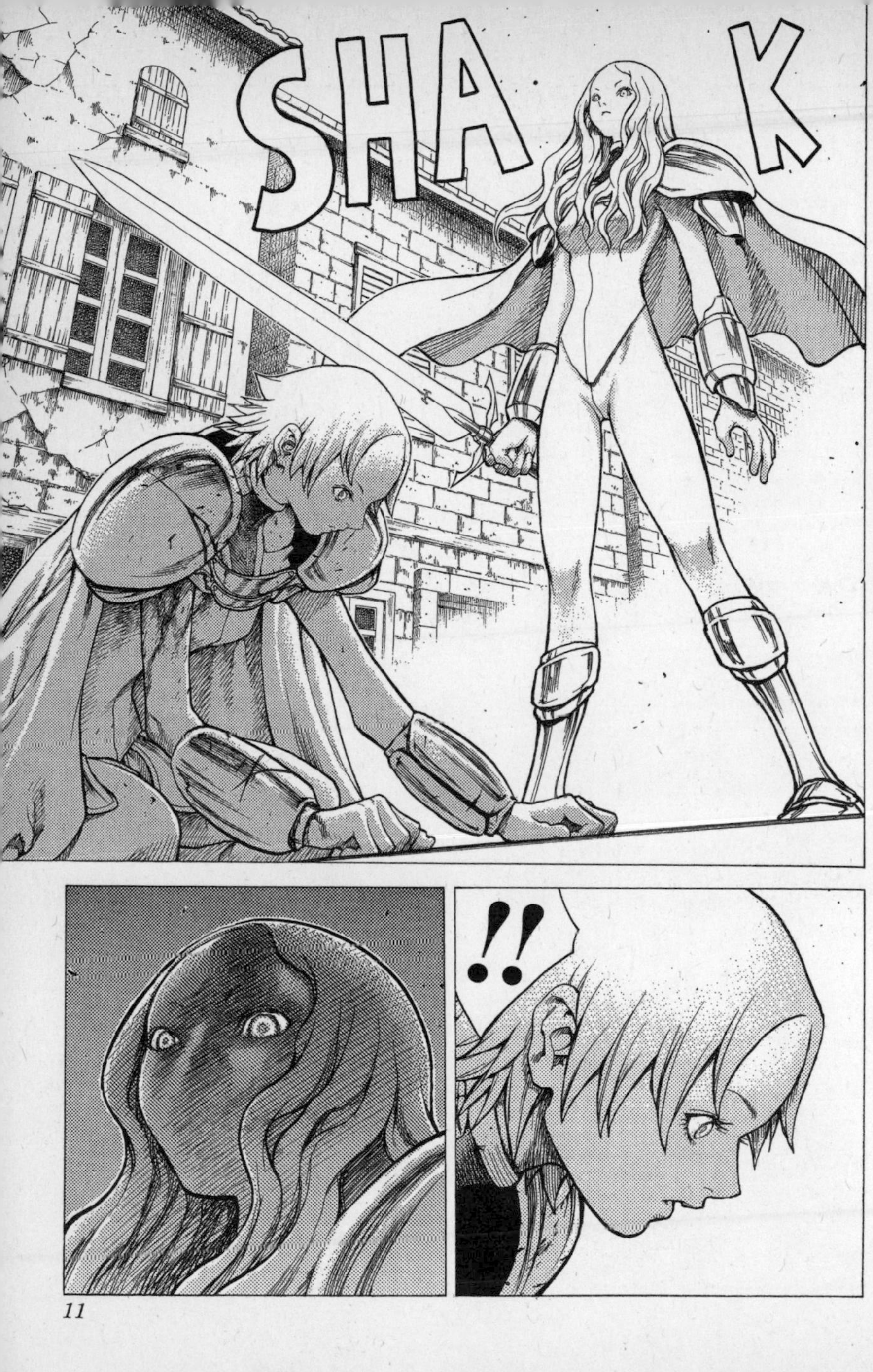
SHAK
!!

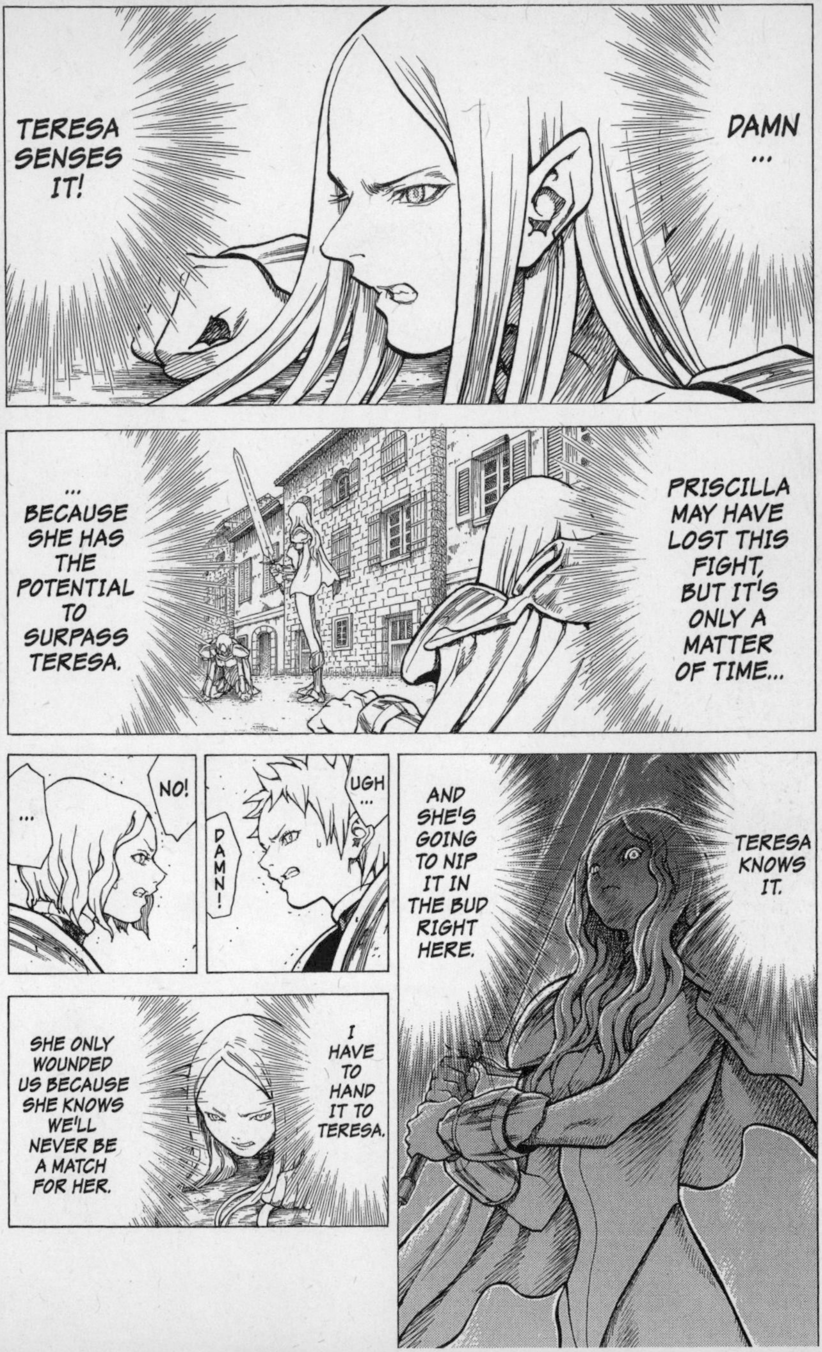
DAMN ...
TERESA SENSES IT!
PRISCILLA MAY HAVE LOST THIS FIGHT, BUT IT'S ONLY A MATTER OF TIME...
... BECAUSE SHE HAS THE POTENTIAL TO SURPASS TERESA.
TERESA KNOWS IT.
AND SHE'S GOING TO NIP IT IN THE BUD RIGHT HERE.
UGH ...
DAMN!
NO!
...
I HAVE TO HAND IT TO TERESA.
SHE ONLY WOUNDED US BECAUSE SHE KNOWS WE'LL NEVER BE A MATCH FOR HER.

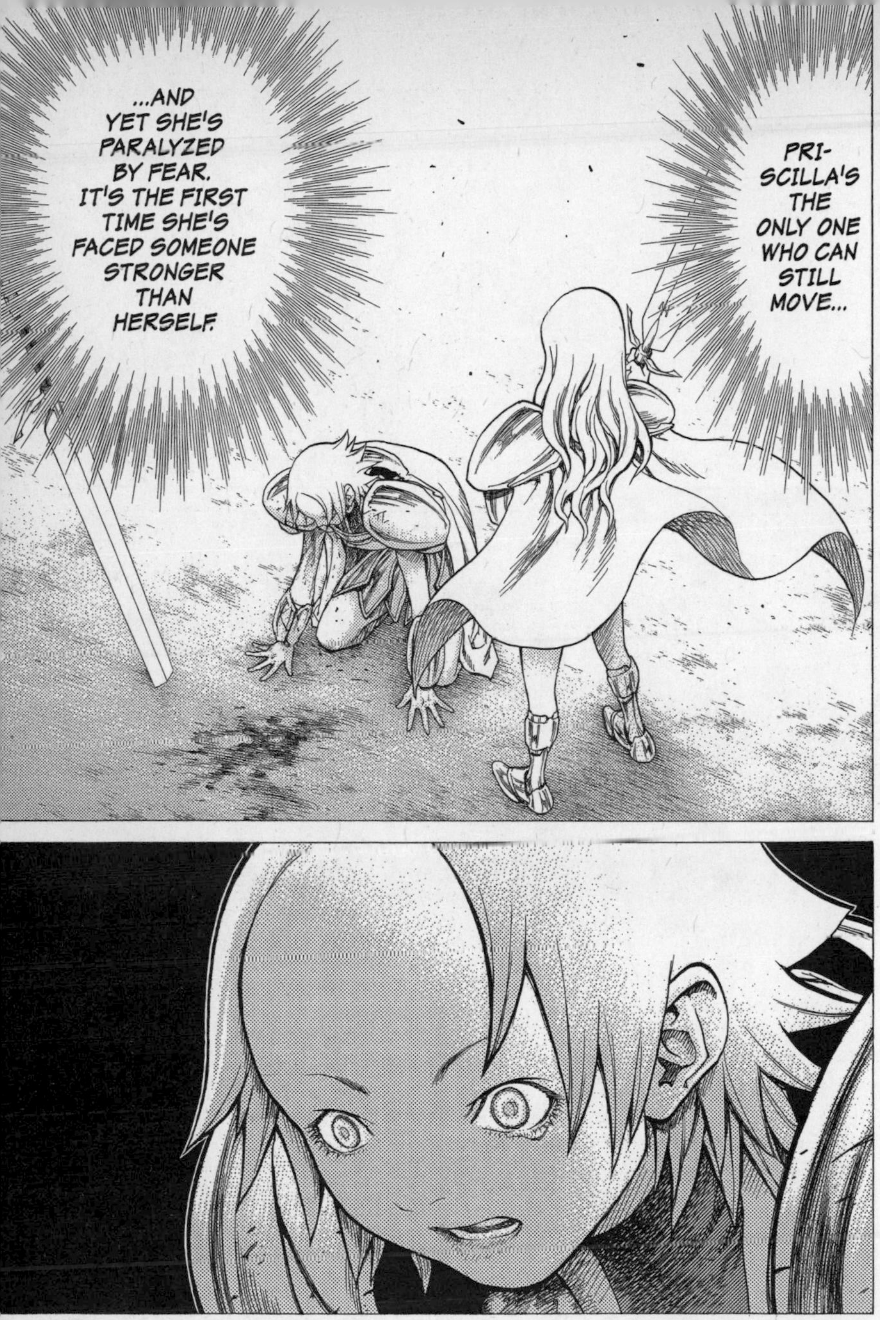
PRI-SCILLA'S THE ONLY ONE WHO CAN STILL MOVE...
...AND YET SHE'S PARALYZED BY FEAR. IT'S THE FIRST TIME SHE'S FACED SOMEONE STRONGER THAN HERSELF.

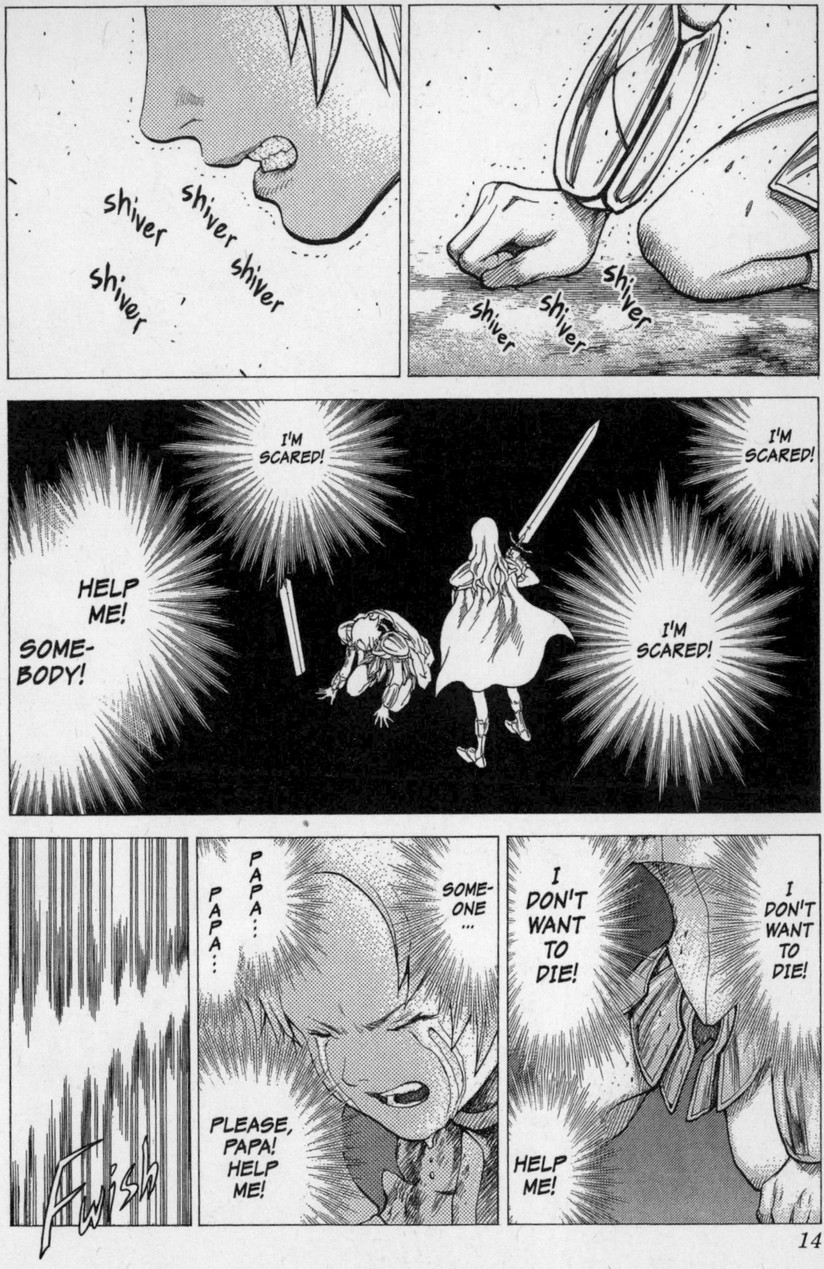
shiver
shiver
shiver
shiver
shiver
shiver
shiver
I'M SCARED!
I'M SCARED!
I'M SCARED!
HELP ME! SOME-BODY!
I DON'T WANT TO DIE!
I DON'T WANT TO DIE!
HELP ME!
SOME-ONE...
PAPA...
PAPA...
PLEASE, PAPA! HELP ME!
Fwish

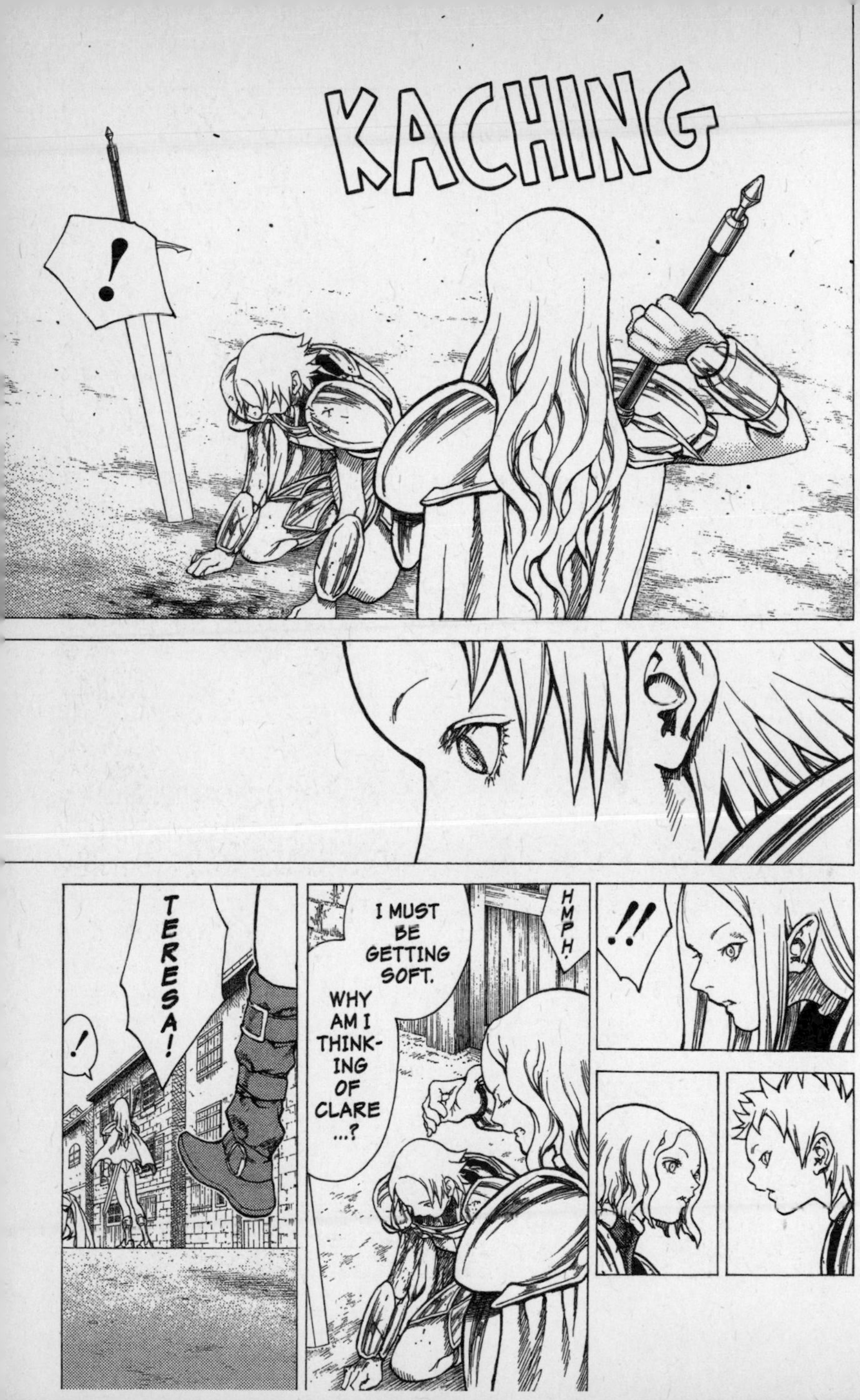
KACHING
!
!!
HMPH!
I MUST BE GETTING SOFT.
WHY AM I THINKING OF CLARE ...?
TERESA!
!

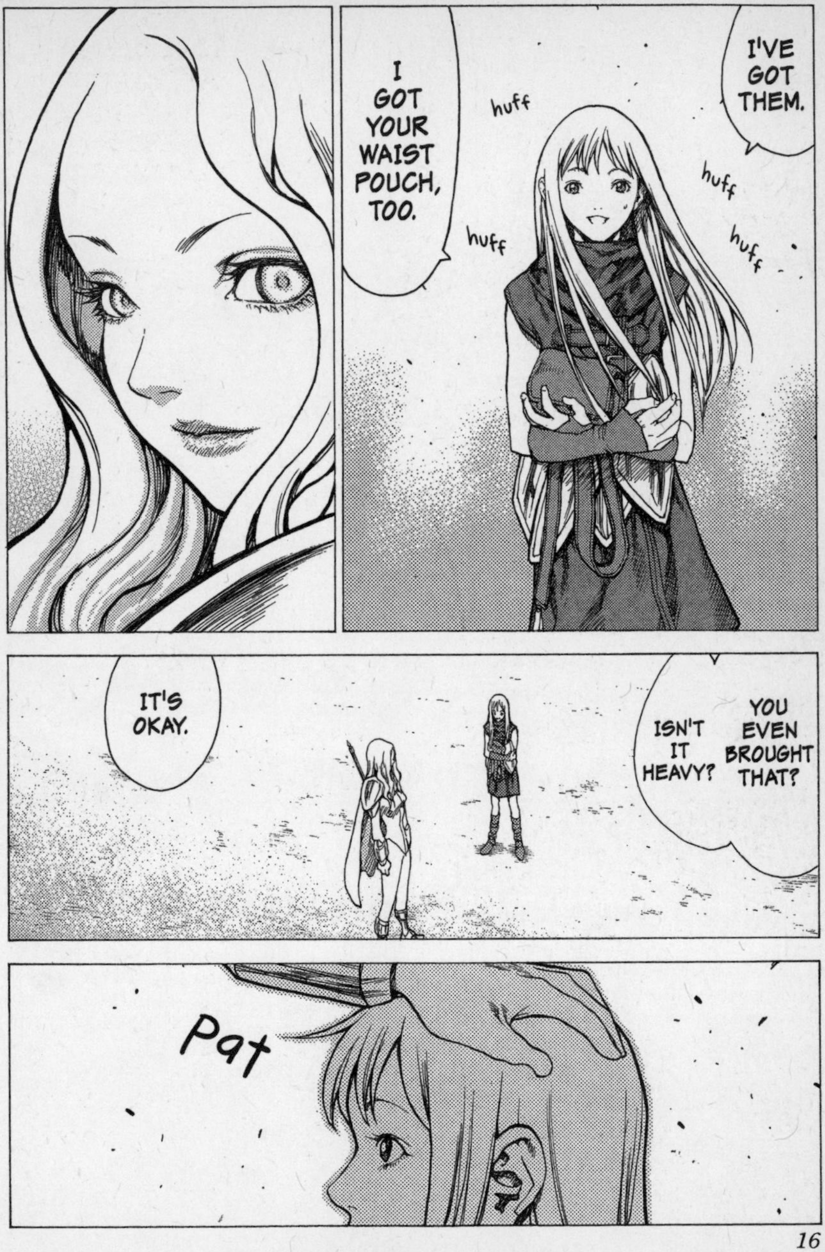
I'VE GOT THEM.
huff
huff
huff
I GOT YOUR WAIST POUCH, TOO.
huff
YOU EVEN BROUGHT THAT?
ISN'T IT HEAVY?
IT'S OKAY.
Pat

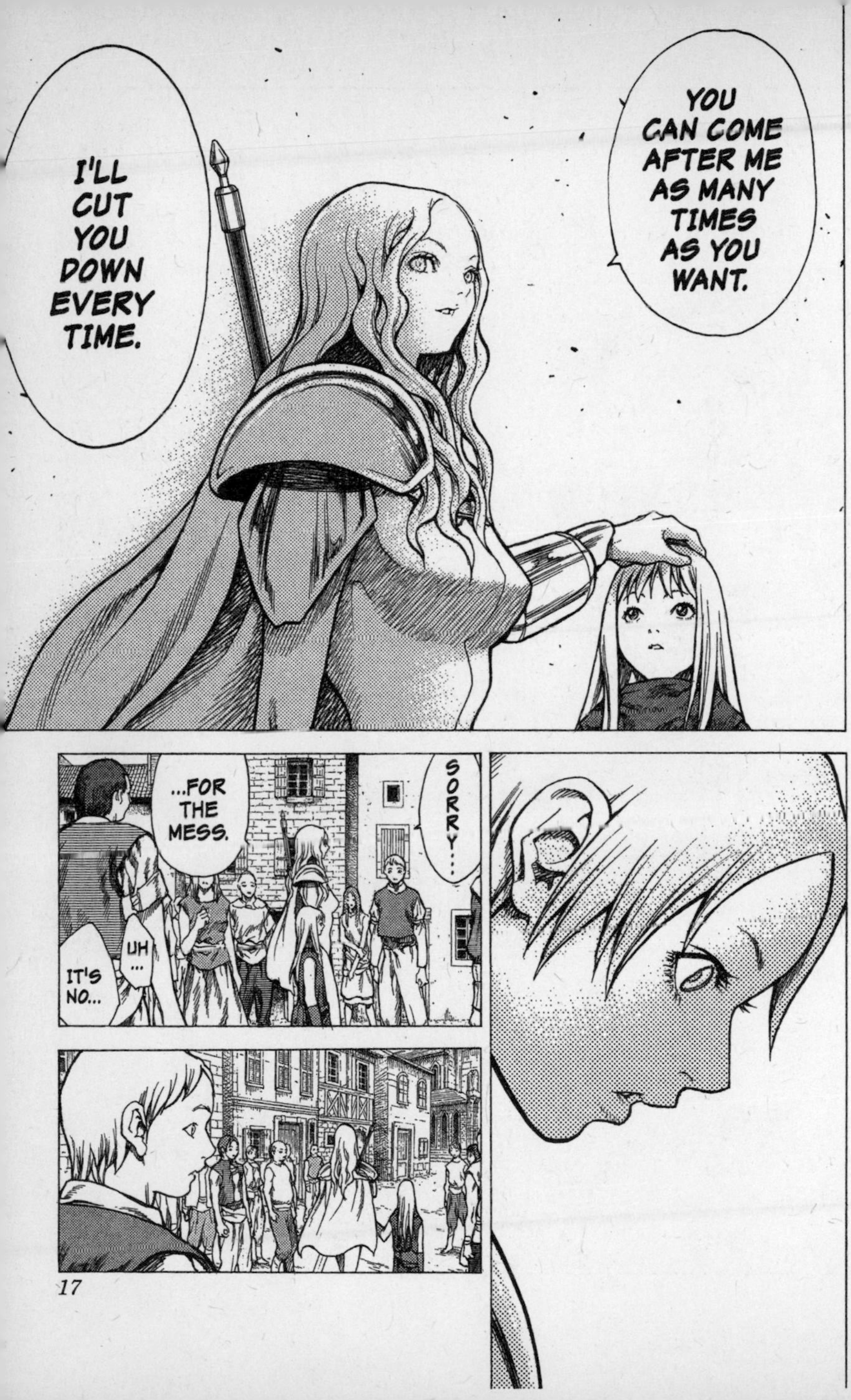
YOU CAN COME AFTER ME AS MANY TIMES AS YOU WANT.
I'LL CUT YOU DOWN EVERY TIME.
SORRY...
...FOR THE MESS.
UH ...
IT'S NO...

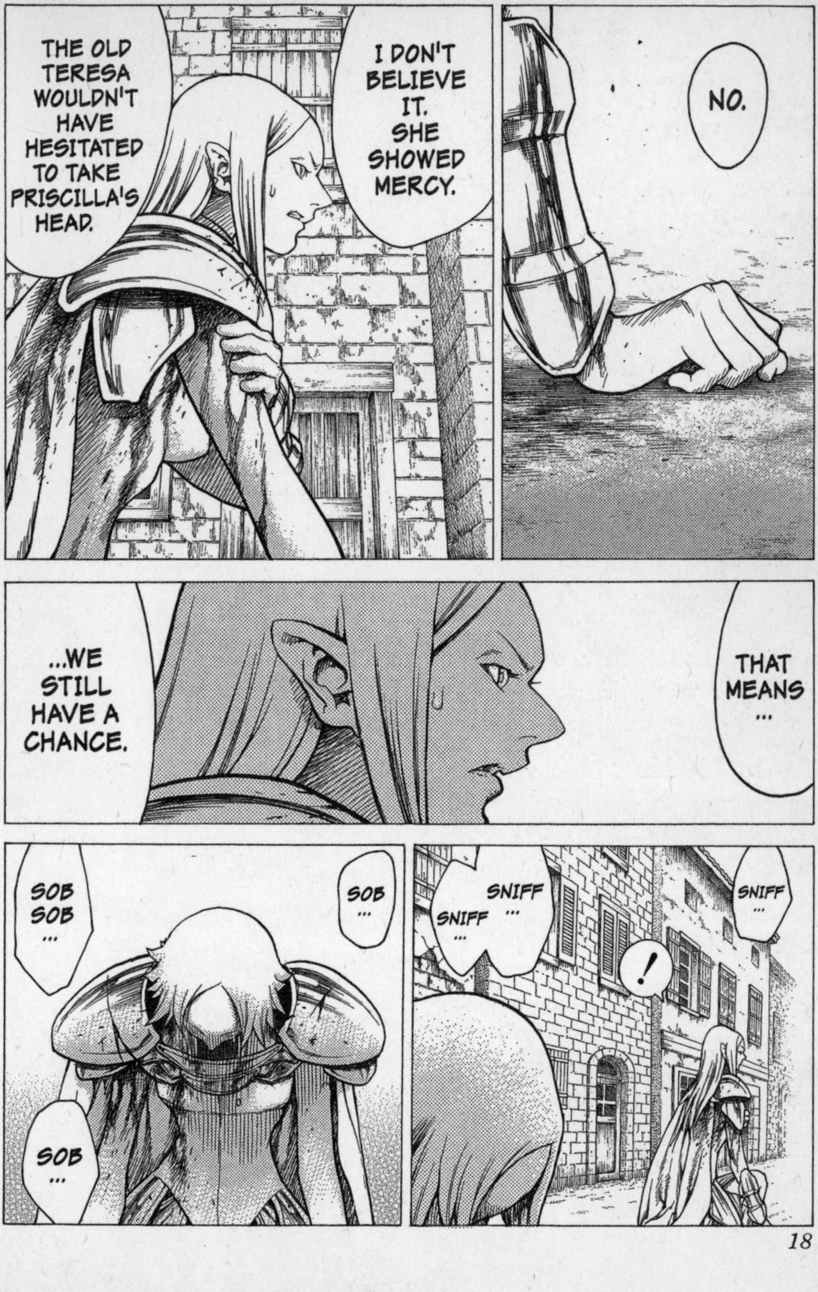
NO.
I DON'T BELIEVE IT. SHE SHOWED MERCY.
THE OLD TERESA WOULDN'T HAVE HESITATED TO TAKE PRISCILLA'S HEAD.
THAT MEANS ...
...WE STILL HAVE A CHANCE.
SNIFF ...
SNIFF ...
SNIFF ...
!
SOB ...
SOB SOB ...
SOB ...

READ THIS WAY

CLOP
DON'T CRY.
IT ISN'T OVER. THE FIGHT ...
... HAS JUST BEGUN.
...WON'T ...
!
... WON'T STAND ...
I WON'T STAND ...
...FOR IT.
I...
I...
I...
... WON'T ...

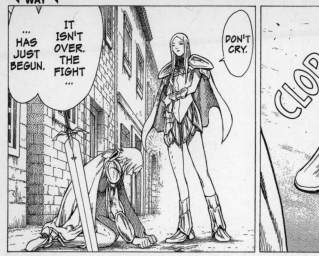

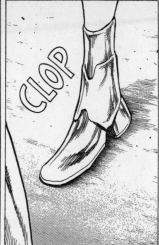

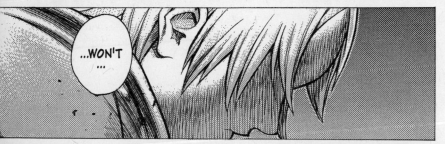

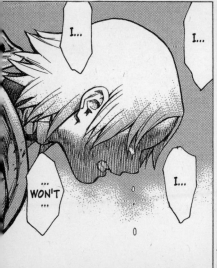

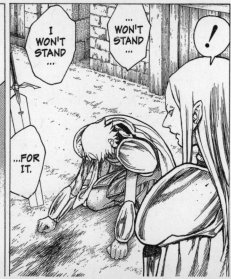

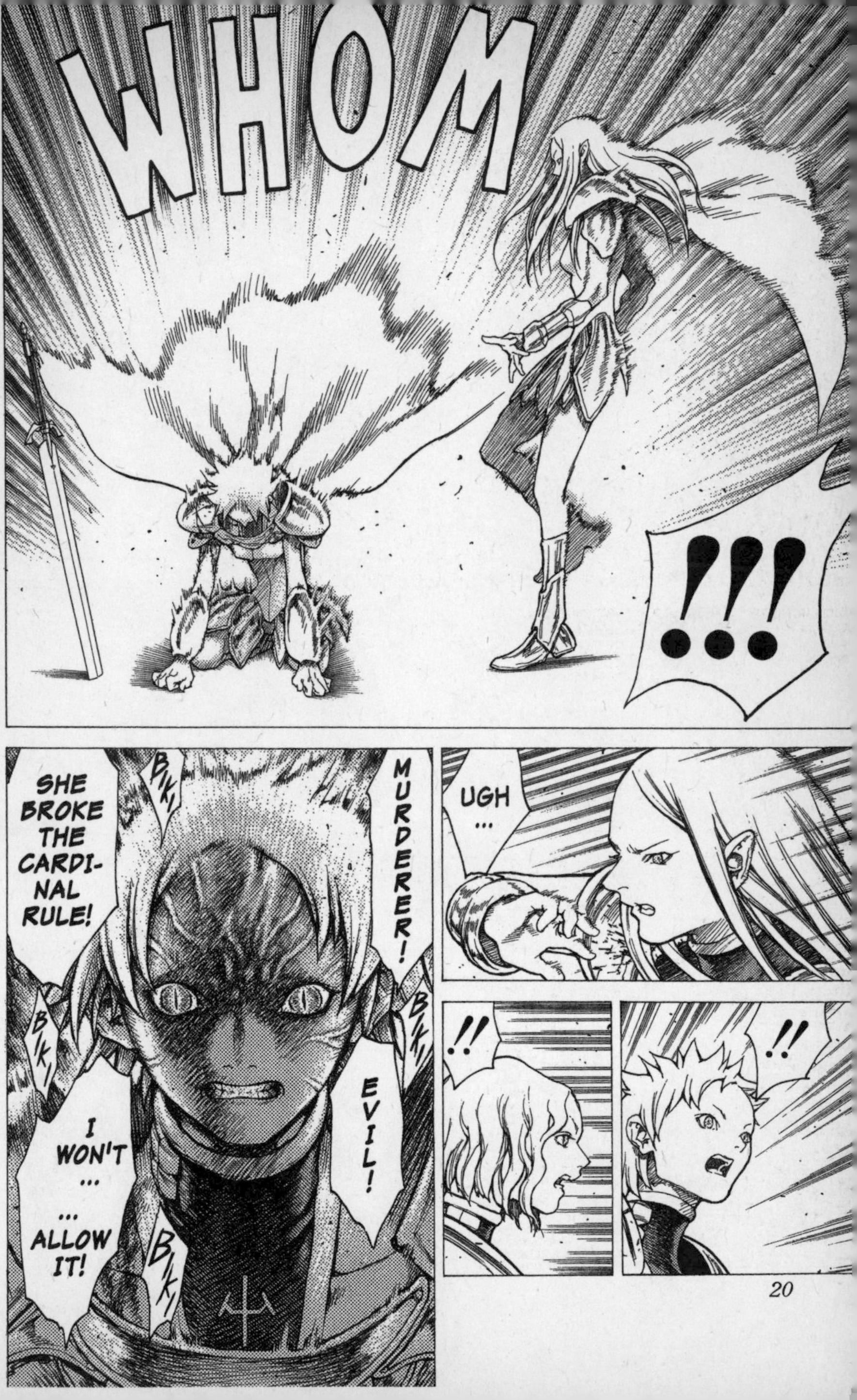
WHOM
!!!
UGH ...
!!
!!
MURDERER!
SHE BROKE THE CARDINAL RULE!
BIKI
BIKI
BIKI
EVIL!
I WON'T ...
... ALLOW IT!
BIKI

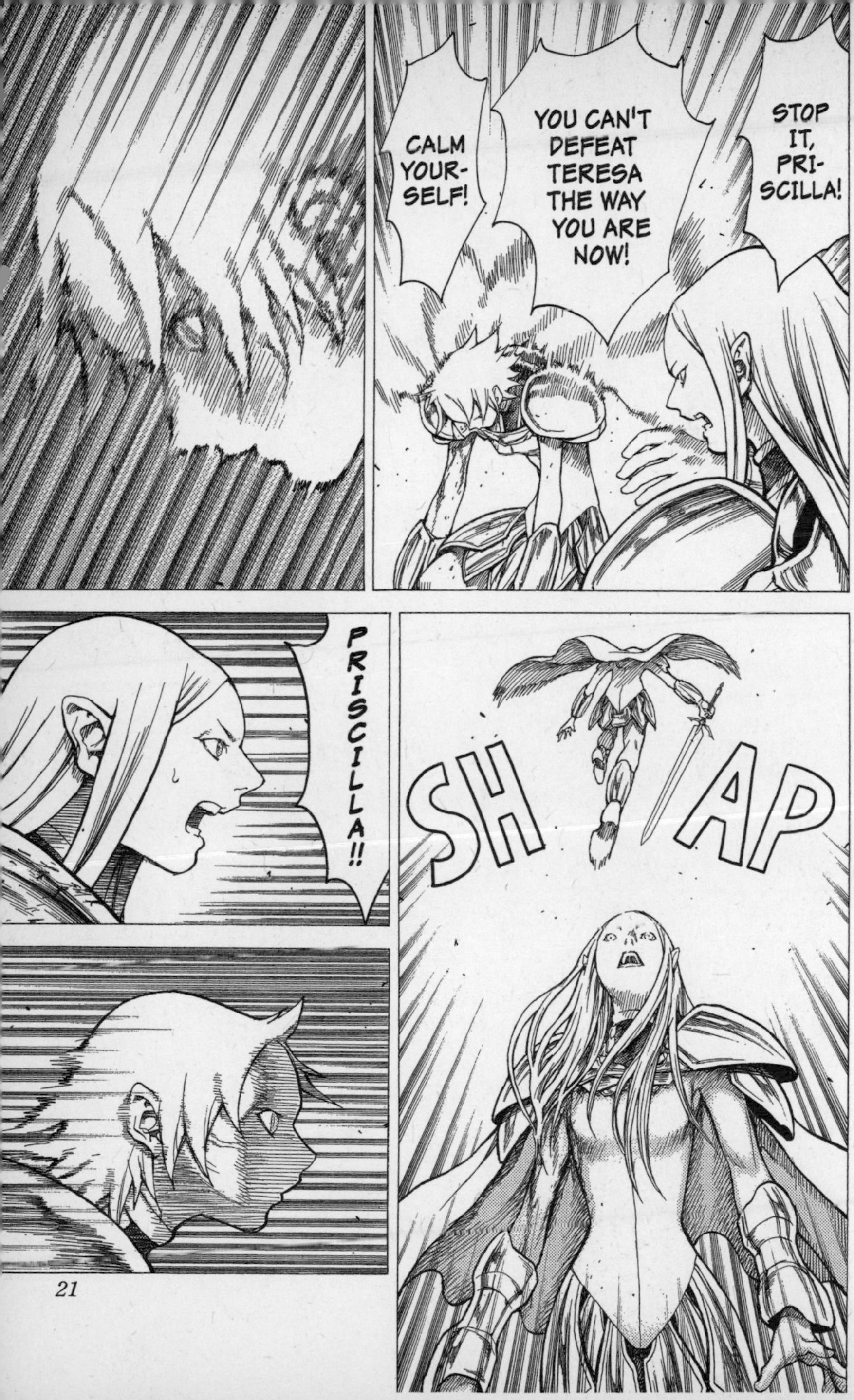
STOP IT, PRI-SCILLA!
YOU CAN'T DEFEAT TERESA THE WAY YOU ARE NOW!
CALM YOUR-SELF!
SHAP
PRISCILLA!!

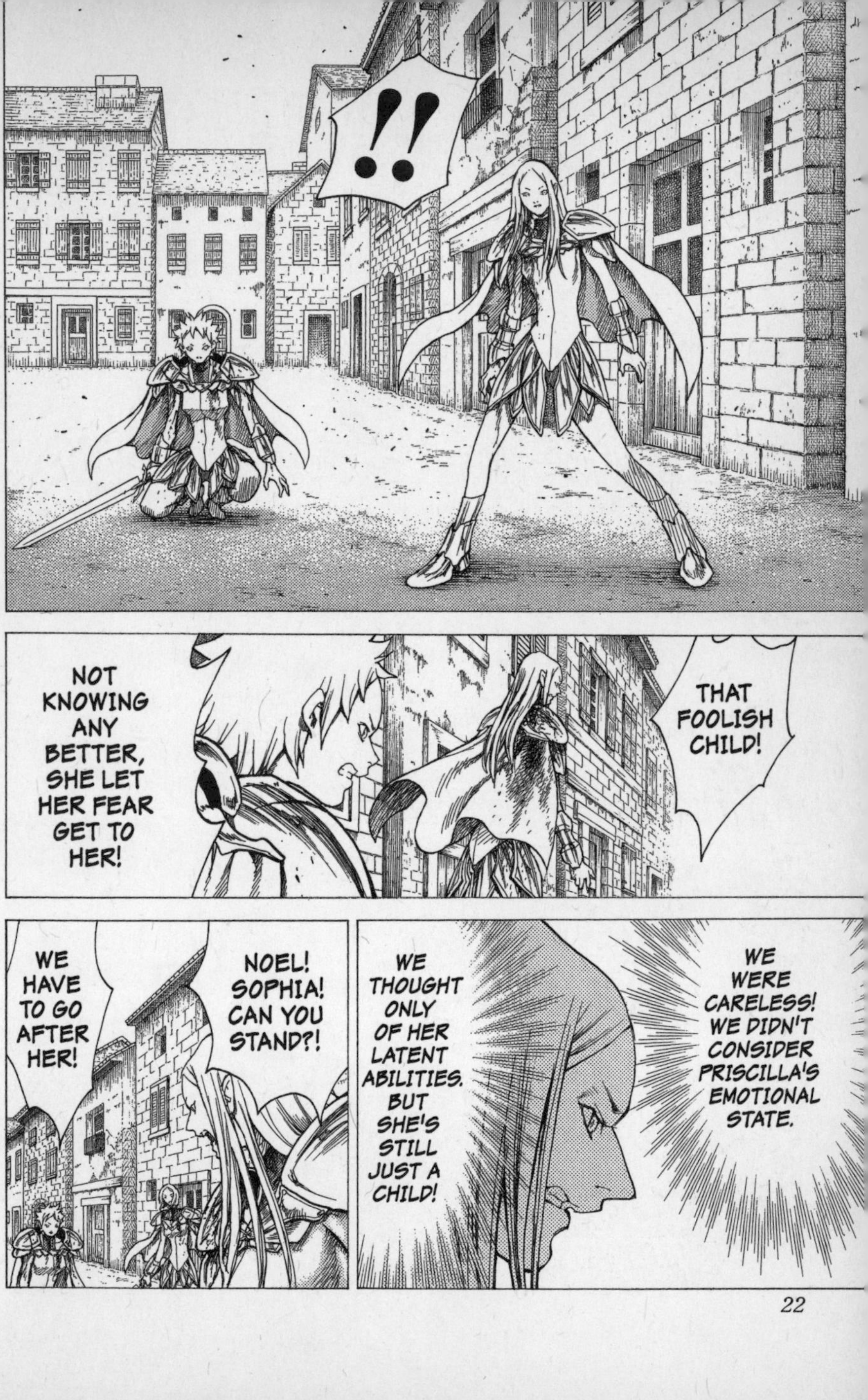
!!
THAT FOOLISH CHILD!
NOT KNOWING ANY BETTER, SHE LET HER FEAR GET TO HER!
WE WERE CARELESS! WE DIDN'T CONSIDER PRISCILLA'S EMOTIONAL STATE.
WE THOUGHT ONLY OF HER LATENT ABILITIES. BUT SHE'S STILL JUST A CHILD!
NOEL! SOPHIA! CAN YOU STAND?!
WE HAVE TO GO AFTER HER!

READ THIS WAY

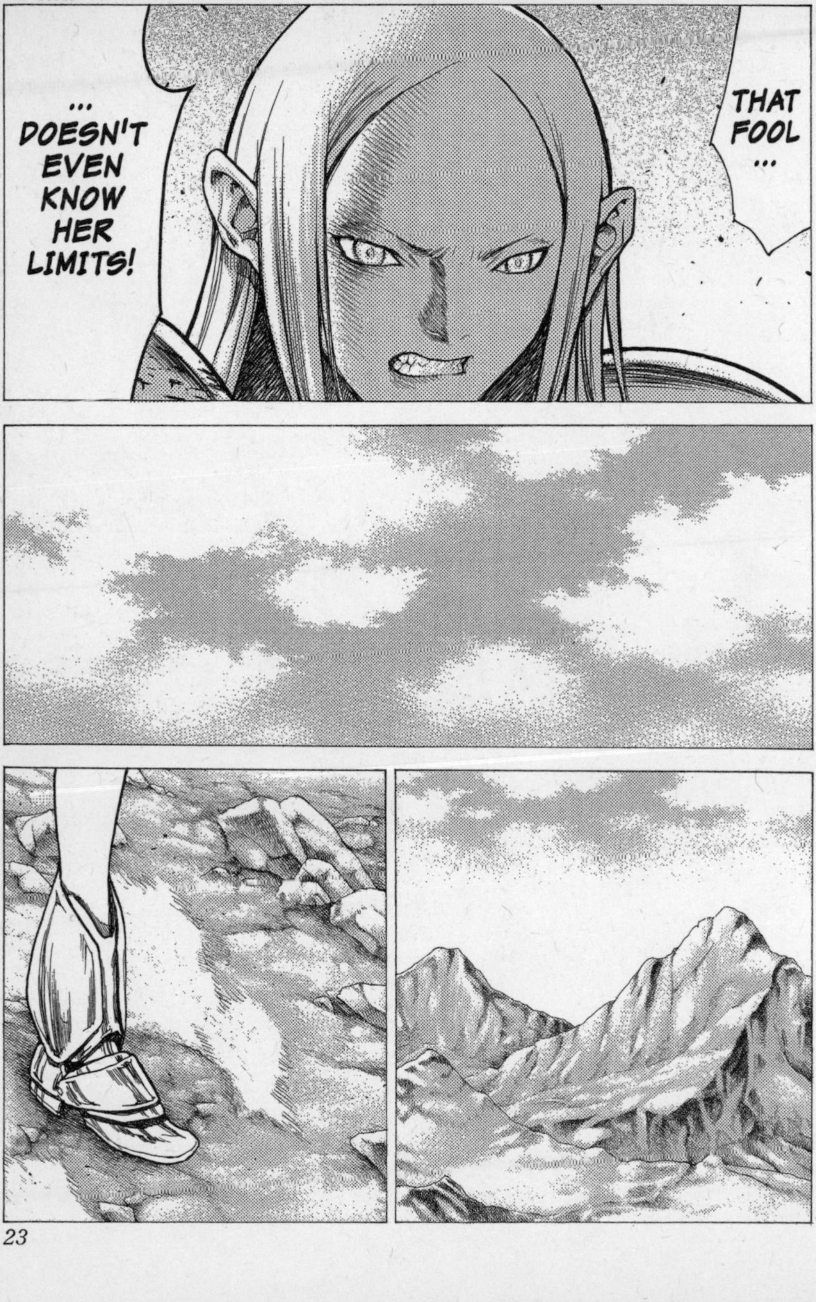
THAT FOOL ...
... DOESN'T EVEN KNOW HER LIMITS!

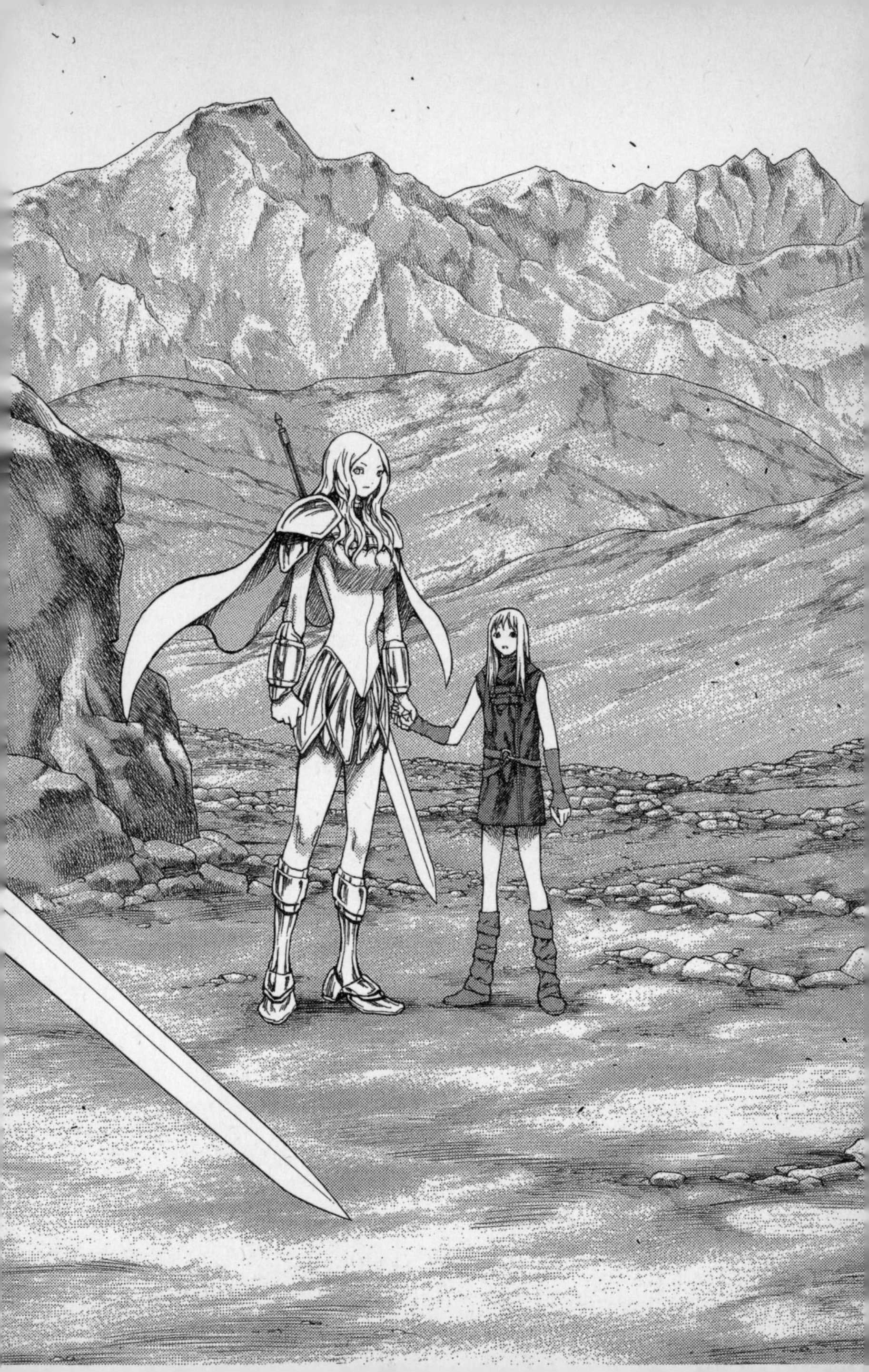

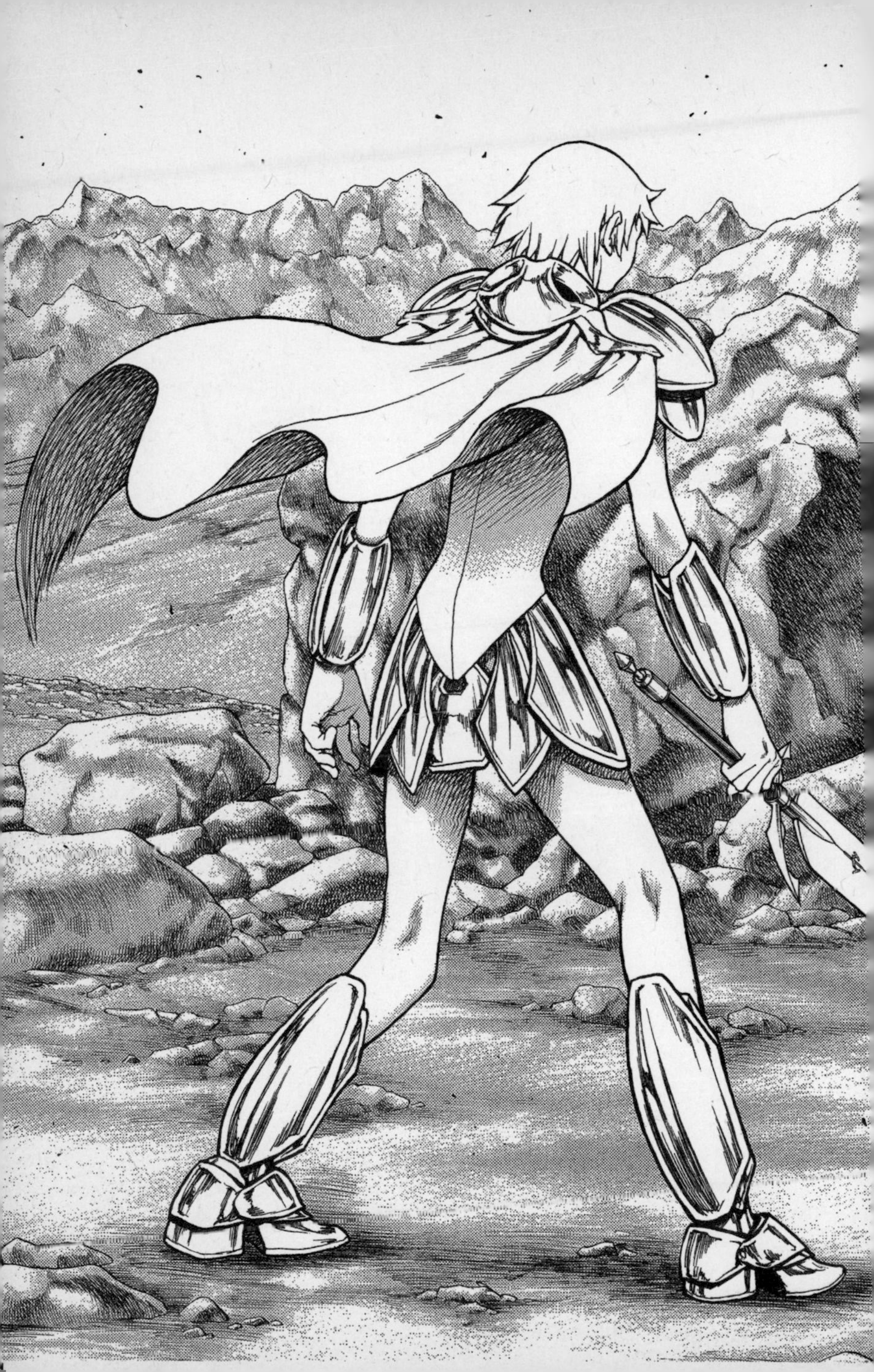

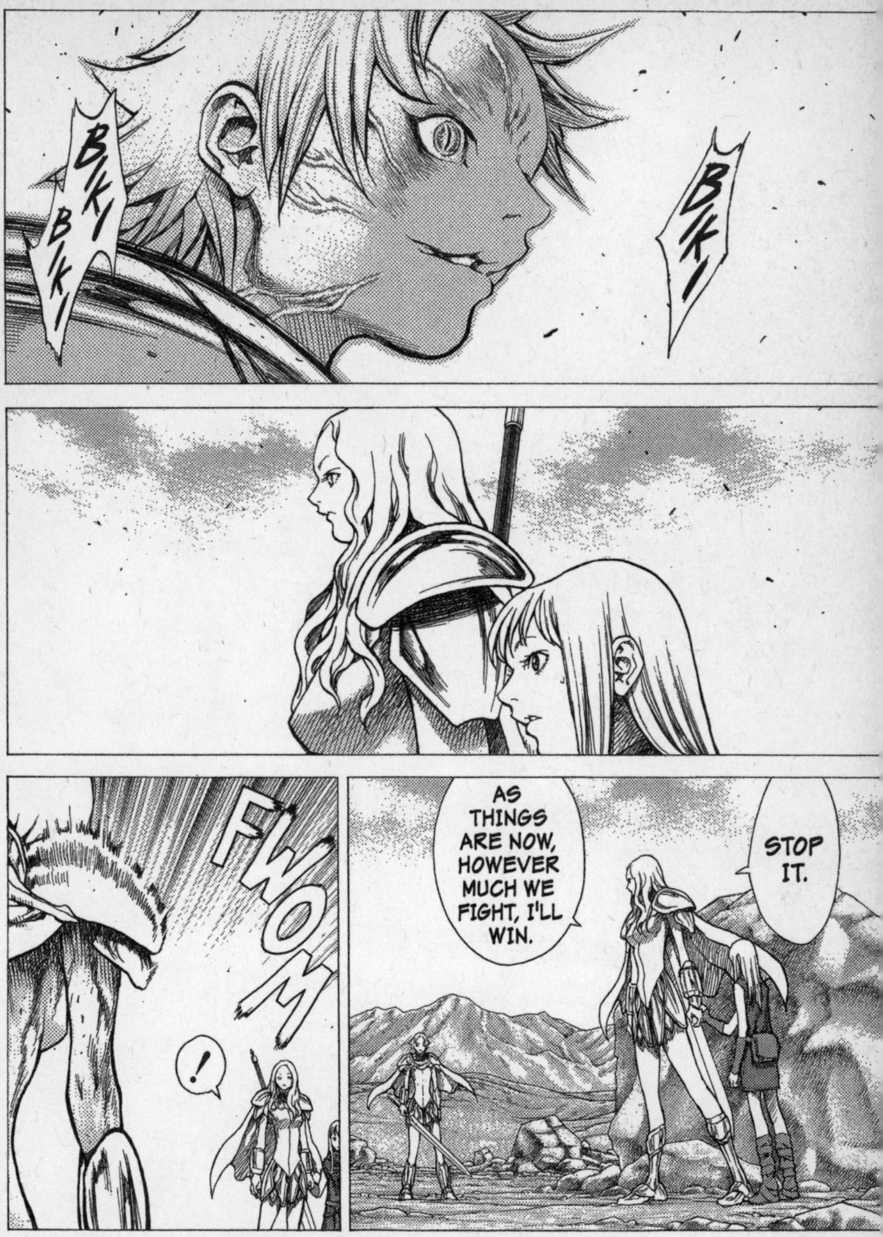
BIKI
BIKI BIKI
STOP IT.
AS THINGS ARE NOW, HOWEVER MUCH WE FIGHT, I'LL WIN.
FWOM
!

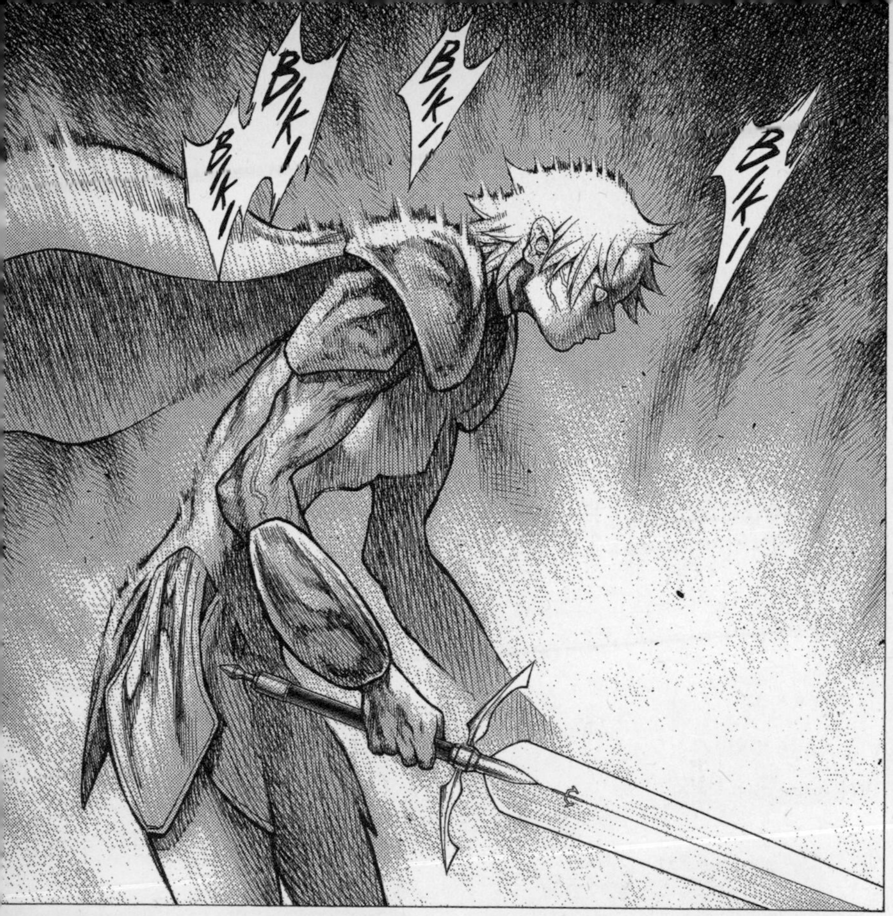
BIKI
BIKI
BIKI
BIKI
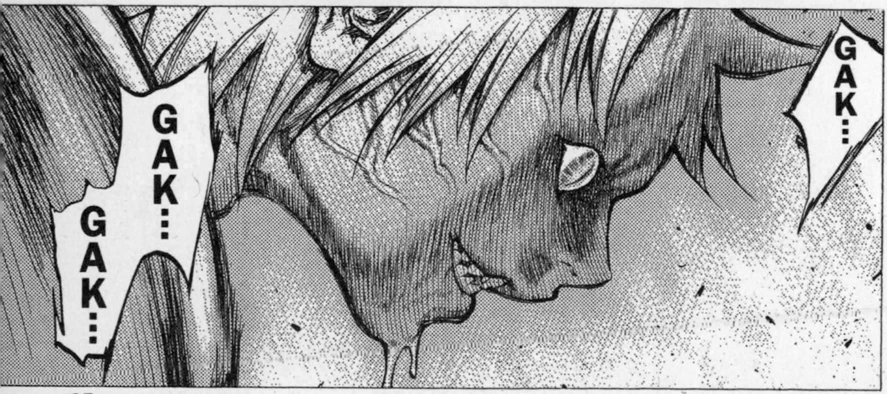
GAK…
GAK…
GAK…

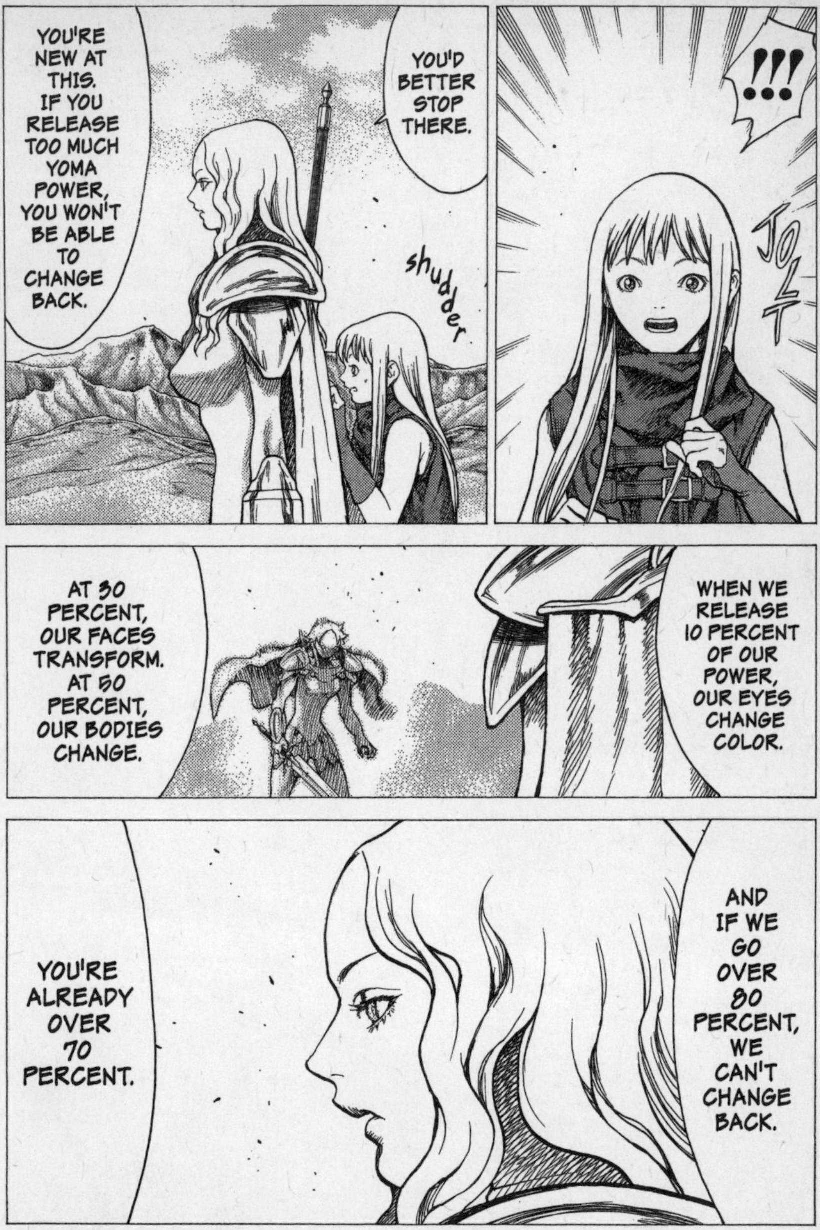
!!!
JOLT
YOU'D BETTER STOP THERE.
shudder
YOU'RE NEW AT THIS. IF YOU RELEASE TOO MUCH YOMA POWER, YOU WON'T BE ABLE TO CHANGE BACK.
WHEN WE RELEASE 10 PERCENT OF OUR POWER, OUR EYES CHANGE COLOR.
AT 30 PERCENT, OUR FACES TRANSFORM. AT 50 PERCENT, OUR BODIES CHANGE.
AND IF WE GO OVER 80 PERCENT, WE CAN'T CHANGE BACK.
YOU'RE ALREADY OVER 70 PERCENT.

READ THIS WAY

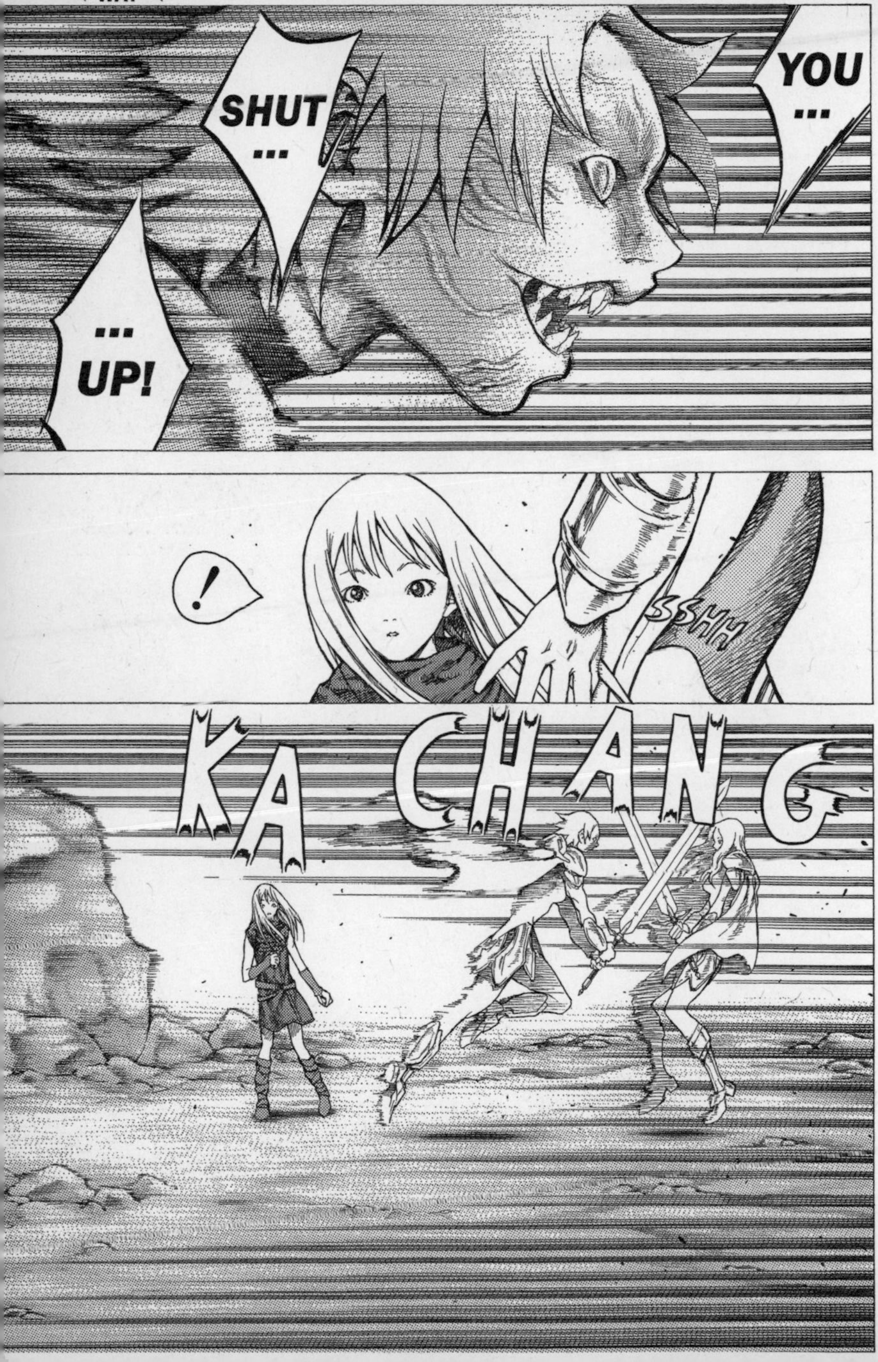
YOU ...
SHUT ...
... UP!
!
SSHH
KA CHANG

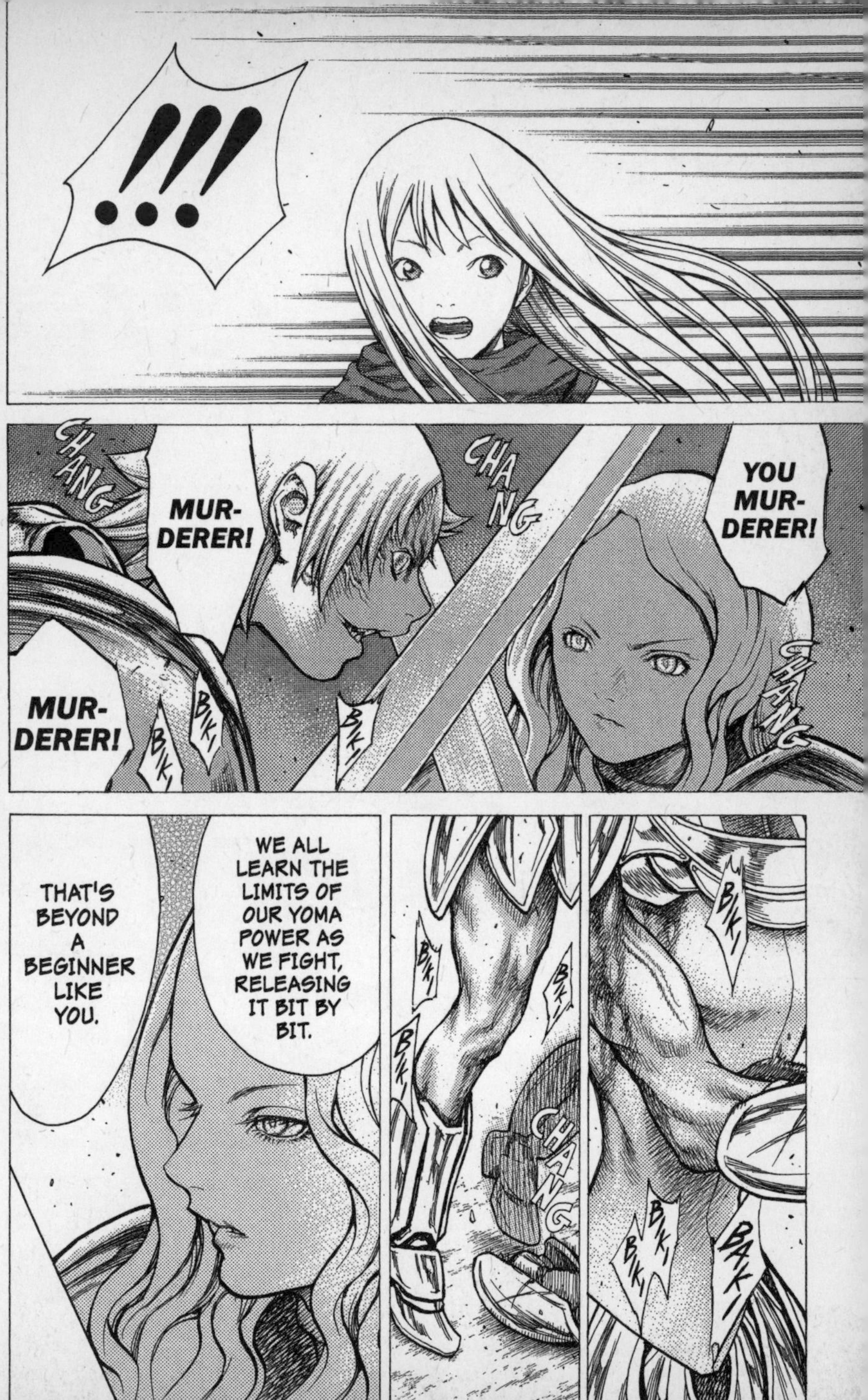
!!!...
CHANG
YOU MURDERER!
CHANG
CHANG
MURDERER!
CHANG
BIKI
MURDERER!
BIKI
BIKI
BIKI
BIKI
BIKI
BAK
BIKI
BIKI
BIKI
CHANG
WE ALL LEARN THE LIMITS OF OUR YOMA POWER AS WE FIGHT, RELEASING IT BIT BY BIT.
THAT'S BEYOND A BEGINNER LIKE YOU.

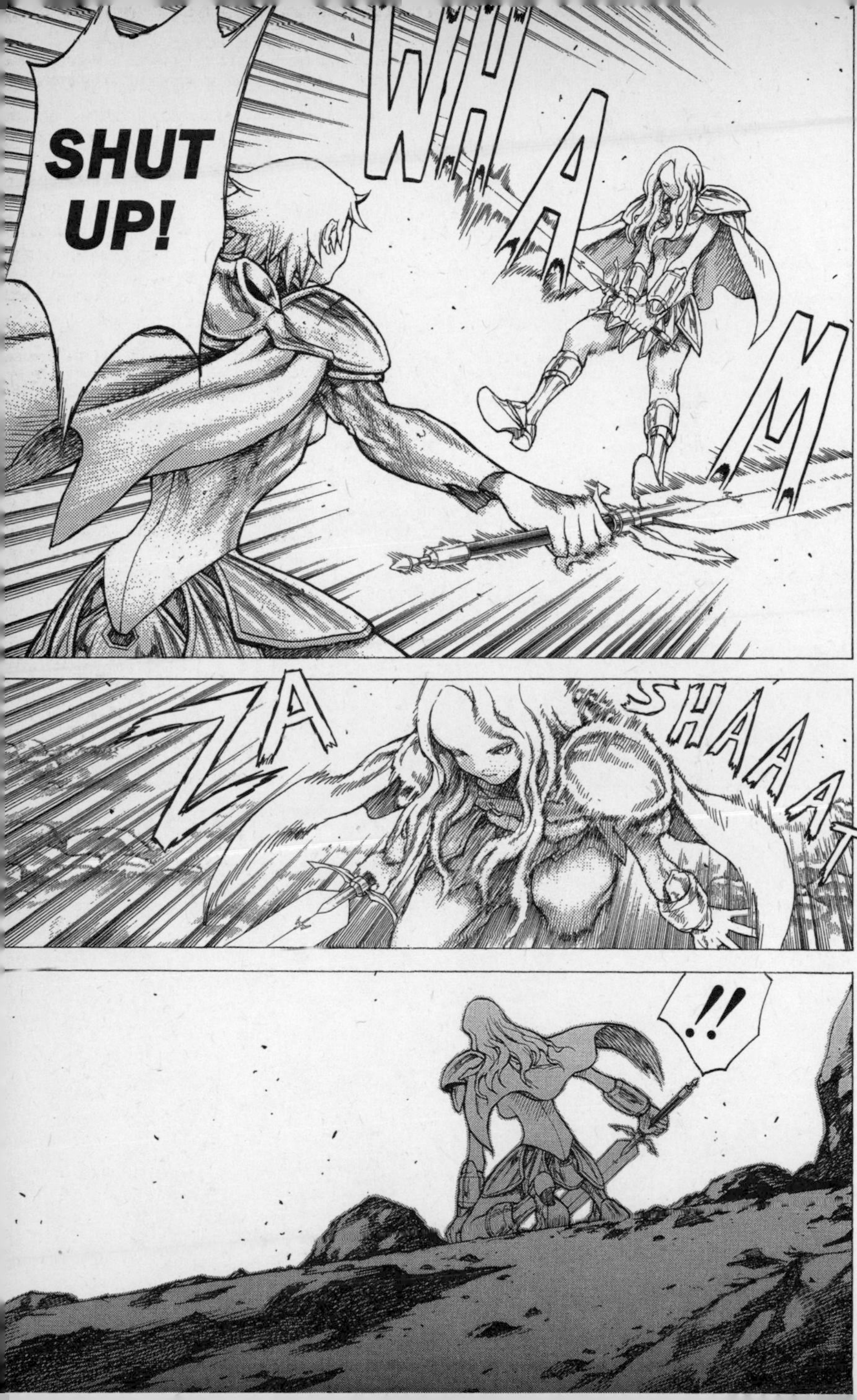
WHAM
SHUT UP!
SHAAAT
ZA
!!

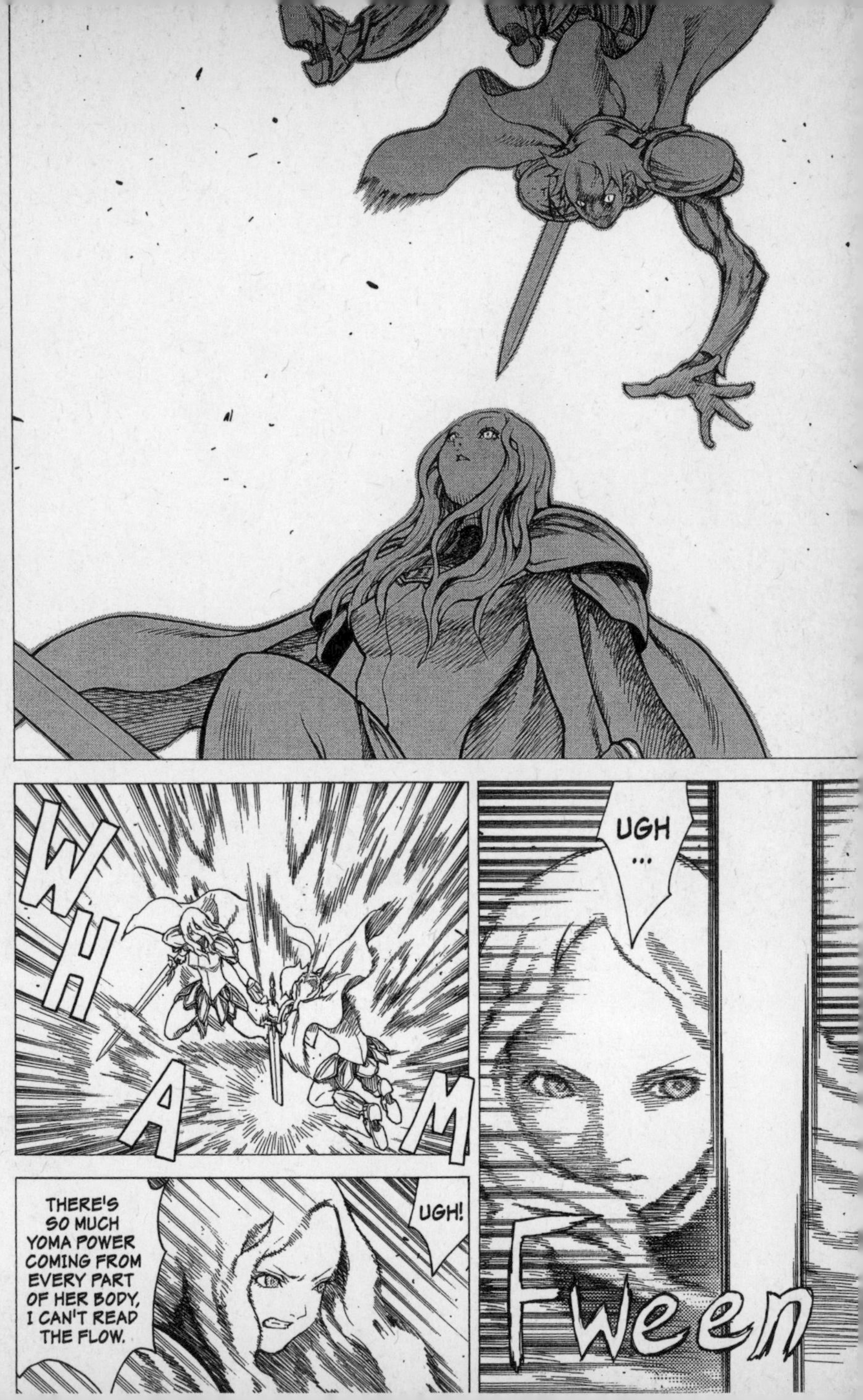
UGH ...
Fween
WHAM
UGH!
THERE'S SO MUCH YOMA POWER COMING FROM EVERY PART OF HER BODY, I CAN'T READ THE FLOW.

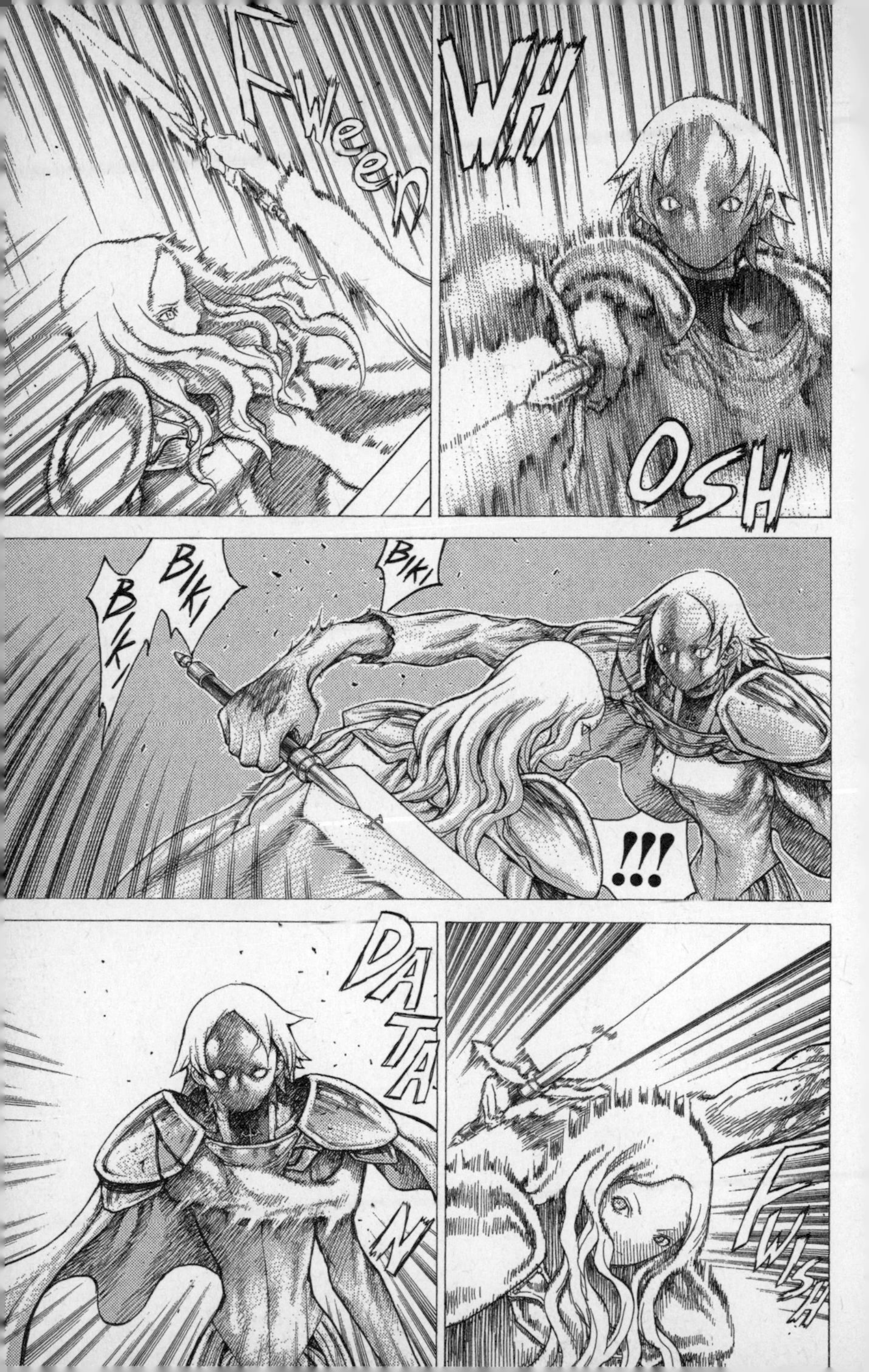
WH
OSH
Fween
BIKI
BIKI
BIKI
!!!
FWISH
DATA
N

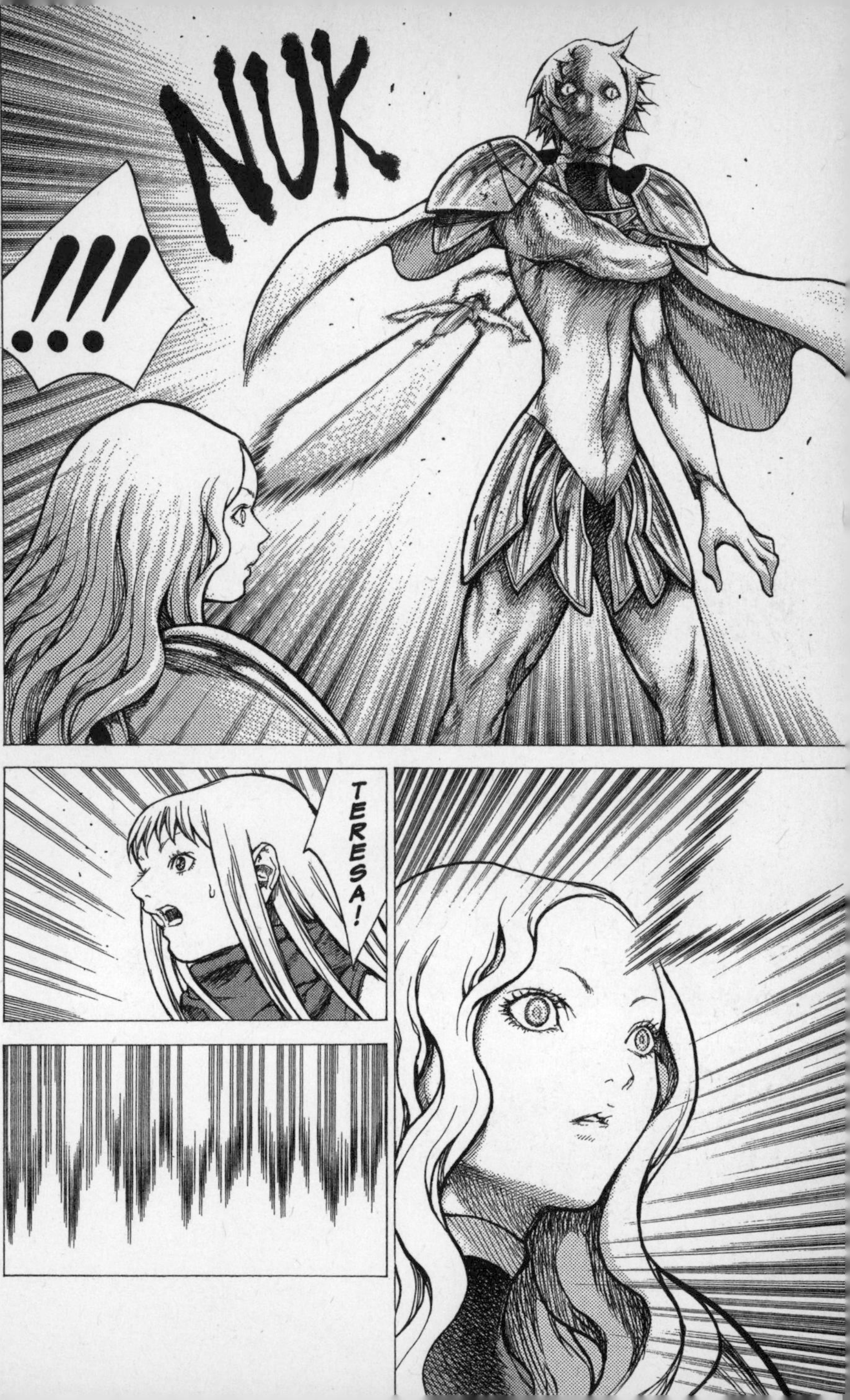
NUK
!!!
TERESA!

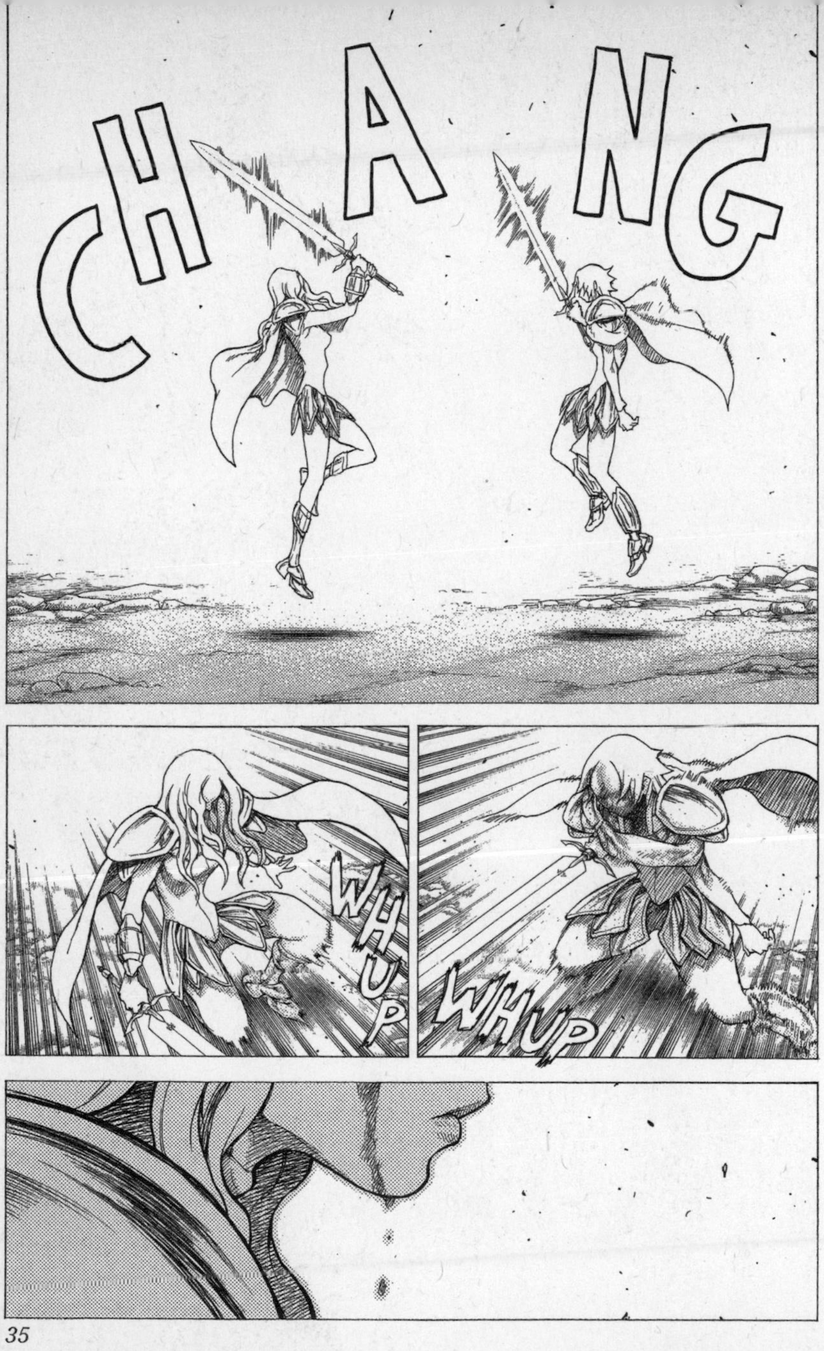
CHANG
WHUP
WHUP

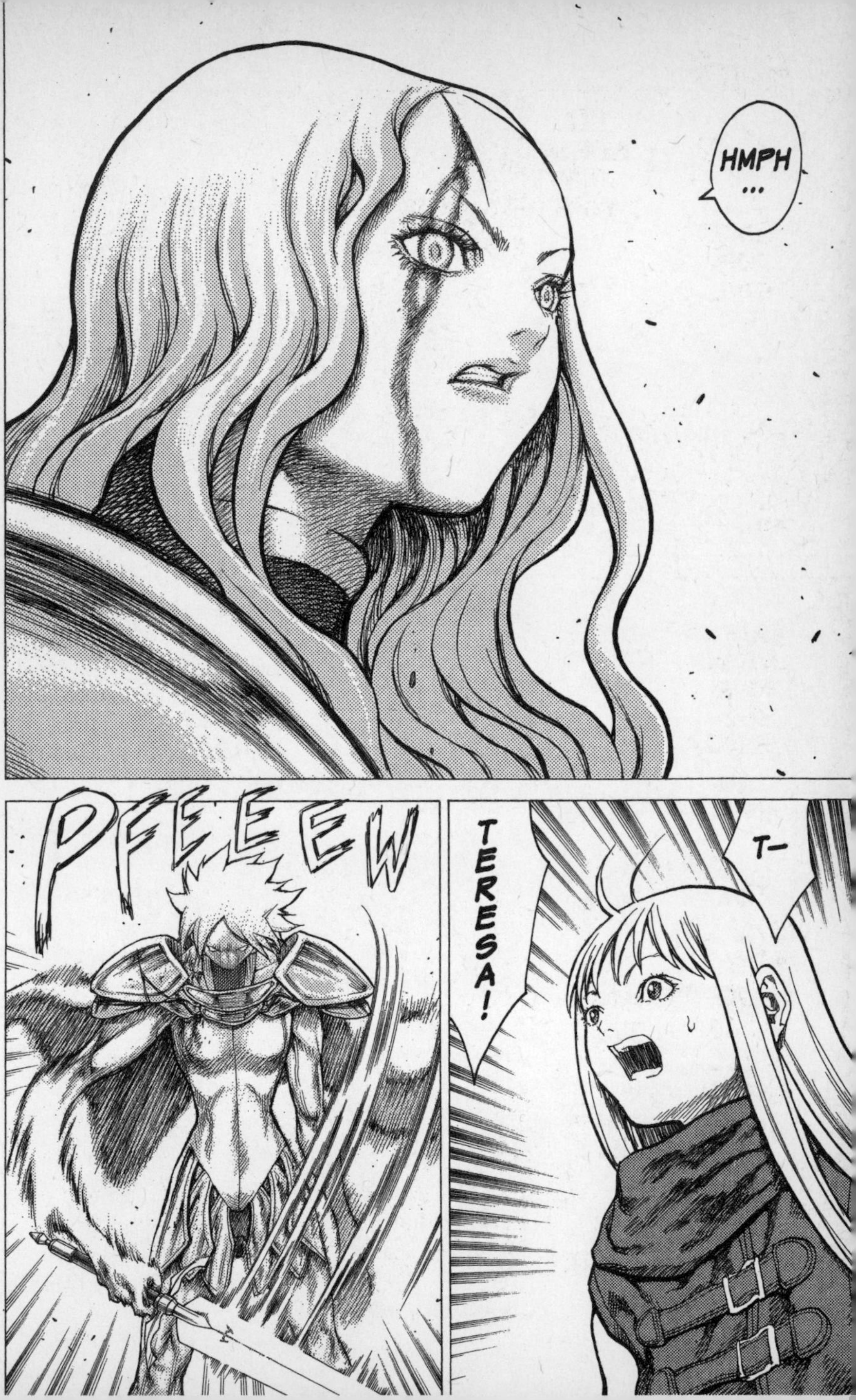
HMPH ...
T—
TERESA!
PFEEEW

READ THIS WAY

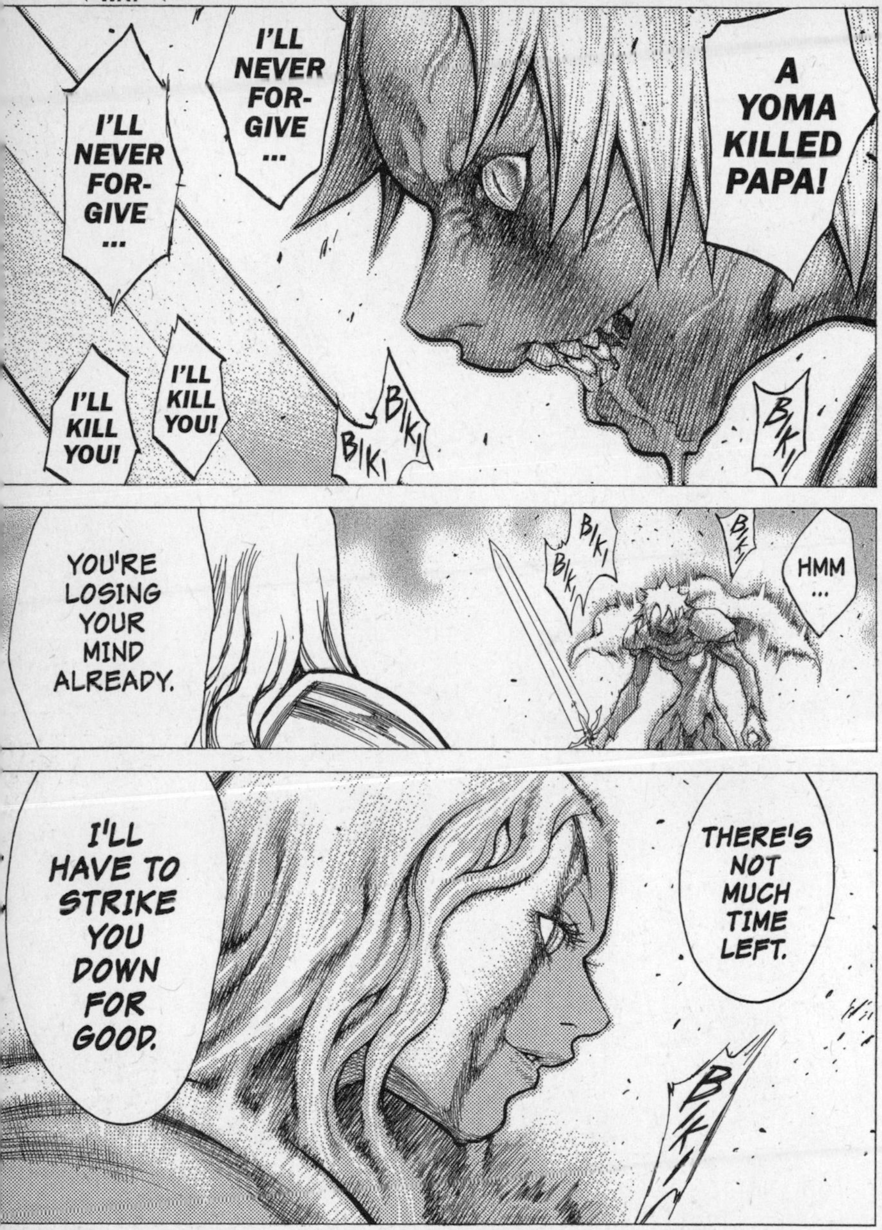
A YOMA KILLED PAPA!
BIKI
I'LL NEVER FORGIVE ...
I'LL NEVER FORGIVE ...
BIKI
BIKI
I'LL KILL YOU!
I'LL KILL YOU!
HMM ...
BIKI
BIKI
BIKI
YOU'RE LOSING YOUR MIND ALREADY.
THERE'S NOT MUCH TIME LEFT.
BIKI
I'LL HAVE TO STRIKE YOU DOWN FOR GOOD.

クレイモア
Claymore™

Scene 23: Marked for Death, Part 6

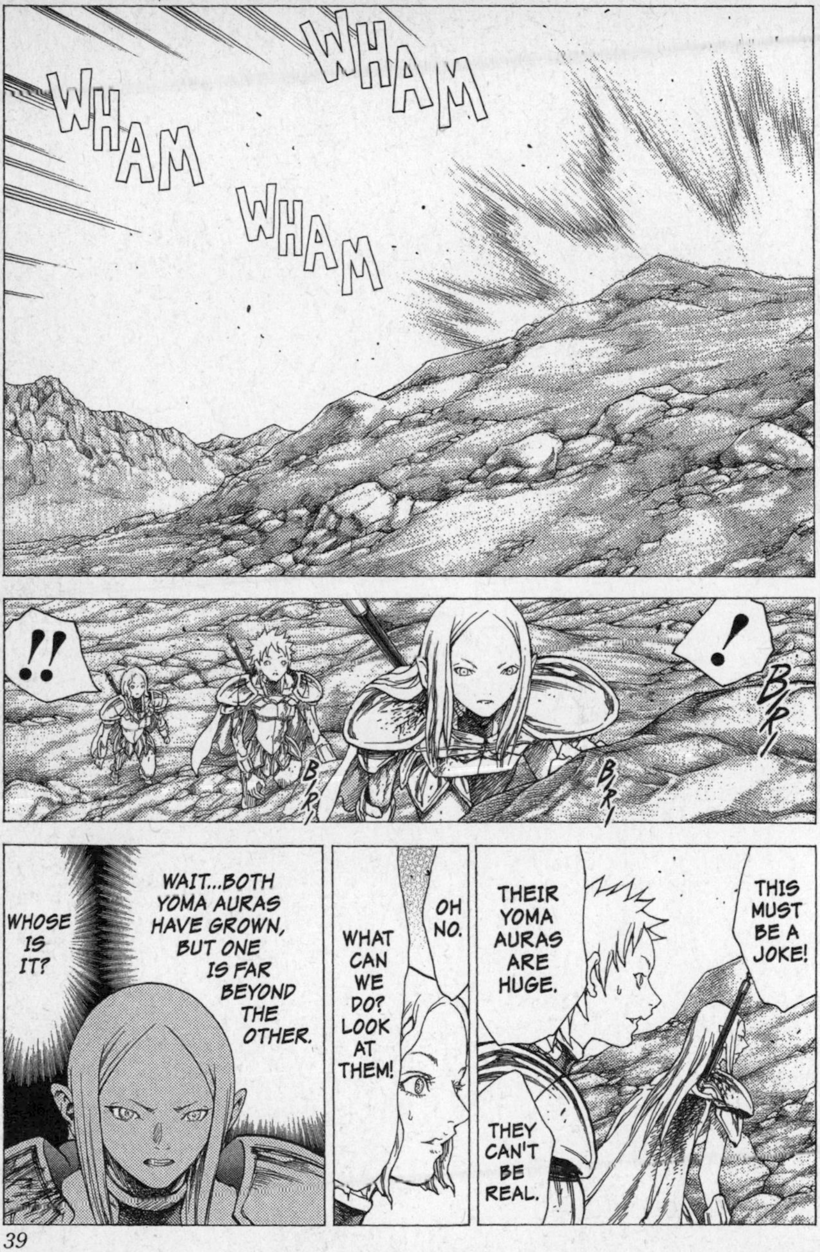
WHAM
WHAM
WHAM
!
BRI
BRI
BRI
!!
THIS MUST BE A JOKE!
THEIR YOMA AURAS ARE HUGE.
THEY CAN'T BE REAL.
OH NO.
WHAT CAN WE DO? LOOK AT THEM!
WAIT...BOTH YOMA AURAS HAVE GROWN, BUT ONE IS FAR BEYOND THE OTHER.
WHOSE IS IT?

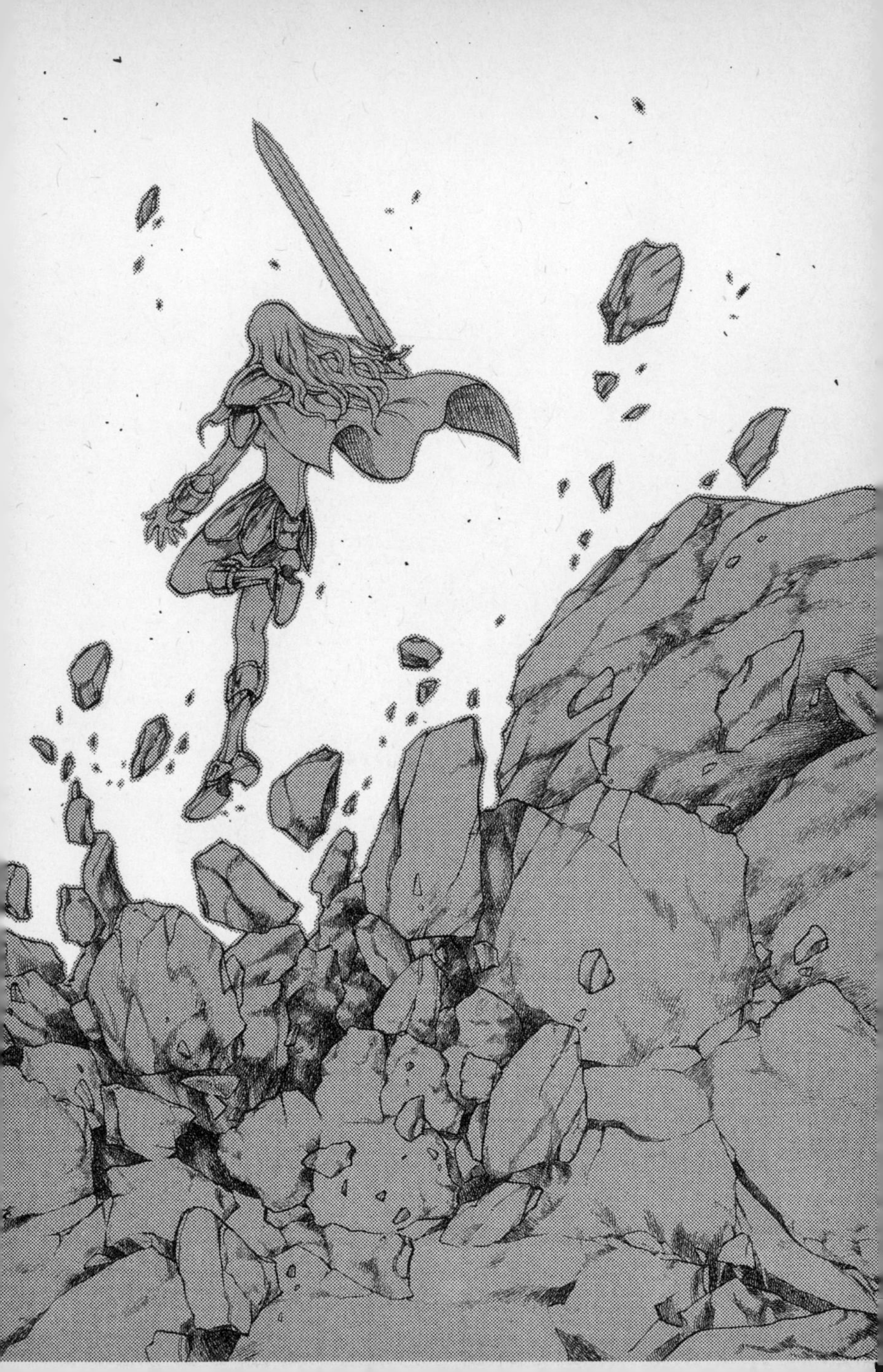

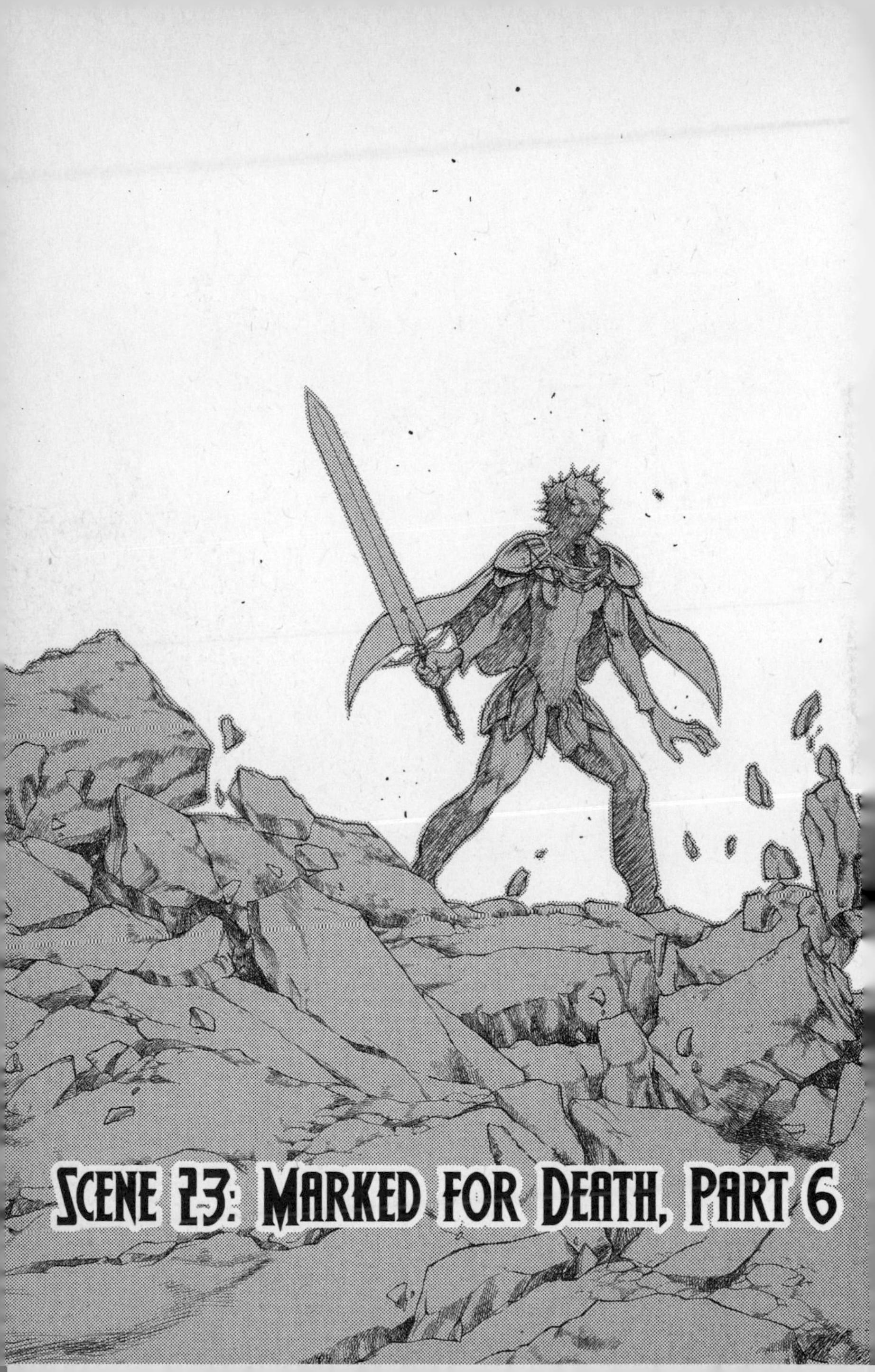
Scene 23: Marked for Death, Part 6

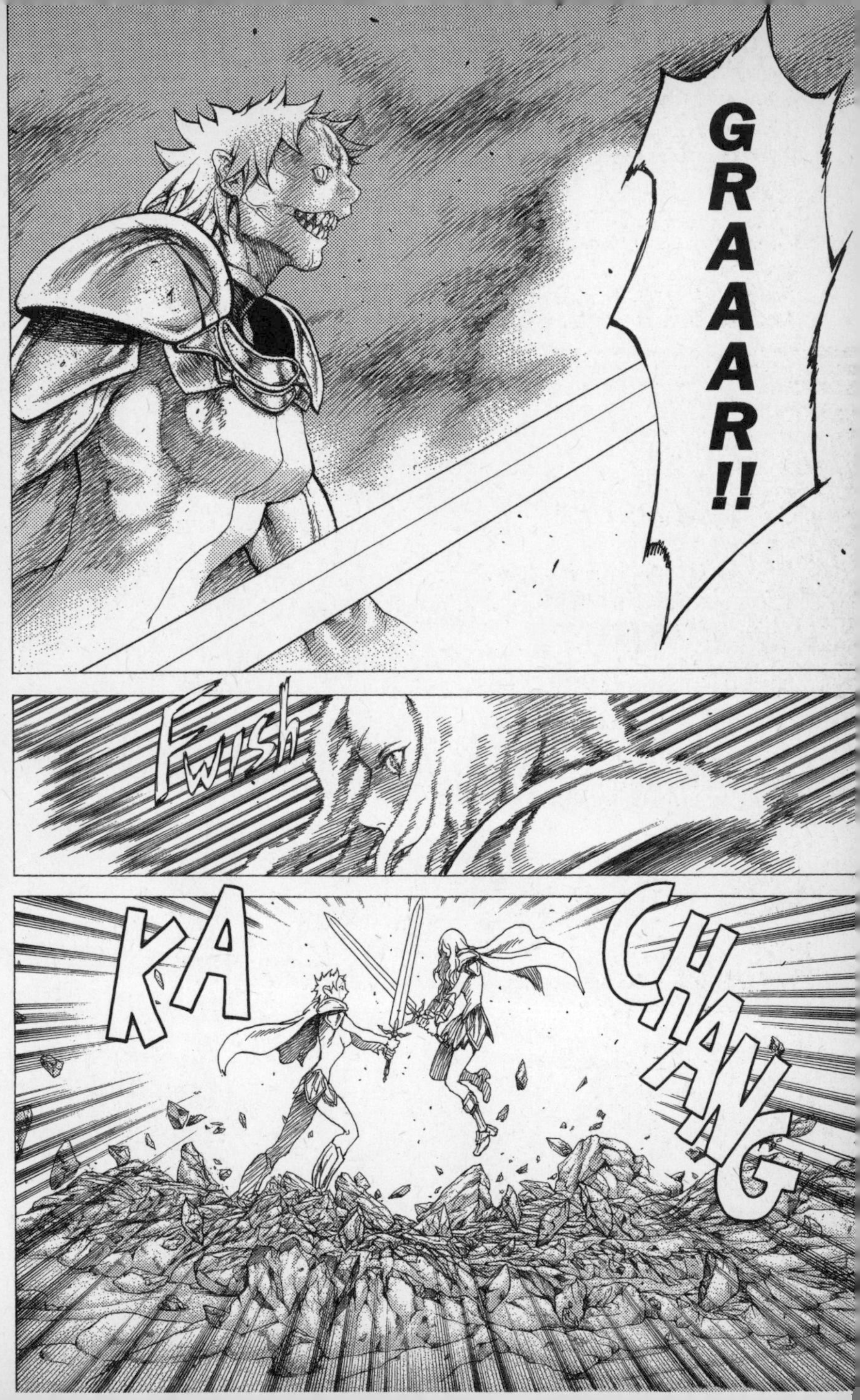
GRAAAR!!
Fwish
KA
CHANG

READ THIS WAY

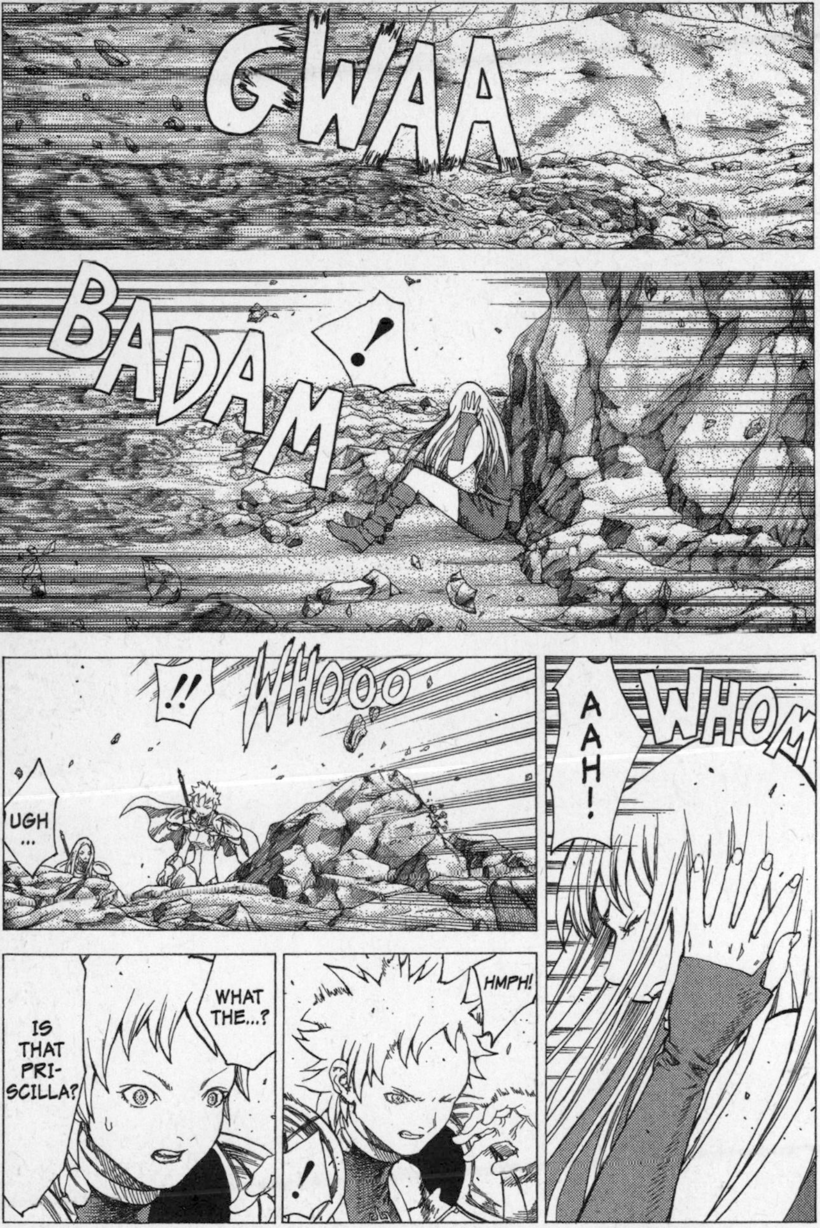

GWAA
BADAM
!
WHOM
AAH!
WHOOO
!!
UGH...
HMPH!
!
WHAT THE...?
IS THAT PRI-SCILLA?

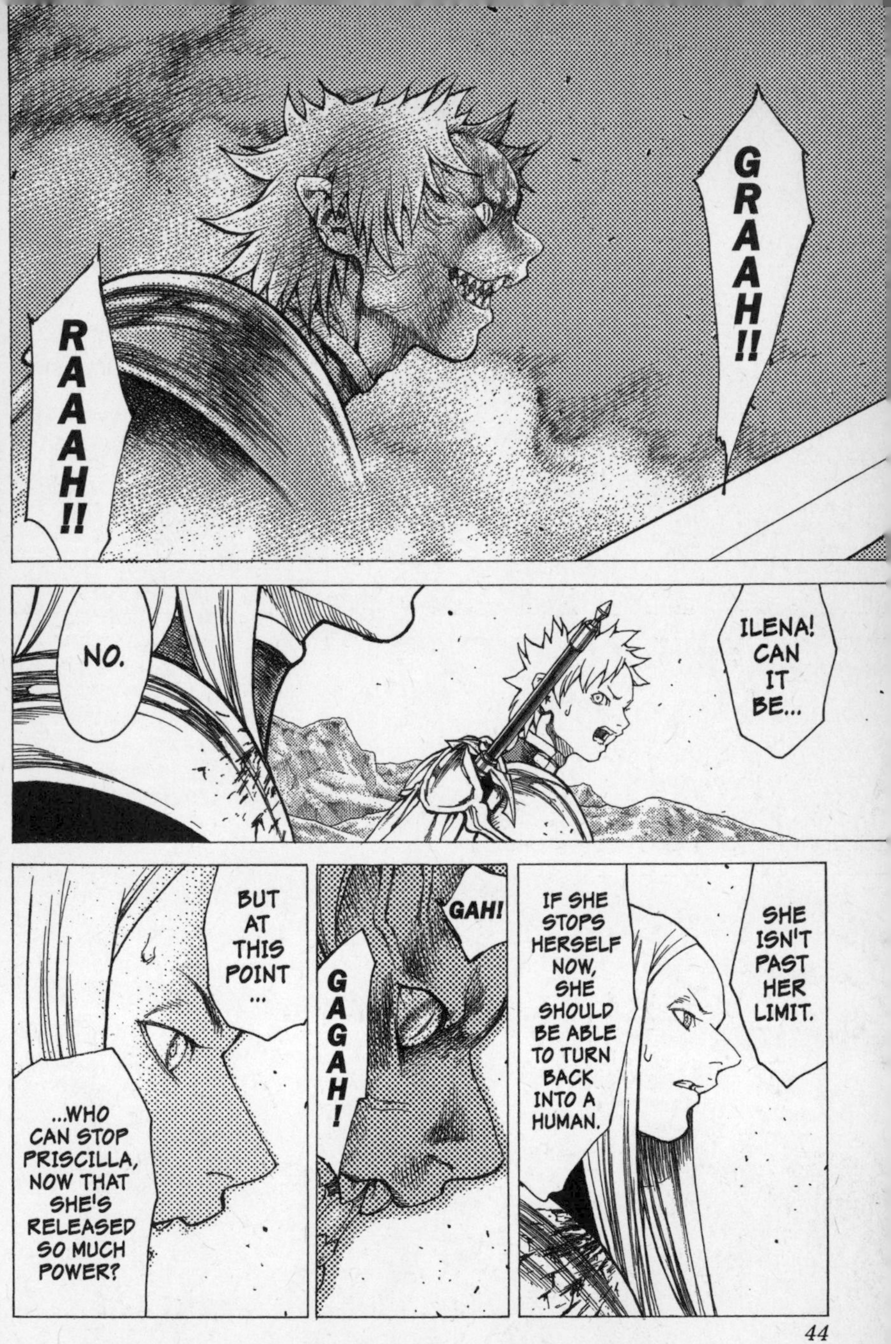
GRAAAH!!
RAAAAH!!
ILENA! CAN IT BE...
NO.
SHE ISN'T PAST HER LIMIT.
IF SHE STOPS HERSELF NOW, SHE SHOULD BE ABLE TO TURN BACK INTO A HUMAN.
GAH!
GAGAH!
BUT AT THIS POINT...
...WHO CAN STOP PRISCILLA, NOW THAT SHE'S RELEASED SO MUCH POWER?

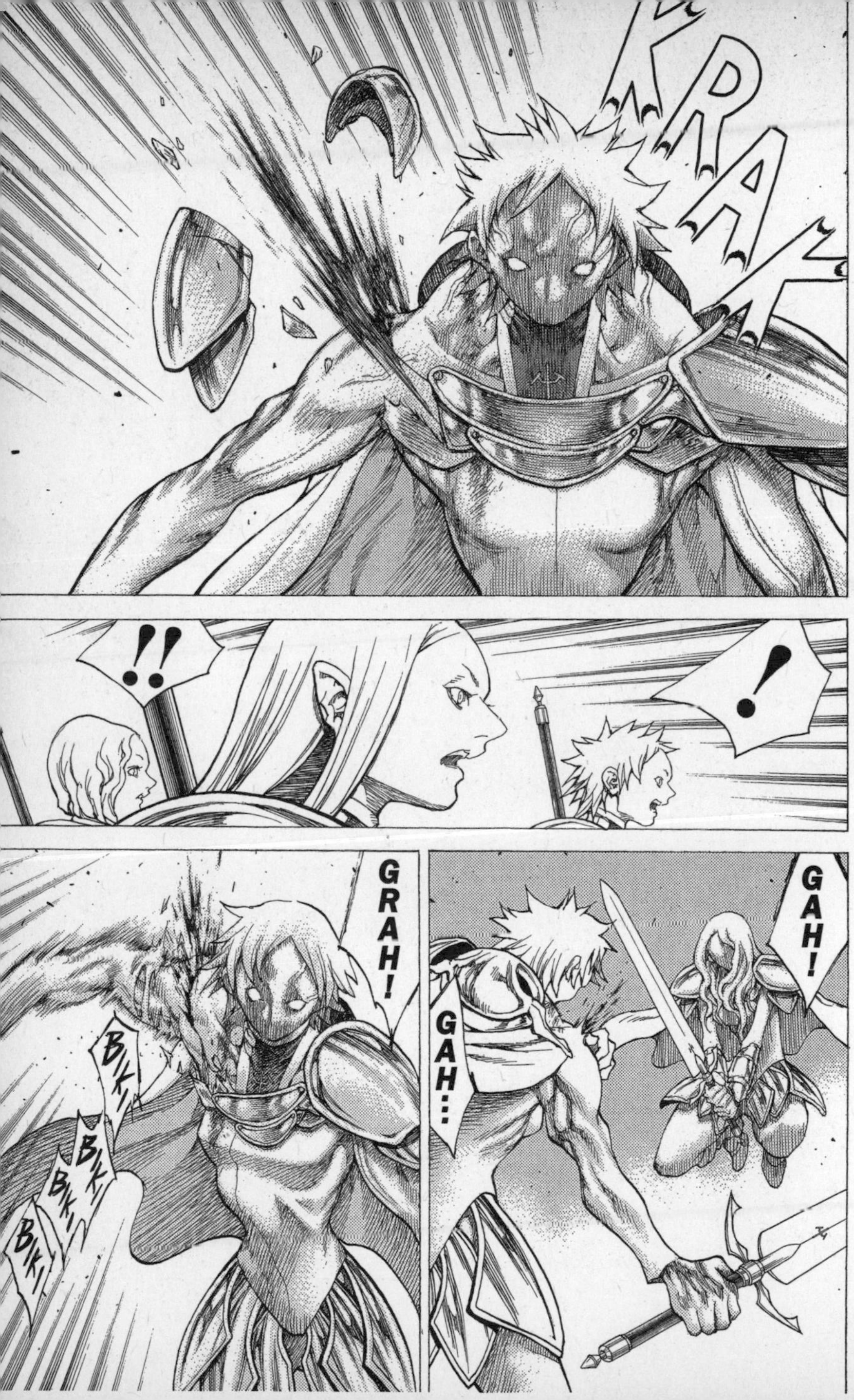
KRAK
!
!!
GAH!
GAH...
GRAH!
BIKI
BIKI
BIKI
BIKI

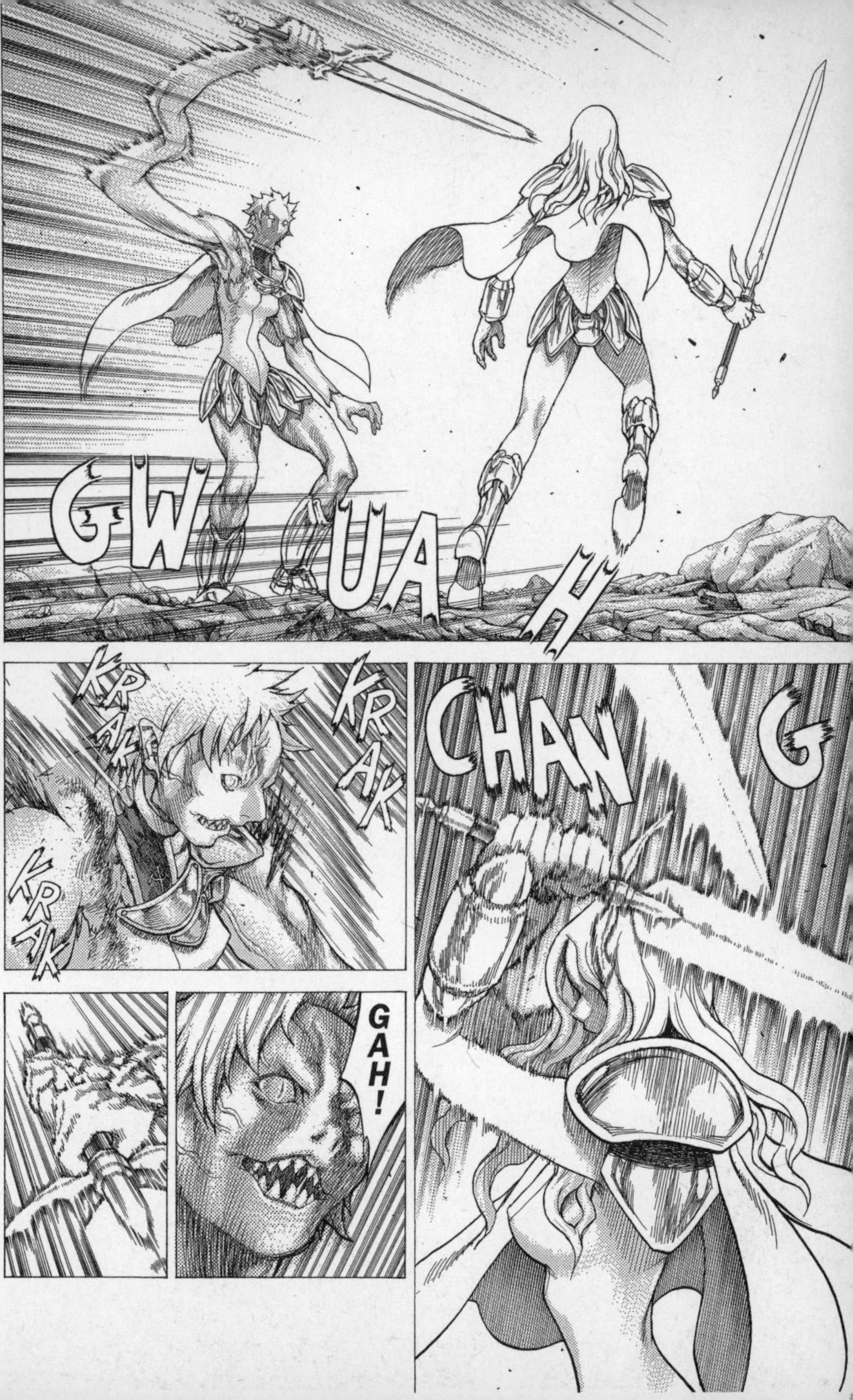
GWUAH
CHANG
KRAK
KRAK
KRAK
GAH!

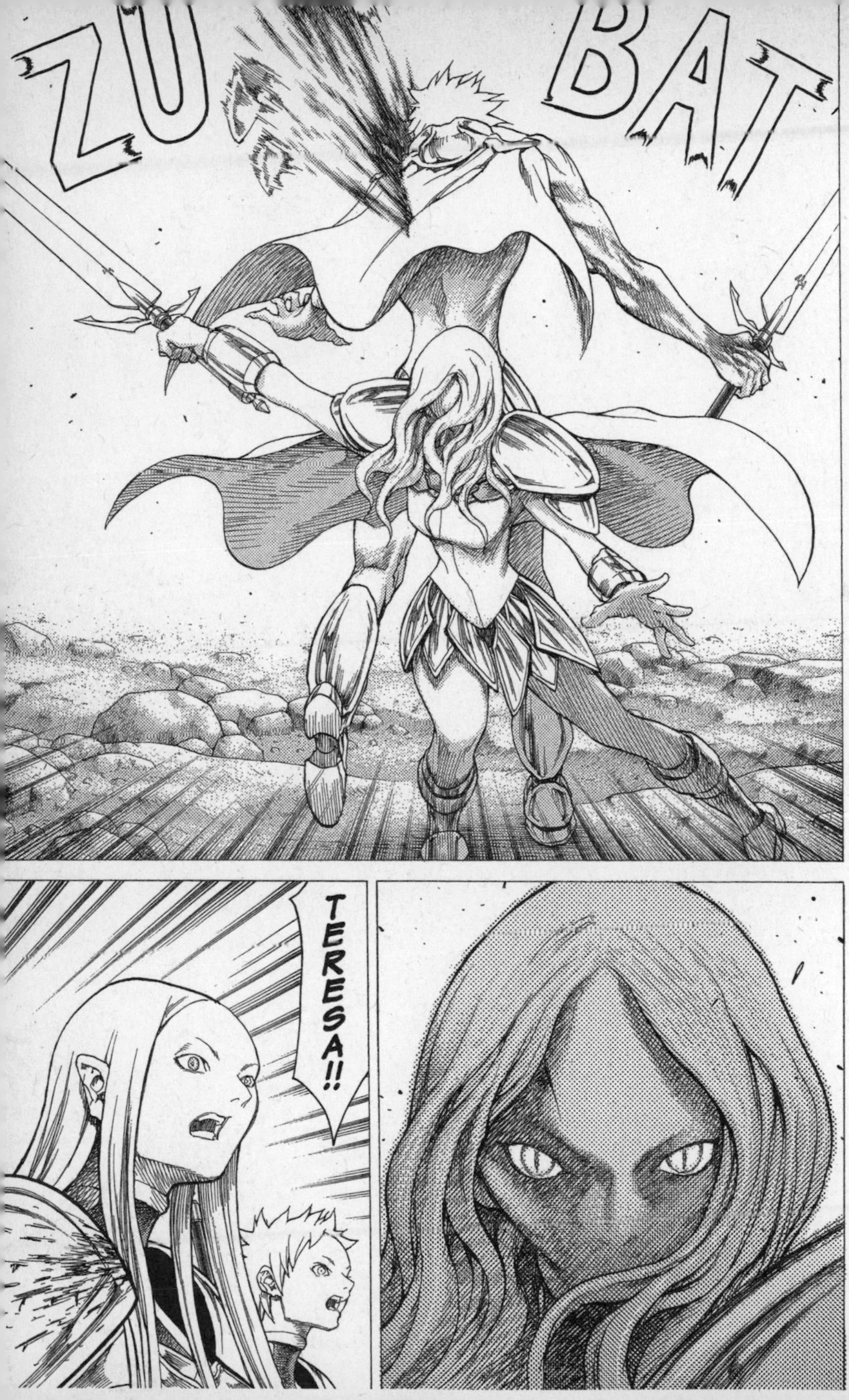
ZU BAT
TERESA!!

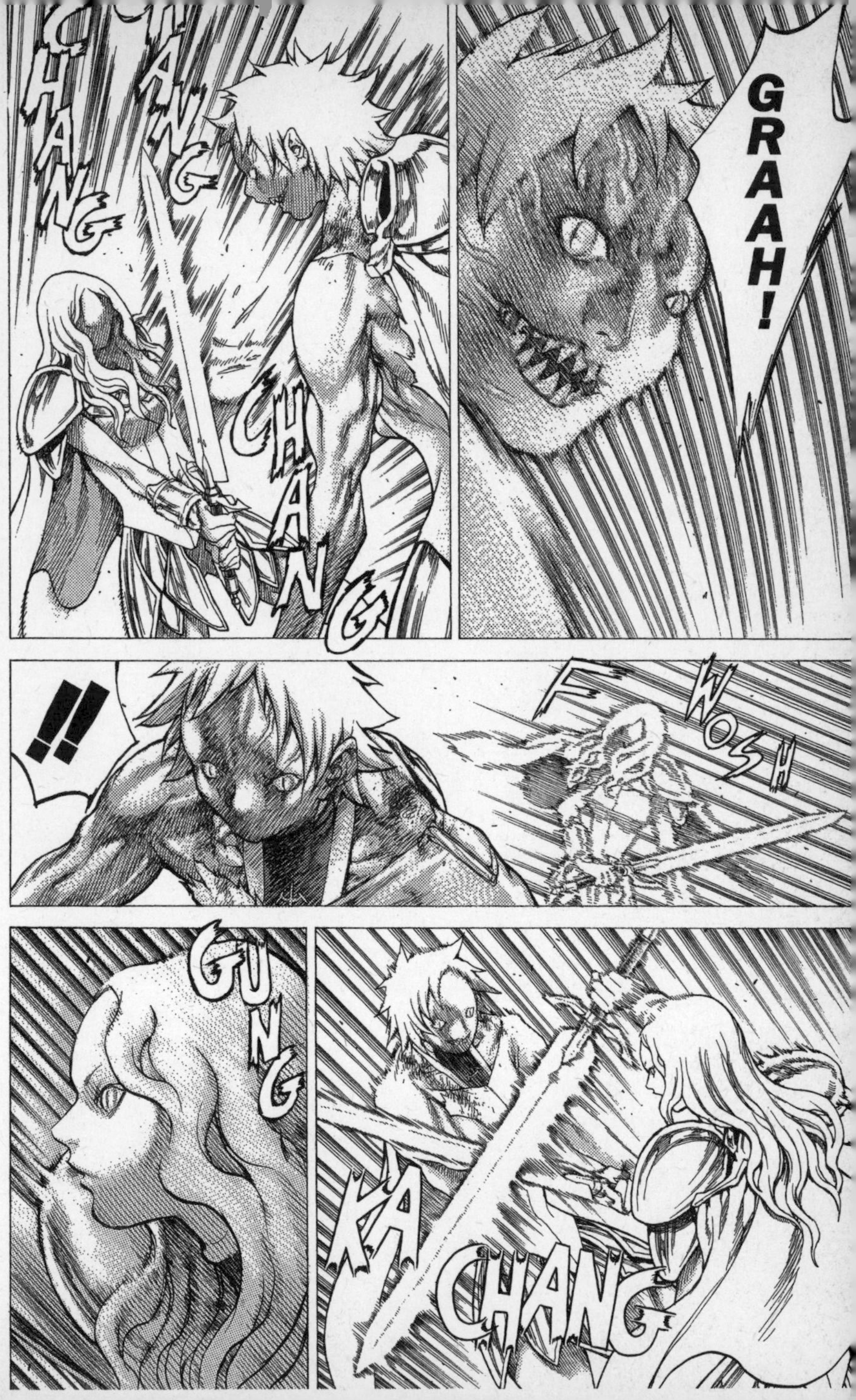
GRAAH!
CHANG
CHANG
CHANG
FWOSH
!!
KA
CHANG
GUNG

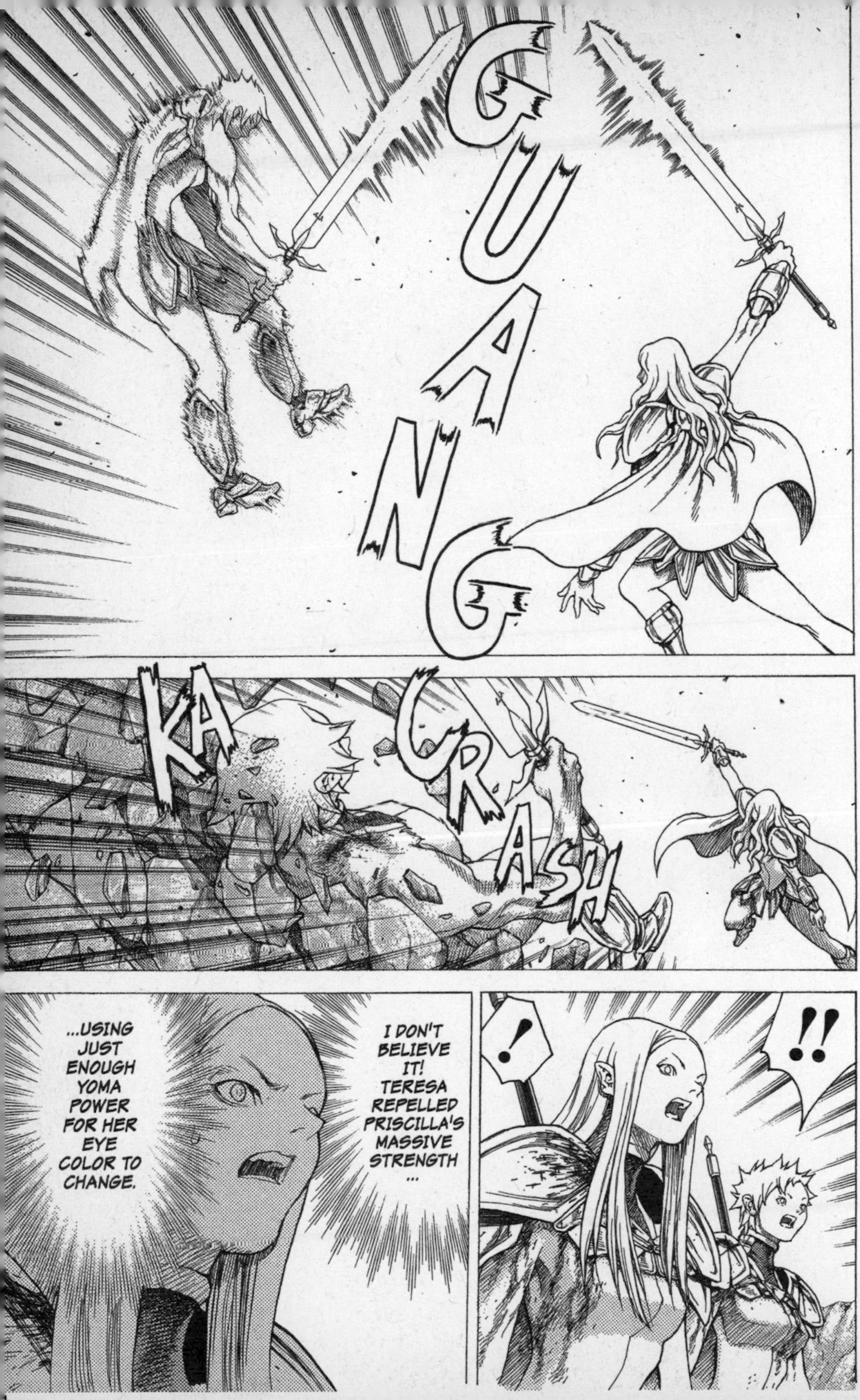
GUANG
KA
CRASH
!!
!
I DON'T BELIEVE IT! TERESA REPELLED PRISCILLA'S MASSIVE STRENGTH ...
...USING JUST ENOUGH YOMA POWER FOR HER EYE COLOR TO CHANGE.

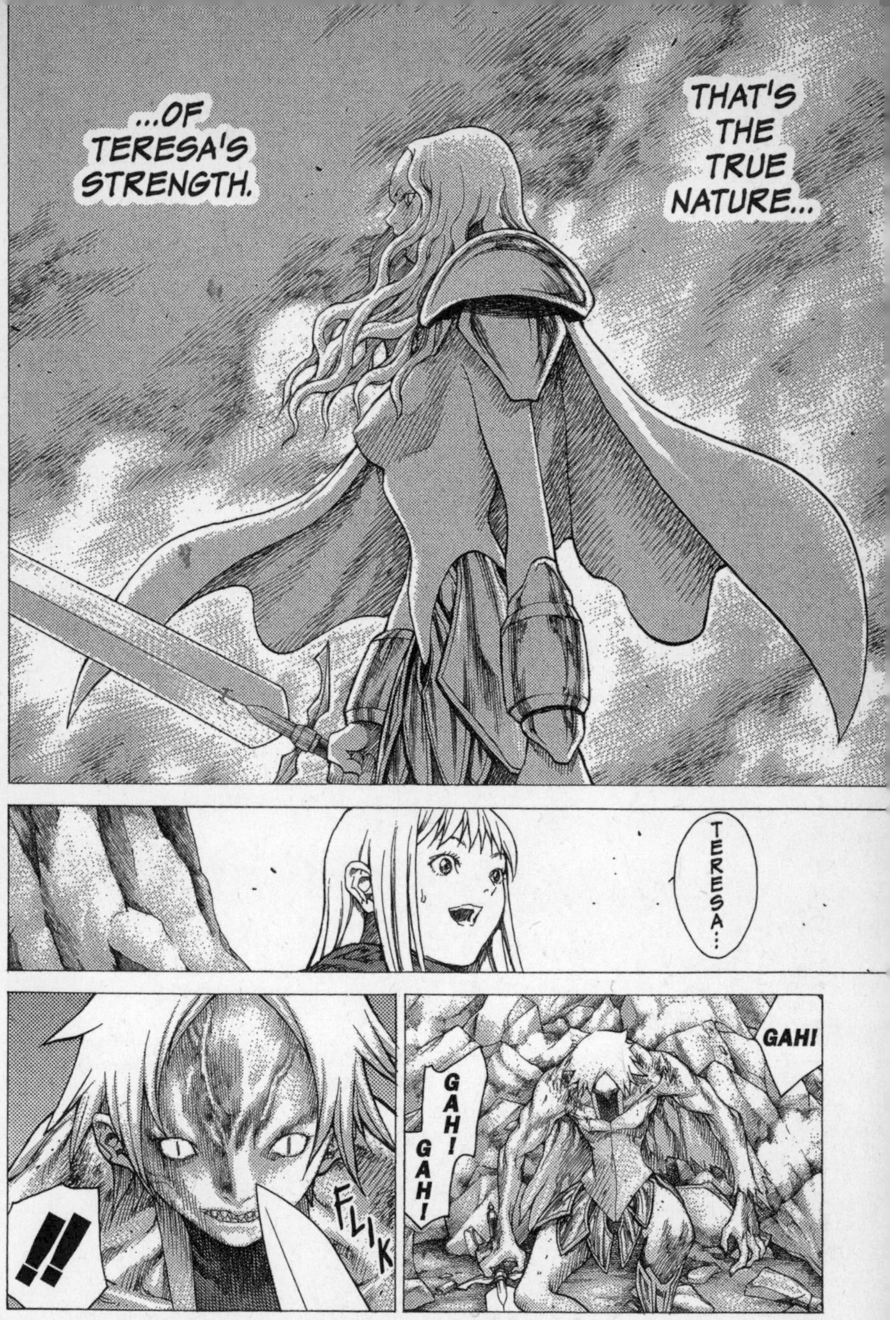
THAT'S THE TRUE NATURE...
...OF TERESA'S STRENGTH.
TERESA...
GAHI
GAHI
GAHI
GAHI
!!
FLIK

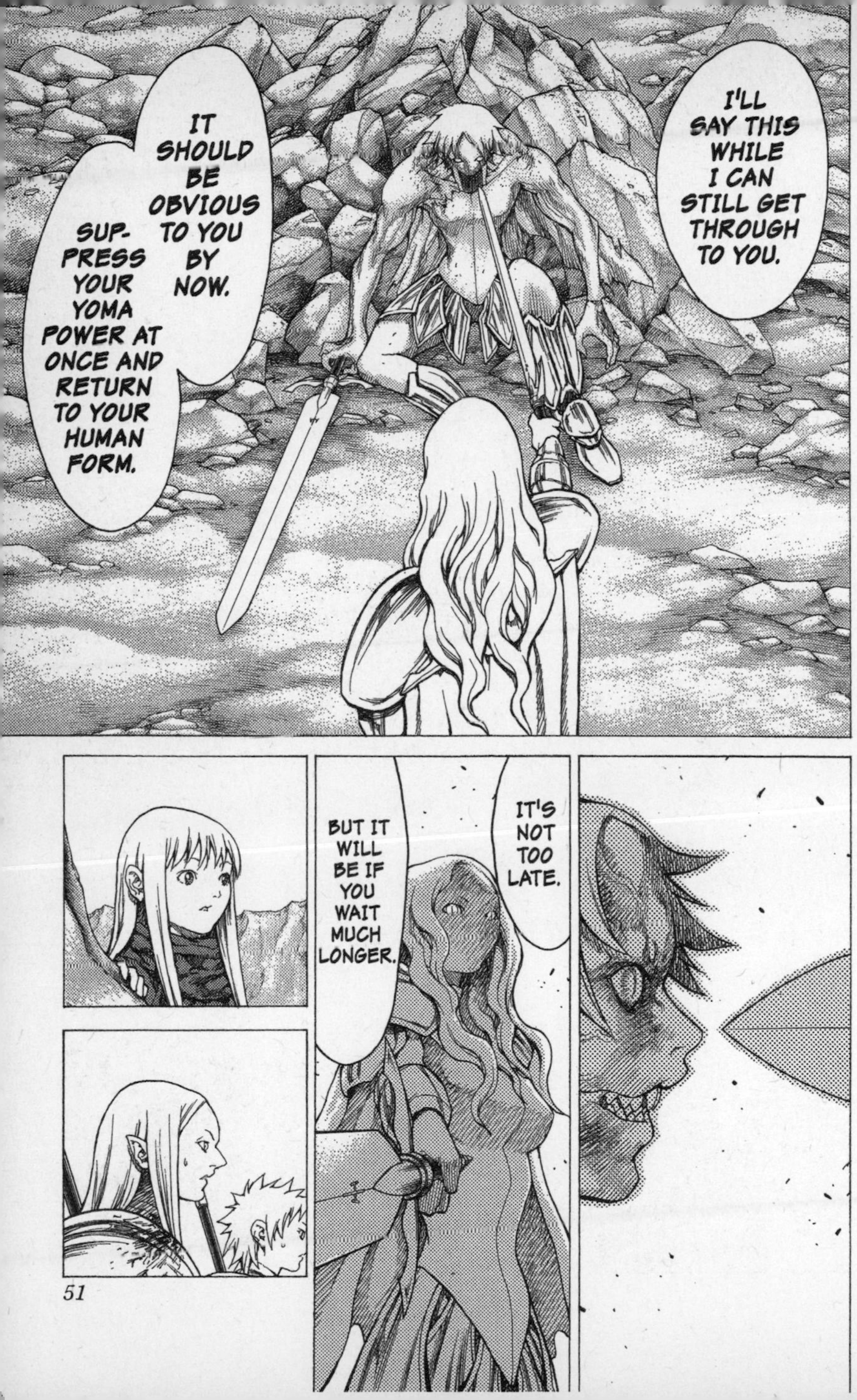
I'LL SAY THIS WHILE I CAN STILL GET THROUGH TO YOU.
IT SHOULD BE OBVIOUS TO YOU BY NOW.
SUP-PRESS YOUR YOMA POWER AT ONCE AND RETURN TO YOUR HUMAN FORM.
IT'S NOT TOO LATE.
BUT IT WILL BE IF YOU WAIT MUCH LONGER.

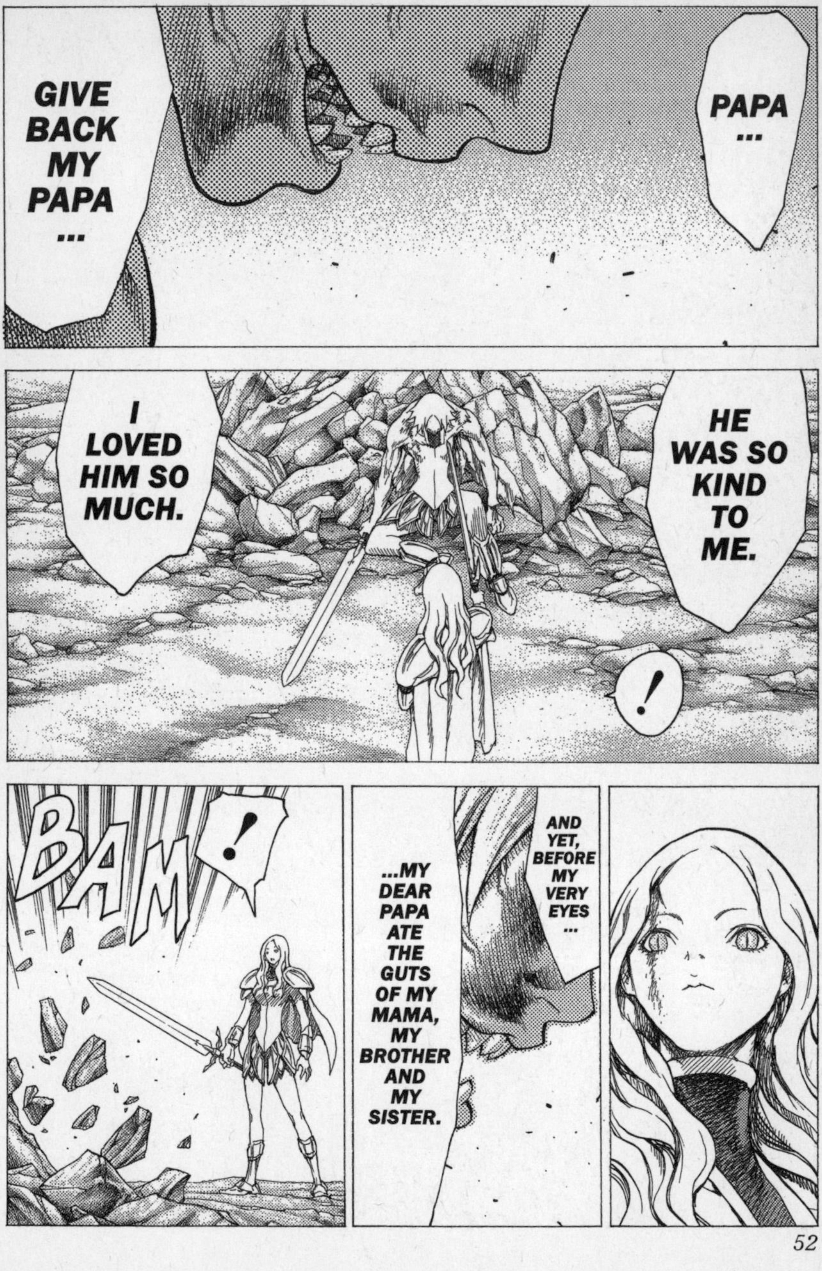
PAPA ...
GIVE BACK MY PAPA ...
HE WAS SO KIND TO ME.
I LOVED HIM SO MUCH.
!
AND YET, BEFORE MY VERY EYES ...
...MY DEAR PAPA ATE THE GUTS OF MY MAMA, MY BROTHER AND MY SISTER.
!
BAM

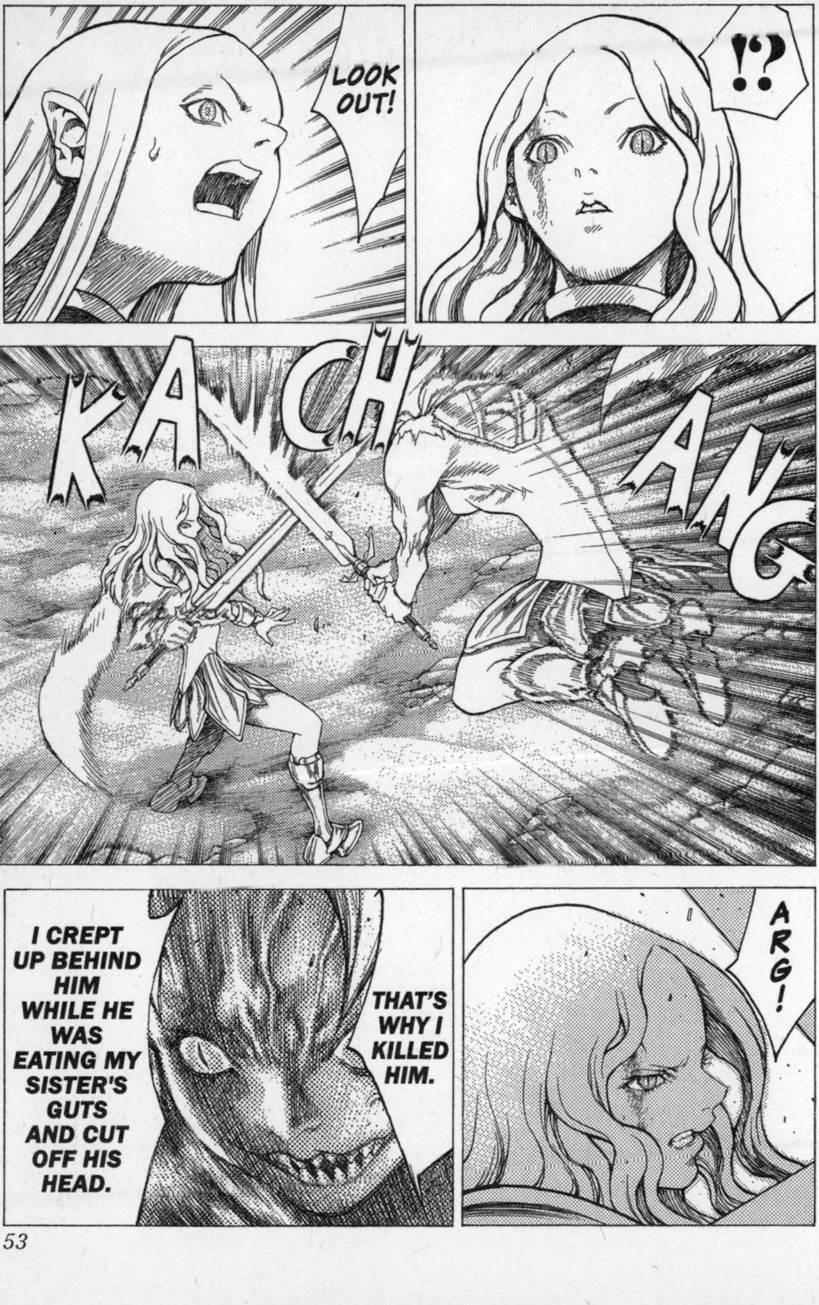
!?
LOOK OUT!
KACH
ANG
ARG!
THAT'S WHY I KILLED HIM.
I CREPT UP BEHIND HIM WHILE HE WAS EATING MY SISTER'S GUTS AND CUT OFF HIS HEAD.

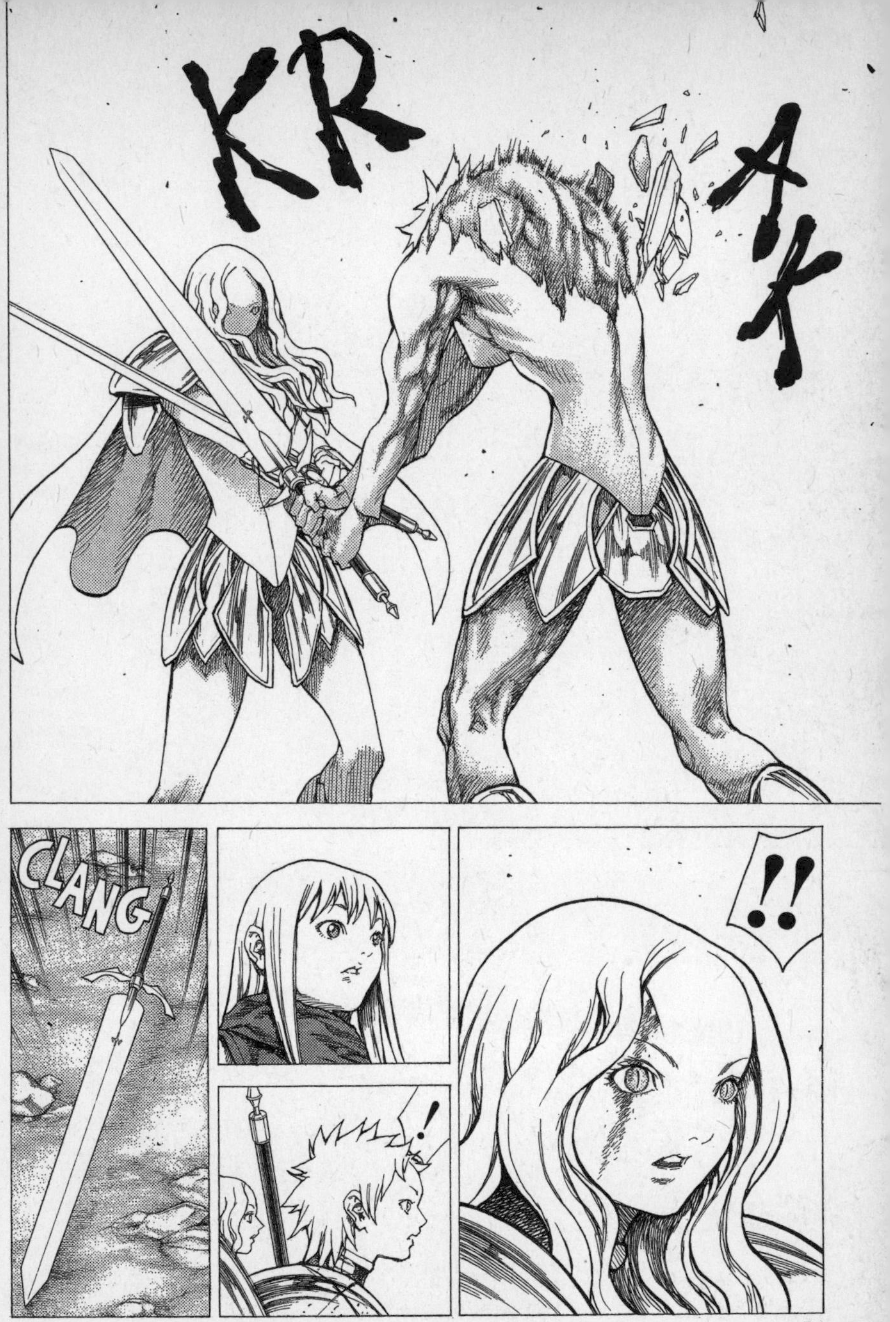
KRAK
!!
!
CLANG

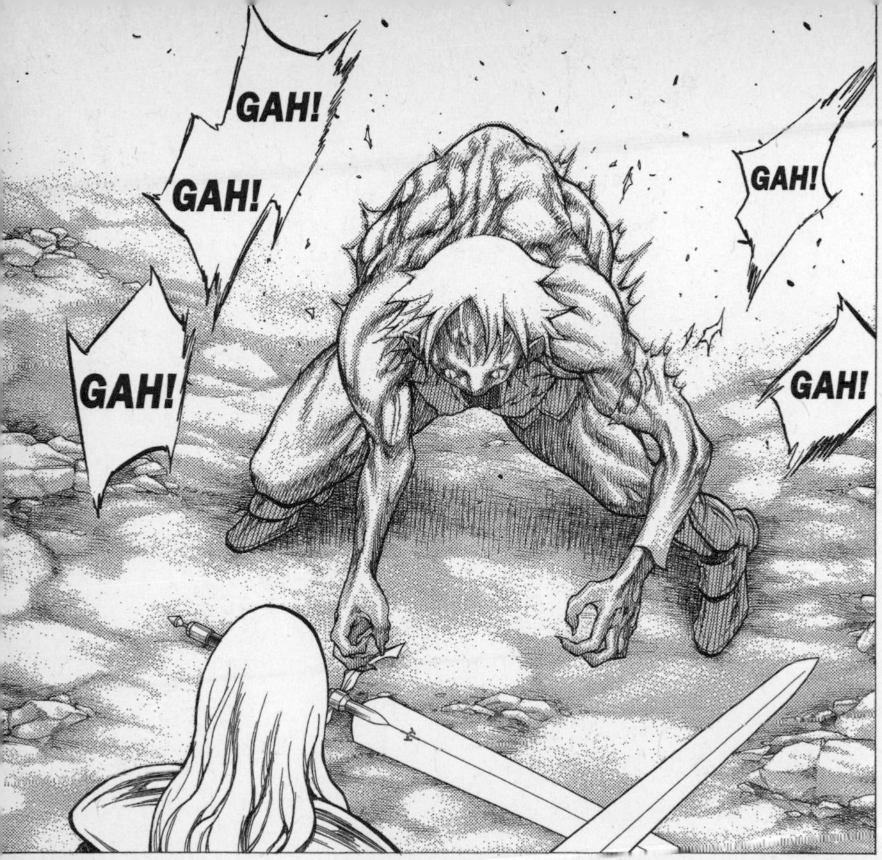
GAH!
GAH!
GAH!
GAH!
GAH!

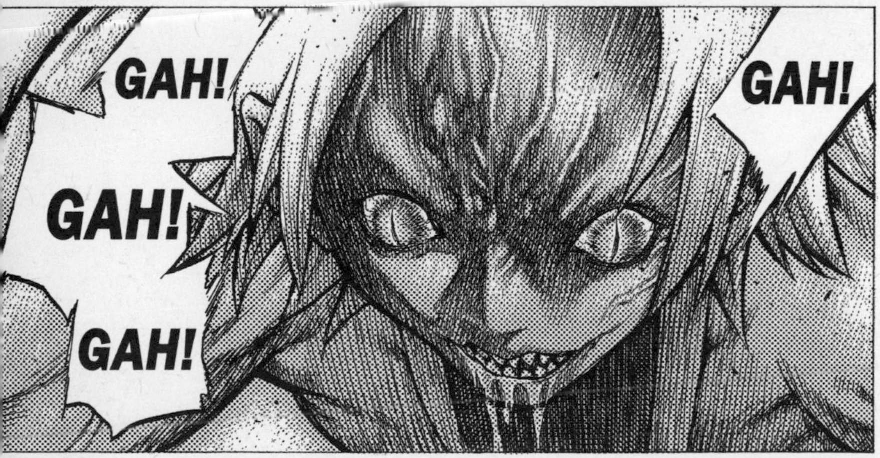
GAH!
GAH!
GAH!
GAH!

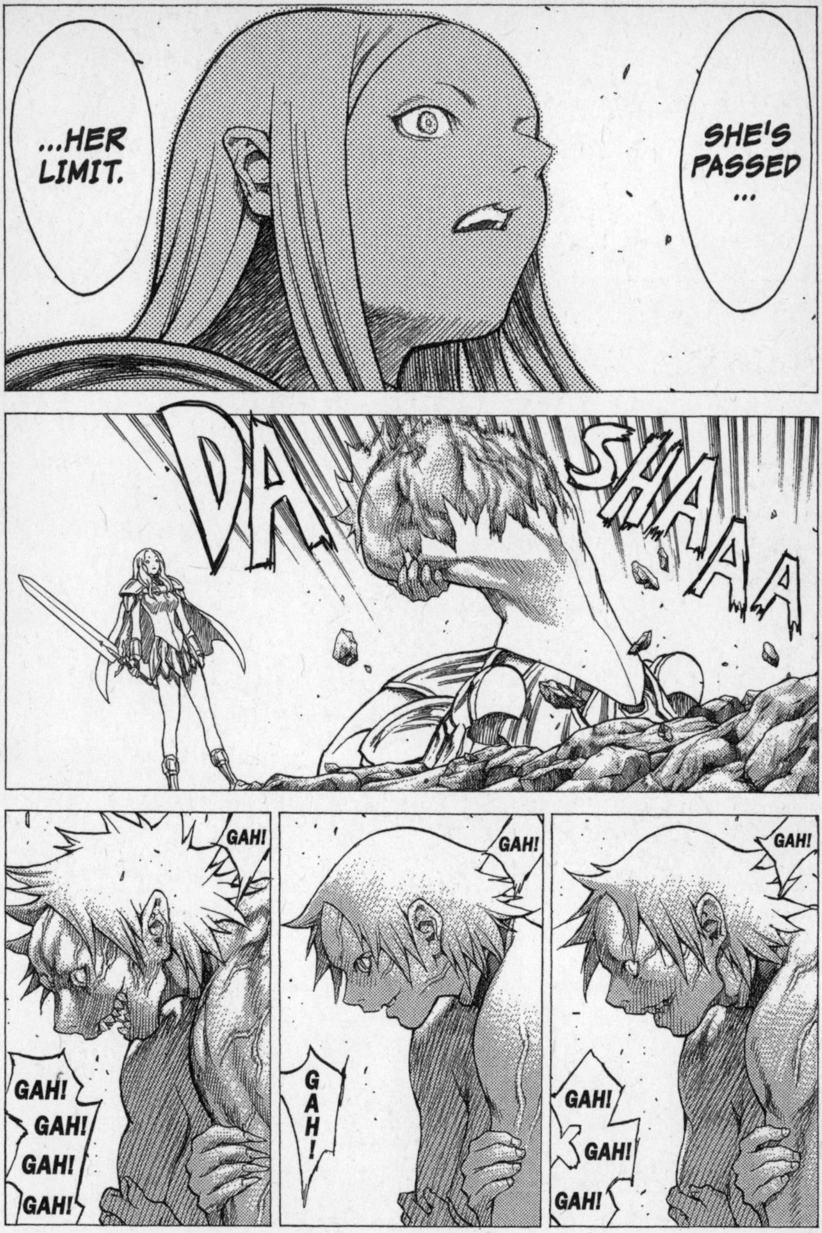
SHE'S PASSED ...
...HER LIMIT.
DA SHAAA
GAH!
GAH!
GAH!
GAH!
GAH!
GAH!
GAH!
GAH!
GAH!
GAH!
GAH!
GAH!

READ THIS WAY

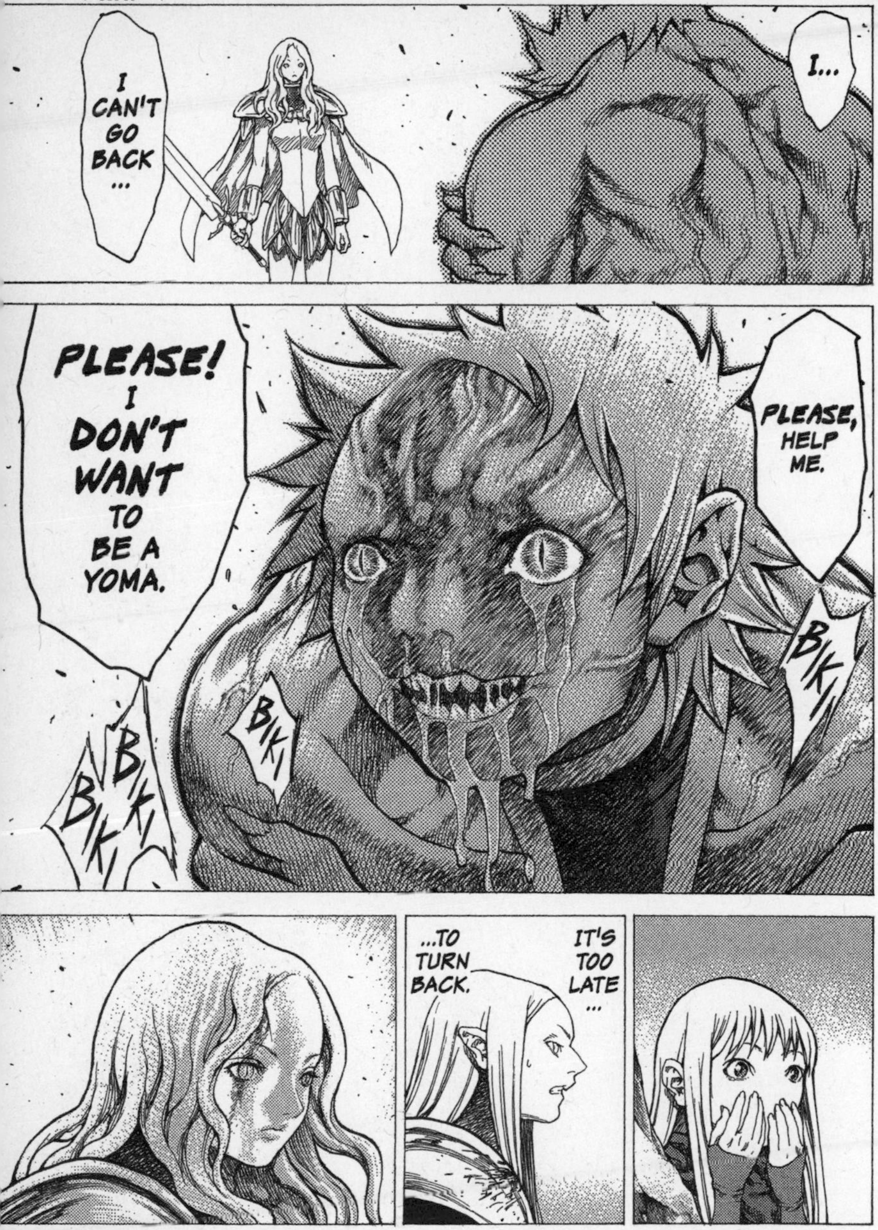

I...
I CAN'T GO BACK ...
PLEASE, HELP ME.
PLEASE! I DON'T WANT TO BE A YOMA.
BIKI
BIKI
BIKI
BIKI
IT'S TOO LATE ...
...TO TURN BACK.

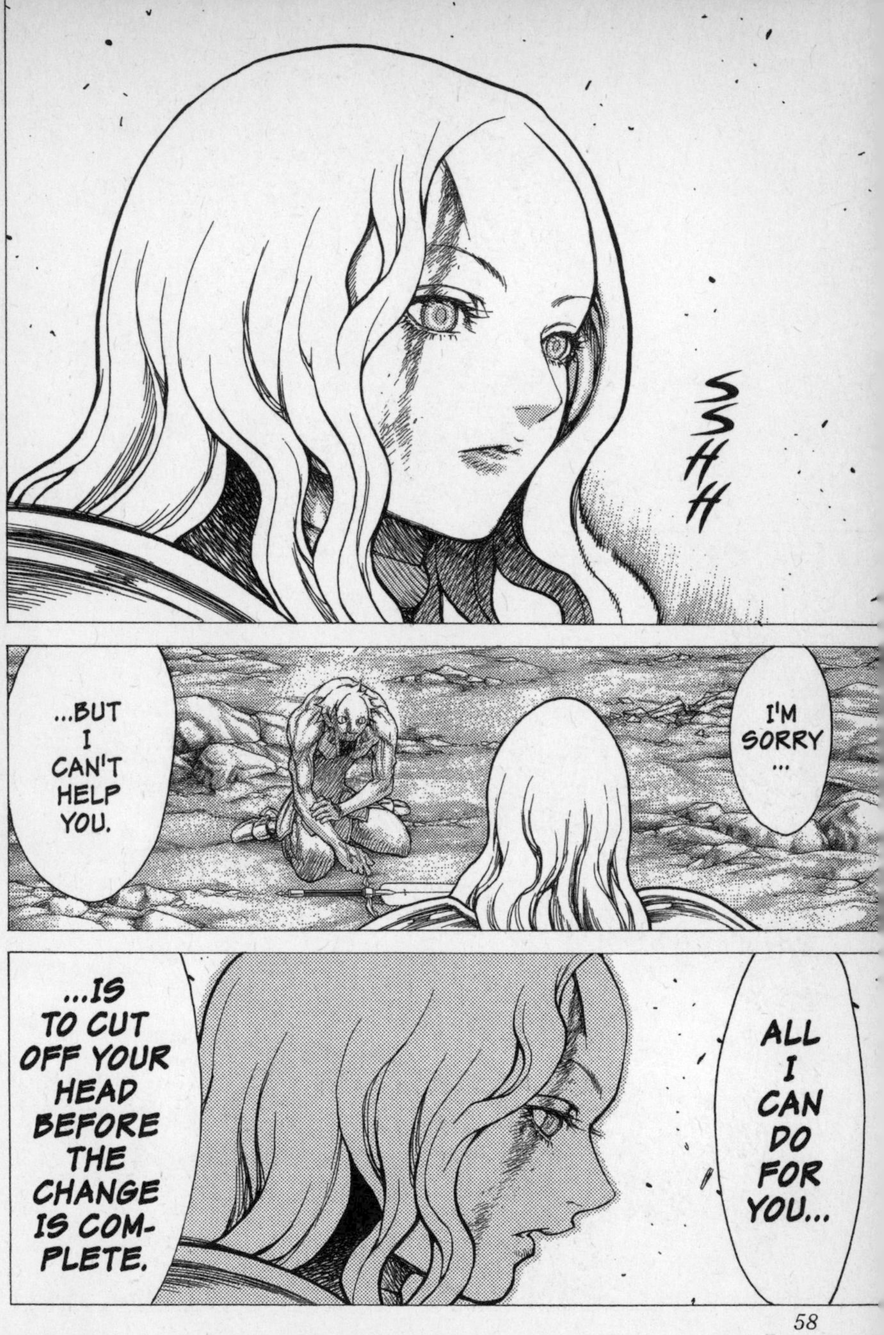
SSHH
I'M SORRY ...
...BUT I CAN'T HELP YOU.
ALL I CAN DO FOR YOU...
...IS TO CUT OFF YOUR HEAD BEFORE THE CHANGE IS COM-PLETE.

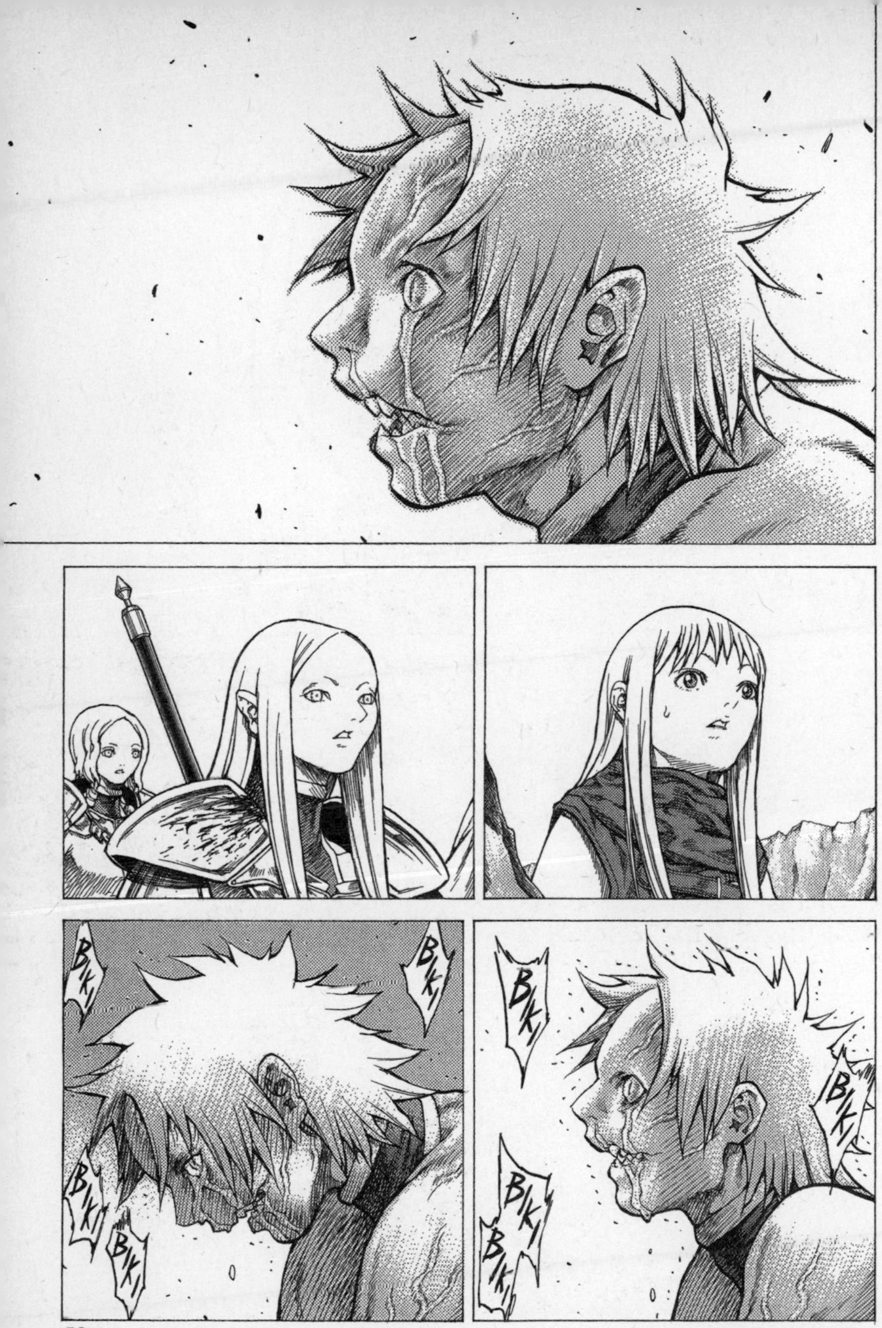
BIKI
BIKI
BIKI
BIKI
BIKI
BIKI
BIKI
BIKI

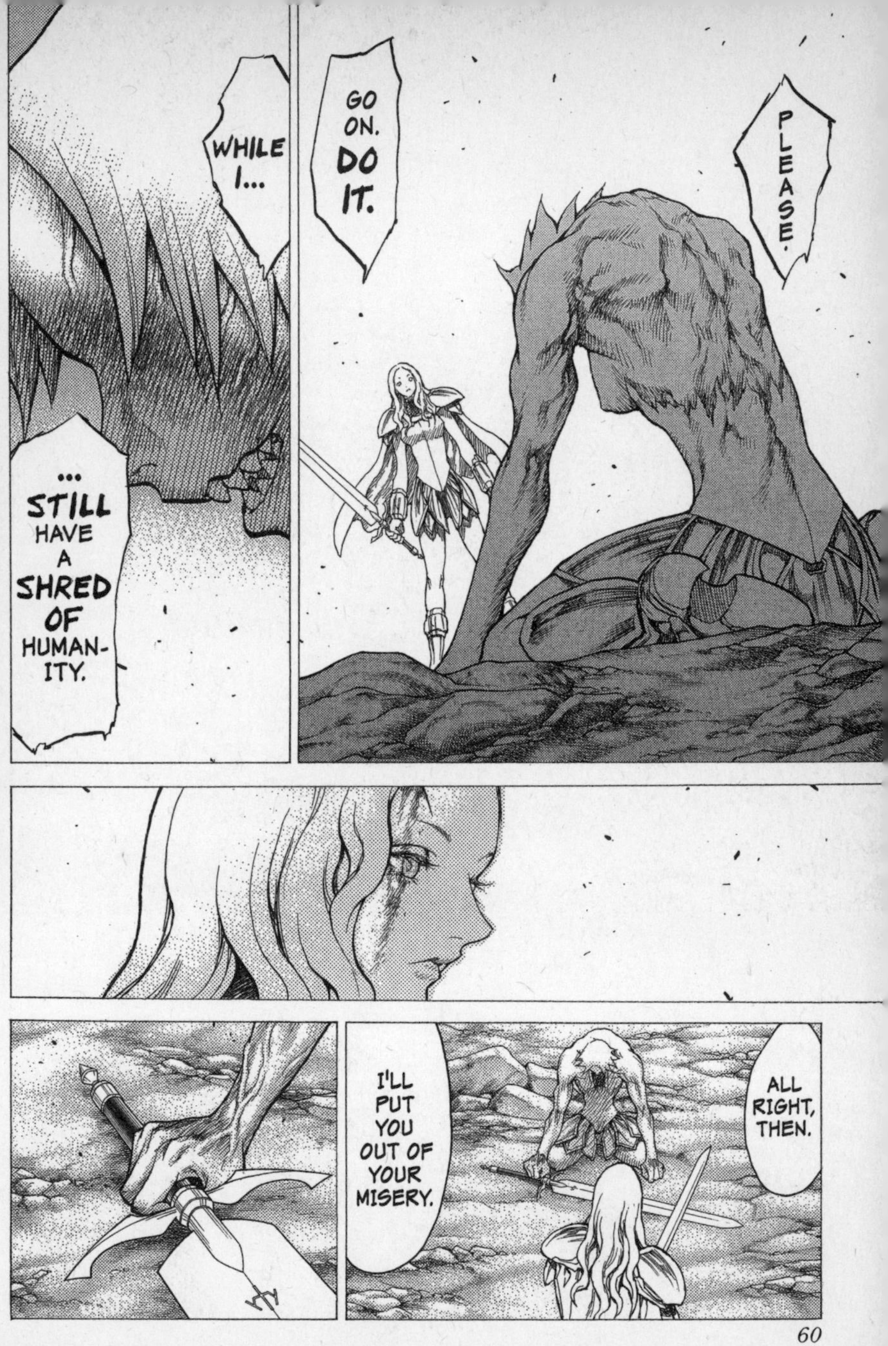
PLEASE.
GO ON. DO IT.
WHILE I...
...STILL HAVE A SHRED OF HUMANITY.
ALL RIGHT, THEN.
I'LL PUT YOU OUT OF YOUR MISERY.

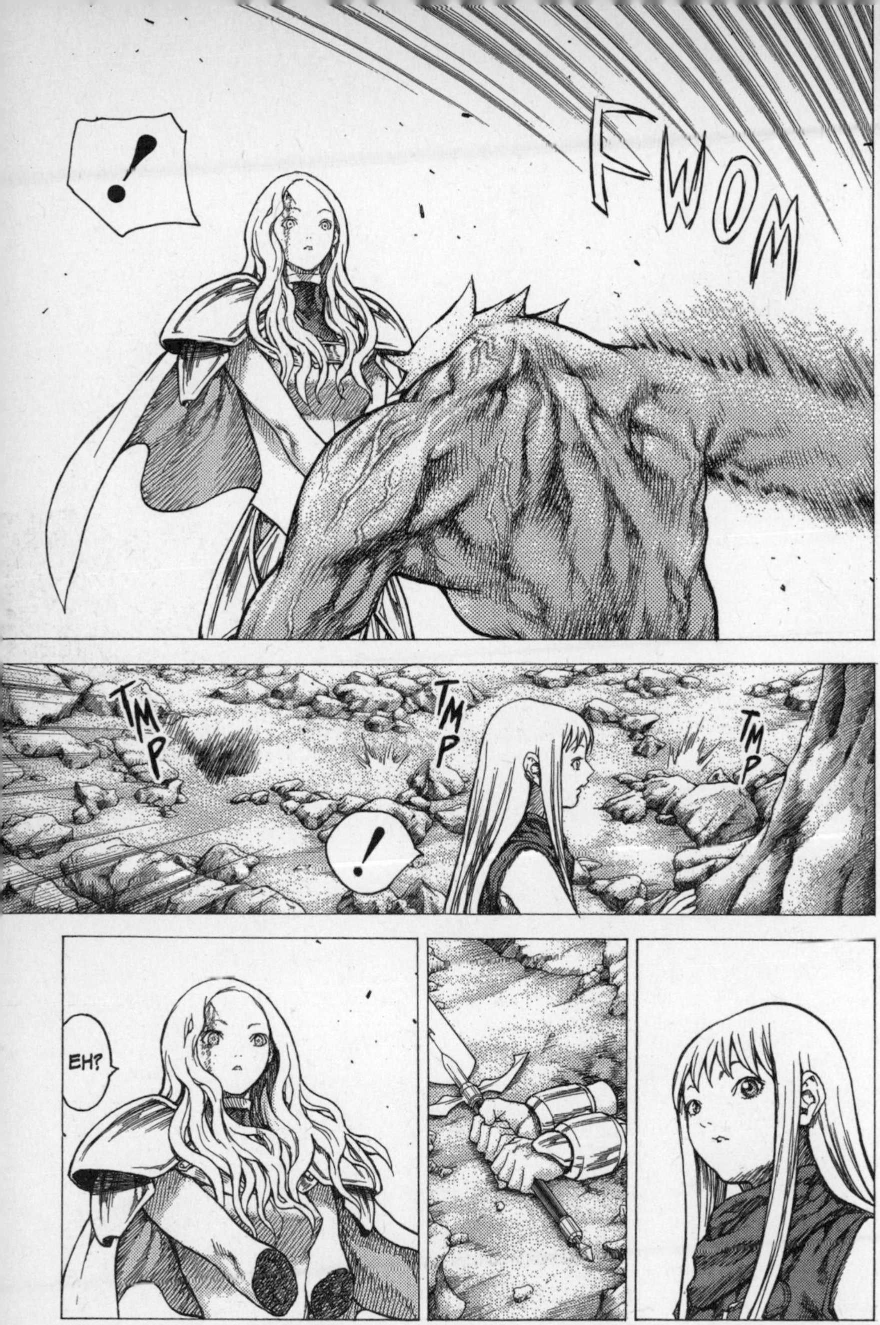
FWOM
!
TMP
TMP
TMP
!
EH?

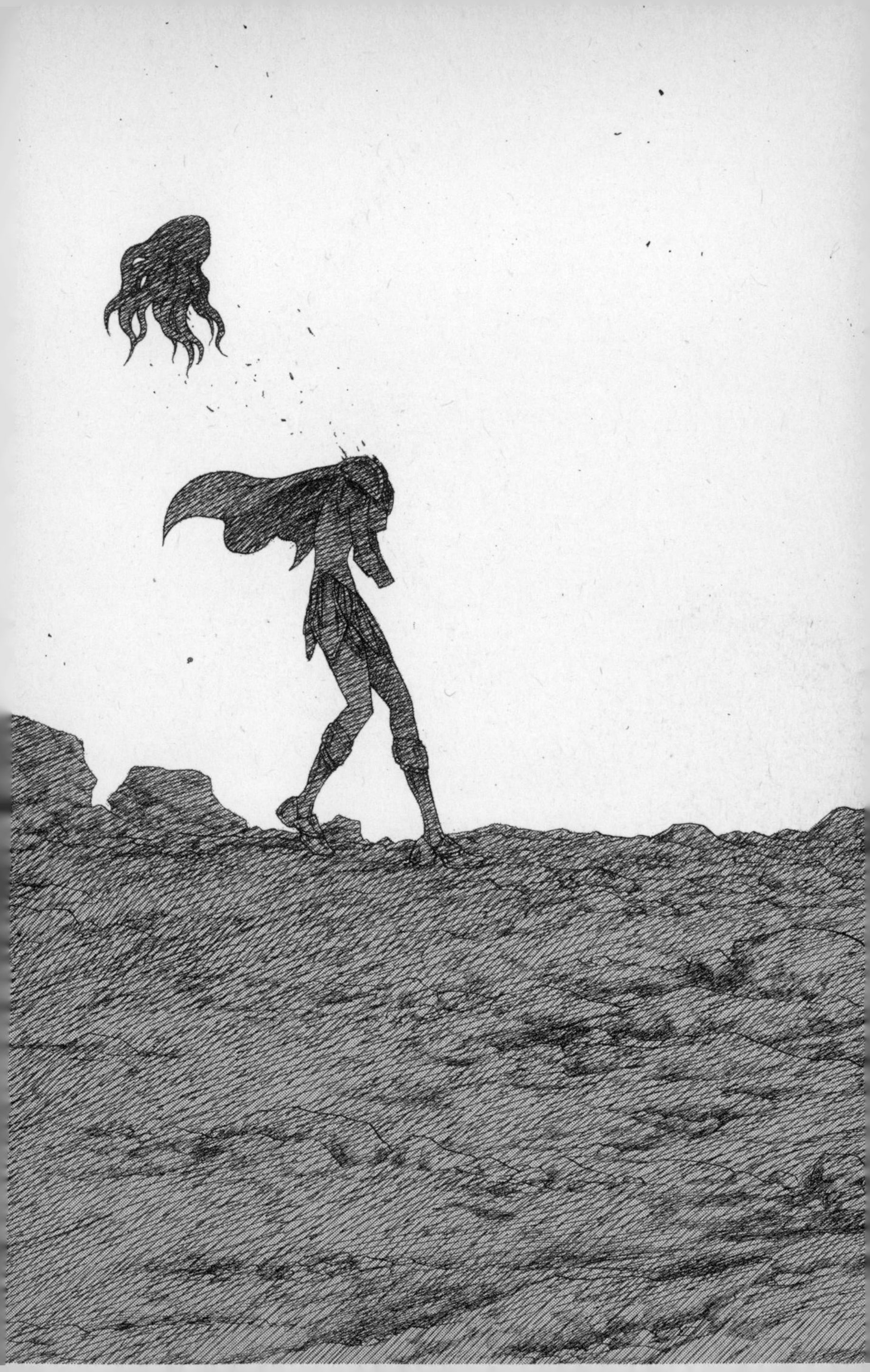

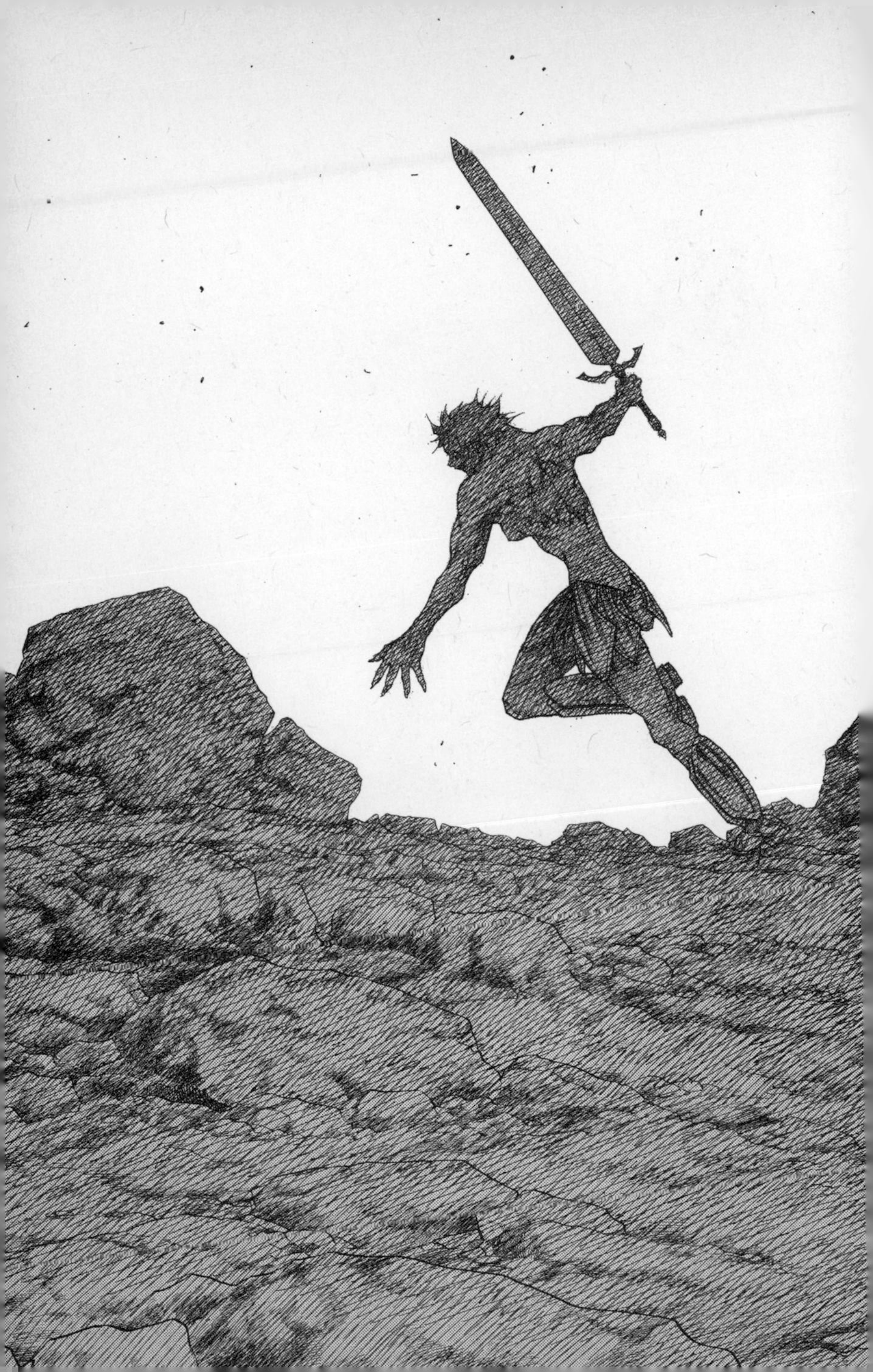

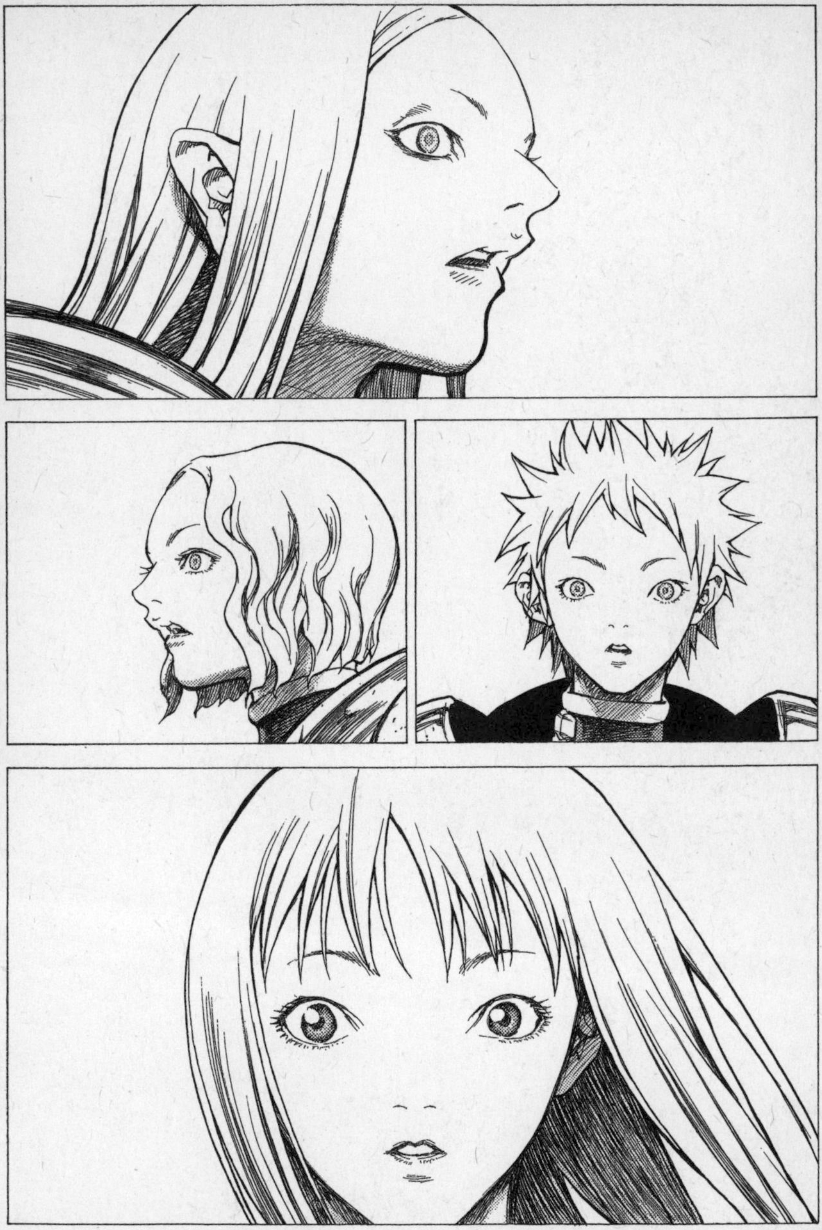

READ THIS WAY

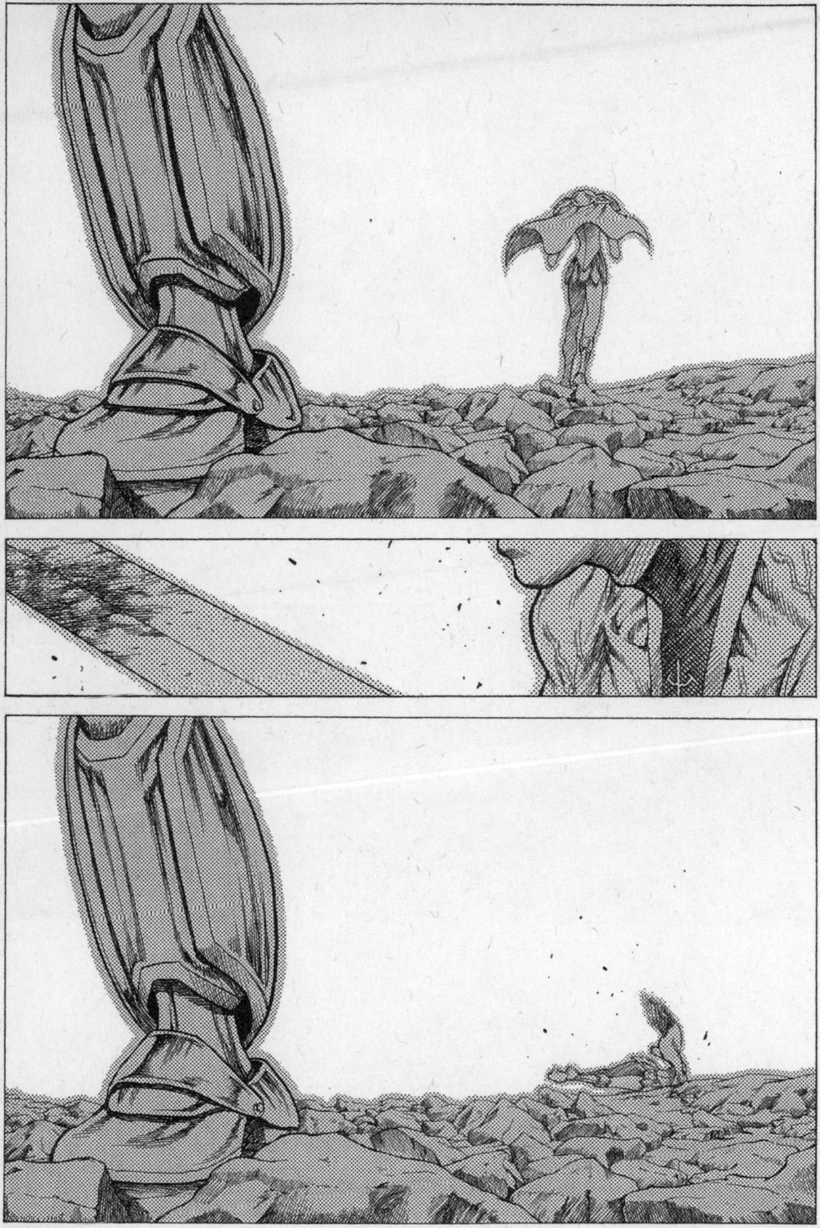

IT WAS
THEN...

...AMID BRUTAL
PAIN AND
INTENSE
PLEASURE...

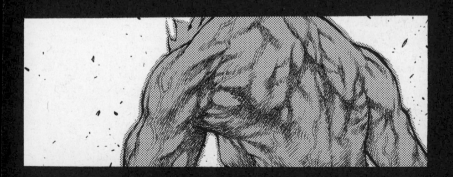

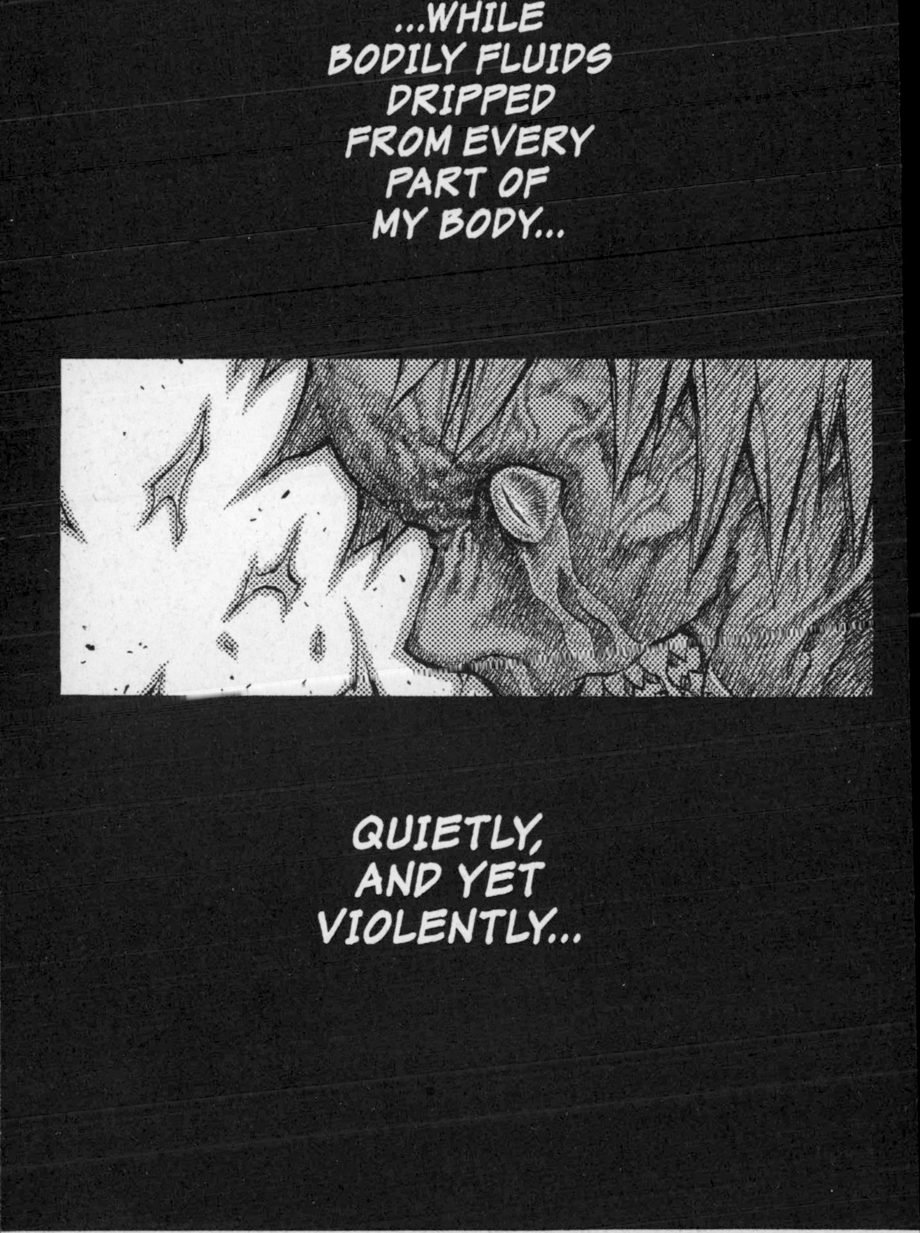
...WHILE BODILY FLUIDS DRIPPED FROM EVERY PART OF MY BODY...
QUIETLY, AND YET VIOLENTLY...

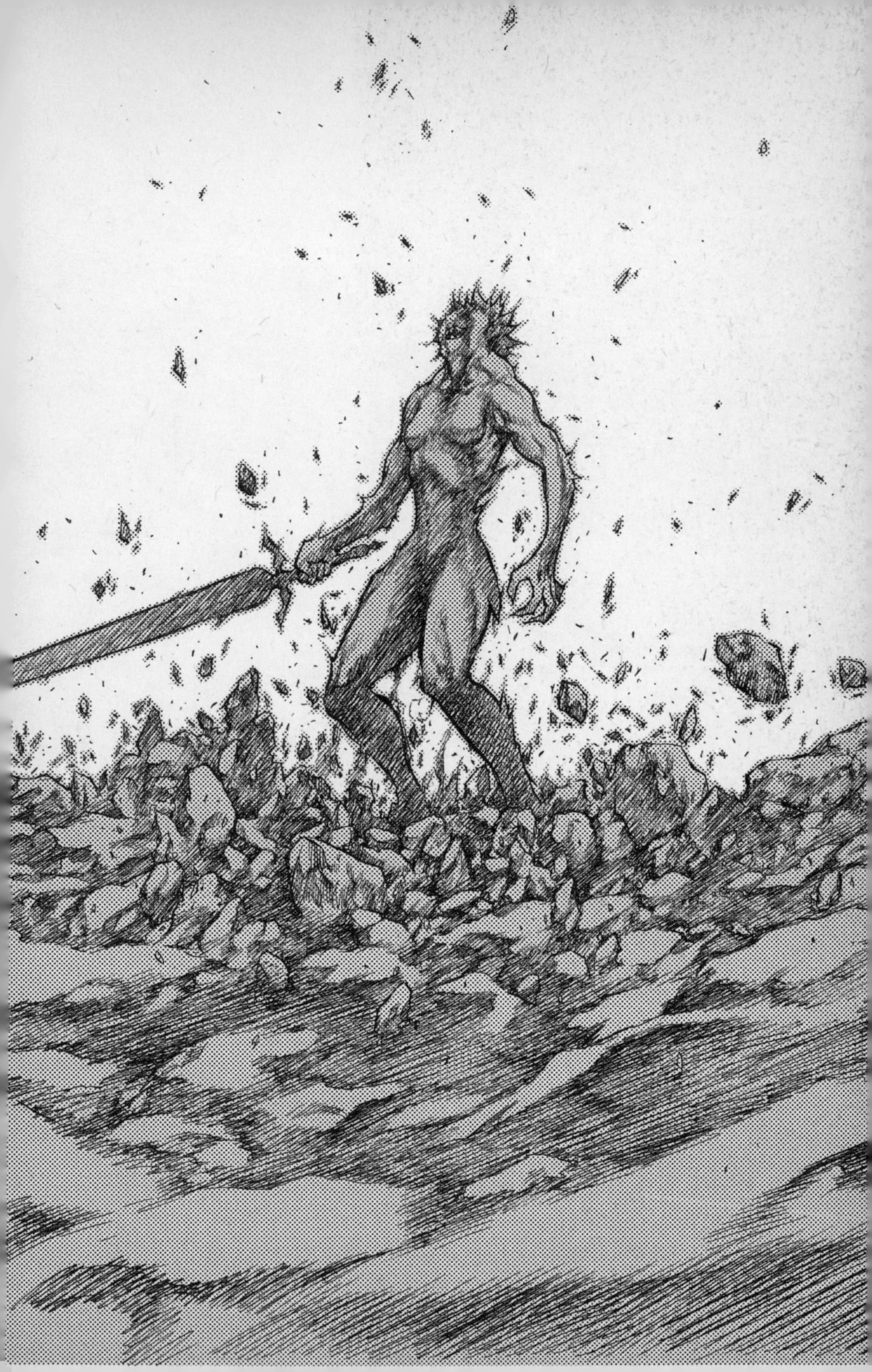

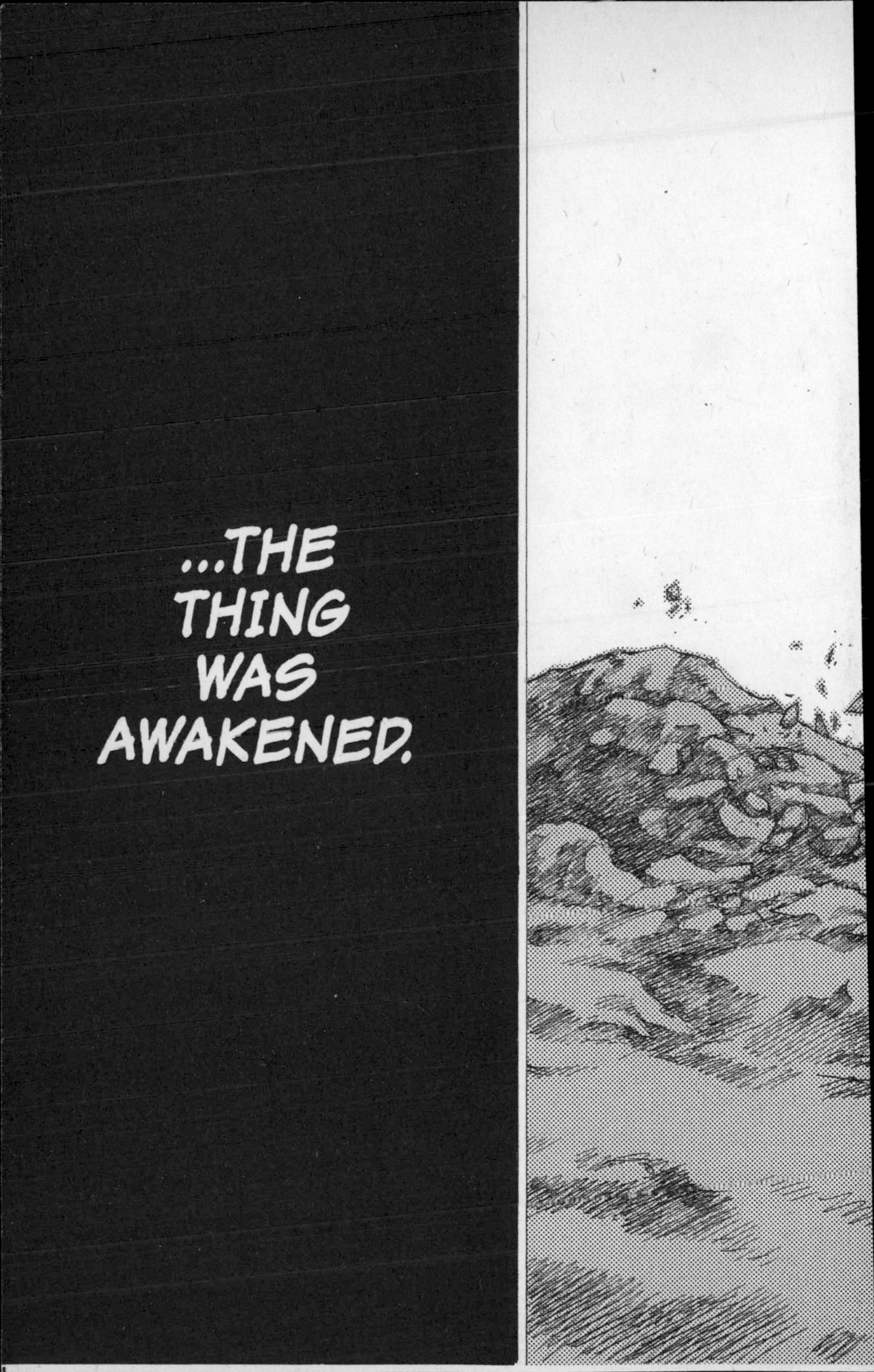
...THE THING WAS AWAKENED.

クレイモア
Claymore™

Scene 24: Marked for Death, Part 7

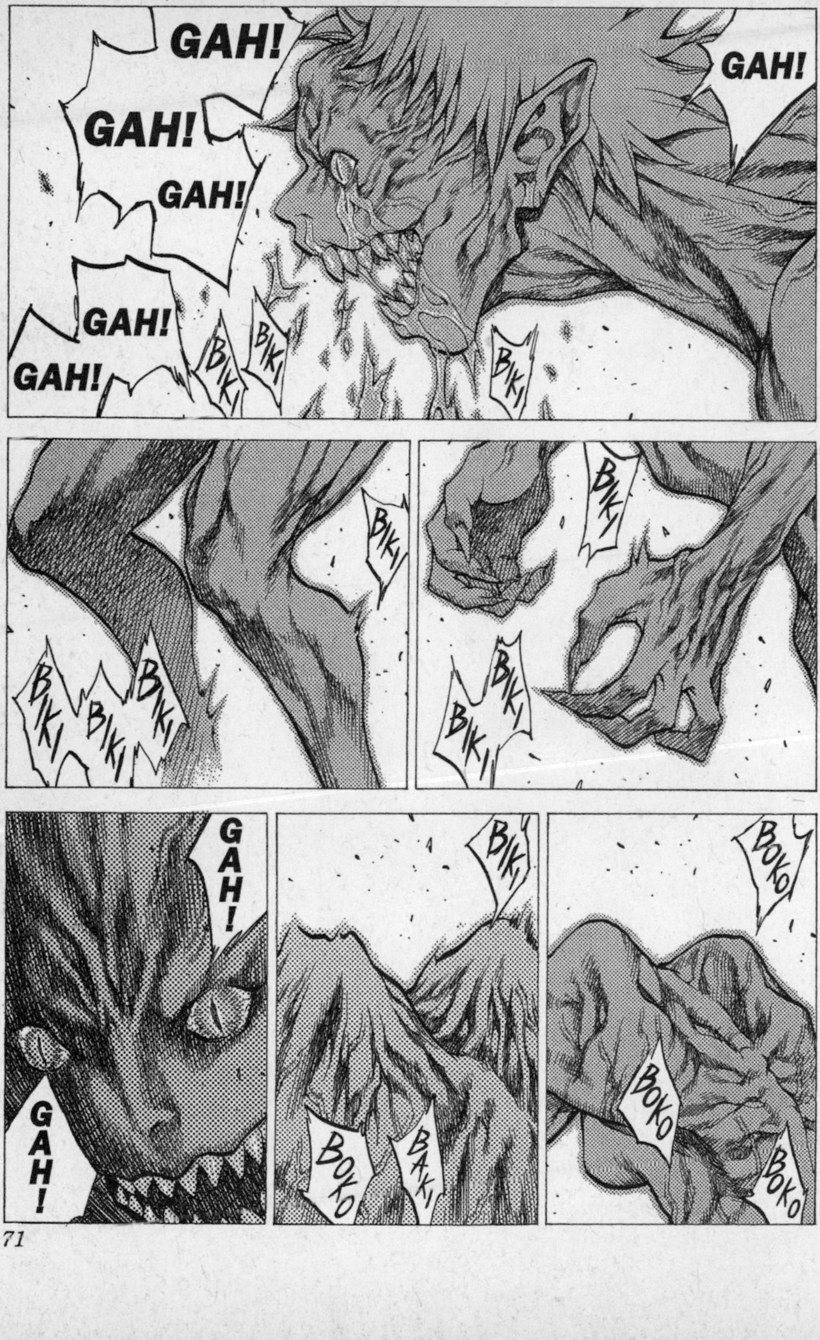
GAH!
GAH!
GAH!
GAH!
BIKI
BIKI
BIKI
GAH!
GAH!
BIKI
BIKI
BIKI
BIKI
BIKI
BIKI
BIKI
BIKI
BOKO
BOKO
BOKO
BIKI
BAKI
BOKO
GAH!
GAH!

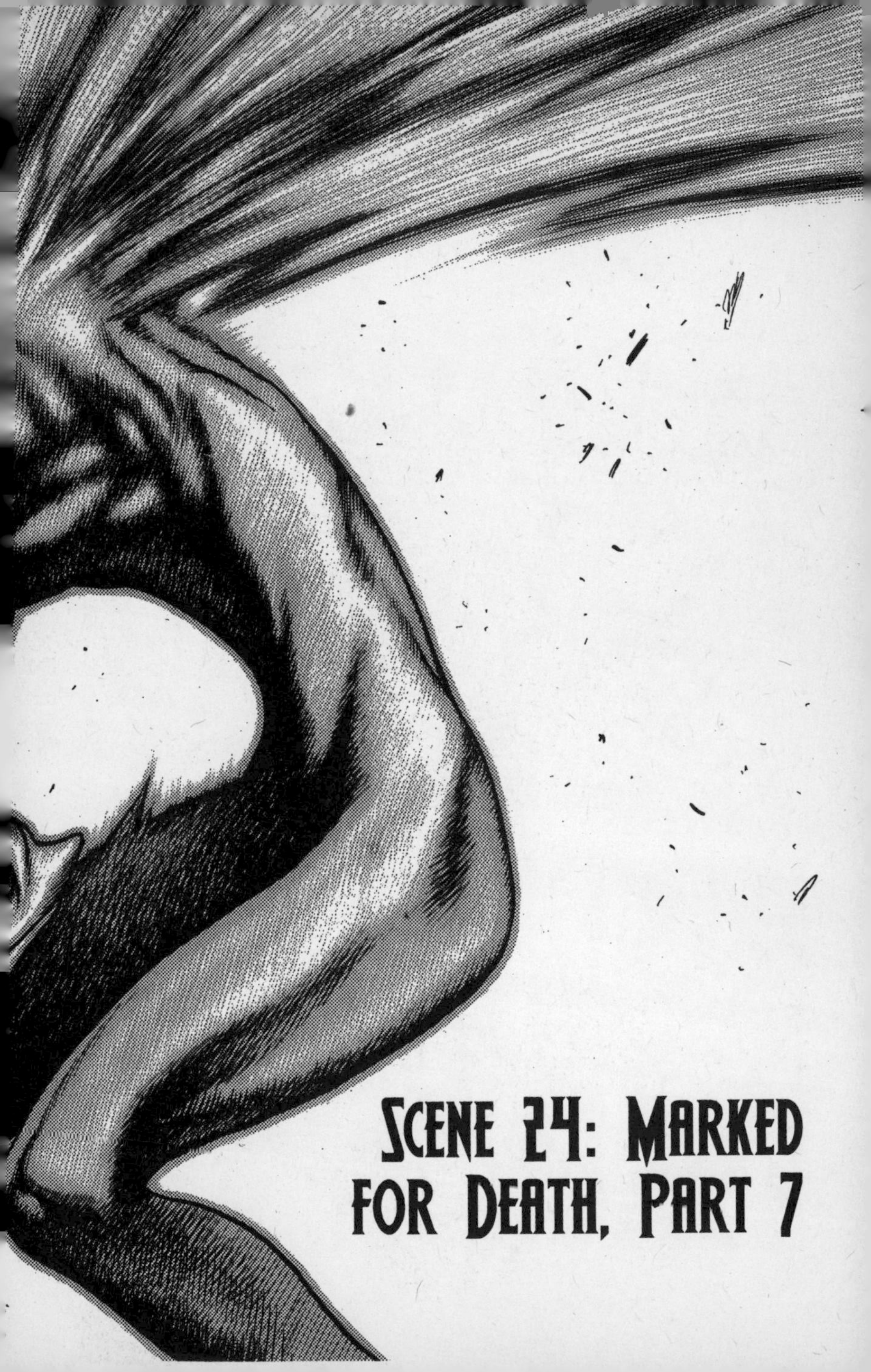

Scene 24: Marked for Death, Part 7

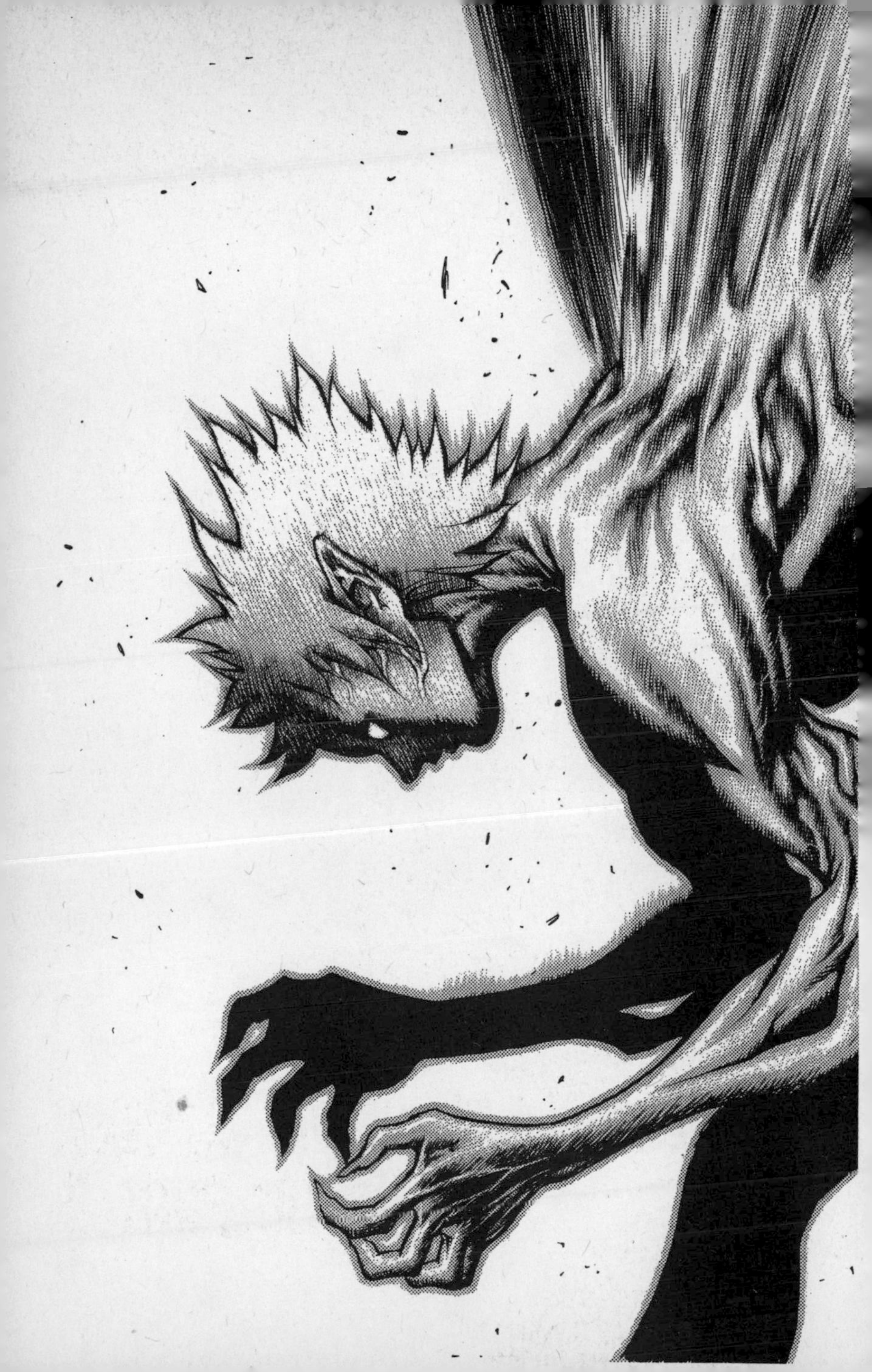

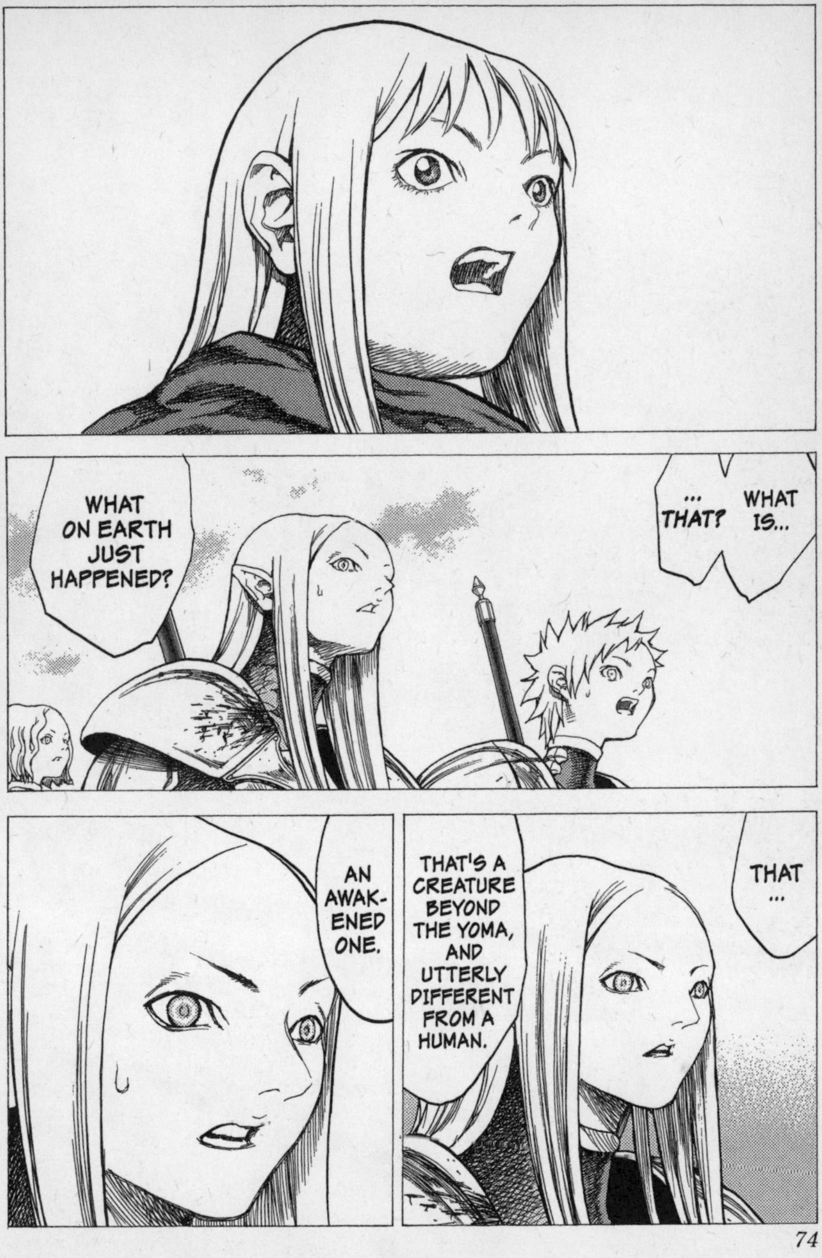
WHAT IS...
... THAT?
WHAT ON EARTH JUST HAPPENED?
THAT ...
THAT'S A CREATURE BEYOND THE YOMA, AND UTTERLY DIFFERENT FROM A HUMAN.
AN AWAK-ENED ONE.

...THERE WAS NO REASON AT ALL TO HOLD BACK.

IT...

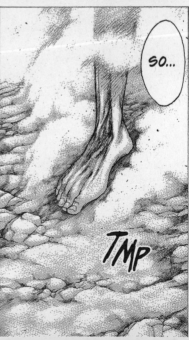

SO...

TMP

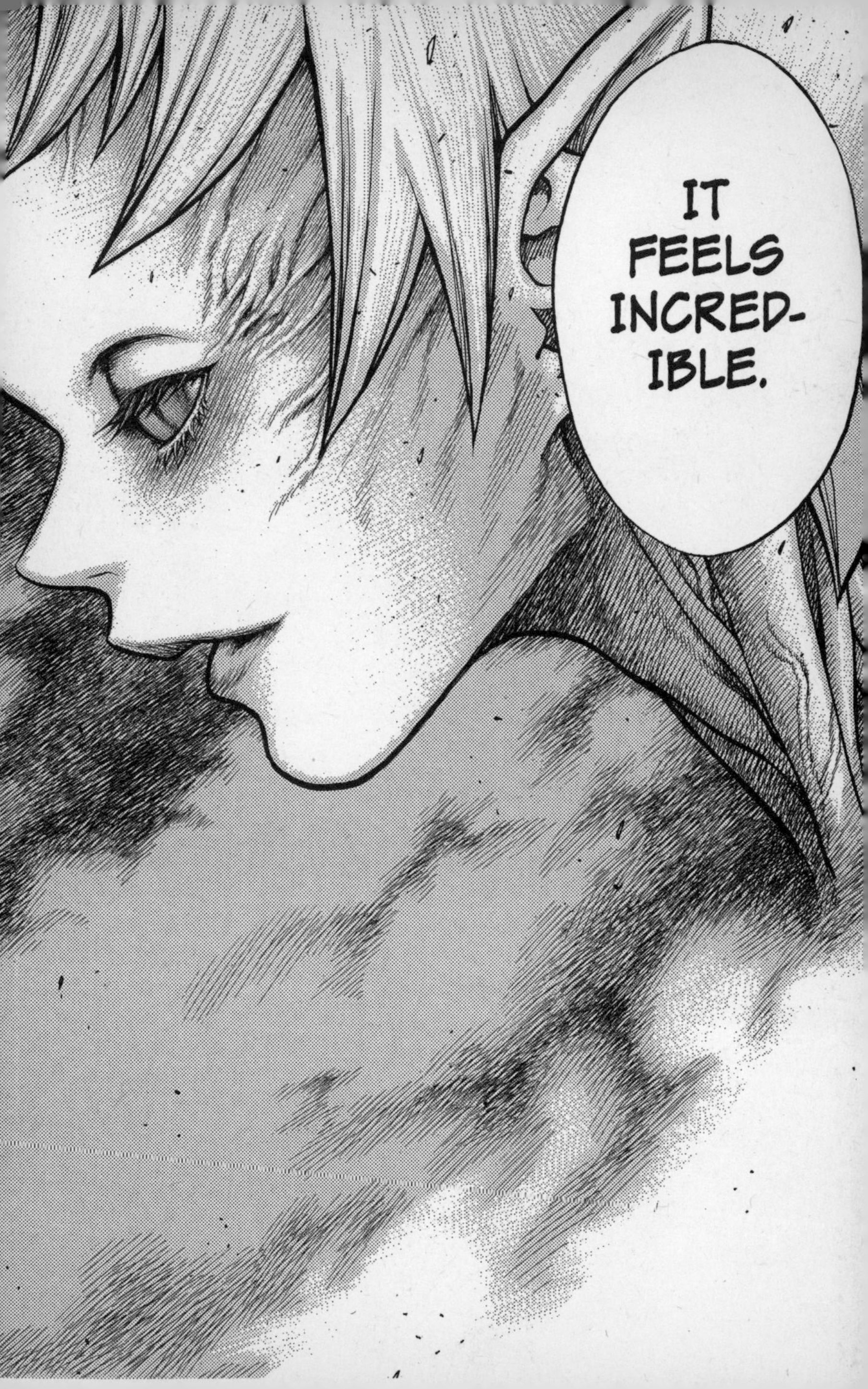
IT FEELS INCRED- IBLE.

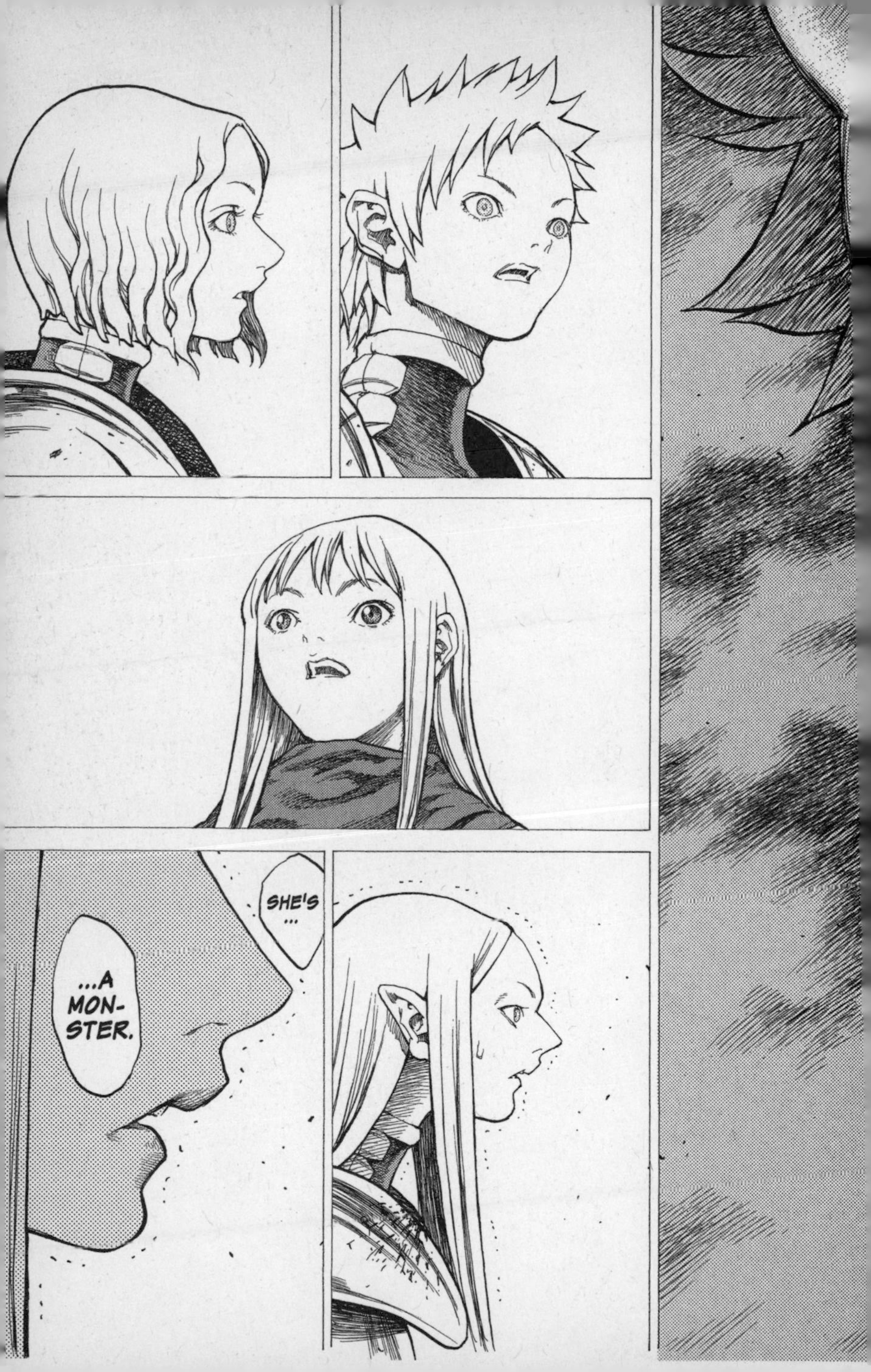
SHE'S ...
...A MONSTER.

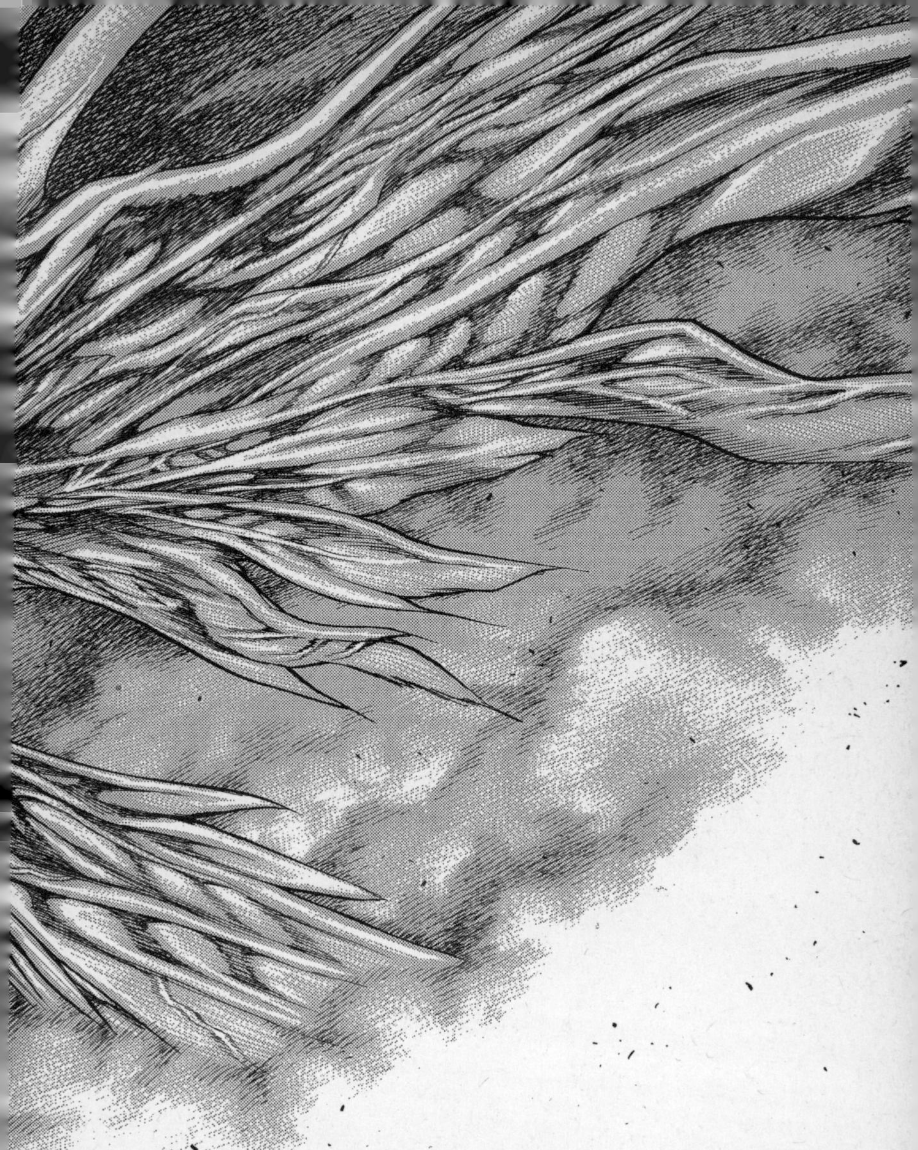

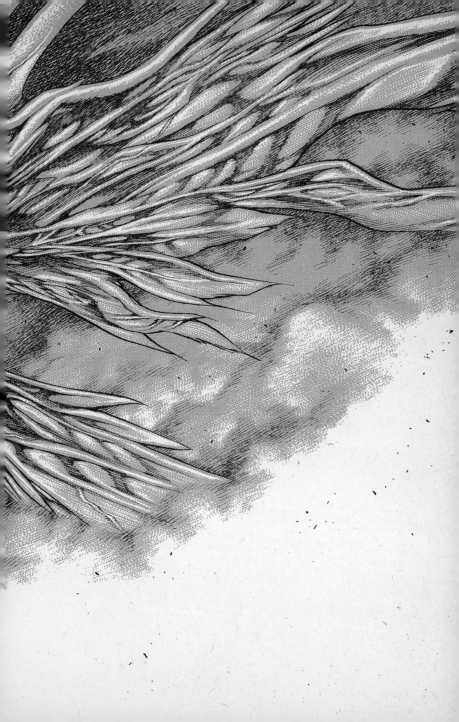

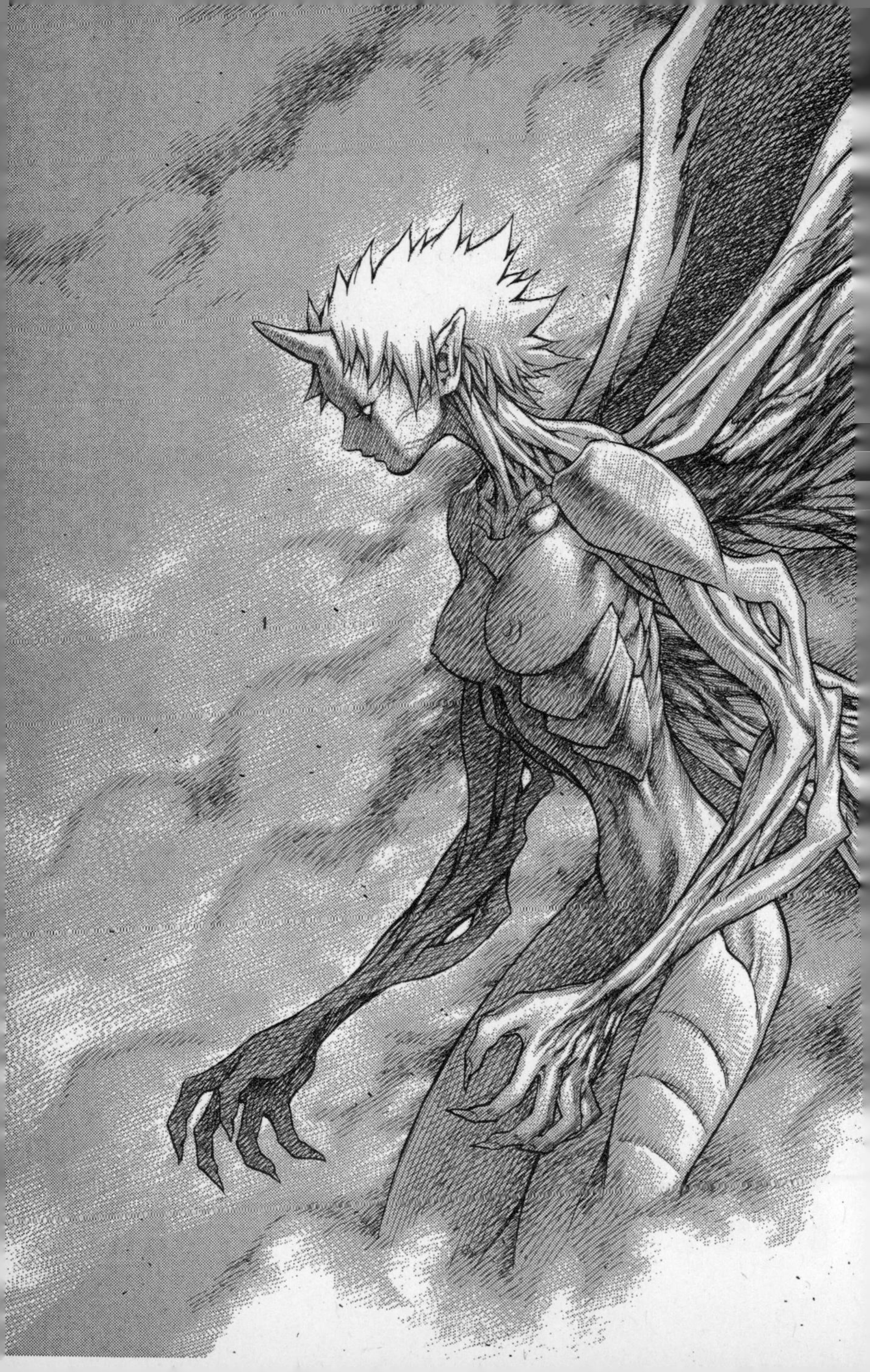

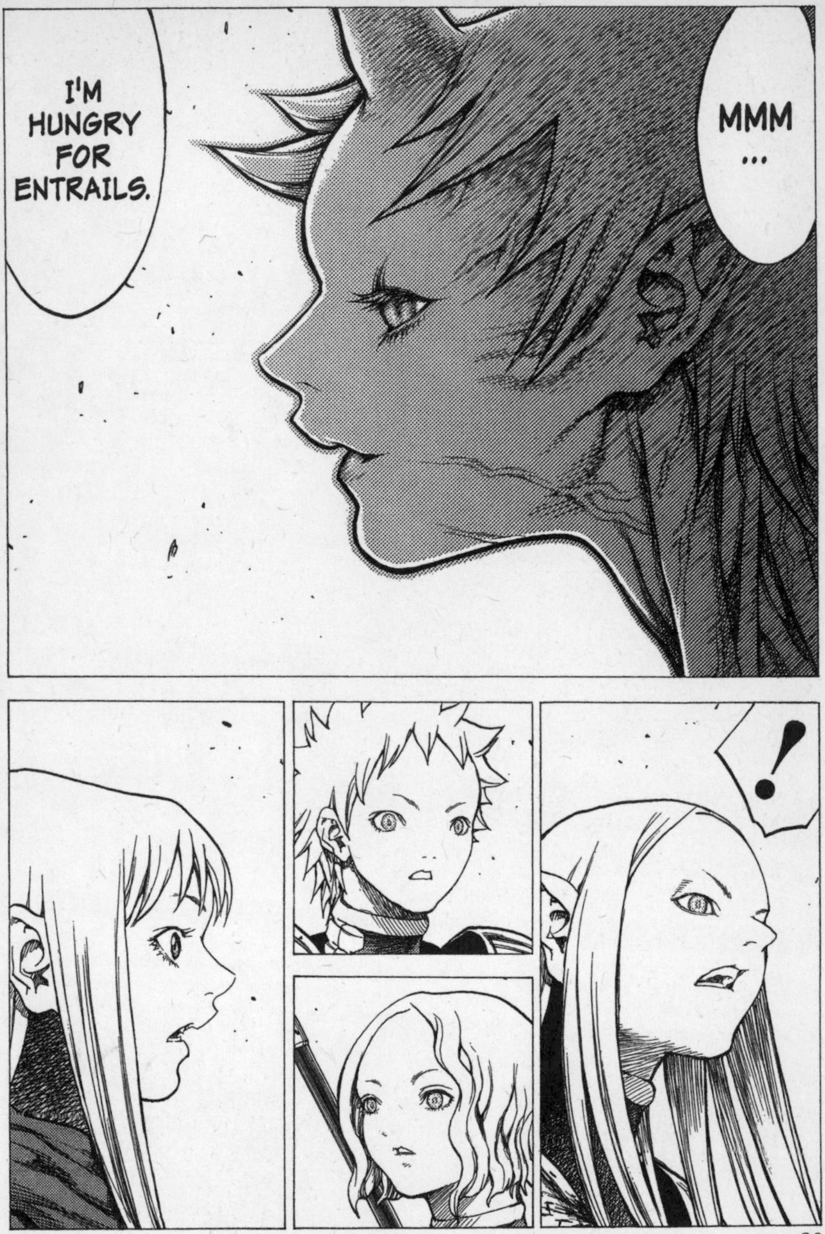
MMM ...
I'M HUNGRY FOR ENTRAILS.
!

READ THIS WAY

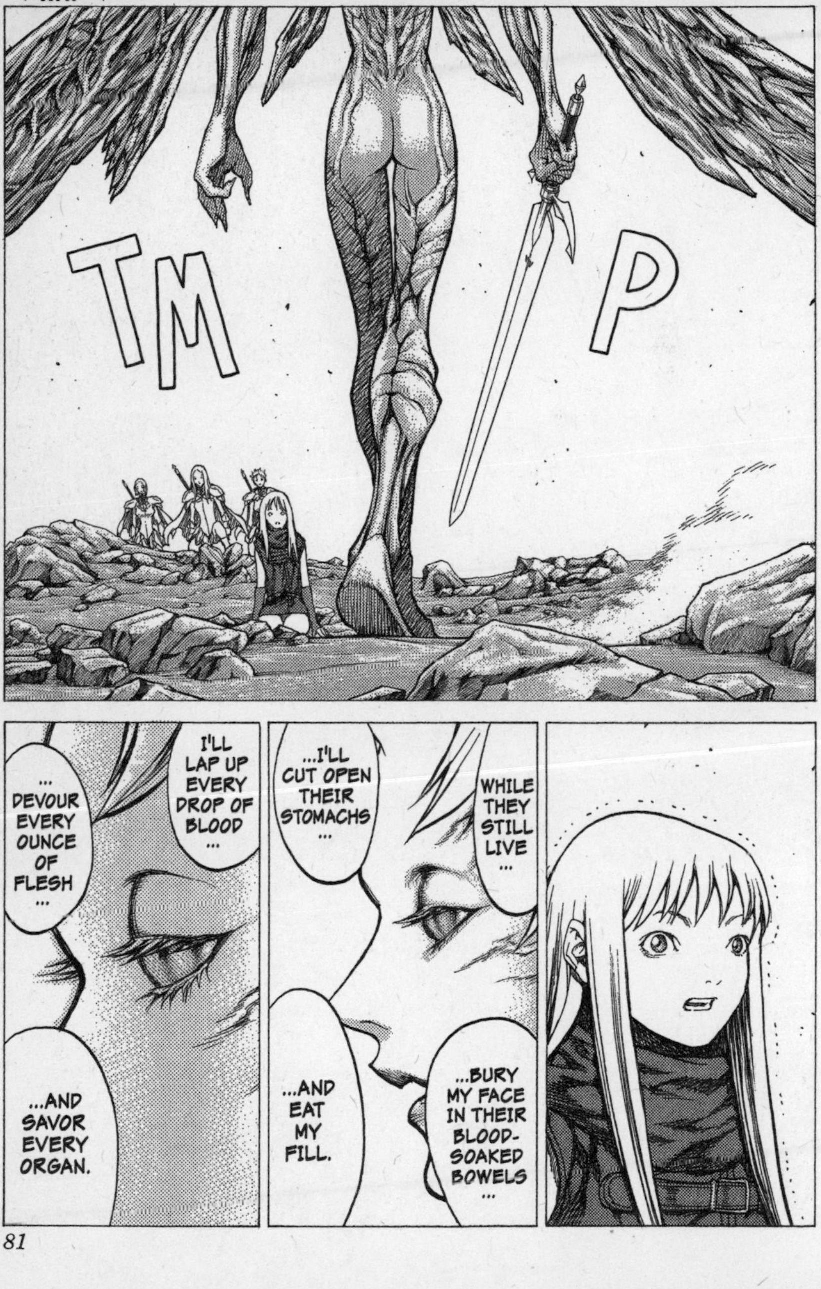
TMP
WHILE THEY STILL LIVE...
...I'LL CUT OPEN THEIR STOMACHS...
...BURY MY FACE IN THEIR BLOOD-SOAKED BOWELS...
...AND EAT MY FILL.
I'LL LAP UP EVERY DROP OF BLOOD...
...DEVOUR EVERY OUNCE OF FLESH...
...AND SAVOR EVERY ORGAN.

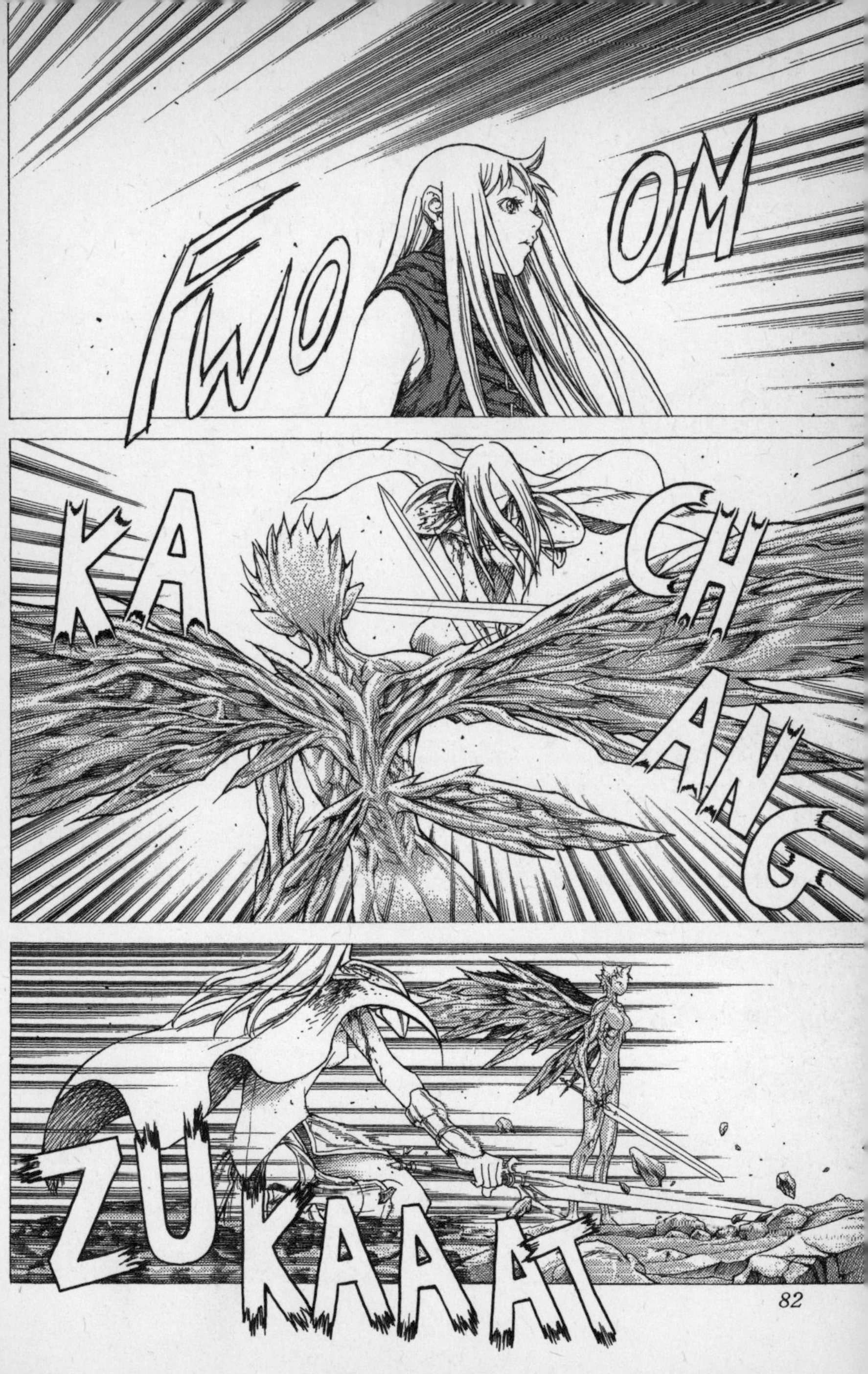
FWO OM
KA CH ANG
ZUKAAAT

READ THIS WAY

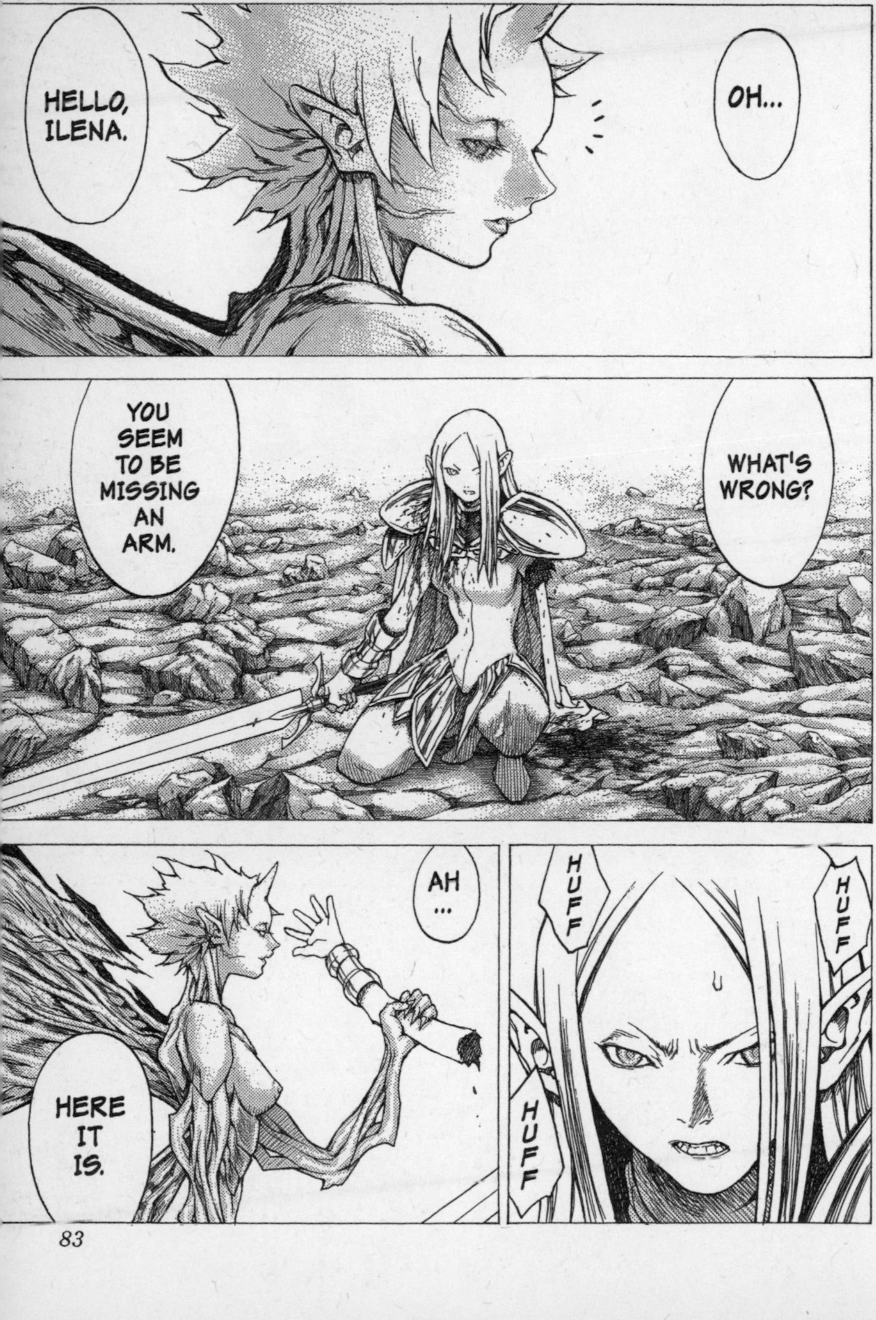
OH...
HELLO, ILENA.
WHAT'S WRONG?
YOU SEEM TO BE MISSING AN ARM.
HUFF
HUFF
HUFF
AH ...
HERE IT IS.

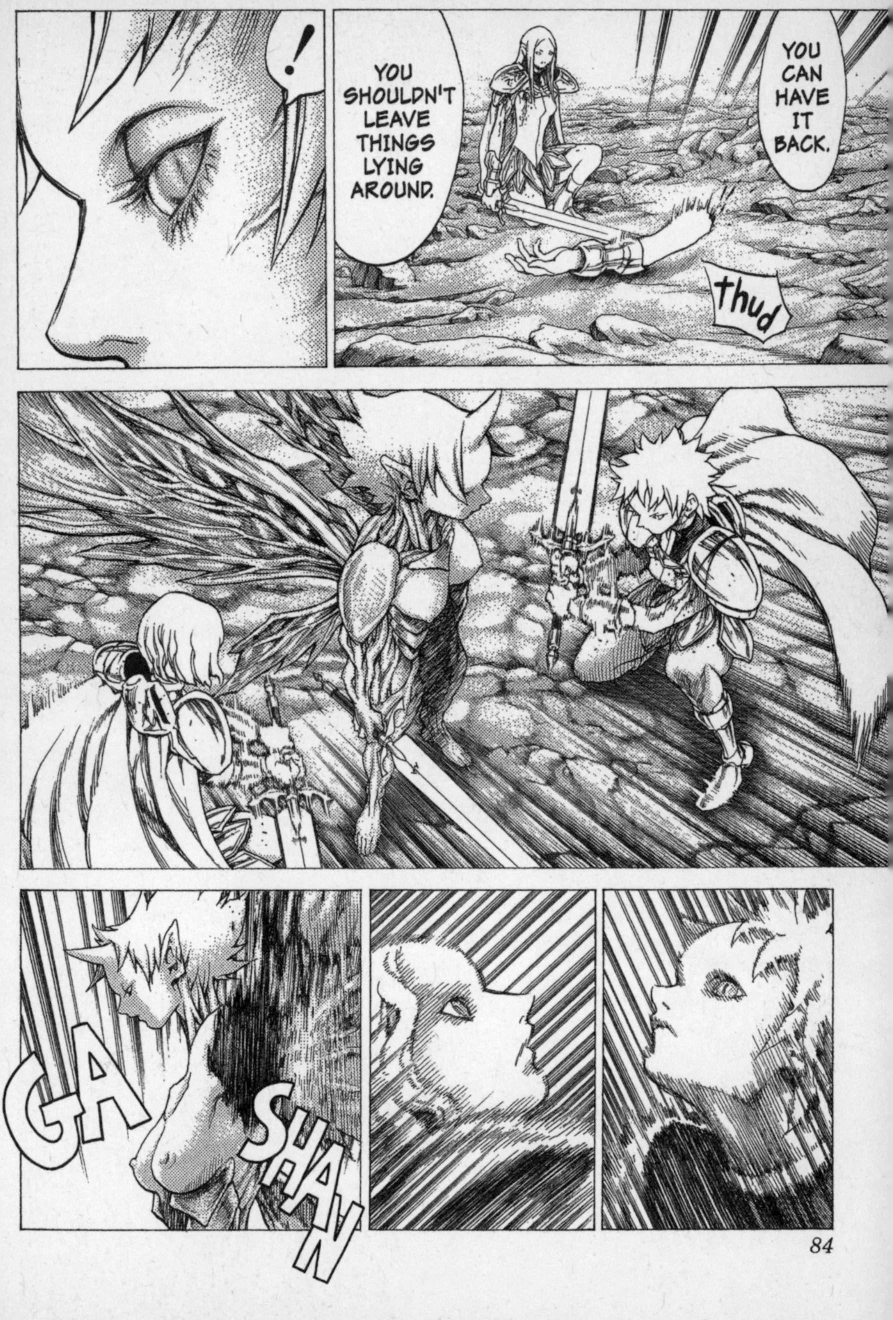
YOU CAN HAVE IT BACK.
thud
YOU SHOULDN'T LEAVE THINGS LYING AROUND.
!
GA SHAN

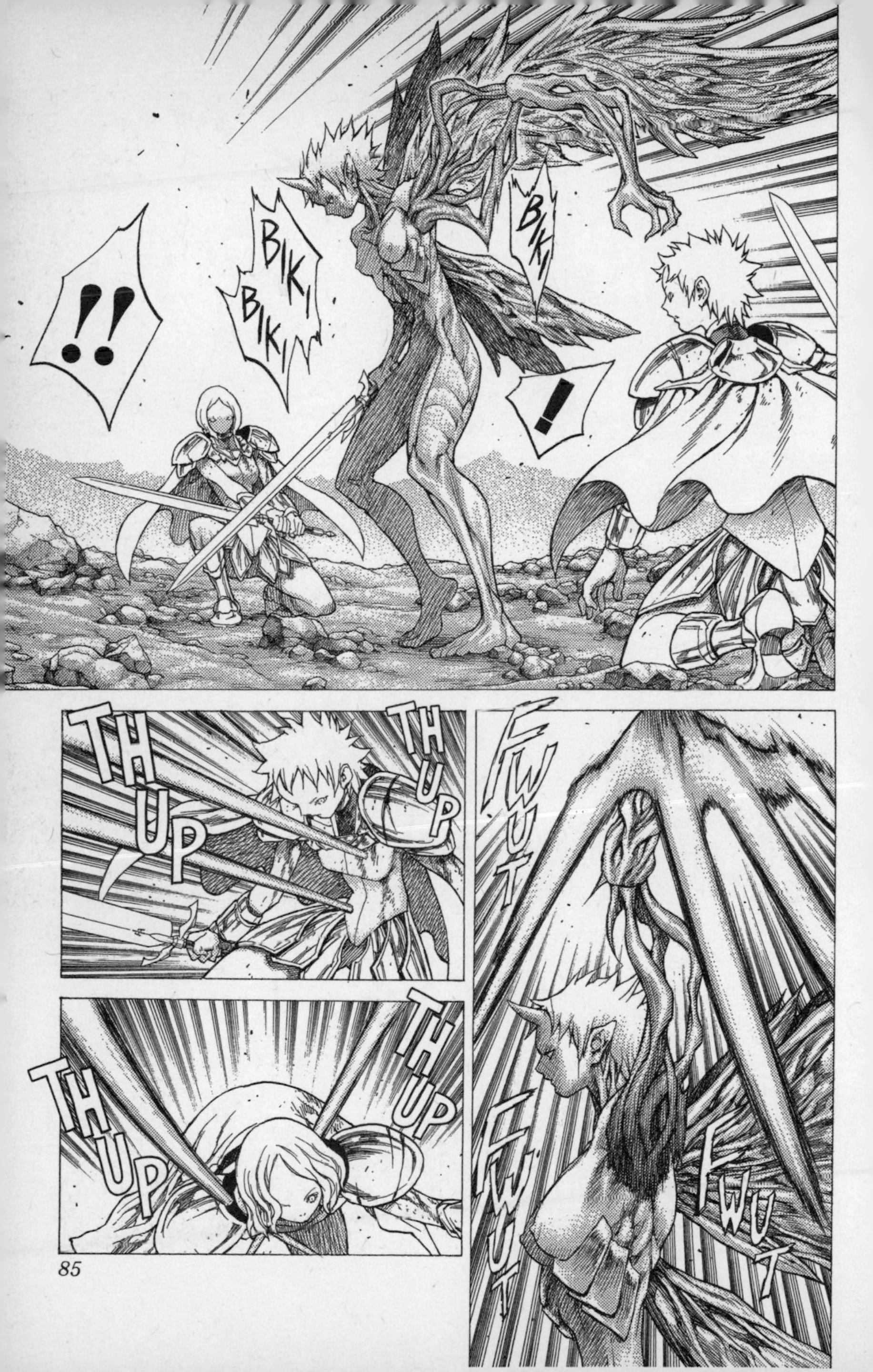

BIKI
!
BIKI BIKI
!!
FWUT
FWUT
FWUT
THUP
THUP
THUP
THUP

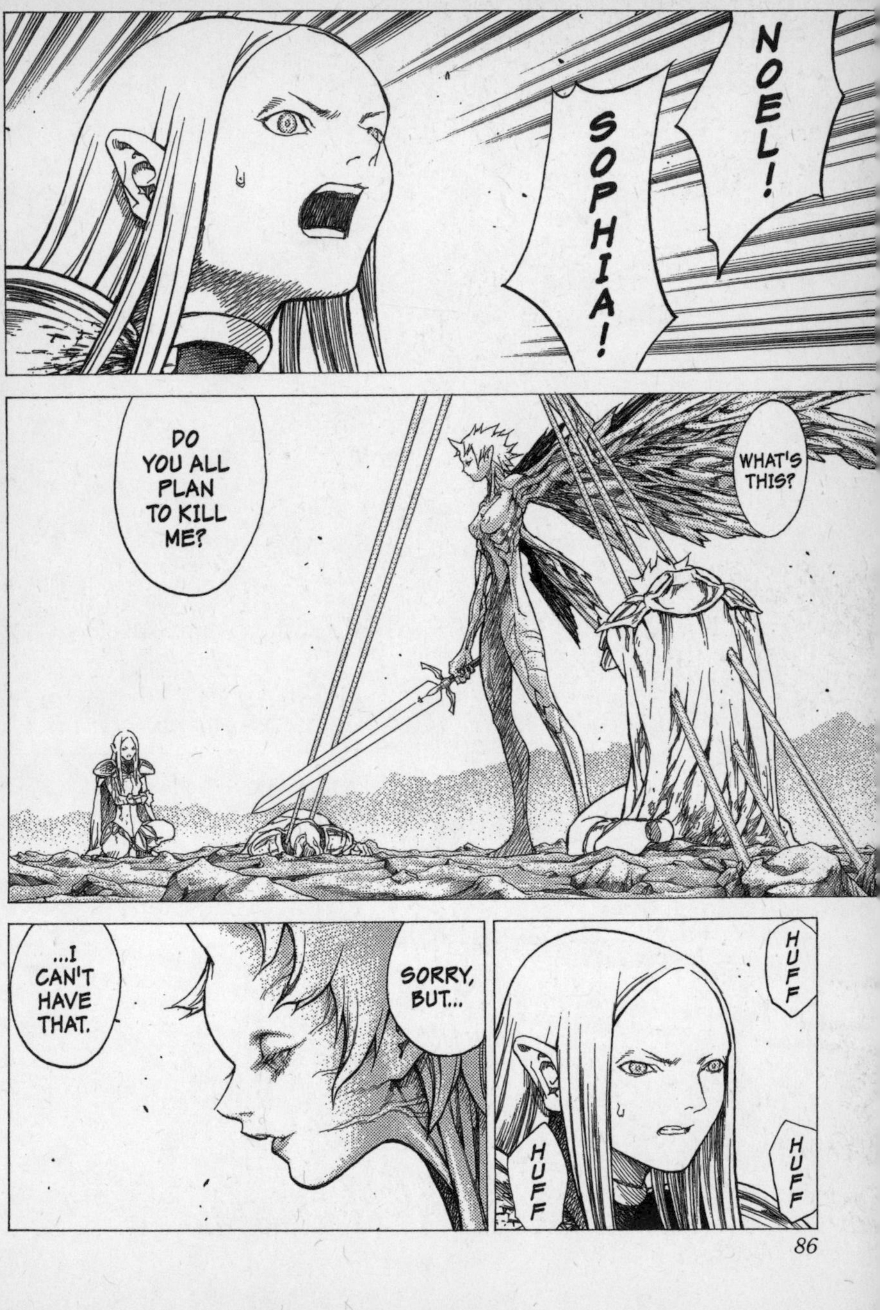
NOEL!
SOPHIA!
WHAT'S THIS?
DO YOU ALL PLAN TO KILL ME?
HUFF
HUFF
HUFF
SORRY, BUT...
...I CAN'T HAVE THAT.

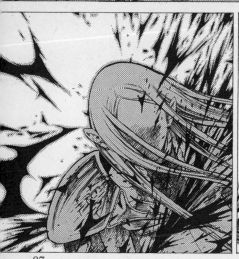

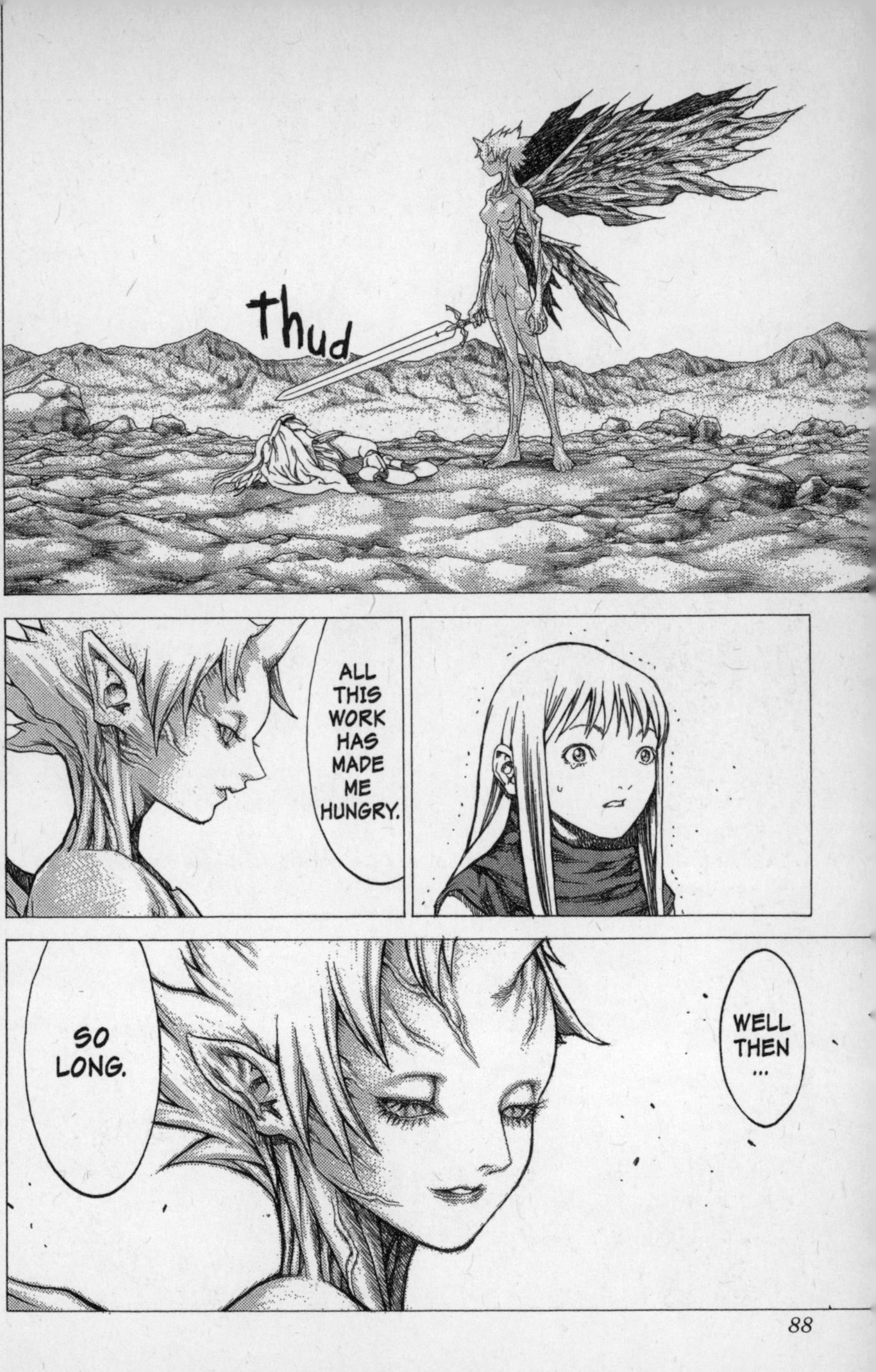
thud
ALL THIS WORK HAS MADE ME HUNGRY.
WELL THEN ...
SO LONG.

READ THIS WAY

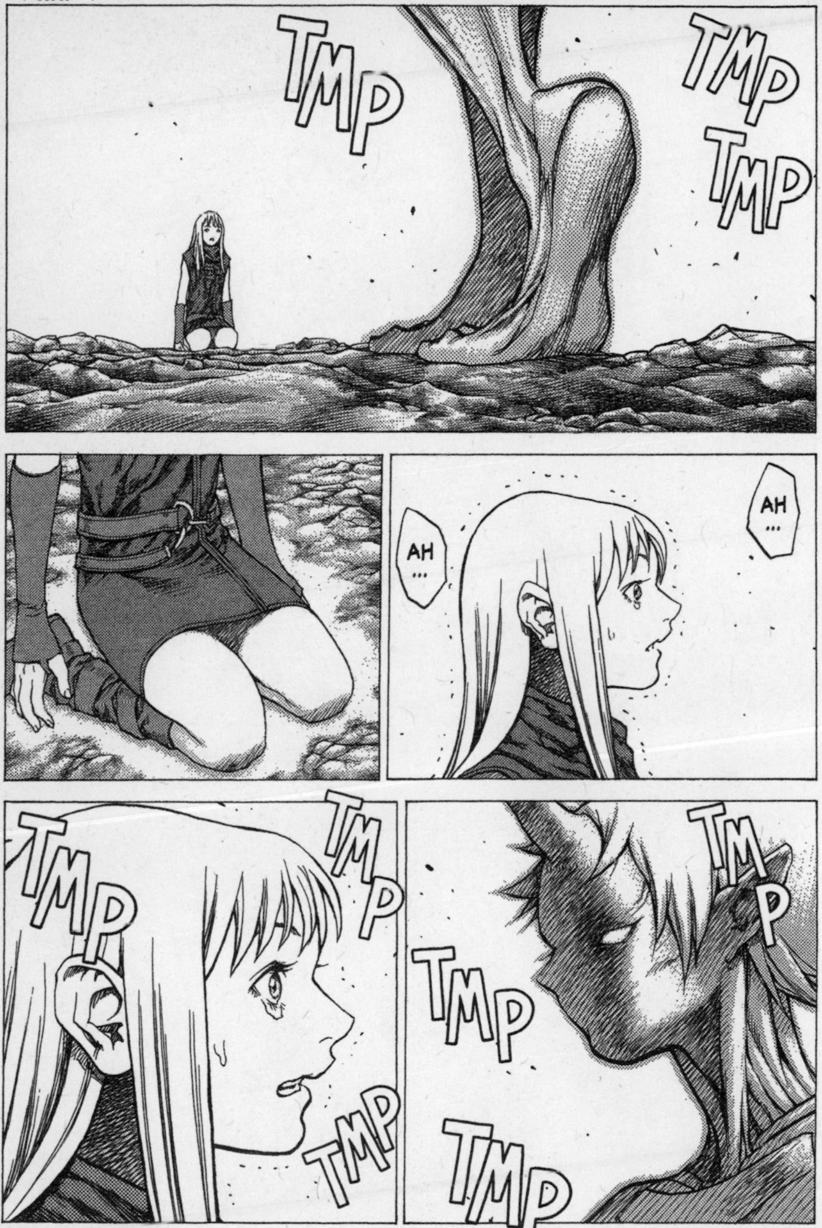
TMP
TMP
TMP
TMP
AH ...
AH ...
TMP
TMP
TMP
TMP
TMP
TMP

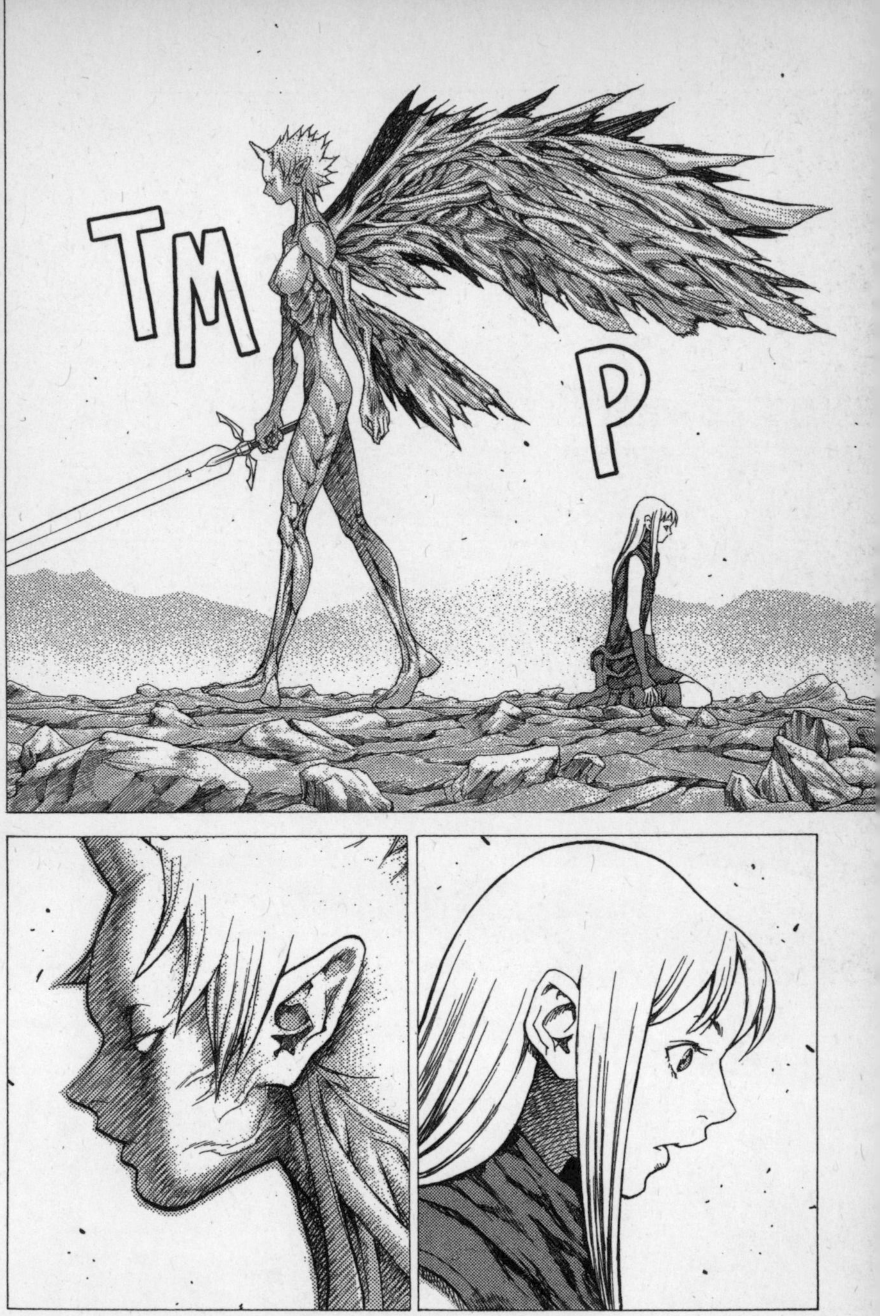
TMP

READ THIS WAY

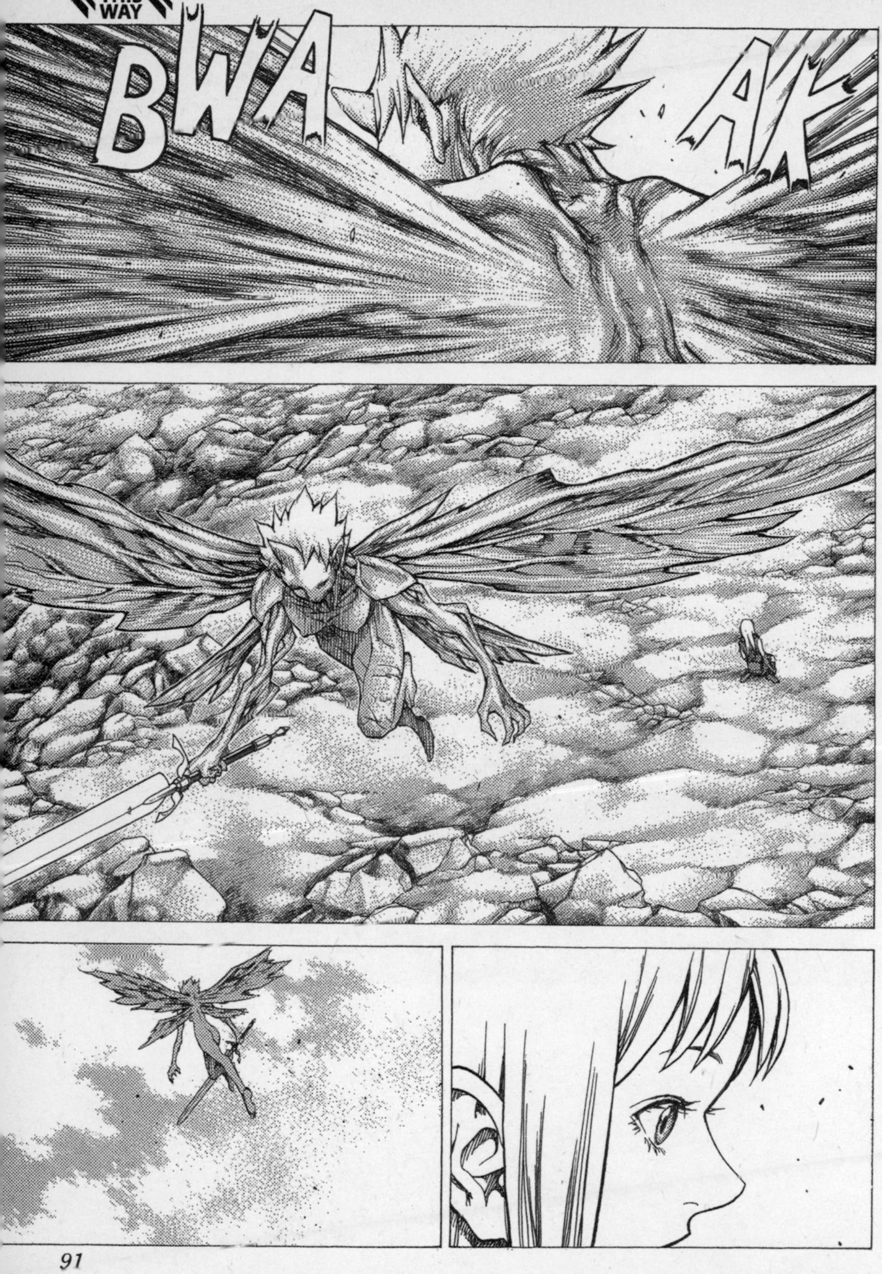
BWA AK

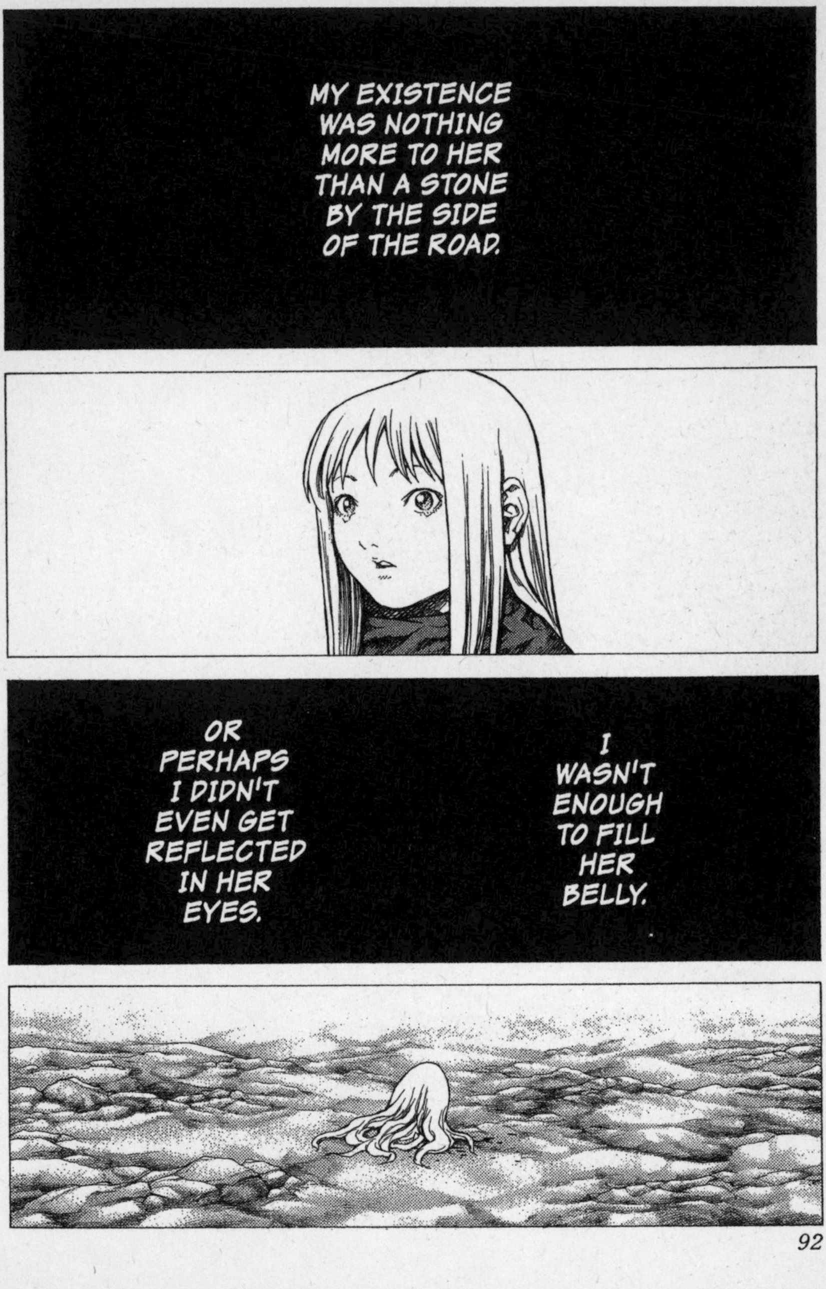
MY EXISTENCE WAS NOTHING MORE TO HER THAN A STONE BY THE SIDE OF THE ROAD.
I WASN'T ENOUGH TO FILL HER BELLY.
OR PERHAPS I DIDN'T EVEN GET REFLECTED IN HER EYES.

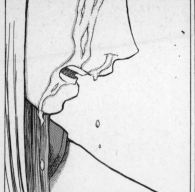

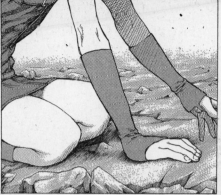

READ THIS WAY

I COULDN'T EVEN HATE THE BEAST THAT KILLED TERESA.
IT WAS ME, OVERCOME BY FEAR, THAT I COULDN'T FORGIVE.

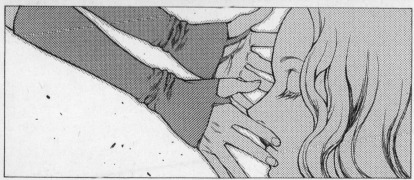

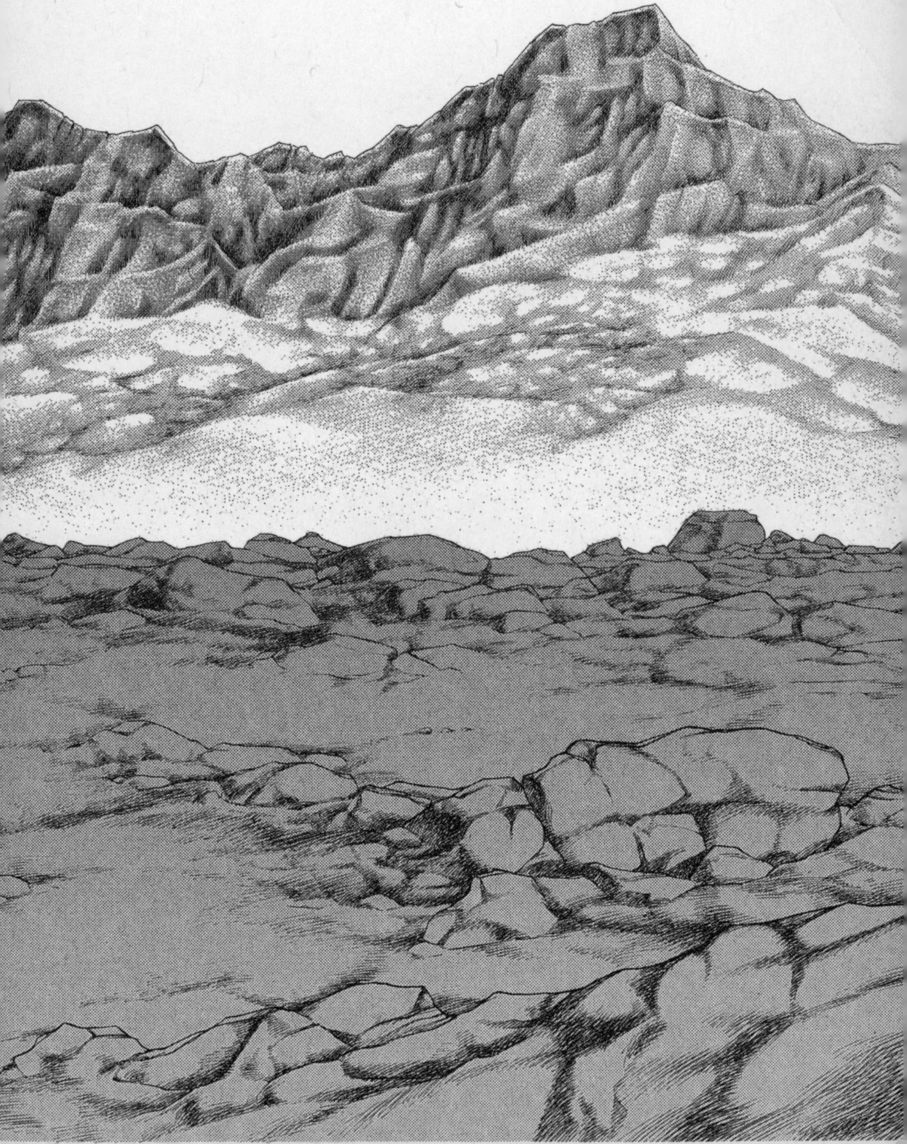

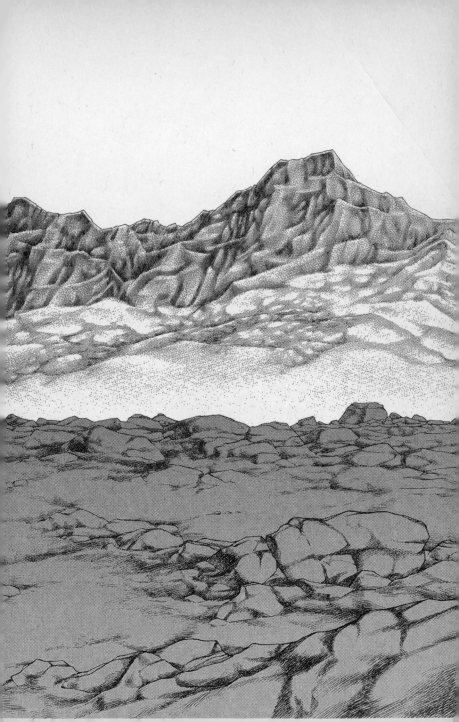

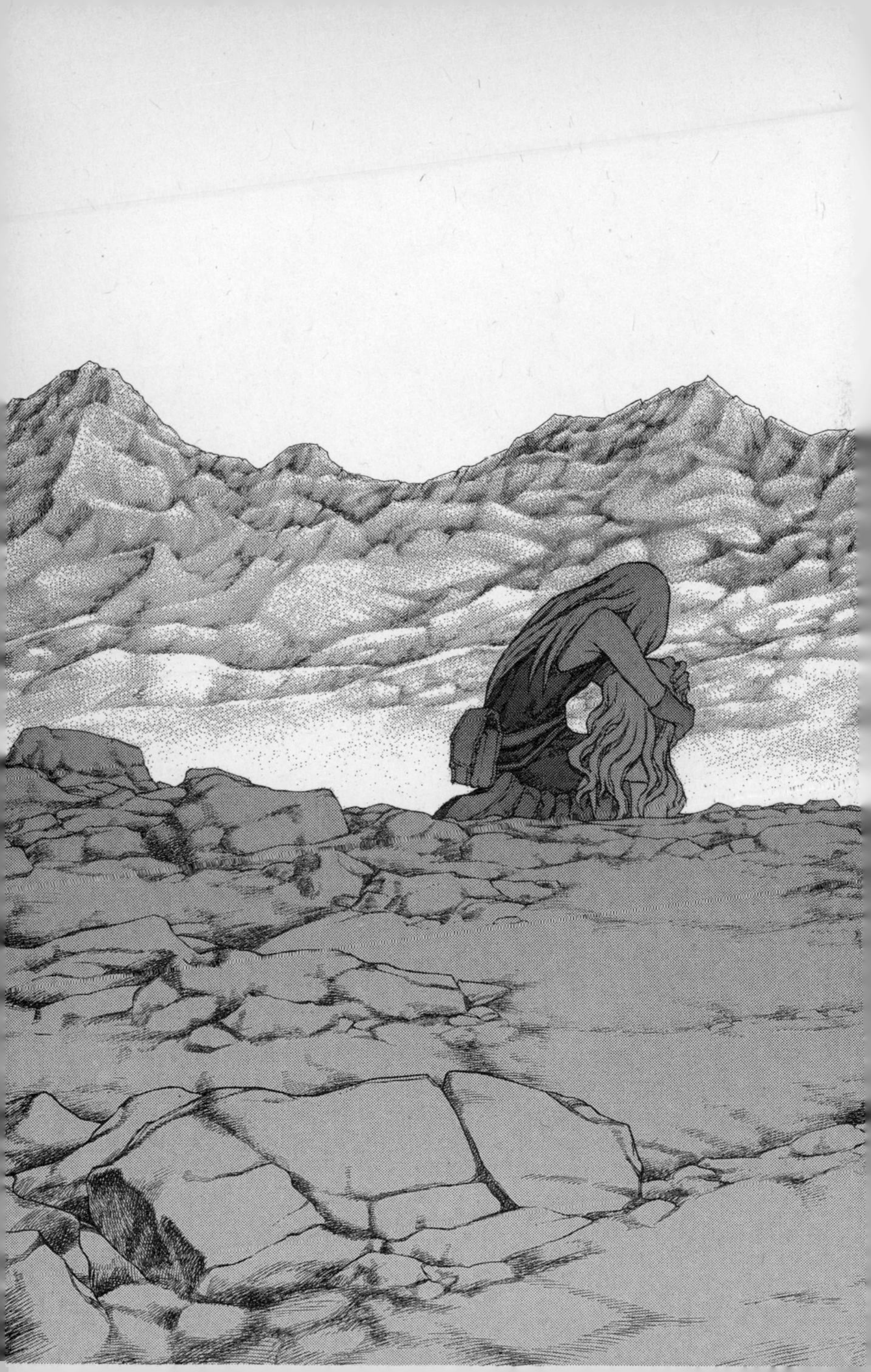

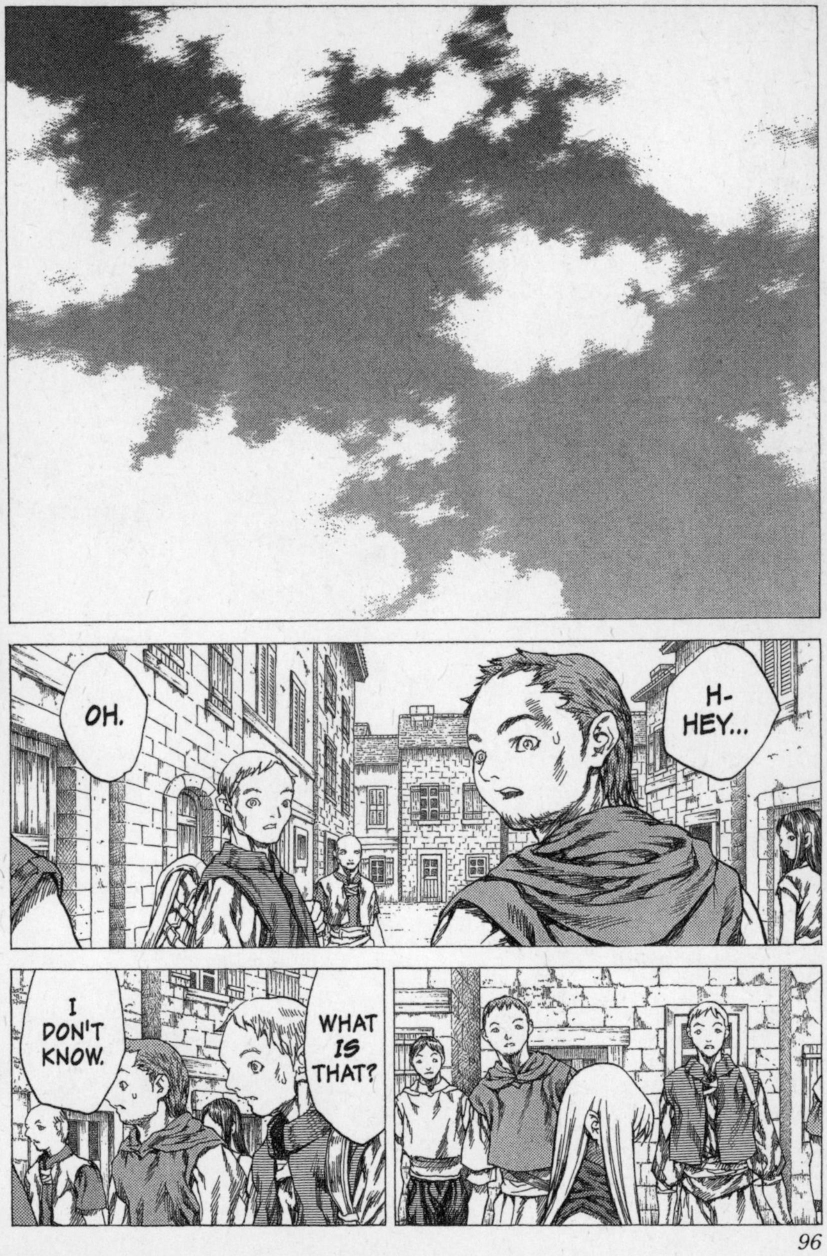
H-
HEY...
OH.
WHAT IS THAT?
I DON'T KNOW.

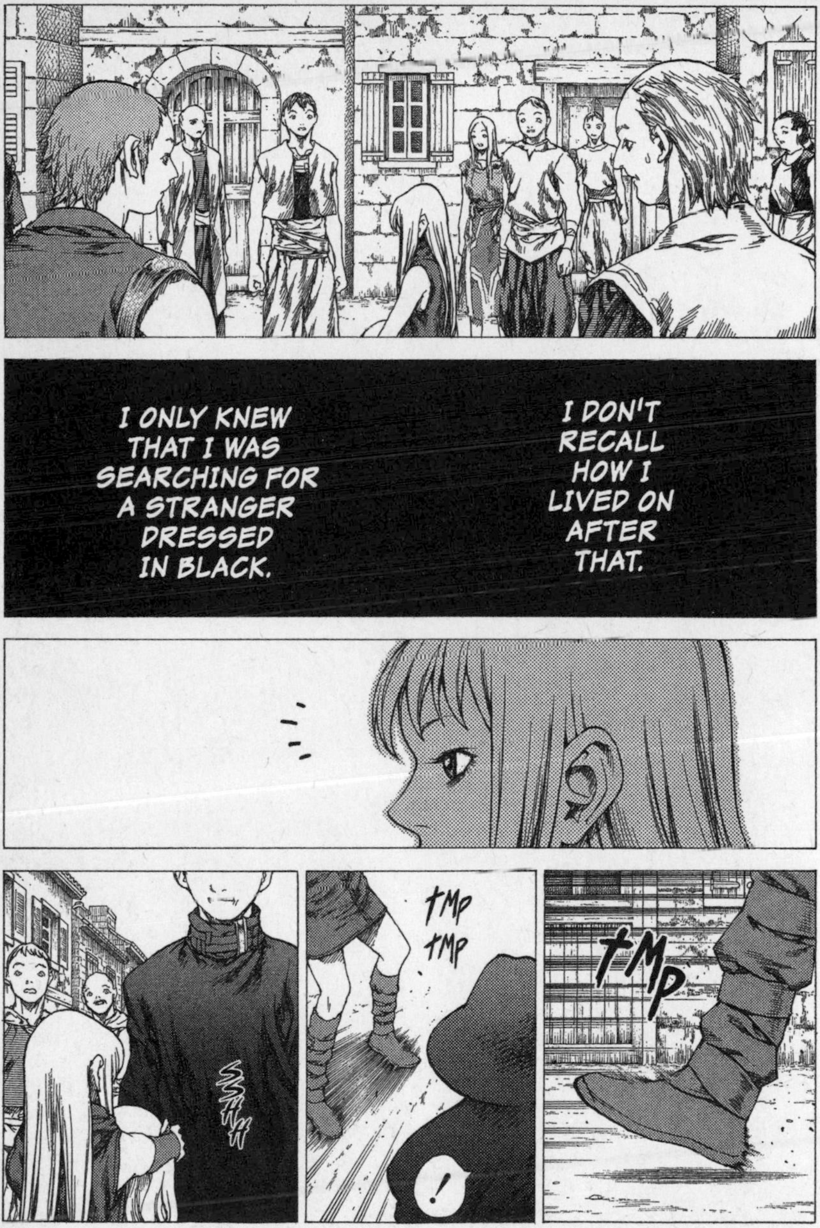
I DON'T RECALL HOW I LIVED ON AFTER THAT.
I ONLY KNEW THAT I WAS SEARCHING FOR A STRANGER DRESSED IN BLACK.
TMP
TMP TMP
!
SSHH

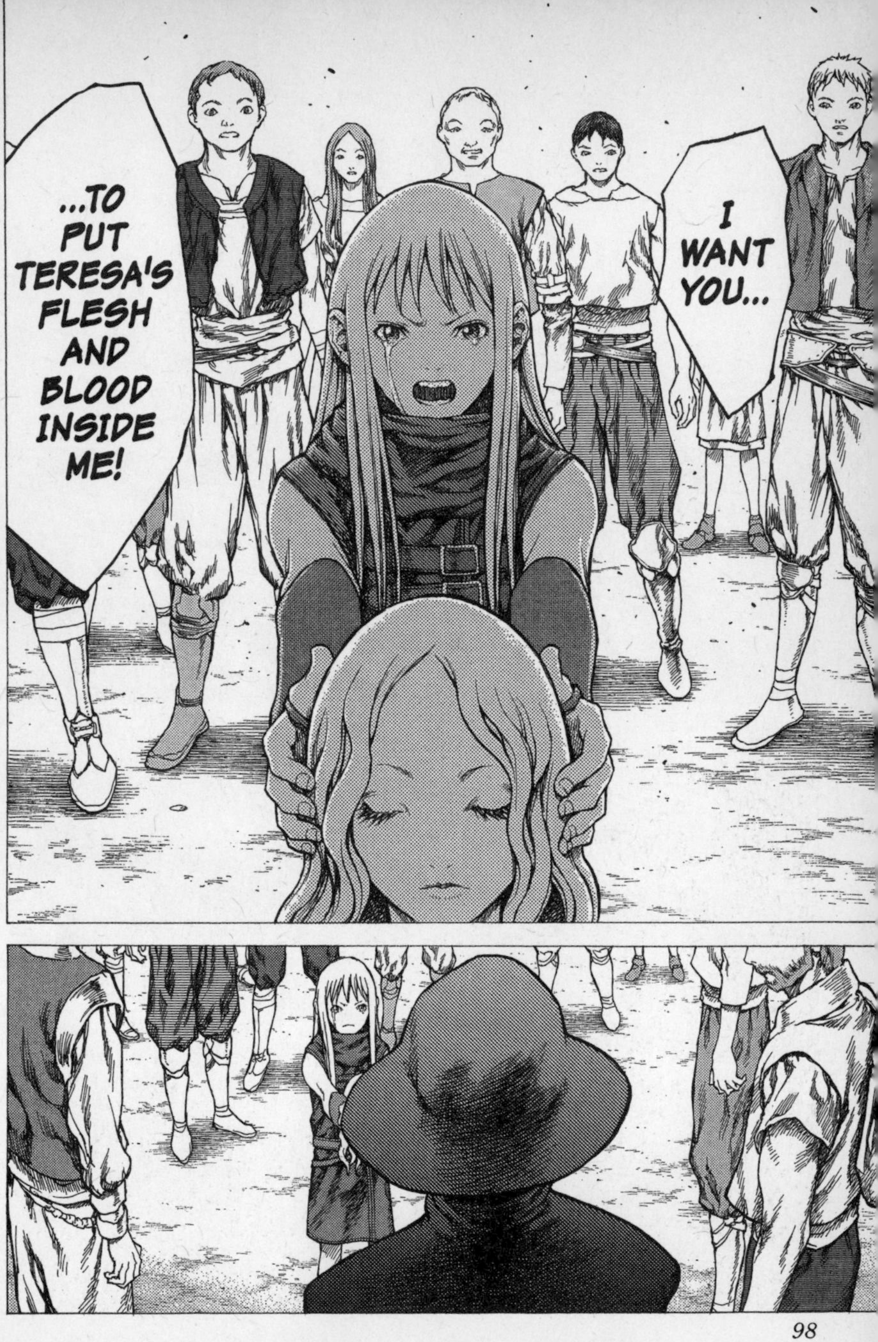
I WANT YOU...
...TO PUT TERESA'S FLESH AND BLOOD INSIDE ME!

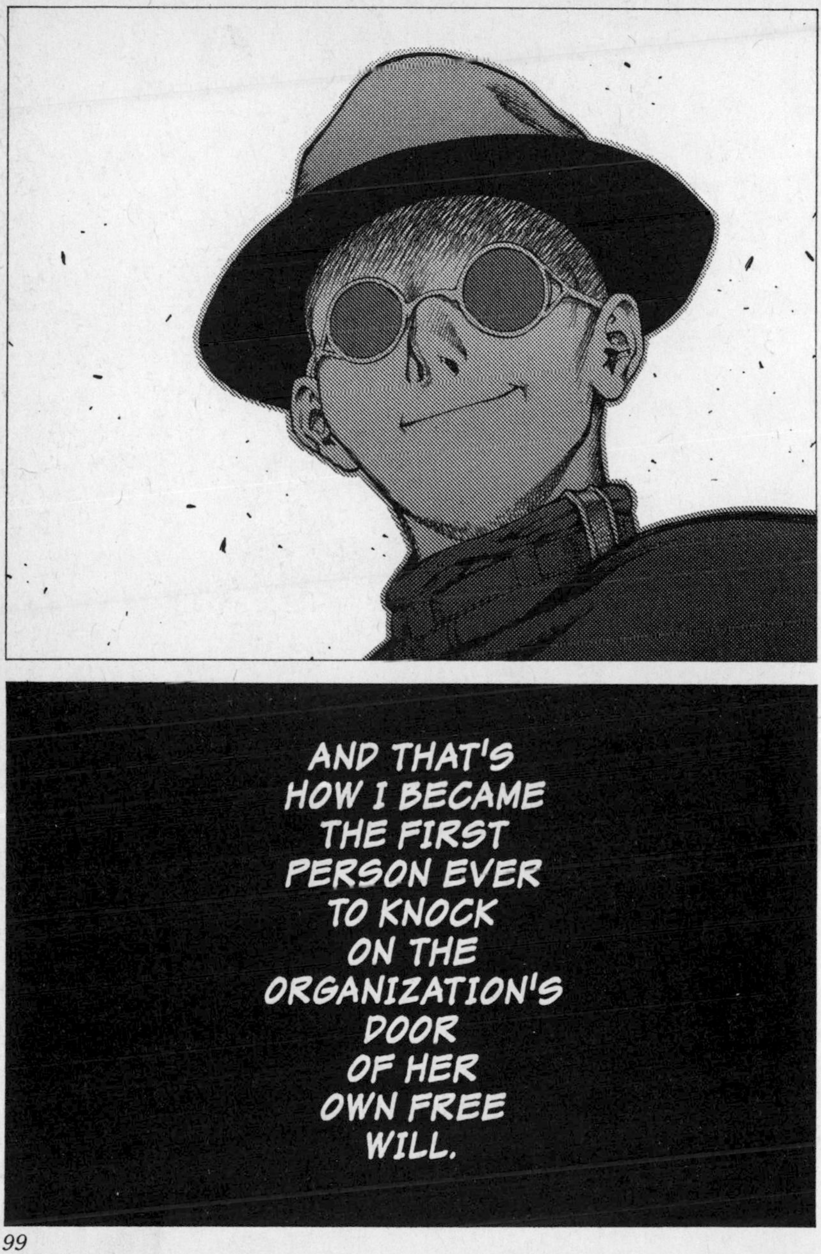
AND THAT'S HOW I BECAME THE FIRST PERSON EVER TO KNOCK ON THE ORGANIZATION'S DOOR OF HER OWN FREE WILL.

クレイモア
Claymore™

Scene 25: The Slashers, Part 1

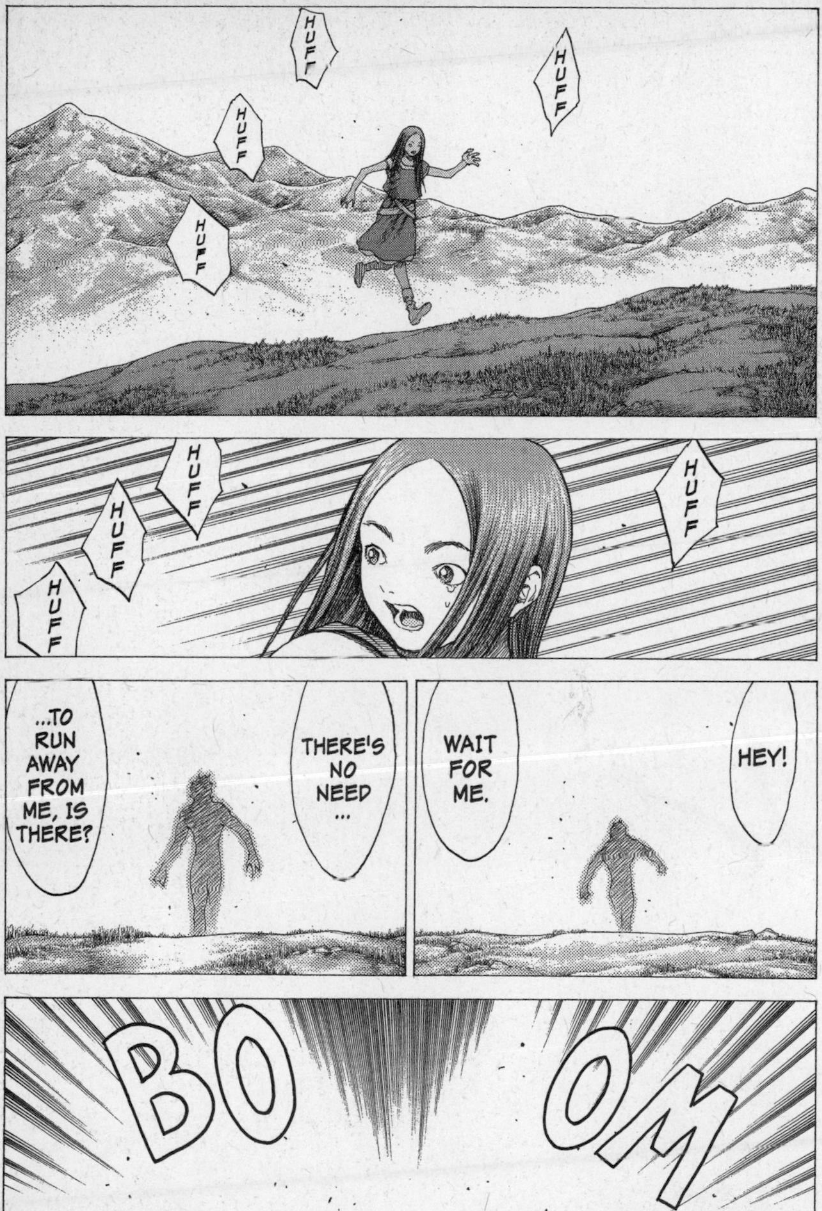
HUFF
HUFF
HUFF
HUFF
HUFF
HUFF
HUFF
HUFF
HEY!
WAIT FOR ME.
THERE'S NO NEED...
...TO RUN AWAY FROM ME, IS THERE?
BOOM

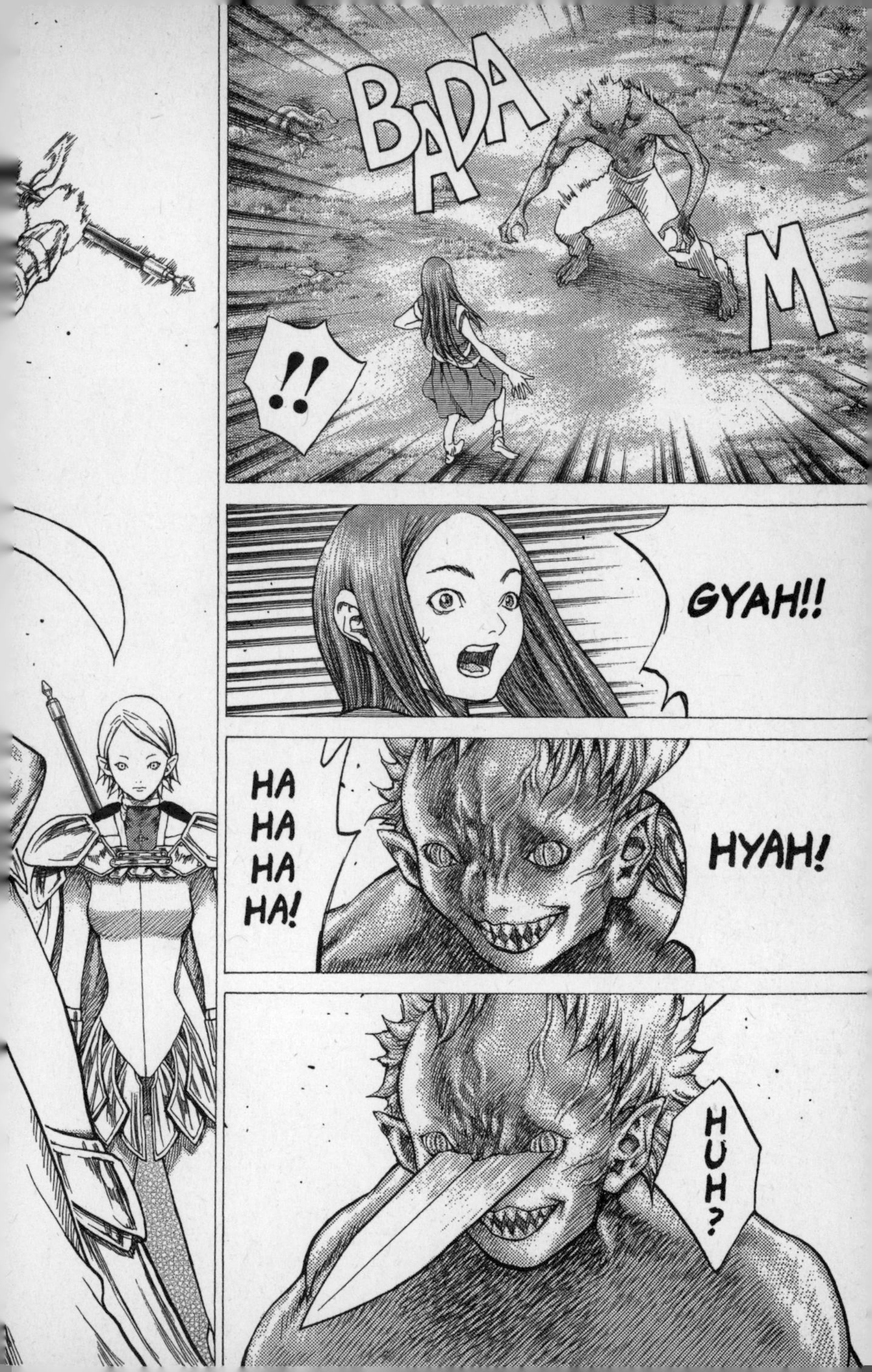
BADADAM
!!
GYAH!!
HYAH!
HA HA HA HA!
HUH?

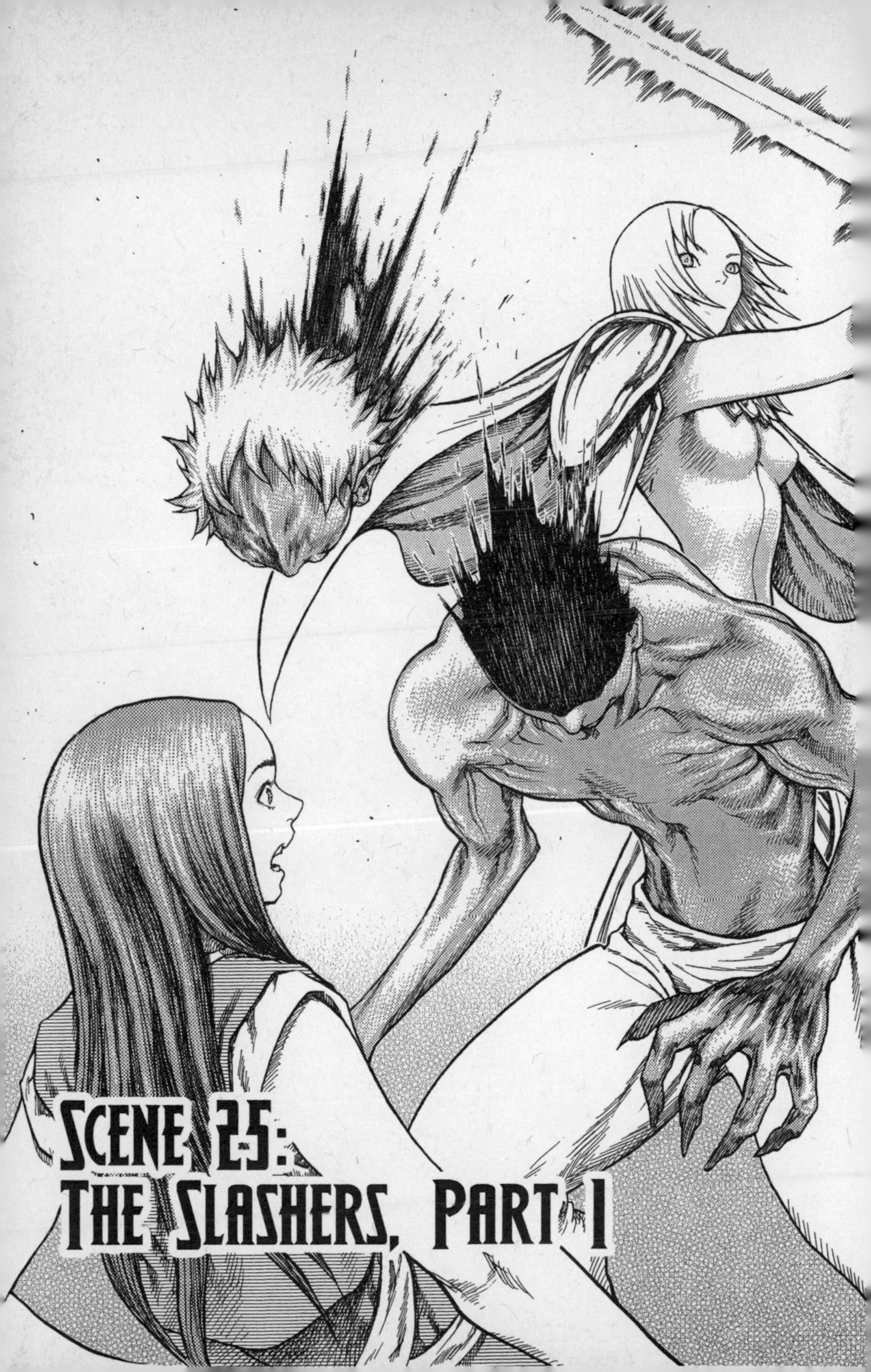
SCENE 25:
THE SLASHERS, PART 1

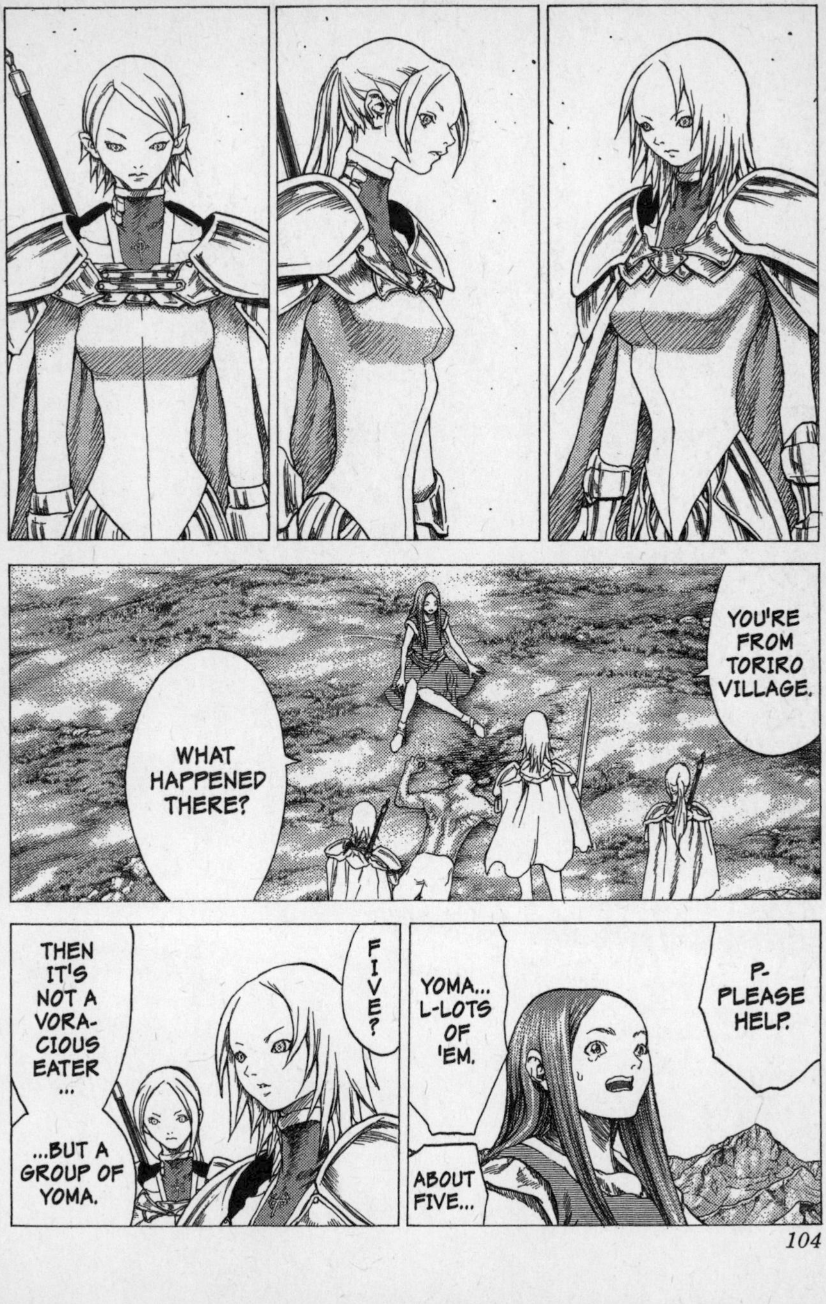
YOU'RE FROM TORIRO VILLAGE.
WHAT HAPPENED THERE?
P-PLEASE HELP.
YOMA... L-LOTS OF 'EM.
ABOUT FIVE...
FIVE?
THEN IT'S NOT A VORACIOUS EATER...
...BUT A GROUP OF YOMA.

READ THIS WAY

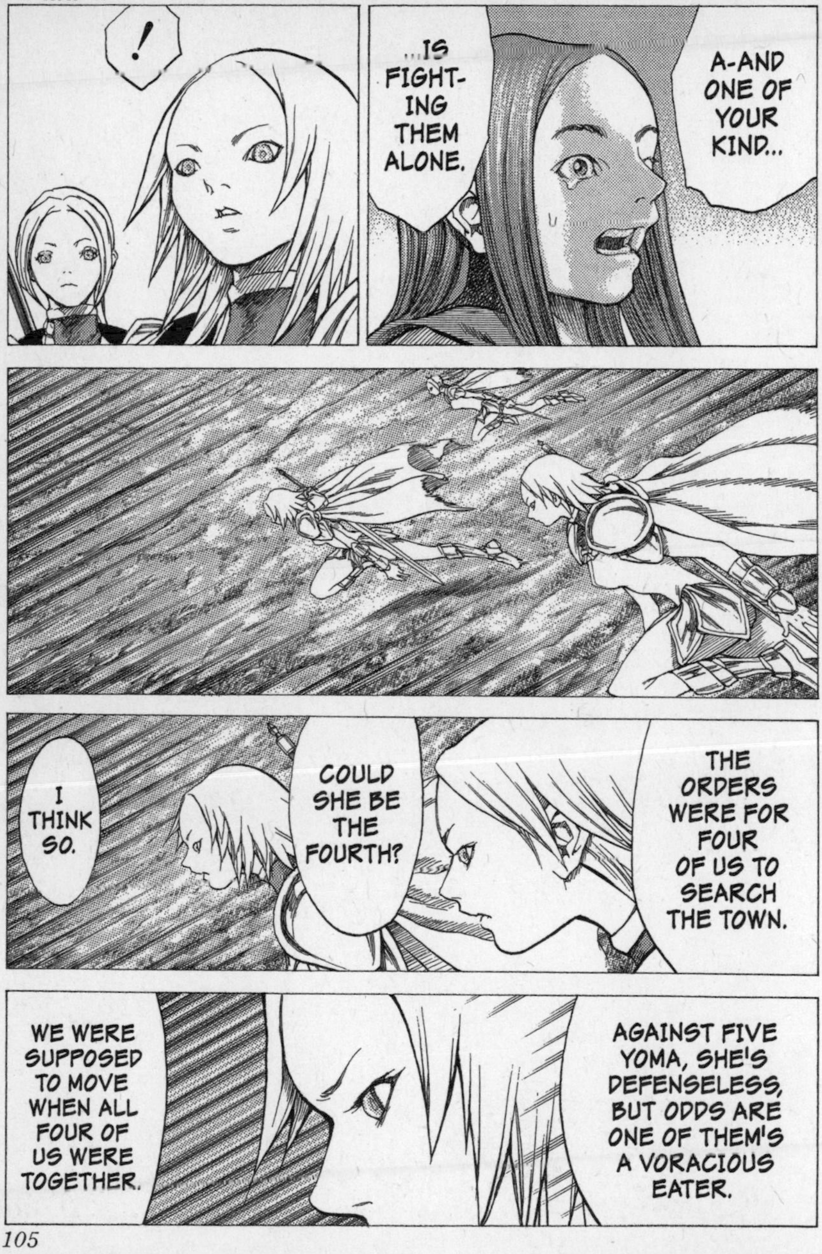
A-AND ONE OF YOUR KIND...
...IS FIGHTING THEM ALONE.
!
THE ORDERS WERE FOR FOUR OF US TO SEARCH THE TOWN.
COULD SHE BE THE FOURTH?
I THINK SO.
AGAINST FIVE YOMA, SHE'S DEFENSELESS, BUT ODDS ARE ONE OF THEM'S A VORACIOUS EATER.
WE WERE SUPPOSED TO MOVE WHEN ALL FOUR OF US WERE TOGETHER.

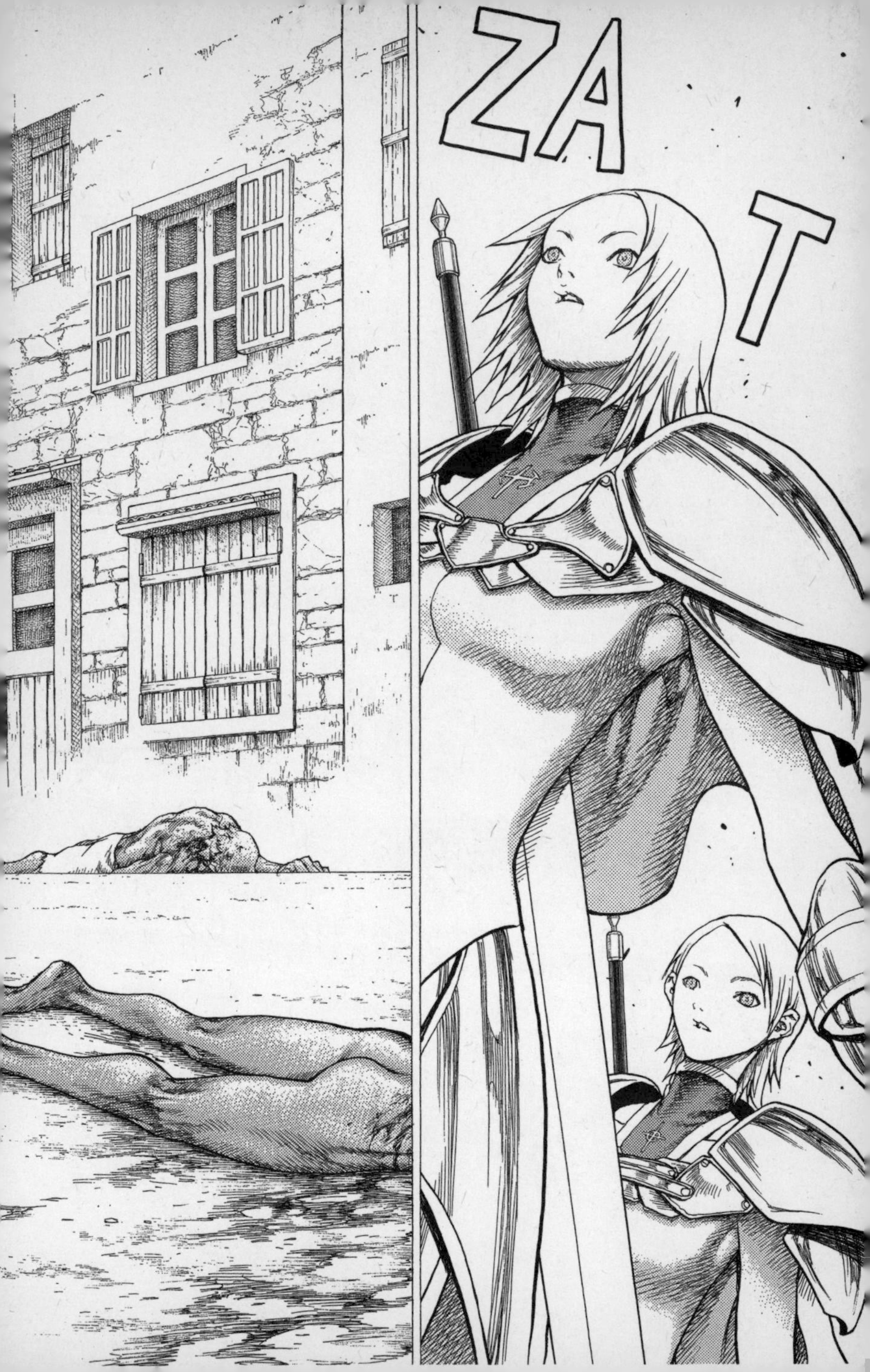
ZAT

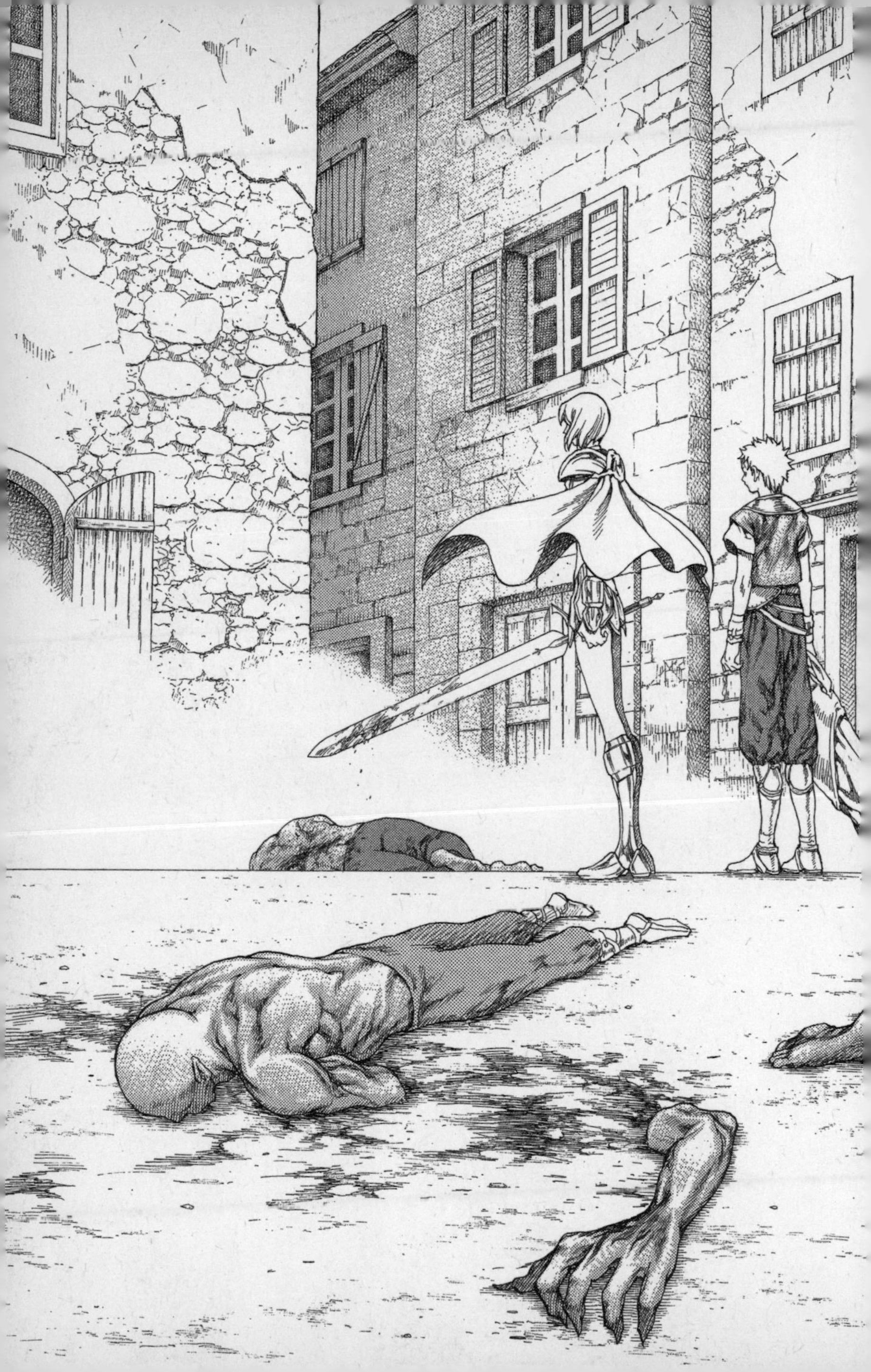

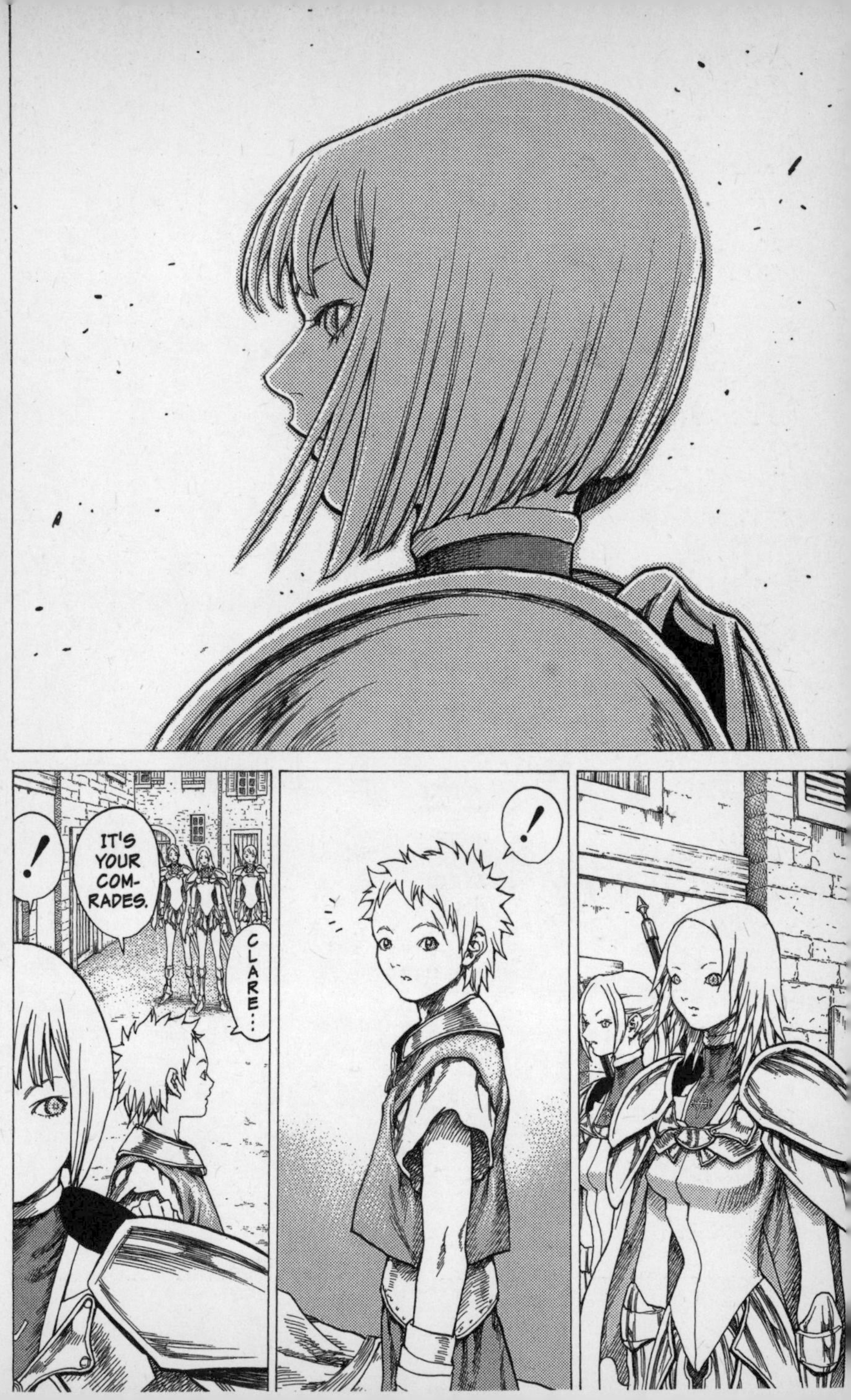
!
!
IT'S YOUR COM-RADES.
CLARE...

READ THIS WAY

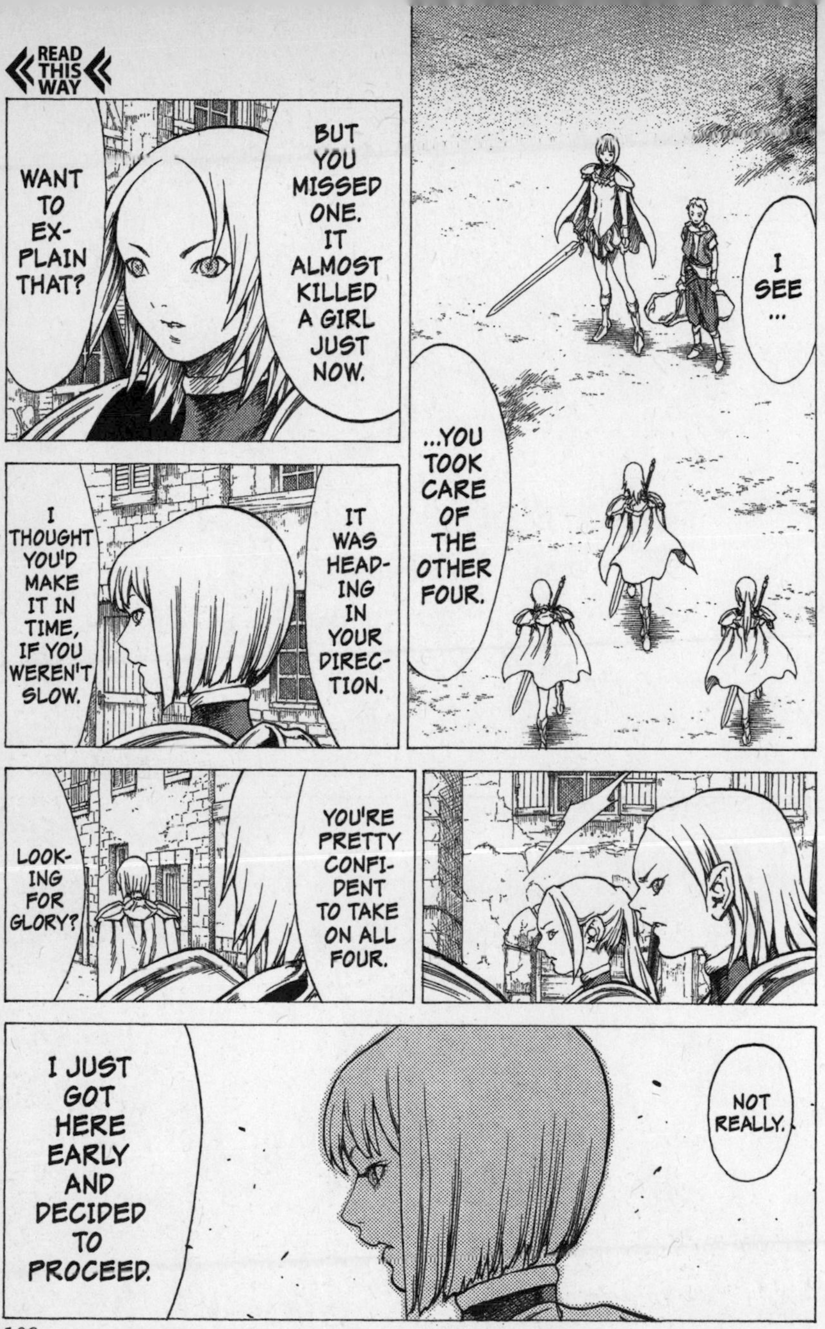
I SEE ...
...YOU TOOK CARE OF THE OTHER FOUR.
BUT YOU MISSED ONE. IT ALMOST KILLED A GIRL JUST NOW.
WANT TO EX-PLAIN THAT?
IT WAS HEAD-ING IN YOUR DIREC-TION.
I THOUGHT YOU'D MAKE IT IN TIME, IF YOU WEREN'T SLOW.
YOU'RE PRETTY CONFI-DENT TO TAKE ON ALL FOUR.
LOOK-ING FOR GLORY?
NOT REALLY.
I JUST GOT HERE EARLY AND DECIDED TO PROCEED.

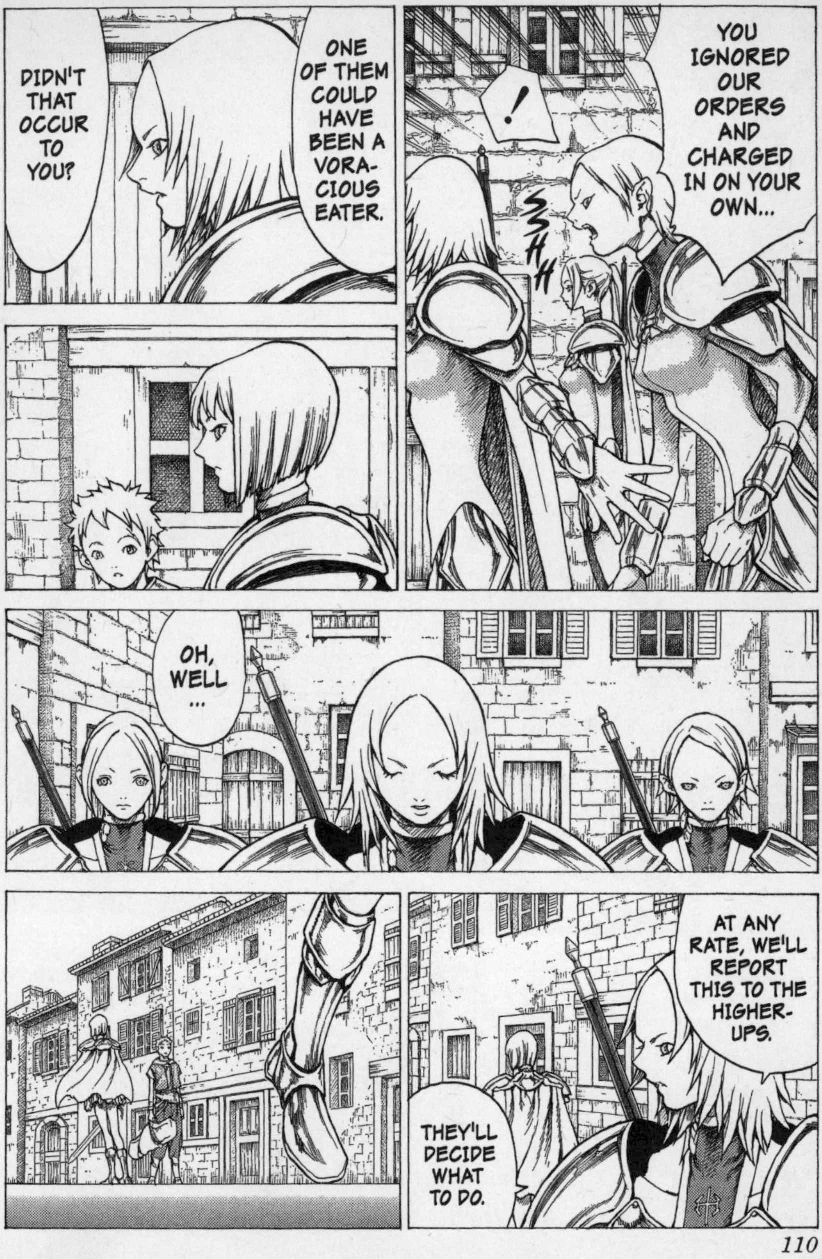
YOU IGNORED OUR ORDERS AND CHARGED IN ON YOUR OWN...
!
SSHH
ONE OF THEM COULD HAVE BEEN A VORACIOUS EATER.
DIDN'T THAT OCCUR TO YOU?
OH, WELL ...
AT ANY RATE, WE'LL REPORT THIS TO THE HIGHER-UPS.
THEY'LL DECIDE WHAT TO DO.

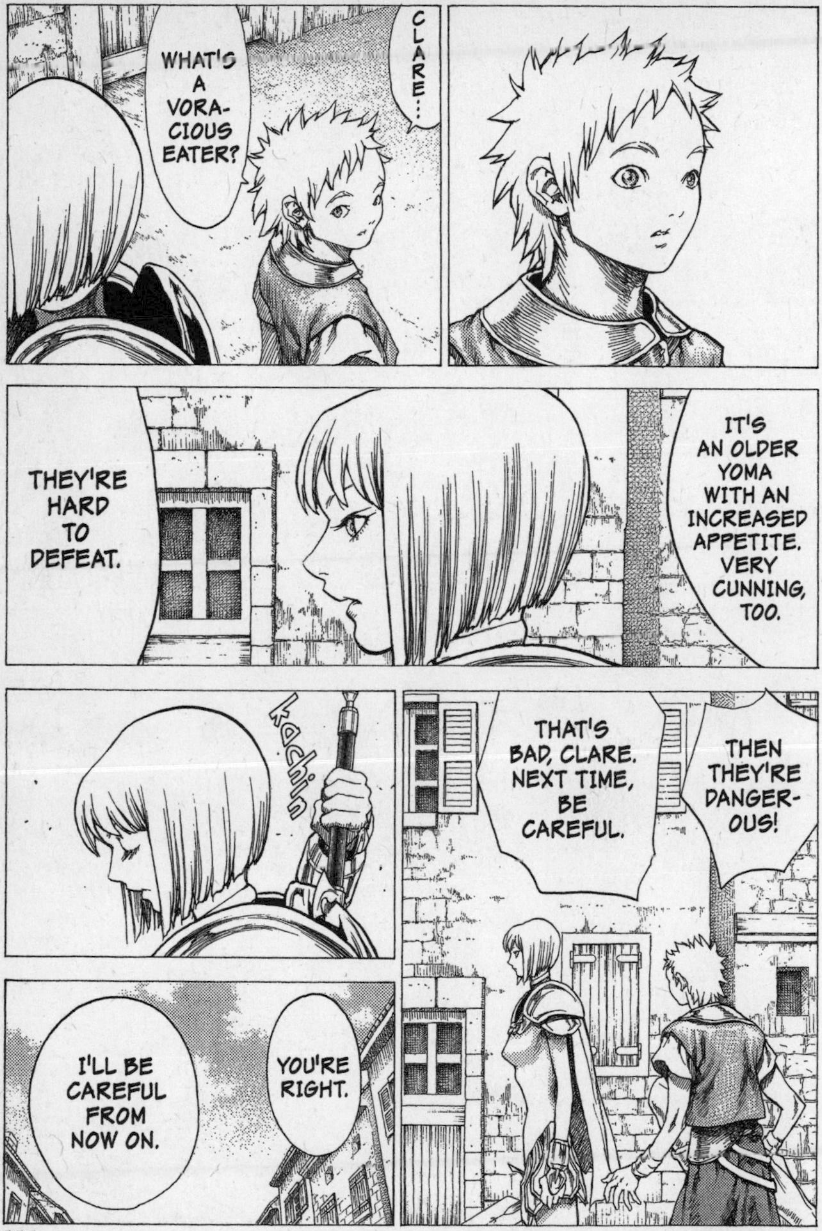
CLARE...
WHAT'S A VORACIOUS EATER?
IT'S AN OLDER YOMA WITH AN INCREASED APPETITE. VERY CUNNING, TOO.
THEY'RE HARD TO DEFEAT.
THEN THEY'RE DANGEROUS!
THAT'S BAD, CLARE. NEXT TIME, BE CAREFUL.
kachin
YOU'RE RIGHT.
I'LL BE CAREFUL FROM NOW ON.

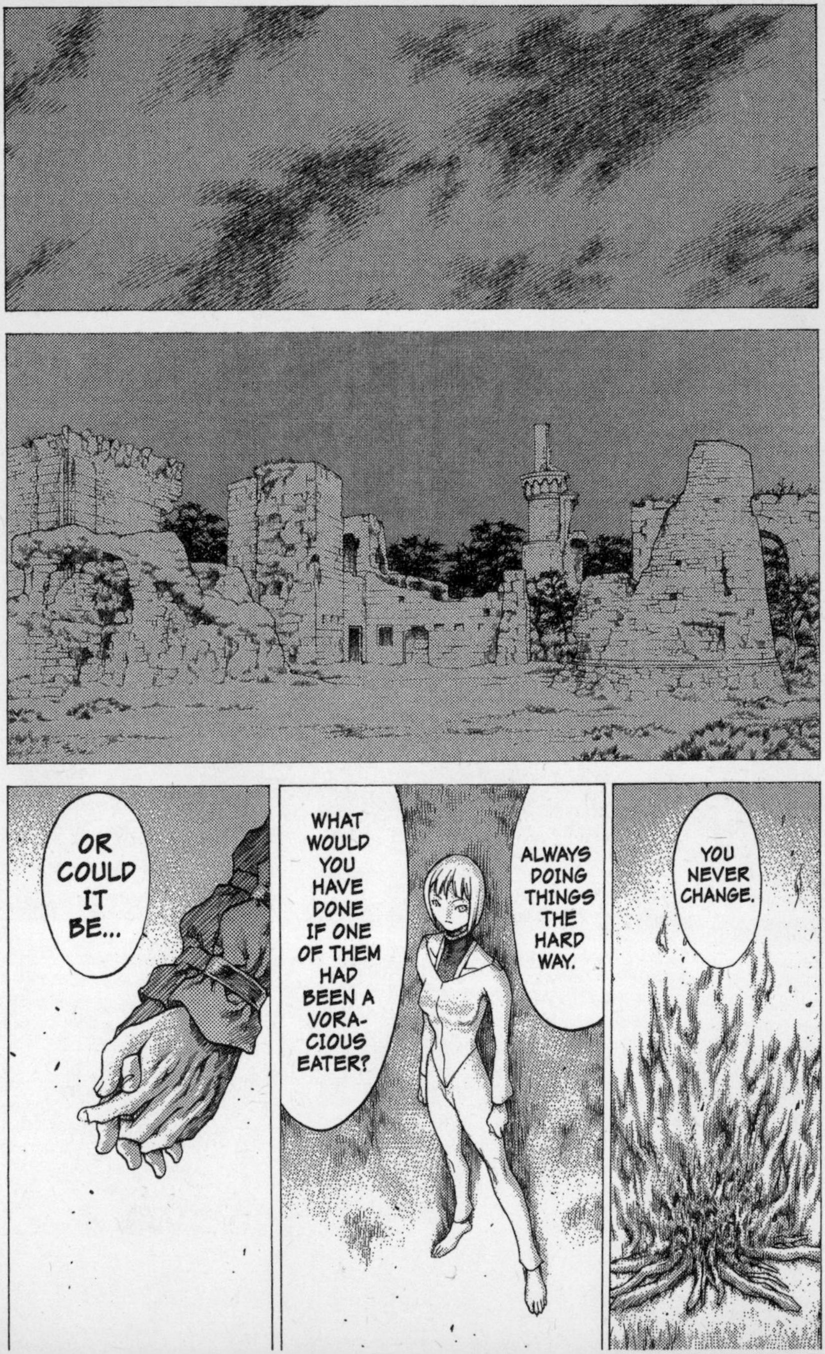
YOU NEVER CHANGE.
ALWAYS DOING THINGS THE HARD WAY.
WHAT WOULD YOU HAVE DONE IF ONE OF THEM HAD BEEN A VORA-CIOUS EATER?
OR COULD IT BE...

READ THIS WAY

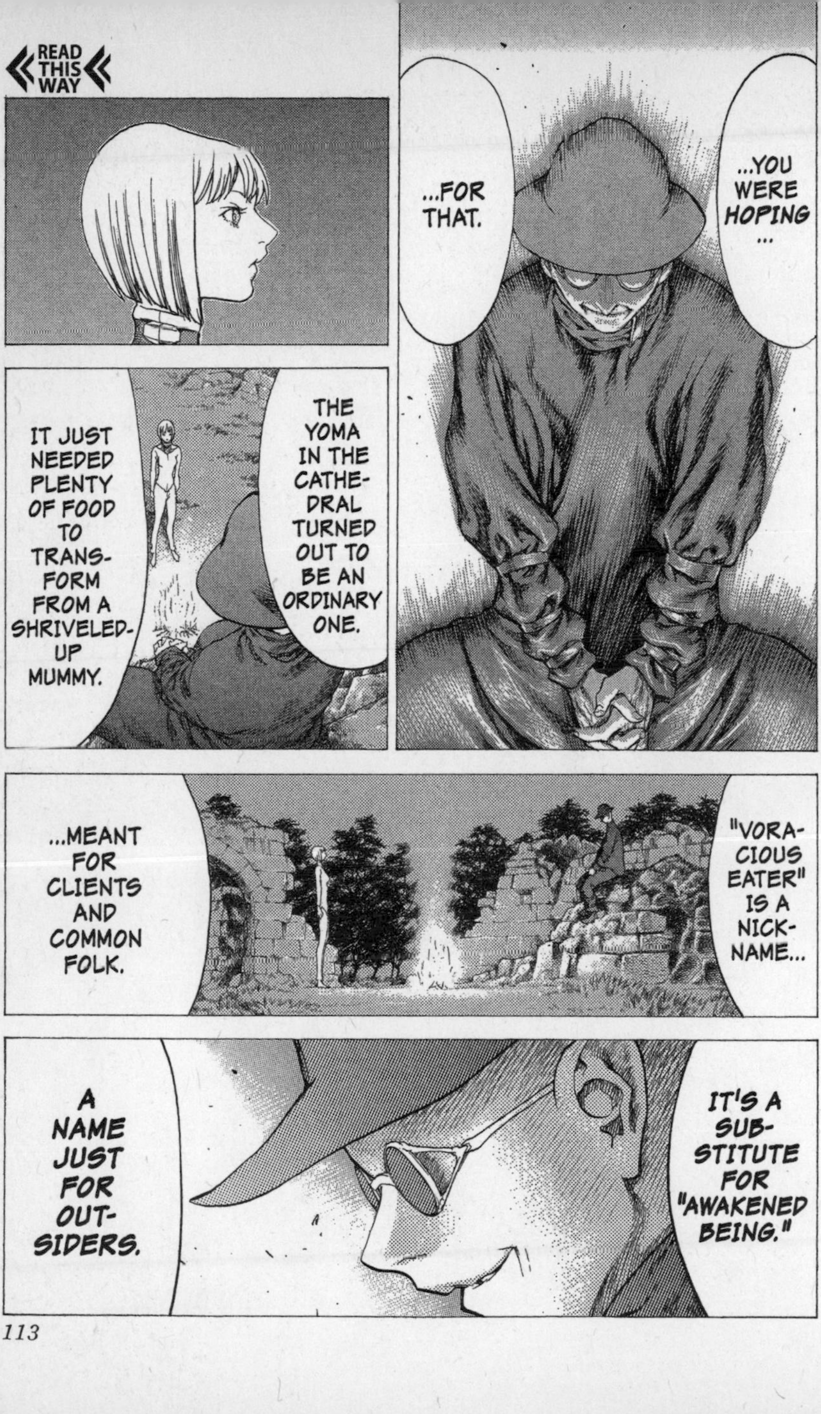

...YOU WERE HOPING ...
...FOR THAT.
THE YOMA IN THE CATHE-DRAL TURNED OUT TO BE AN ORDINARY ONE.
IT JUST NEEDED PLENTY OF FOOD TO TRANS-FORM FROM A SHRIVELED-UP MUMMY.
"VORA-CIOUS EATER" IS A NICK-NAME...
...MEANT FOR CLIENTS AND COMMON FOLK.
IT'S A SUB-STITUTE FOR "AWAKENED BEING."
A NAME JUST FOR OUT-SIDERS.

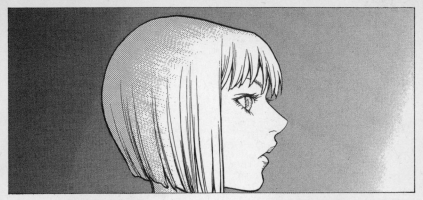

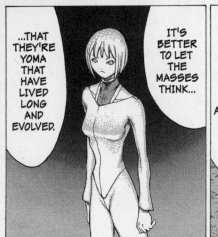

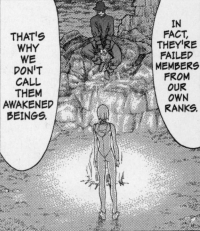

IN FACT, THEY'RE FAILED MEMBERS FROM OUR OWN RANKS.
THAT'S WHY WE DON'T CALL THEM AWAKENED BEINGS.
IT'S BETTER TO LET THE MASSES THINK...
...THAT THEY'RE YOMA THAT HAVE LIVED LONG AND EVOLVED.
IF YOU FACED A VORACIOUS EATER...
...THAT IS, AN AWAKENED BEING, YOU'D BE CUT TO RIBBONS IN SECONDS.

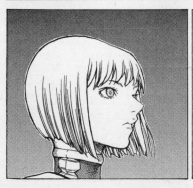

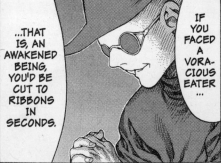

READ THIS WAY

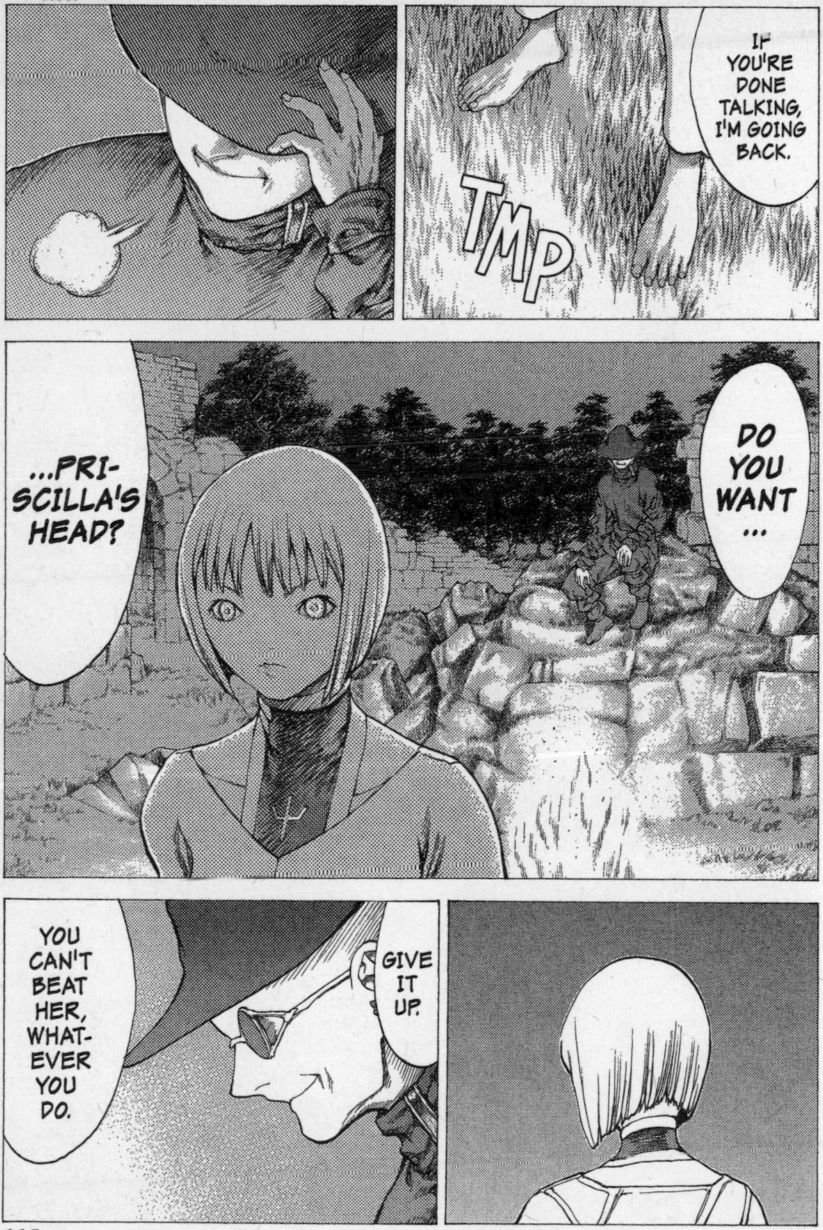
IF YOU'RE DONE TALKING, I'M GOING BACK.
TMP
DO YOU WANT...
...PRISCILLA'S HEAD?
GIVE IT UP.
YOU CAN'T BEAT HER, WHATEVER YOU DO.

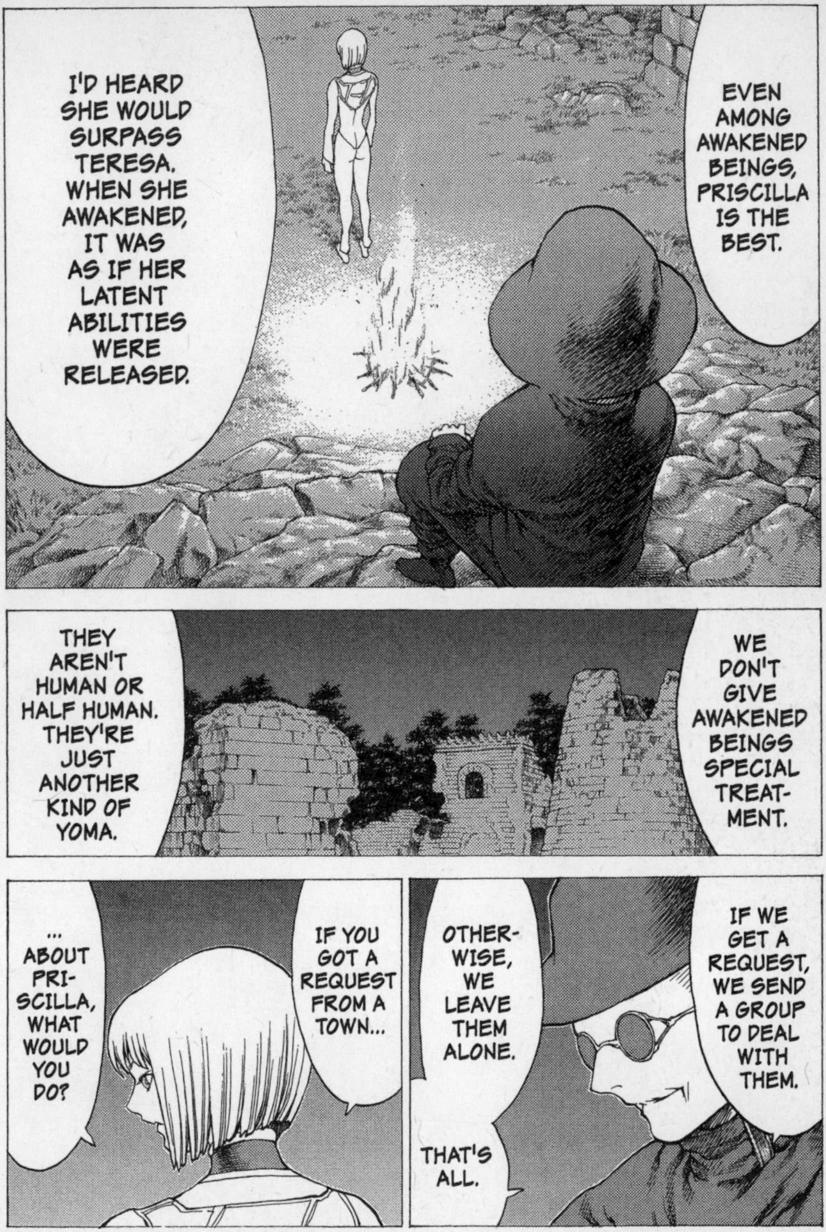
EVEN AMONG AWAKENED BEINGS, PRISCILLA IS THE BEST.
I'D HEARD SHE WOULD SURPASS TERESA. WHEN SHE AWAKENED, IT WAS AS IF HER LATENT ABILITIES WERE RELEASED.
WE DON'T GIVE AWAKENED BEINGS SPECIAL TREAT-MENT.
THEY AREN'T HUMAN OR HALF HUMAN. THEY'RE JUST ANOTHER KIND OF YOMA.
IF WE GET A REQUEST, WE SEND A GROUP TO DEAL WITH THEM.
OTHER-WISE, WE LEAVE THEM ALONE.
THAT'S ALL.
IF YOU GOT A REQUEST FROM A TOWN...
... ABOUT PRI-SCILLA, WHAT WOULD YOU DO?

READ THIS WAY

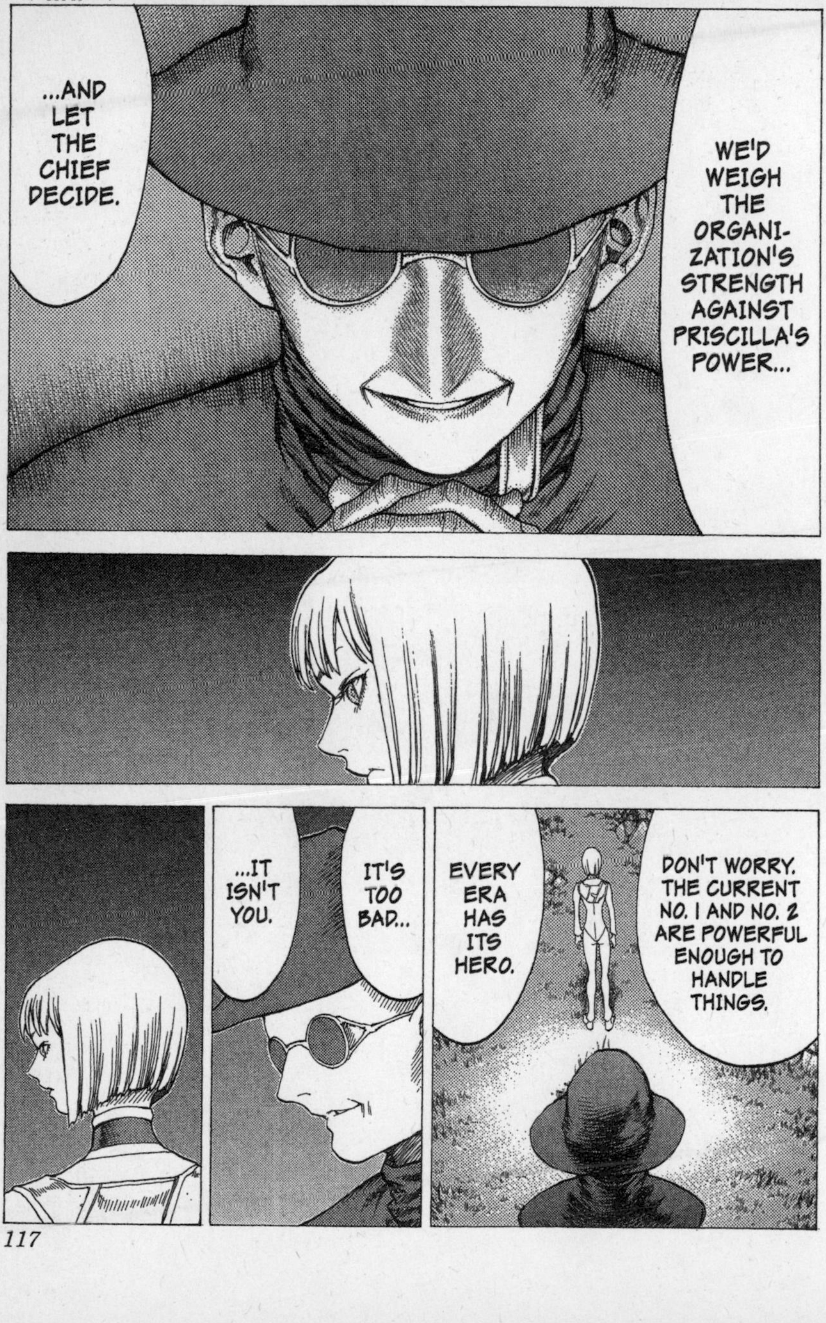
WE'D WEIGH THE ORGANIZATION'S STRENGTH AGAINST PRISCILLA'S POWER...
...AND LET THE CHIEF DECIDE.
DON'T WORRY. THE CURRENT NO. 1 AND NO. 2 ARE POWERFUL ENOUGH TO HANDLE THINGS.
EVERY ERA HAS ITS HERO.
IT'S TOO BAD...
...IT ISN'T YOU.

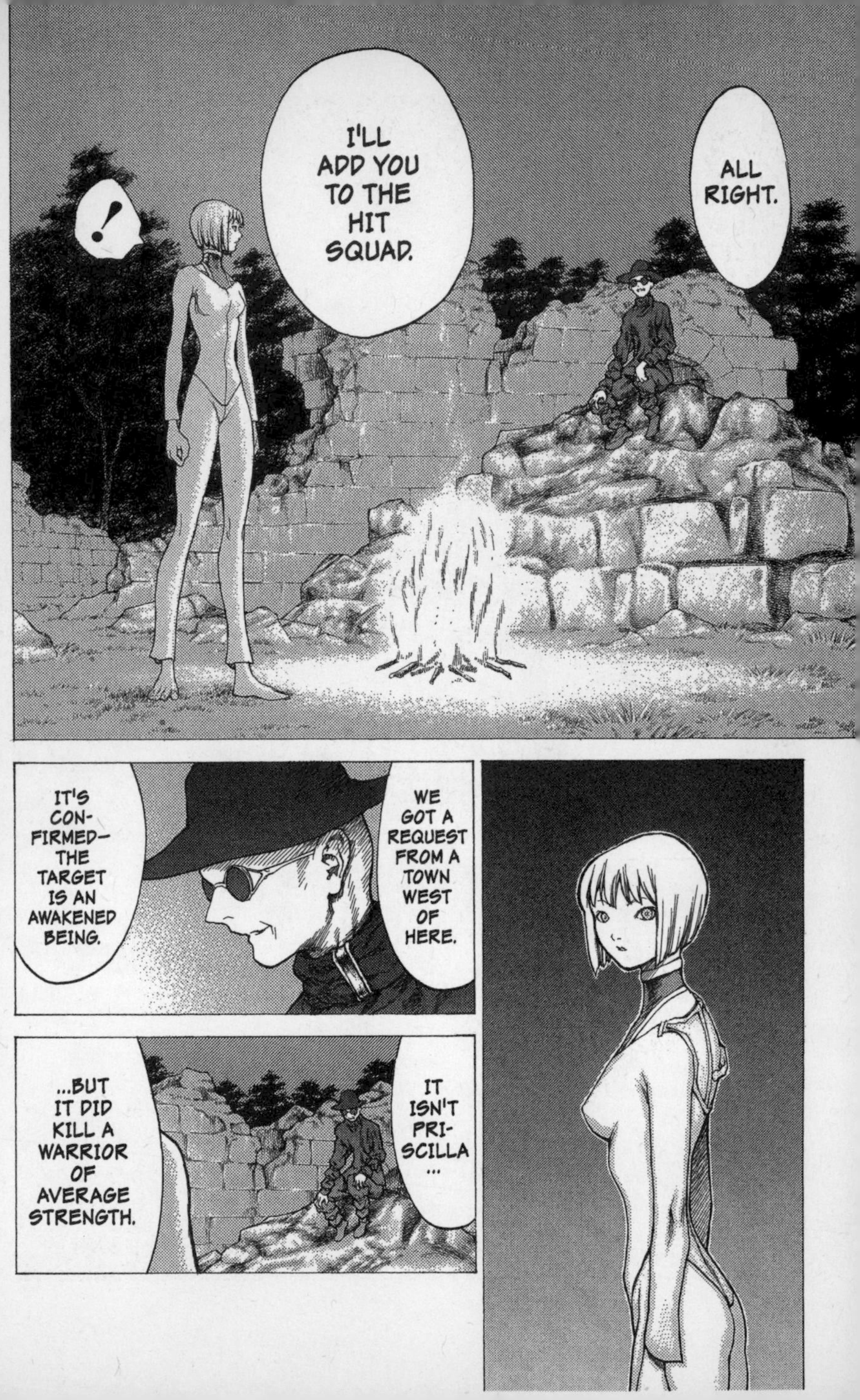
ALL RIGHT.
I'LL ADD YOU TO THE HIT SQUAD.
!
WE GOT A REQUEST FROM A TOWN WEST OF HERE.
IT'S CON-FIRMED—THE TARGET IS AN AWAKENED BEING.
IT ISN'T PRI-SCILLA...
...BUT IT DID KILL A WARRIOR OF AVERAGE STRENGTH.

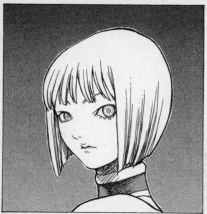

...THIS MIGHT BE A CHANCE FOR YOU TO DISCOVER THE LIMITS OF YOUR STRENGTH.

SO...

ZZZZZ....

ZZZZZ....

KRUK

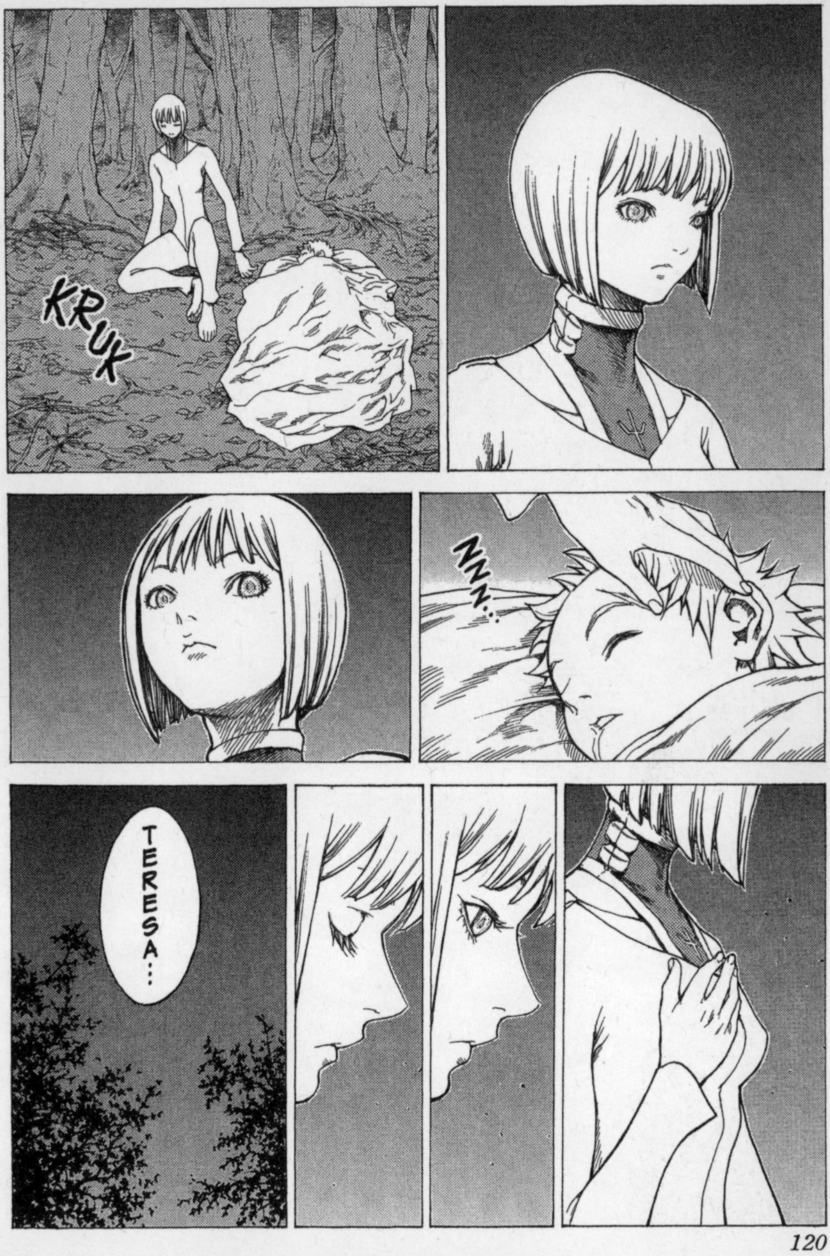
KRUK
ZZZ...
TERESA...

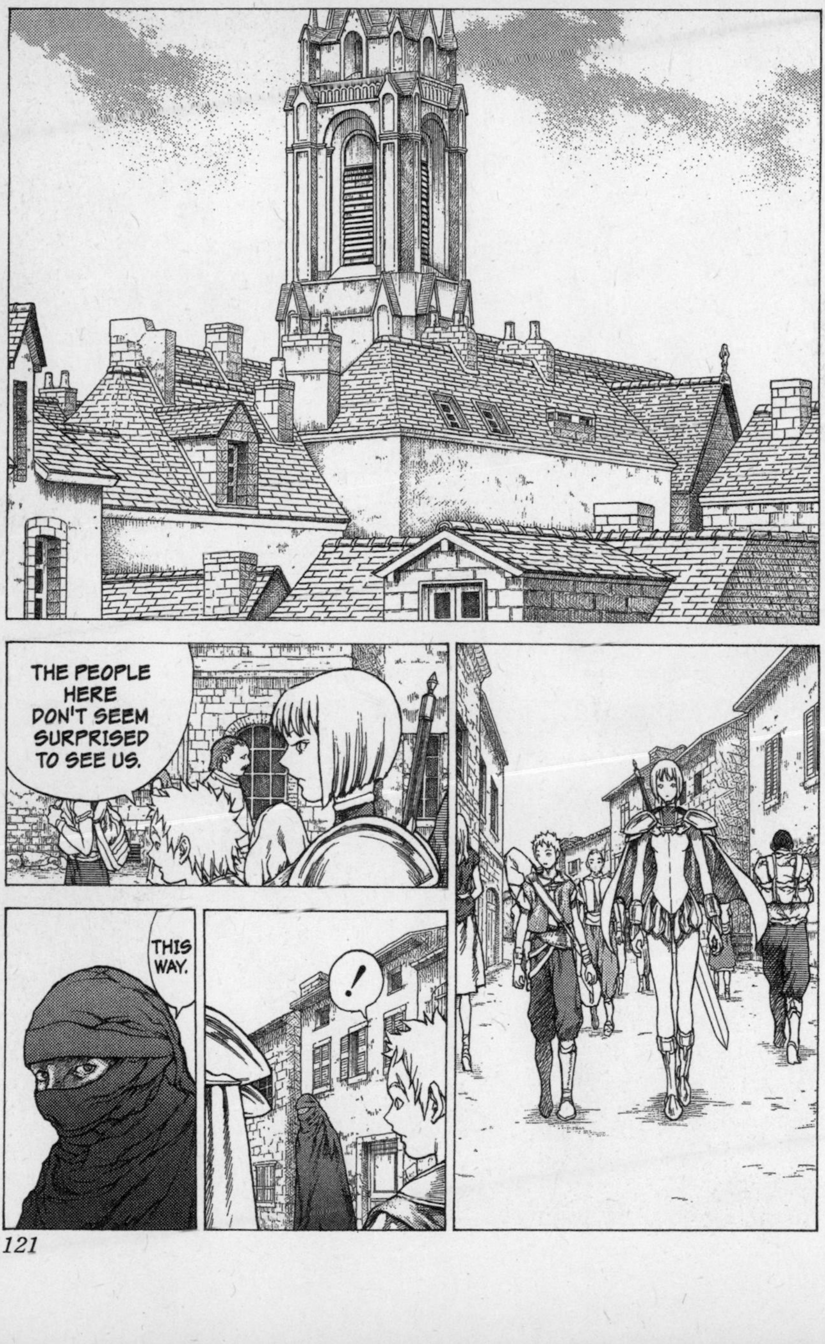
THE PEOPLE HERE DON'T SEEM SURPRISED TO SEE US.
!
THIS WAY.

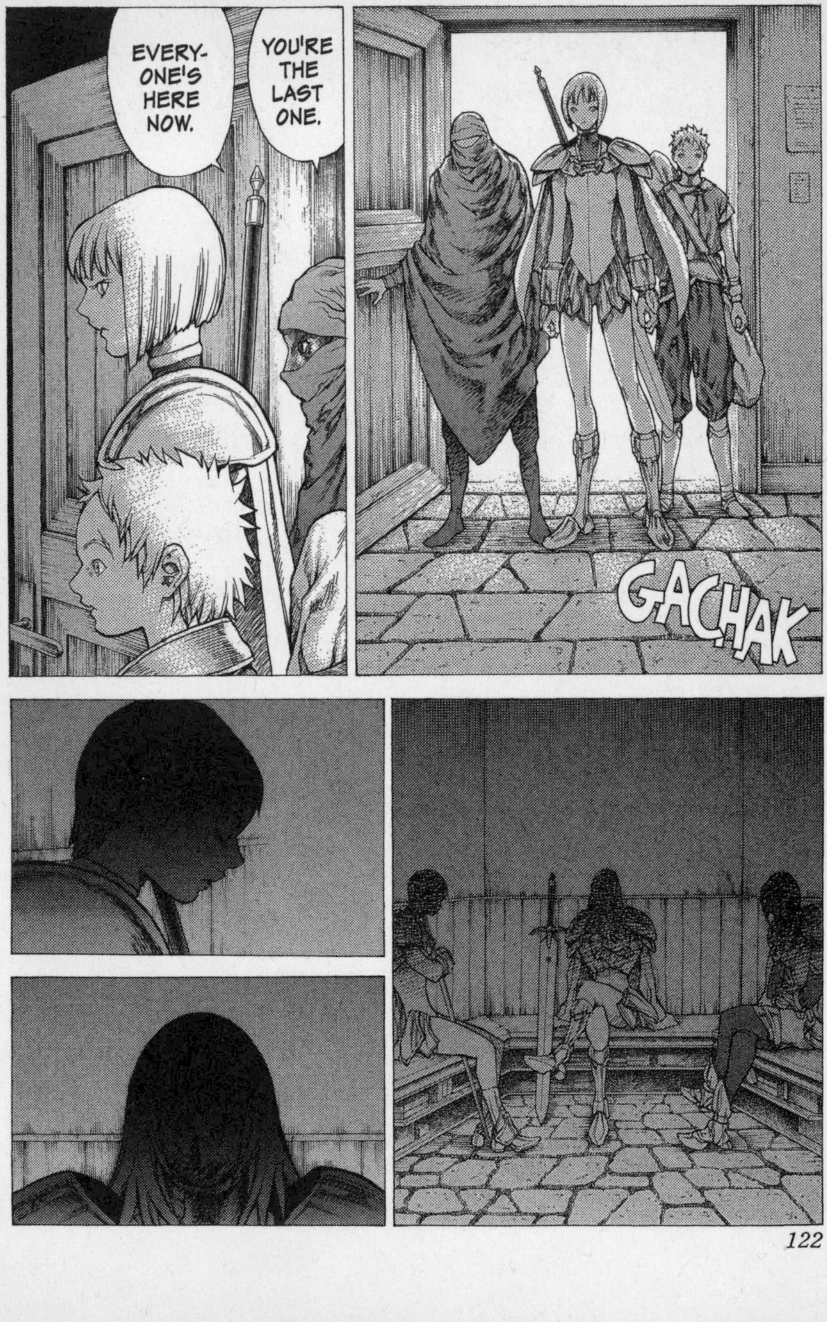
GACHAK
YOU'RE THE LAST ONE.
EVERY-ONE'S HERE NOW.

READ THIS WAY

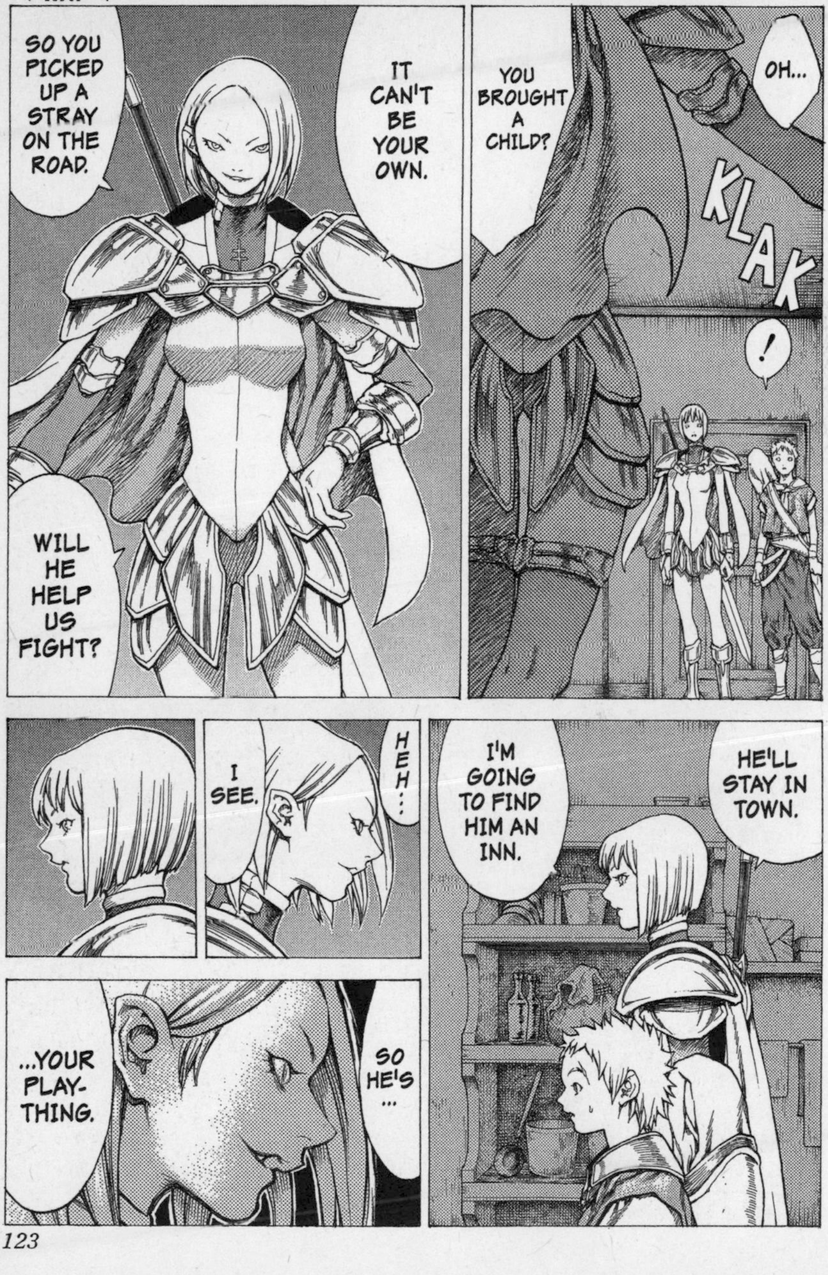
OH...
YOU BROUGHT A CHILD?
KLAK
!
IT CAN'T BE YOUR OWN.
SO YOU PICKED UP A STRAY ON THE ROAD.
WILL HE HELP US FIGHT?
HE'LL STAY IN TOWN.
I'M GOING TO FIND HIM AN INN.
HEH...
I SEE.
SO HE'S...
...YOUR PLAY-THING.

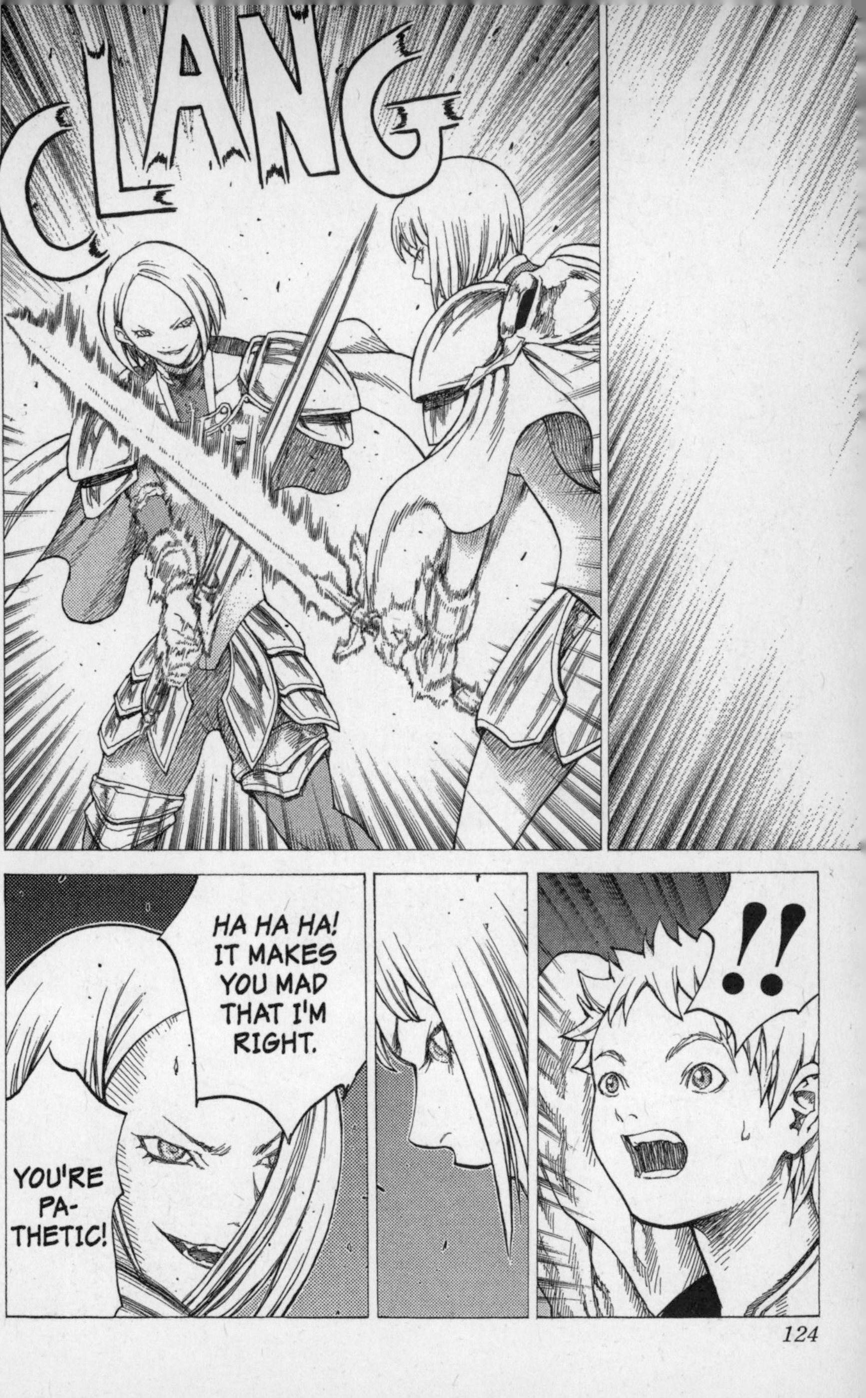
CLANG
!!
HA HA HA! IT MAKES YOU MAD THAT I'M RIGHT.
YOU'RE PA-THETIC!

READ THIS WAY

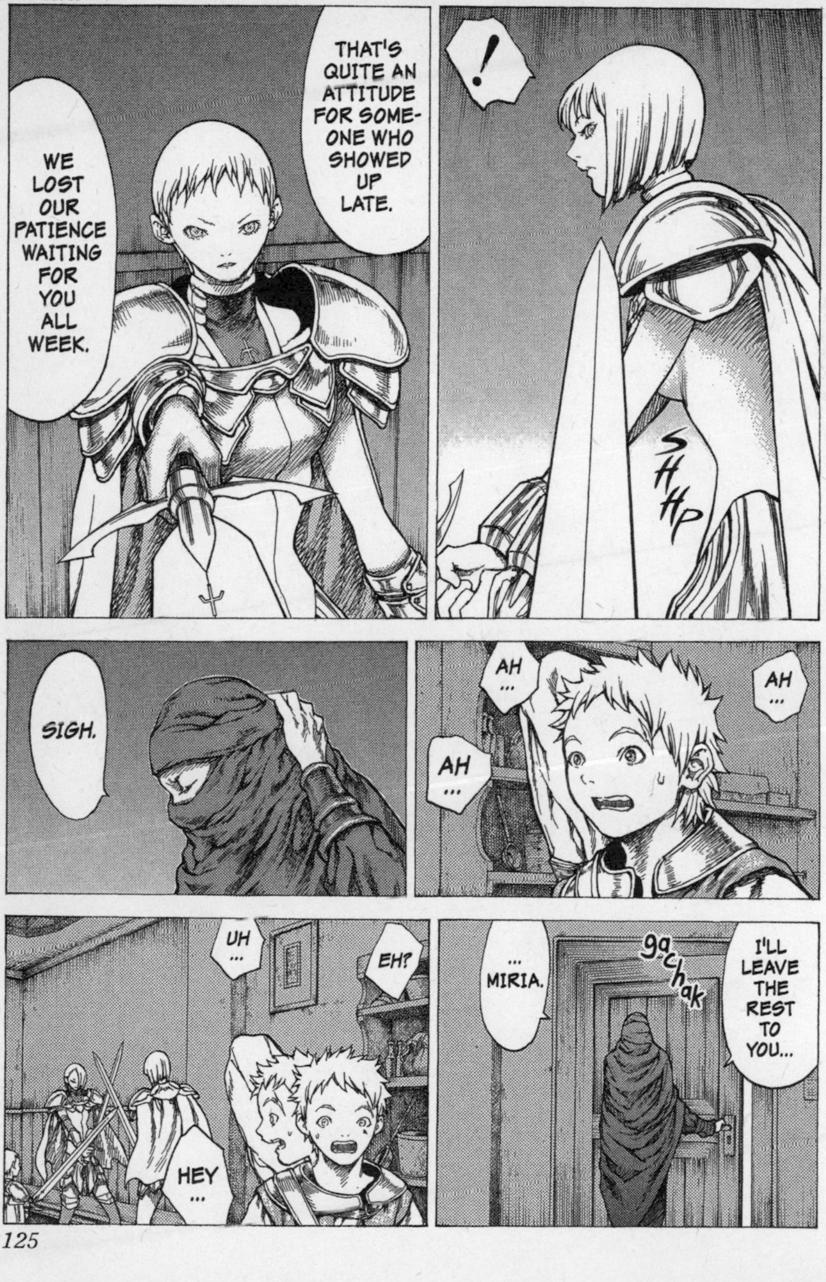
!
SHHP
THAT'S QUITE AN ATTITUDE FOR SOME-ONE WHO SHOWED UP LATE.
WE LOST OUR PATIENCE WAITING FOR YOU ALL WEEK.
AH ...
AH ...
AH ...
SIGH.
I'LL LEAVE THE REST TO YOU...
gachak
... MIRIA.
EH?
UH ...
HEY ...

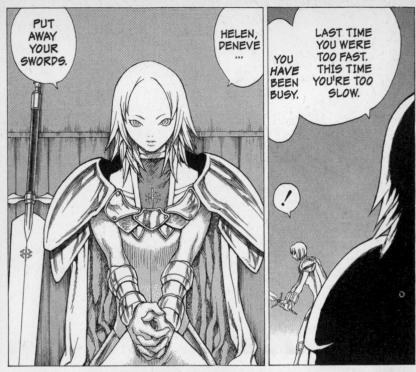

LAST TIME YOU WERE TOO FAST. THIS TIME YOU'RE TOO SLOW.
YOU HAVE BEEN BUSY.
!
HELEN, DENEVE ...
PUT AWAY YOUR SWORDS.
AH!
!
TCHINK
GACHAK

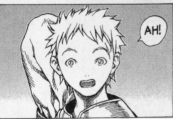

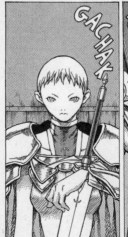

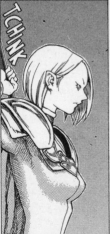

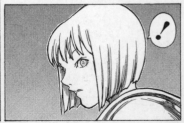

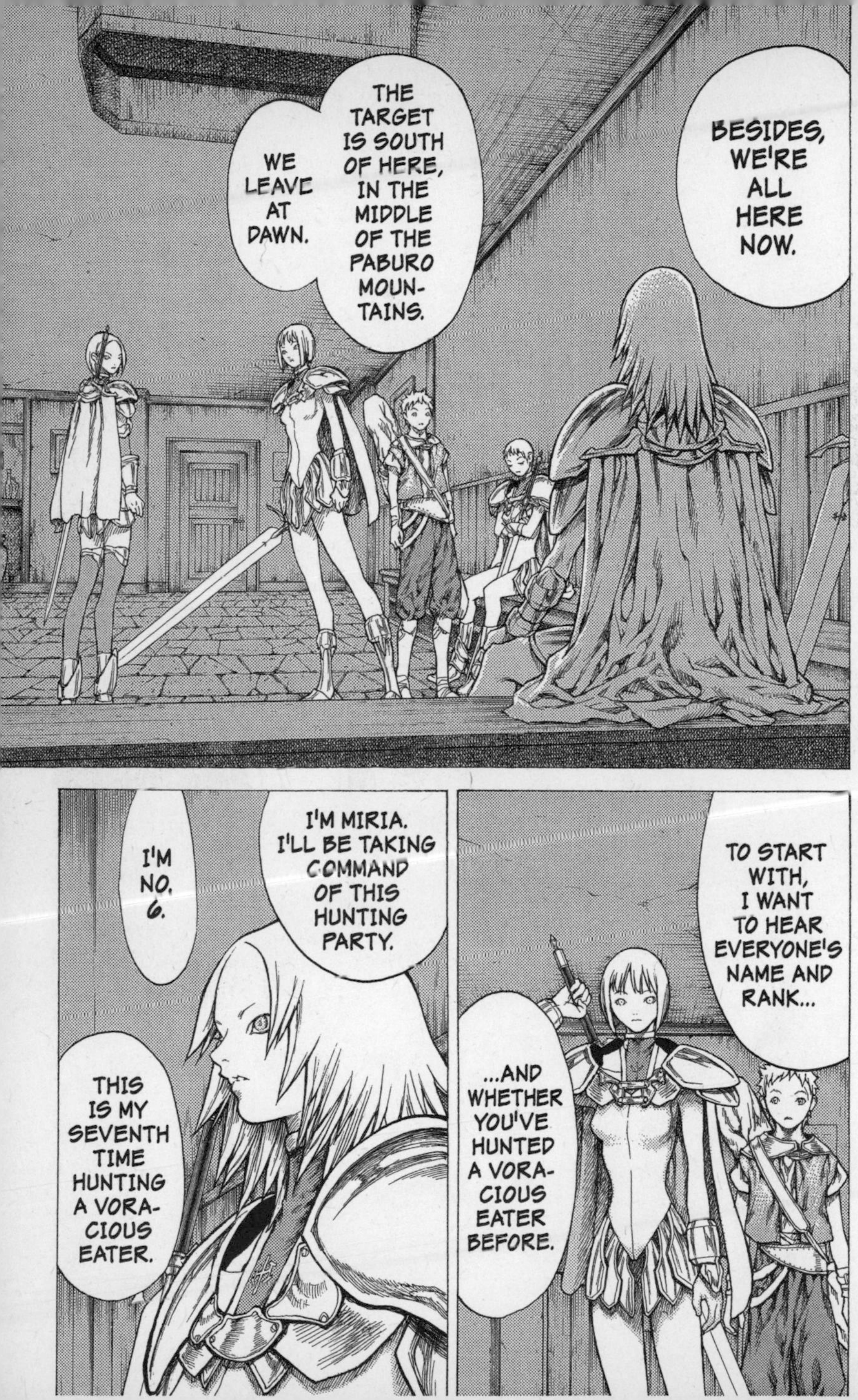
BESIDES, WE'RE ALL HERE NOW.
THE TARGET IS SOUTH OF HERE, IN THE MIDDLE OF THE PABURO MOUNTAINS.
WE LEAVE AT DAWN.
TO START WITH, I WANT TO HEAR EVERYONE'S NAME AND RANK...
...AND WHETHER YOU'VE HUNTED A VORACIOUS EATER BEFORE.
I'M MIRIA. I'LL BE TAKING COMMAND OF THIS HUNTING PARTY.
I'M NO. 6.
THIS IS MY SEVENTH TIME HUNTING A VORACIOUS EATER.

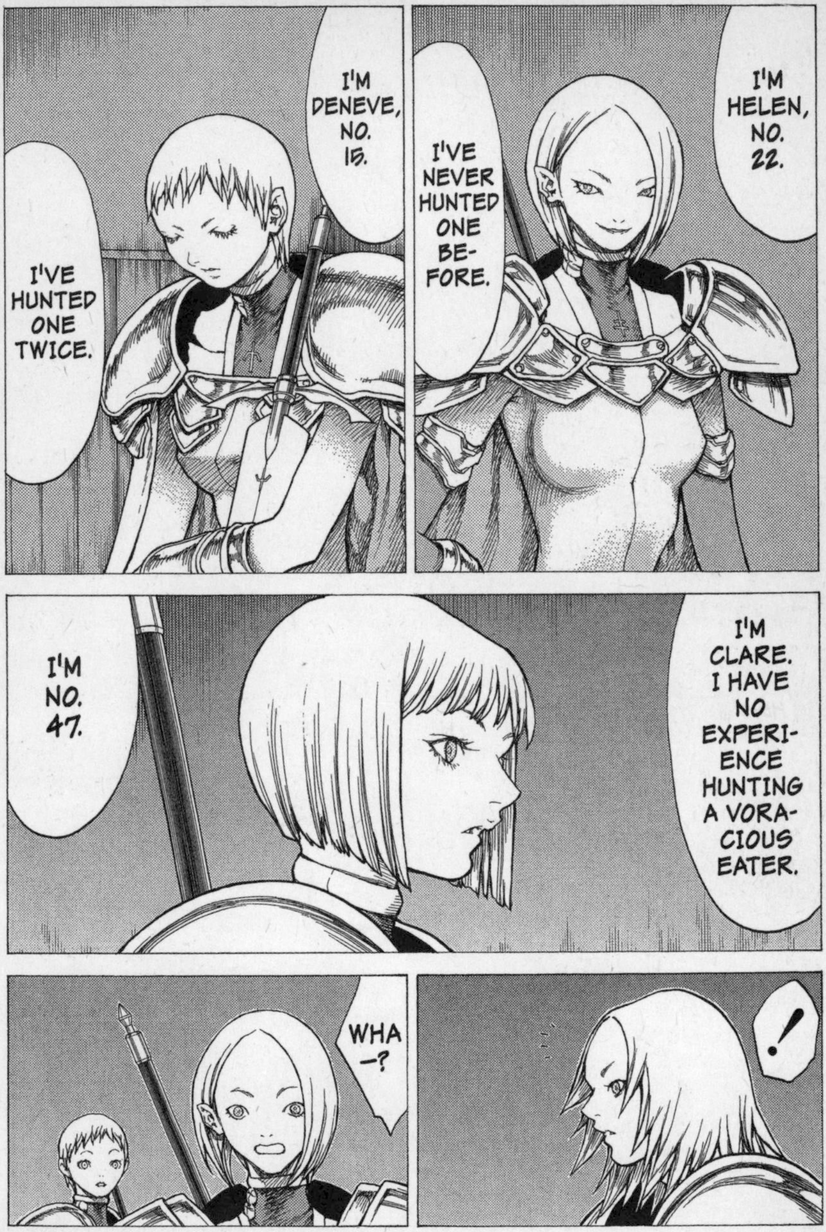
I'M HELEN, NO. 22.
I'VE NEVER HUNTED ONE BEFORE.
I'M DENEVE, NO. 15.
I'VE HUNTED ONE TWICE.
I'M CLARE. I HAVE NO EXPERIENCE HUNTING A VORACIOUS EATER.
I'M NO. 47.
!
WHA—?

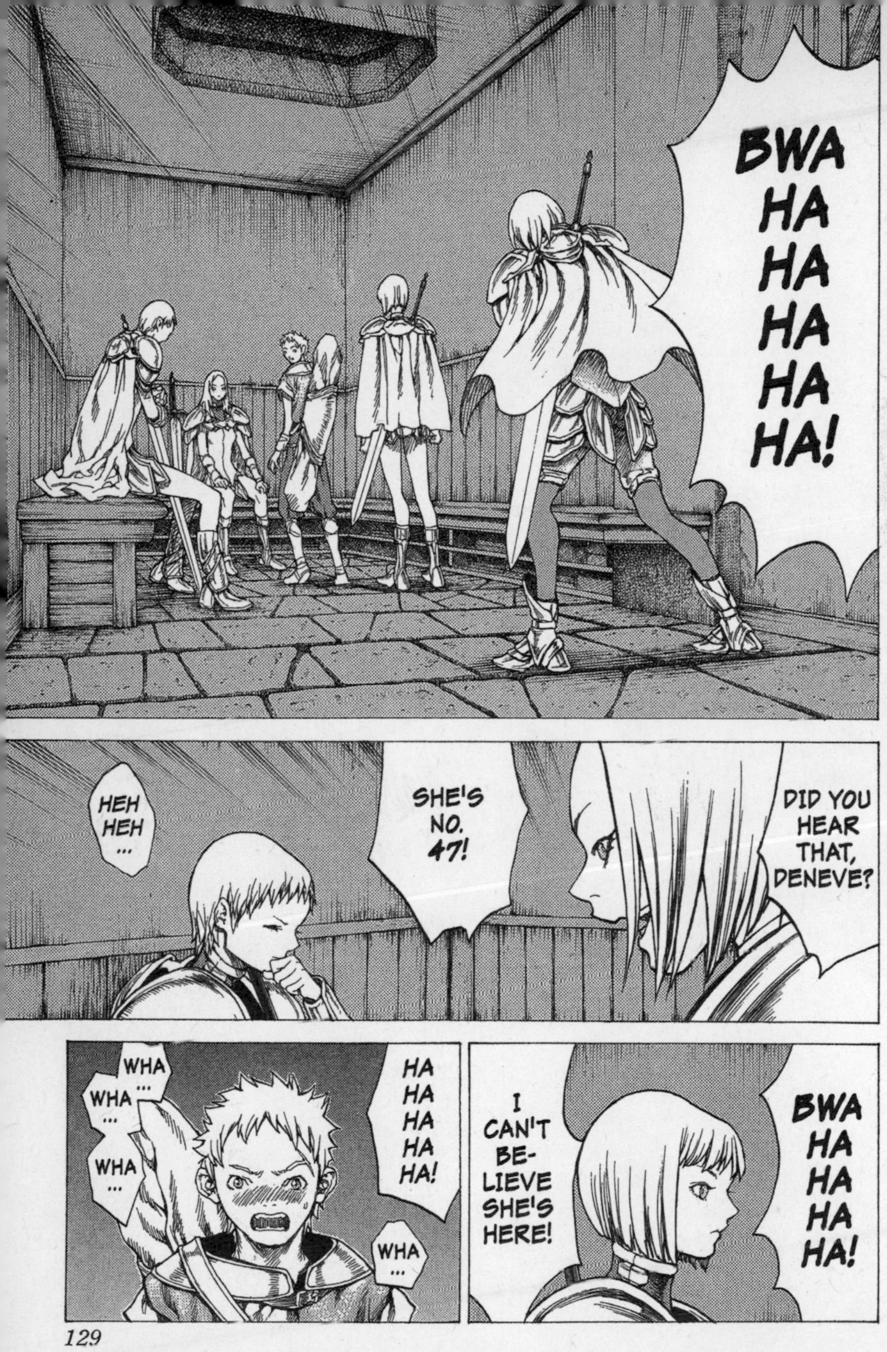
BWA HA HA HA HA HA!
DID YOU HEAR THAT, DENEVE?
SHE'S NO. 47!
HEH HEH ...
BWA HA HA HA HA!
I CAN'T BE-LIEVE SHE'S HERE!
HA HA HA HA HA!
WHA ...
WHA ...
WHA ...
WHA ...

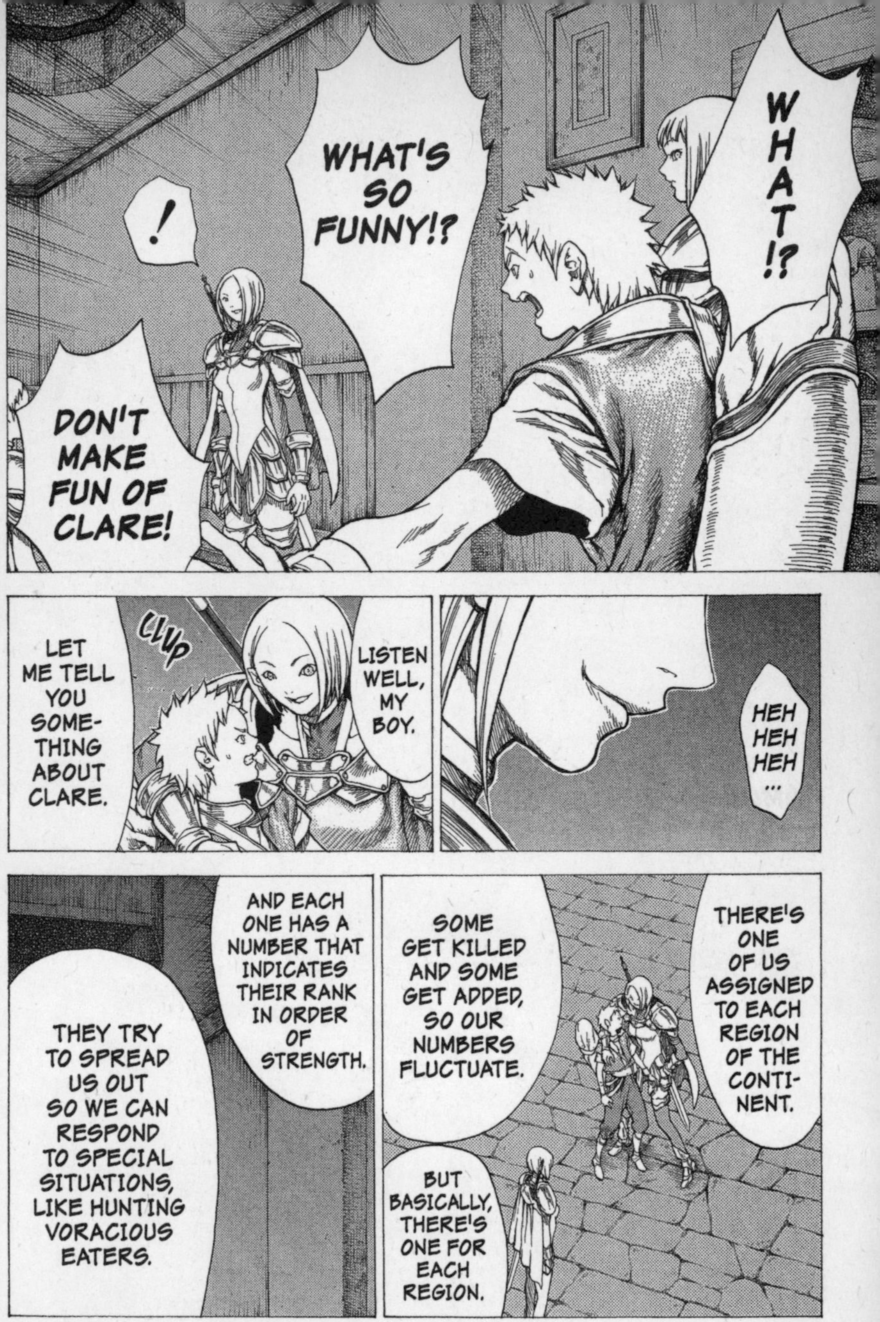
WHAT!?
WHAT'S SO FUNNY!?
!
DON'T MAKE FUN OF CLARE!
HEH HEH HEH ...
LISTEN WELL, MY BOY.
CLUP
LET ME TELL YOU SOME-THING ABOUT CLARE.
THERE'S ONE OF US ASSIGNED TO EACH REGION OF THE CONTI-NENT.
SOME GET KILLED AND SOME GET ADDED, SO OUR NUMBERS FLUCTUATE.
BUT BASICALLY, THERE'S ONE FOR EACH REGION.
AND EACH ONE HAS A NUMBER THAT INDICATES THEIR RANK IN ORDER OF STRENGTH.
THEY TRY TO SPREAD US OUT SO WE CAN RESPOND TO SPECIAL SITUATIONS, LIKE HUNTING VORACIOUS EATERS.

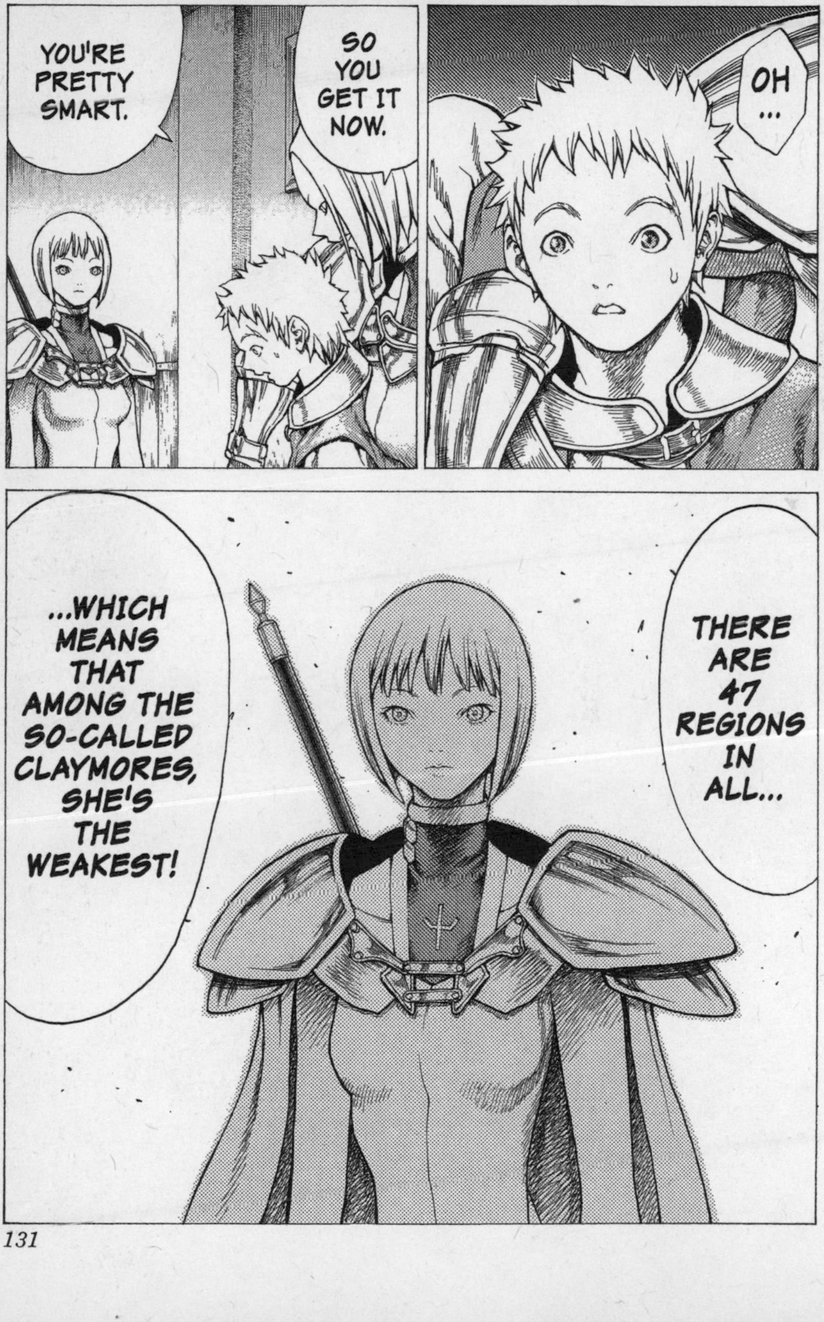
OH ...
SO YOU GET IT NOW.
YOU'RE PRETTY SMART.
THERE ARE 47 REGIONS IN ALL...
...WHICH MEANS THAT AMONG THE SO-CALLED CLAYMORES, SHE'S THE WEAKEST!

クレイモア
Claymore™

Scene 26: The Slashers, Part 2

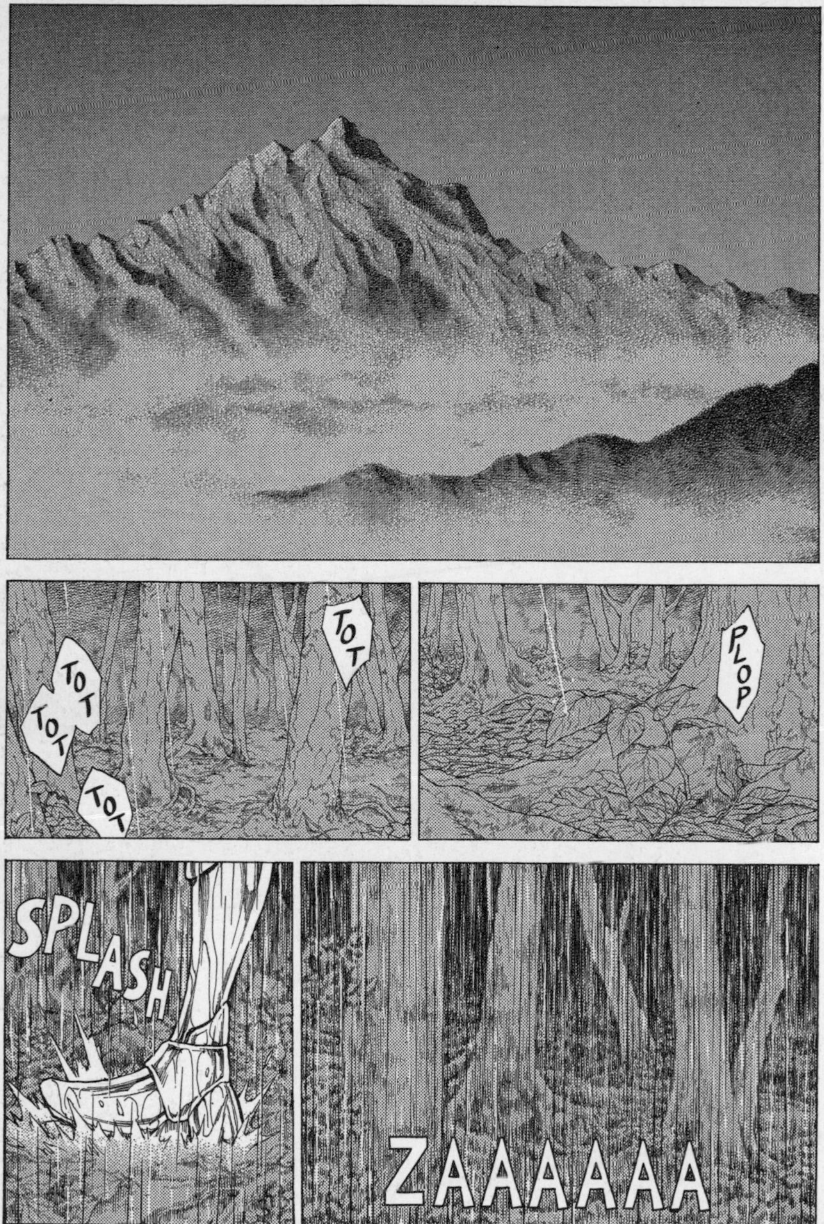
PLOP
TOT
TOT
TOT
TOT
ZAAAAAA
SPLASH

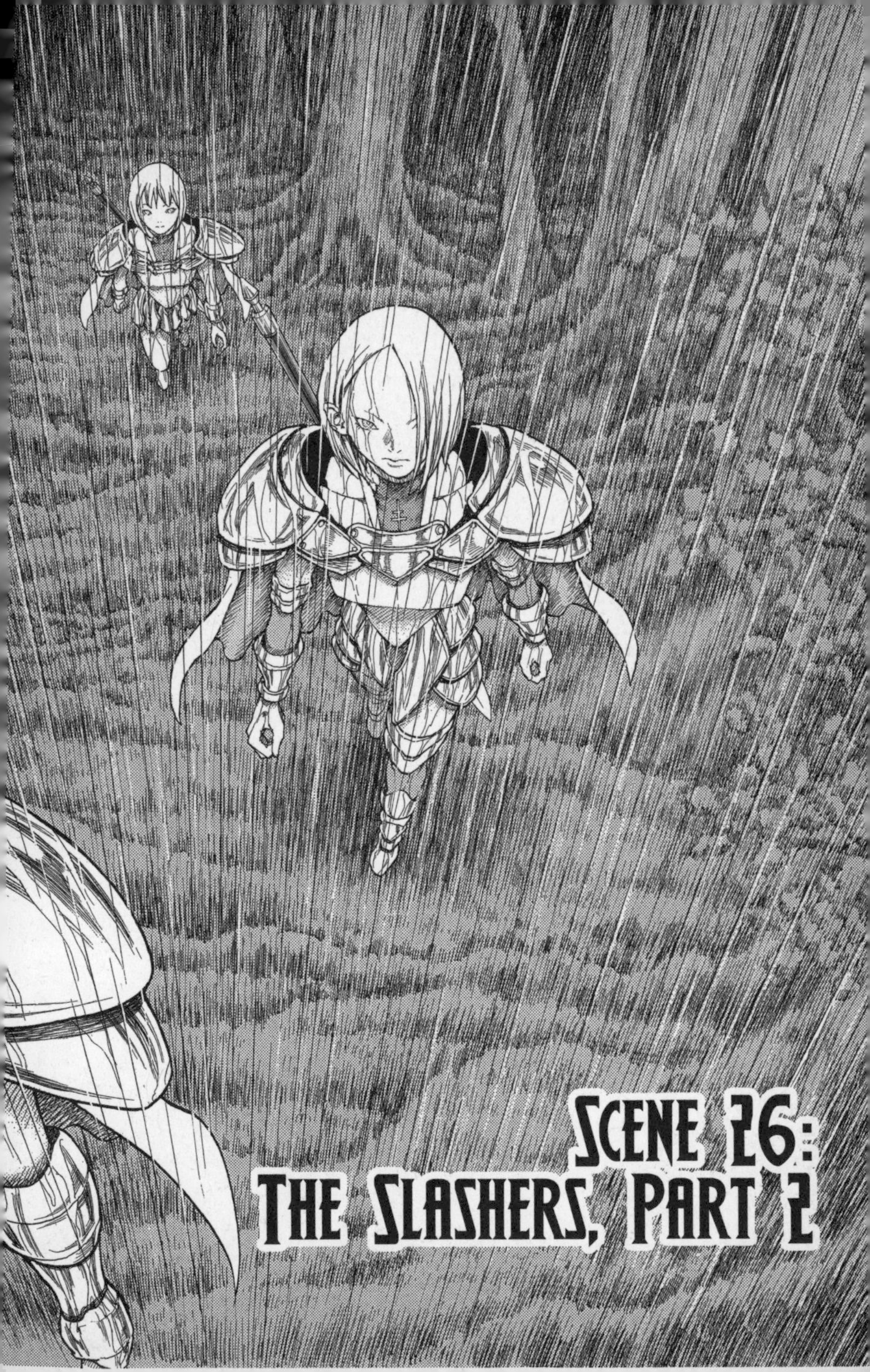
SCENE 26:
THE SLASHERS, PART 2

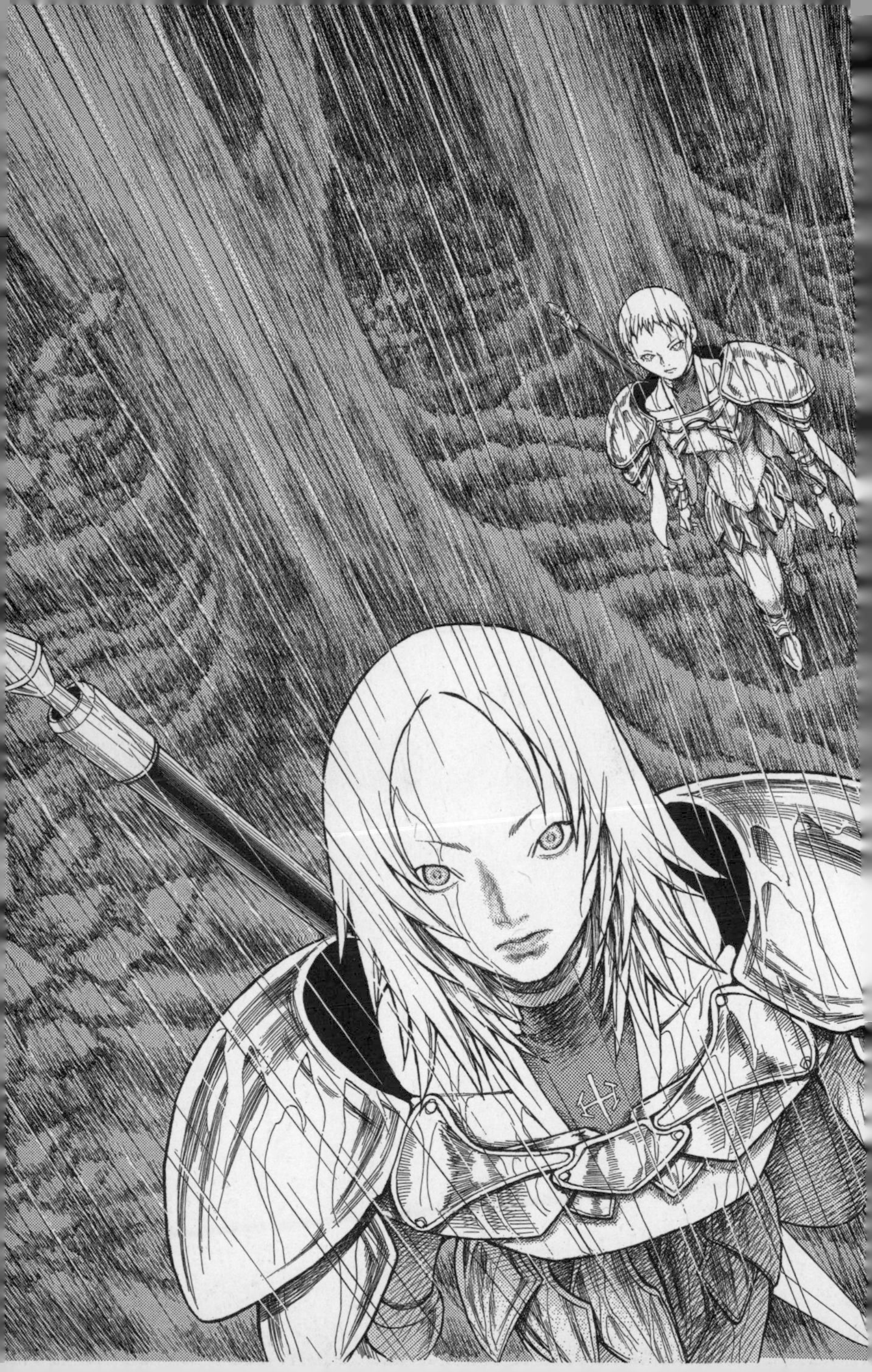

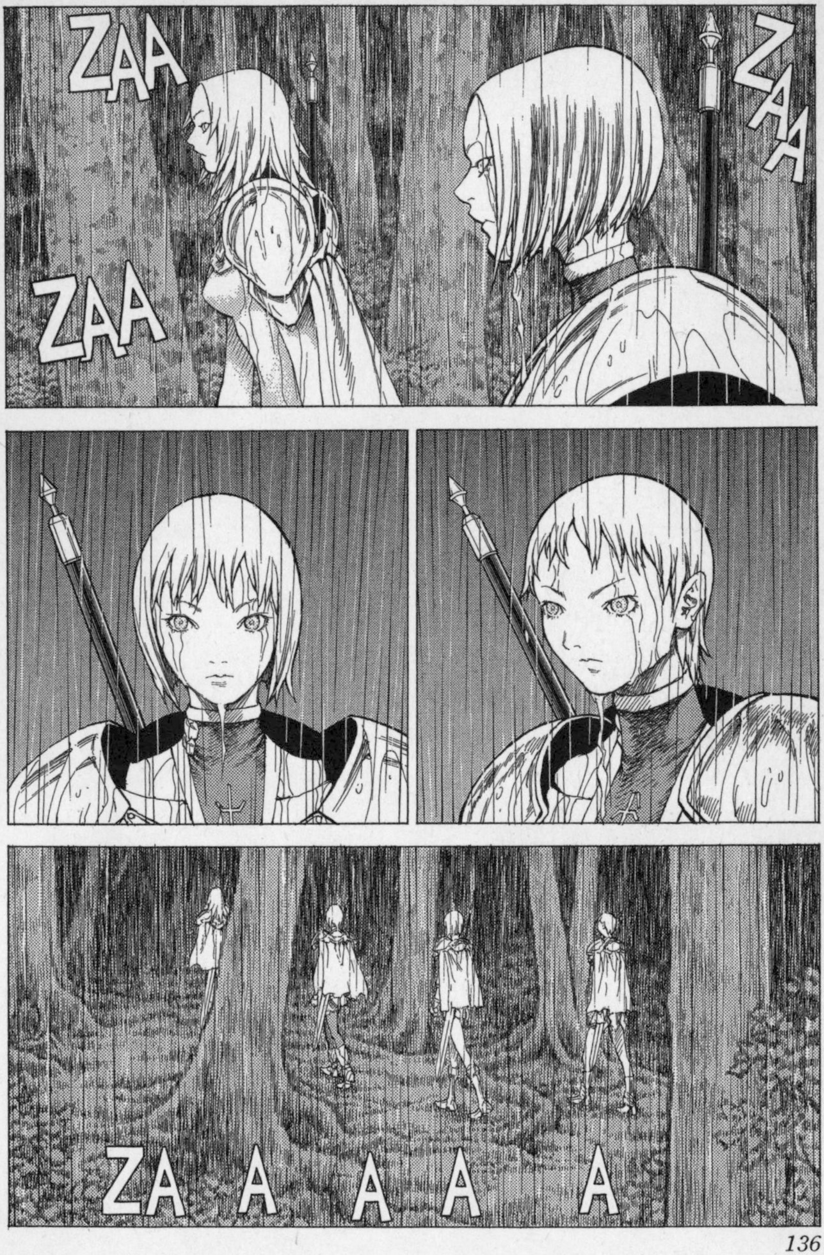
ZAA
ZAA
ZAA
ZA A A A A

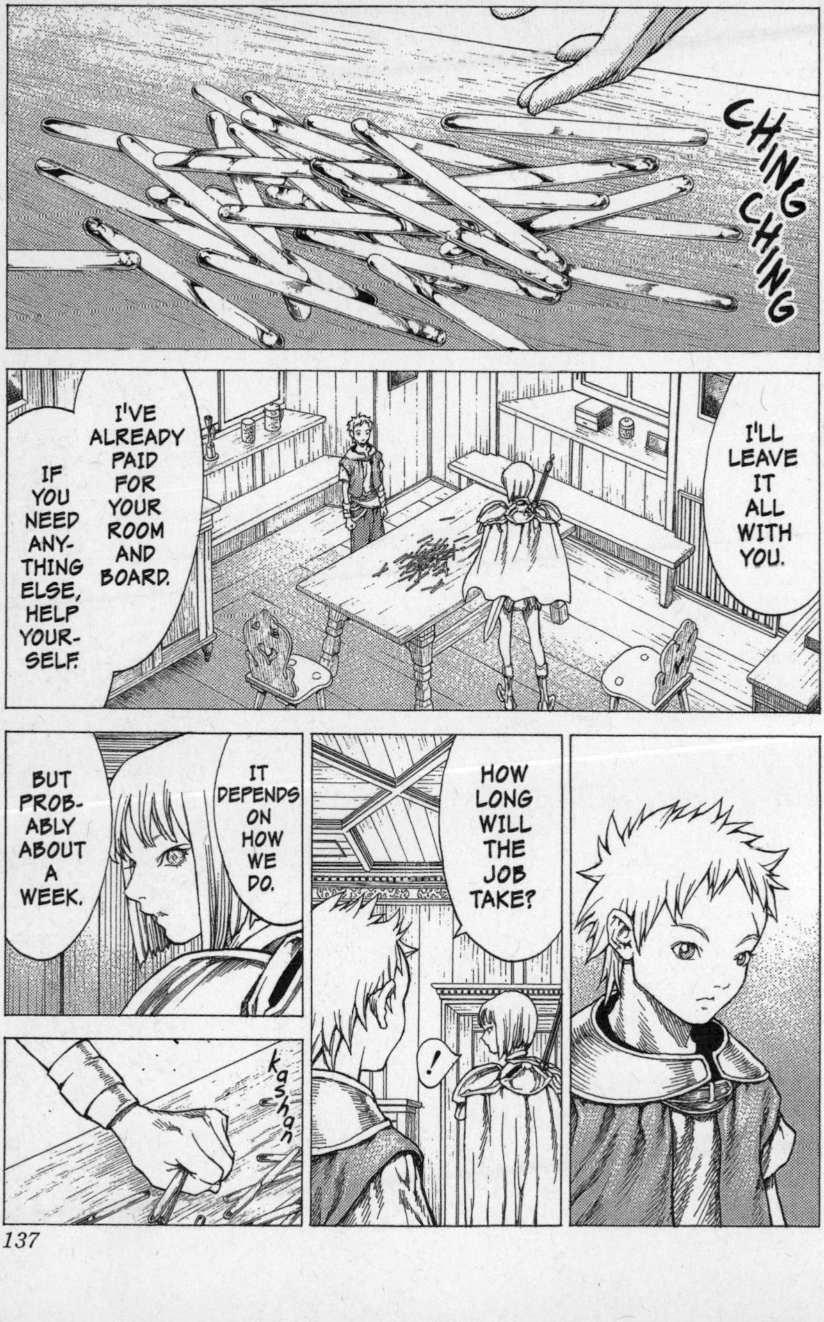
CHING CHING
I'LL LEAVE IT ALL WITH YOU.
I'VE ALREADY PAID FOR YOUR ROOM AND BOARD.
IF YOU NEED ANY-THING ELSE, HELP YOUR-SELF.
HOW LONG WILL THE JOB TAKE?
!
IT DEPENDS ON HOW WE DO.
BUT PROB-ABLY ABOUT A WEEK.
kashan

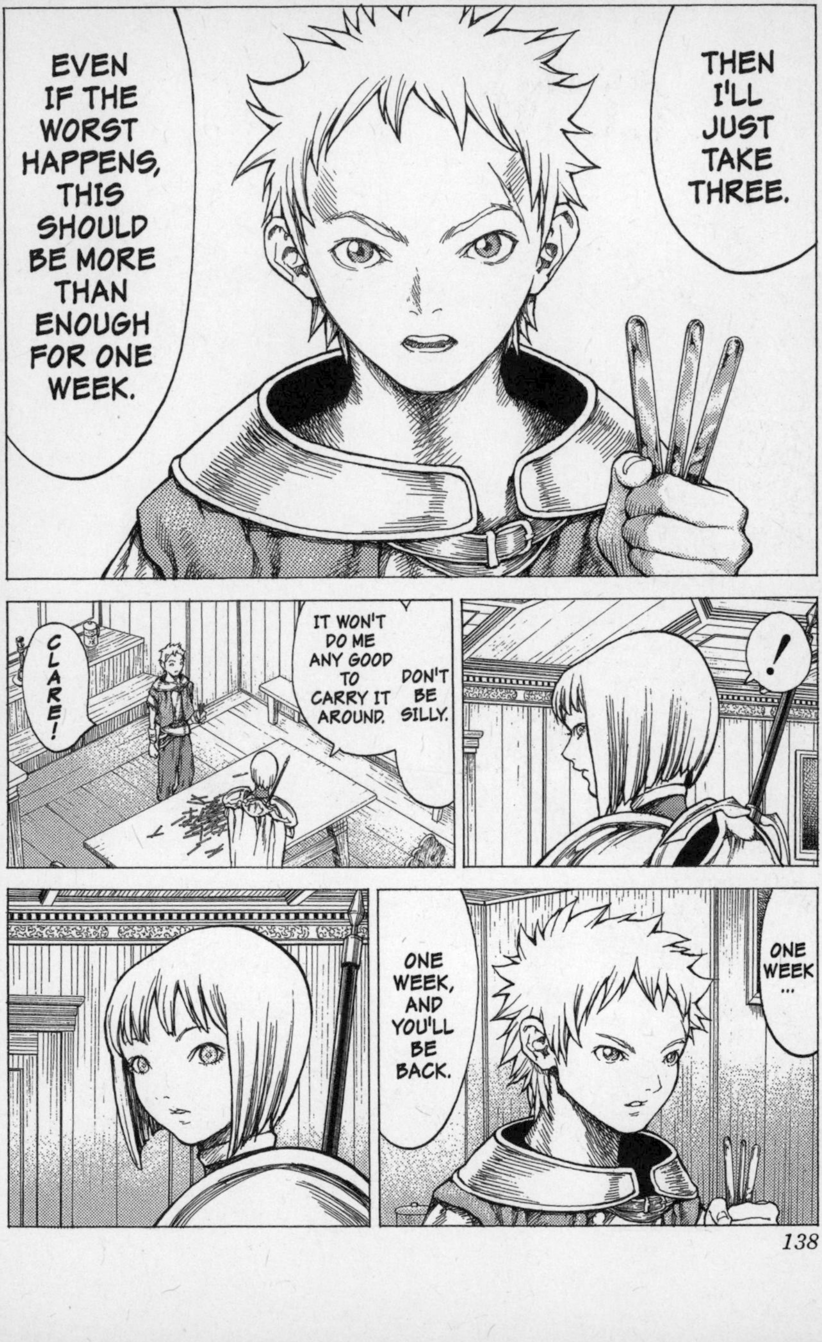
THEN I'LL JUST TAKE THREE.
EVEN IF THE WORST HAPPENS, THIS SHOULD BE MORE THAN ENOUGH FOR ONE WEEK.
!
DON'T BE SILLY.
IT WON'T DO ME ANY GOOD TO CARRY IT AROUND.
CLARE!
ONE WEEK...
ONE WEEK, AND YOU'LL BE BACK.

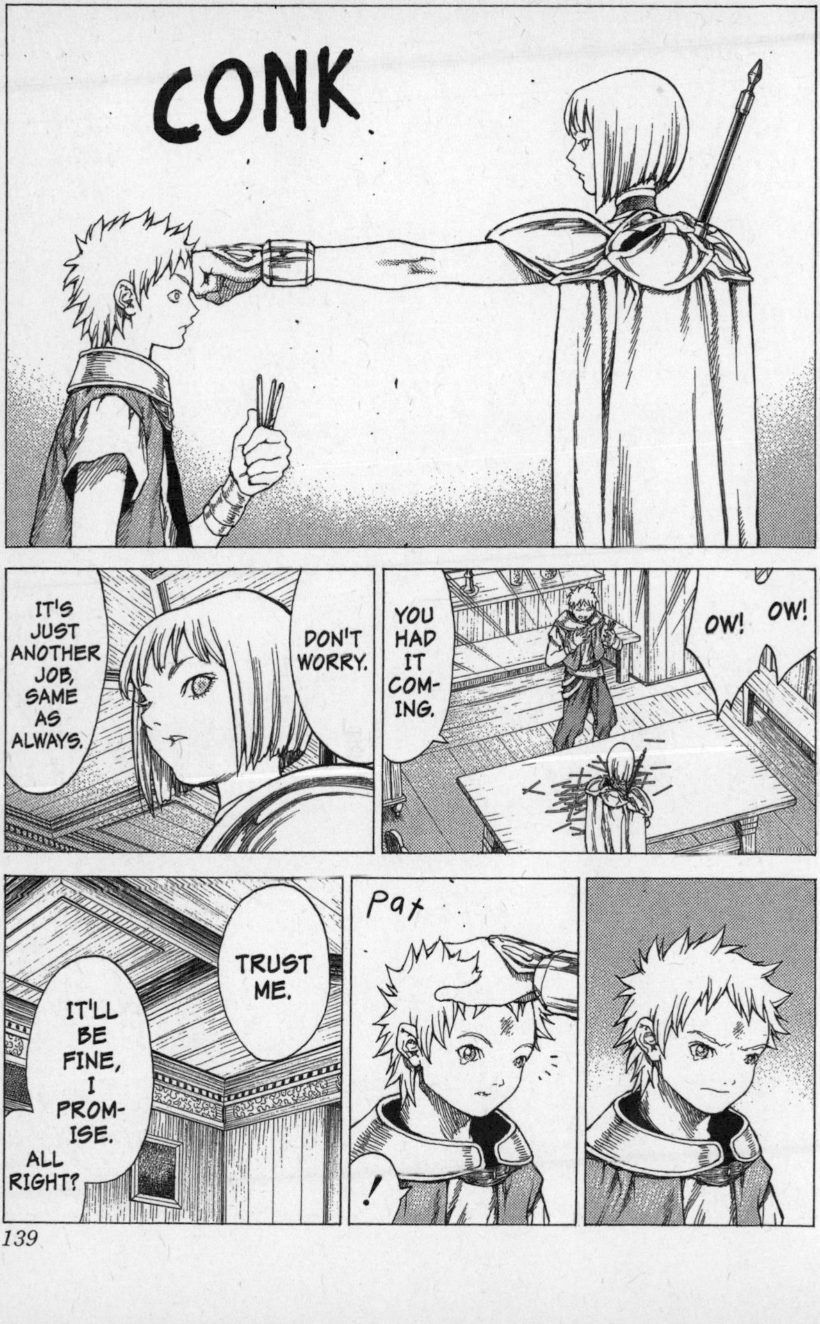
CONK
OW!
OW!
YOU HAD IT COMING.
DON'T WORRY.
IT'S JUST ANOTHER JOB, SAME AS ALWAYS.
Pat
!
TRUST ME.
IT'LL BE FINE, I PROMISE.
ALL RIGHT?

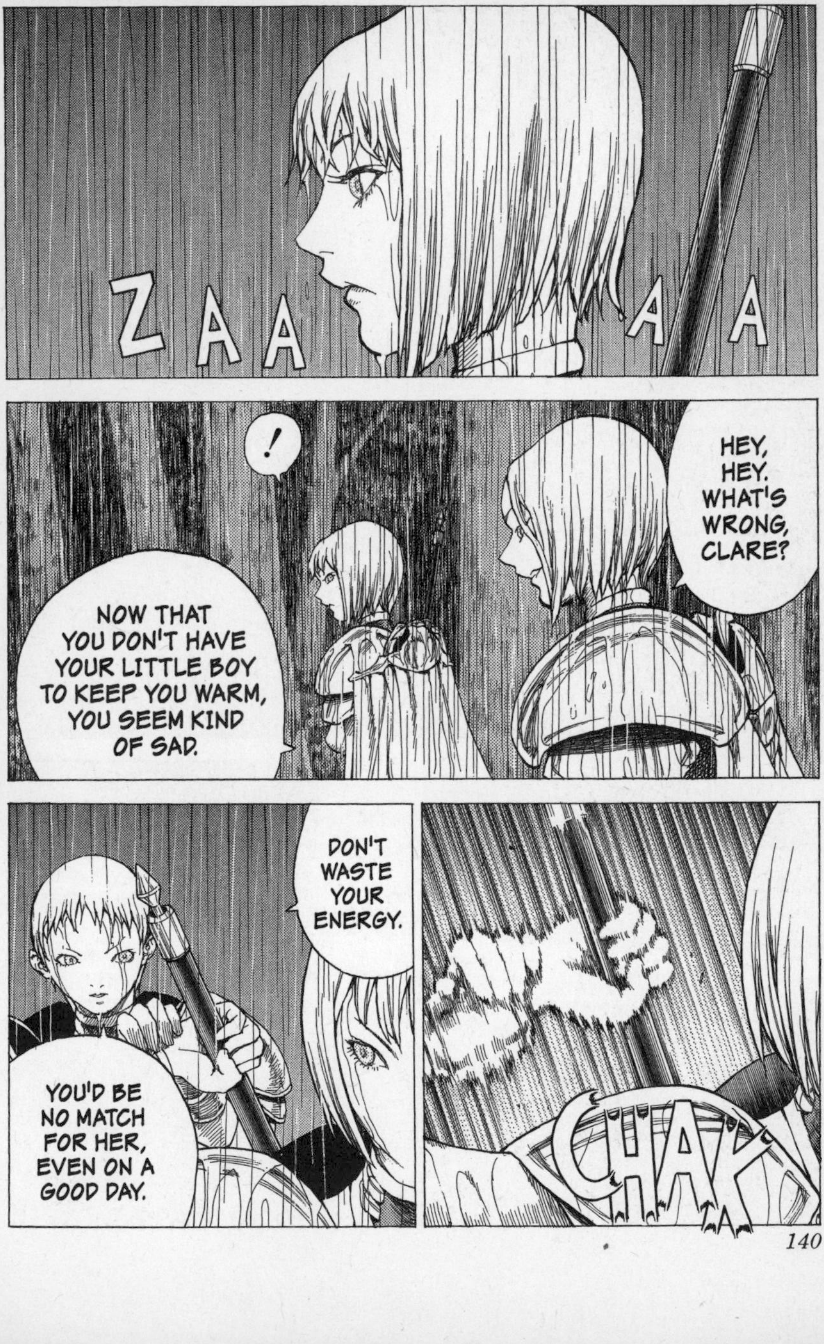
ZAAAA
HEY, HEY. WHAT'S WRONG, CLARE?
!
NOW THAT YOU DON'T HAVE YOUR LITTLE BOY TO KEEP YOU WARM, YOU SEEM KIND OF SAD.
CHAK
TA
DON'T WASTE YOUR ENERGY.
YOU'D BE NO MATCH FOR HER, EVEN ON A GOOD DAY.

READ THIS WAY

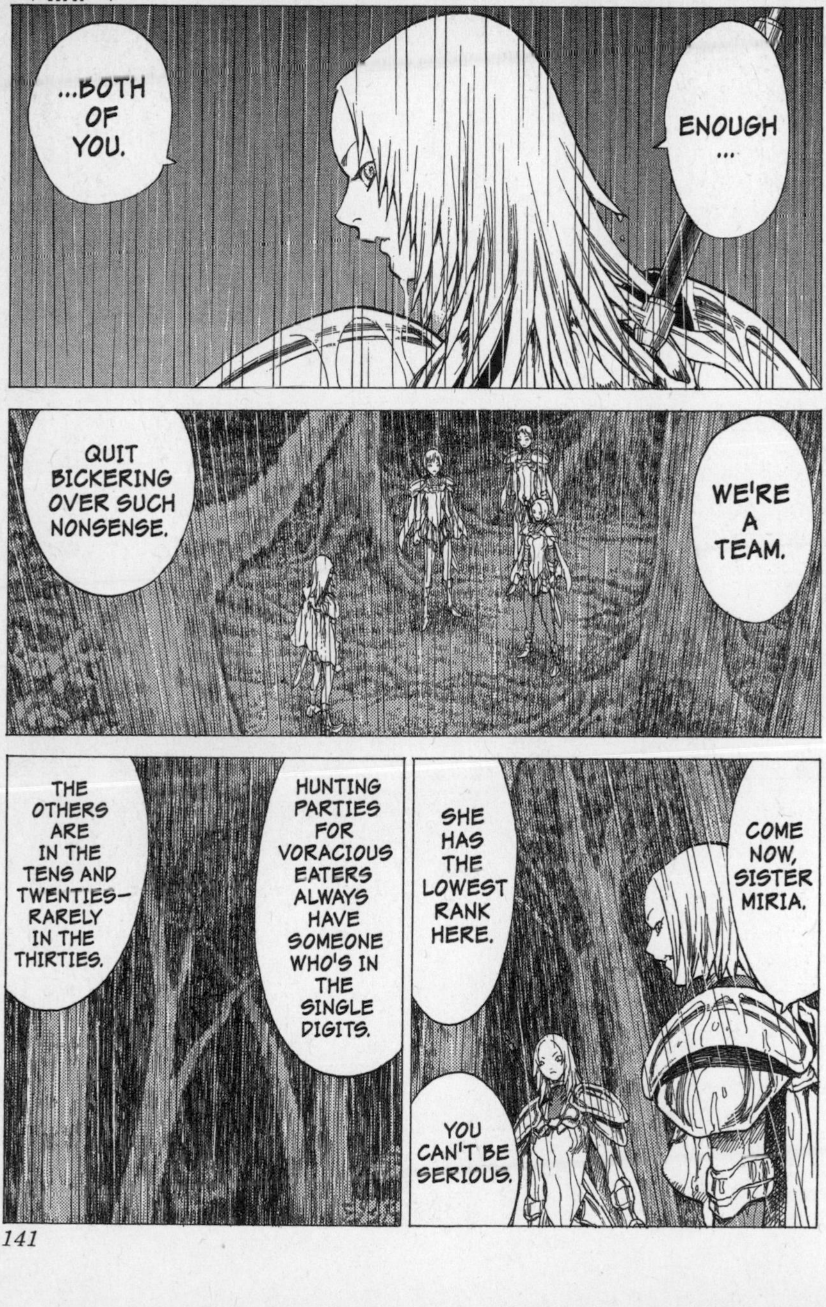

ENOUGH ...
...BOTH OF YOU.
WE'RE A TEAM.
QUIT BICKERING OVER SUCH NONSENSE.
COME NOW, SISTER MIRIA.
SHE HAS THE LOWEST RANK HERE.
YOU CAN'T BE SERIOUS.
HUNTING PARTIES FOR VORACIOUS EATERS ALWAYS HAVE SOMEONE WHO'S IN THE SINGLE DIGITS.
THE OTHERS ARE IN THE TENS AND TWENTIES—RARELY IN THE THIRTIES.

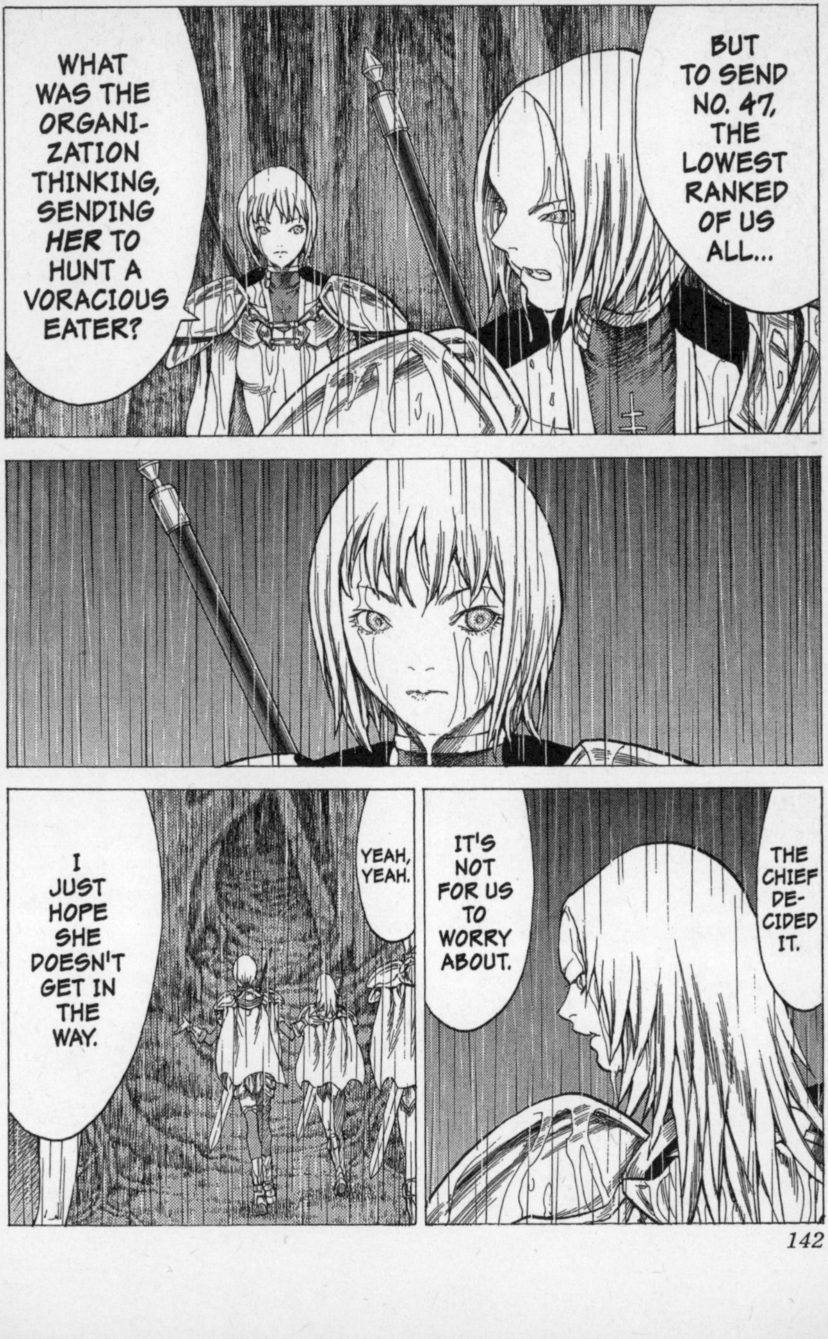
BUT TO SEND NO. 47, THE LOWEST RANKED OF US ALL...
WHAT WAS THE ORGANI-ZATION THINKING, SENDING *HER* TO HUNT A VORACIOUS EATER?
THE CHIEF DE-CIDED IT.
IT'S NOT FOR US TO WORRY ABOUT.
YEAH, YEAH.
I JUST HOPE SHE DOESN'T GET IN THE WAY.

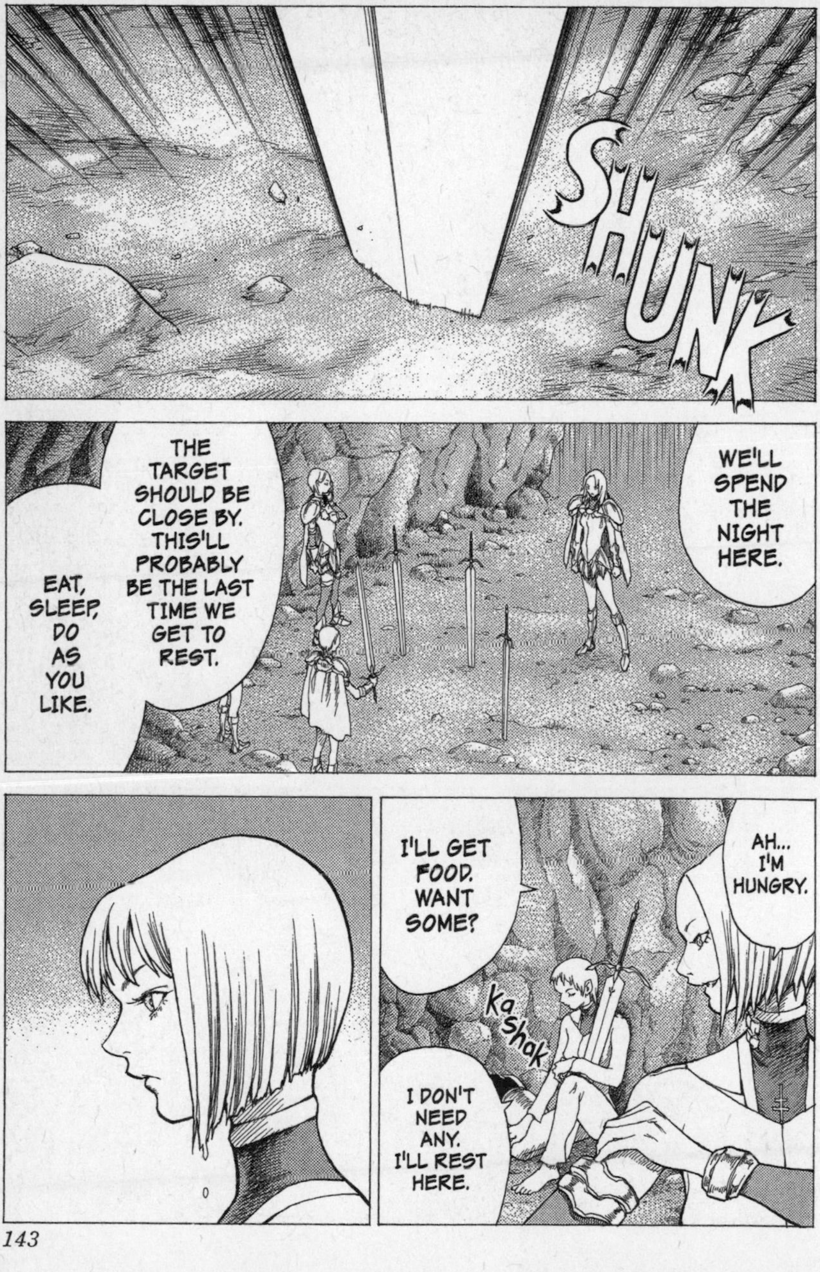
SHUNK
WE'LL SPEND THE NIGHT HERE.
THE TARGET SHOULD BE CLOSE BY. THIS'LL PROBABLY BE THE LAST TIME WE GET TO REST.
EAT, SLEEP, DO AS YOU LIKE.
AH... I'M HUNGRY.
I'LL GET FOOD. WANT SOME?
Ka shak
I DON'T NEED ANY. I'LL REST HERE.

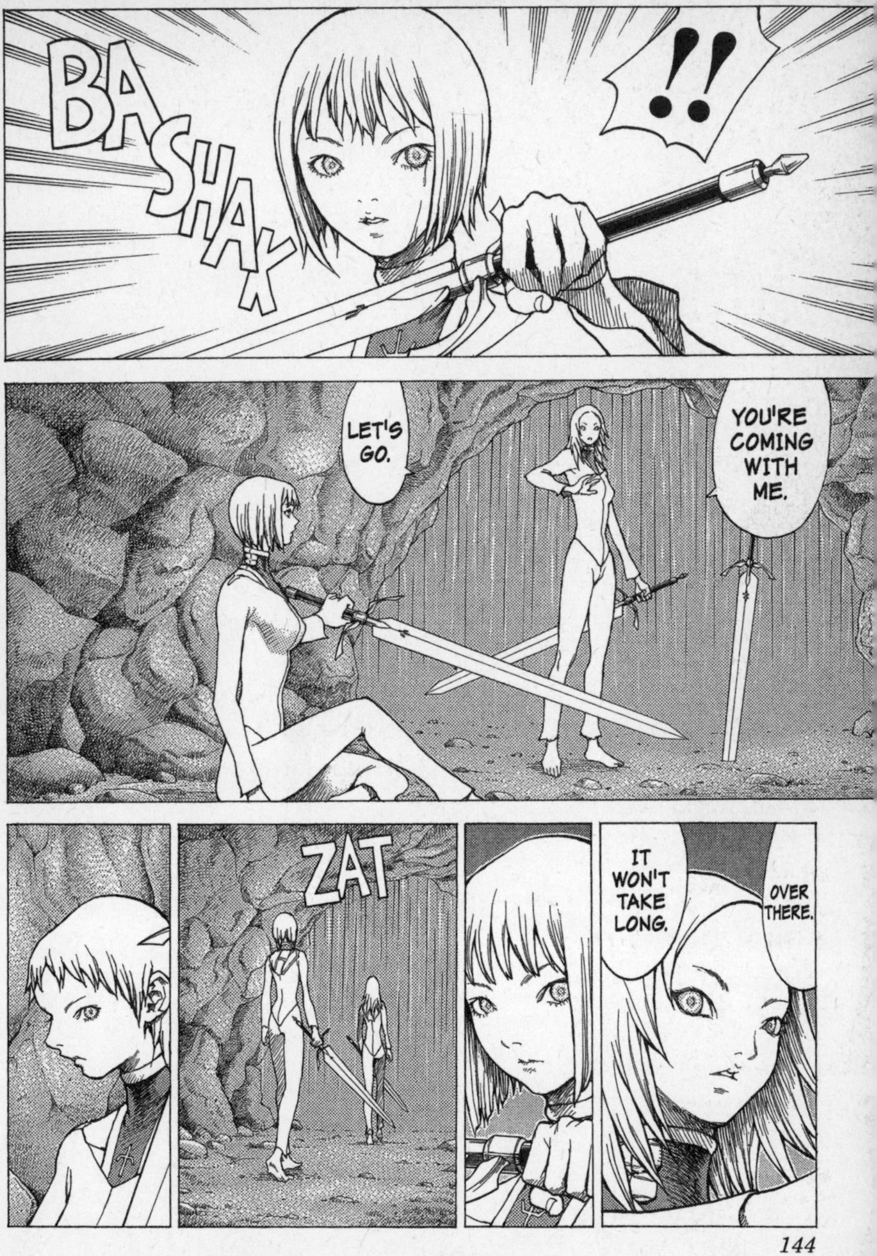
!!
BASHAK
YOU'RE COMING WITH ME.
LET'S GO.
OVER THERE.
IT WON'T TAKE LONG.
ZAT

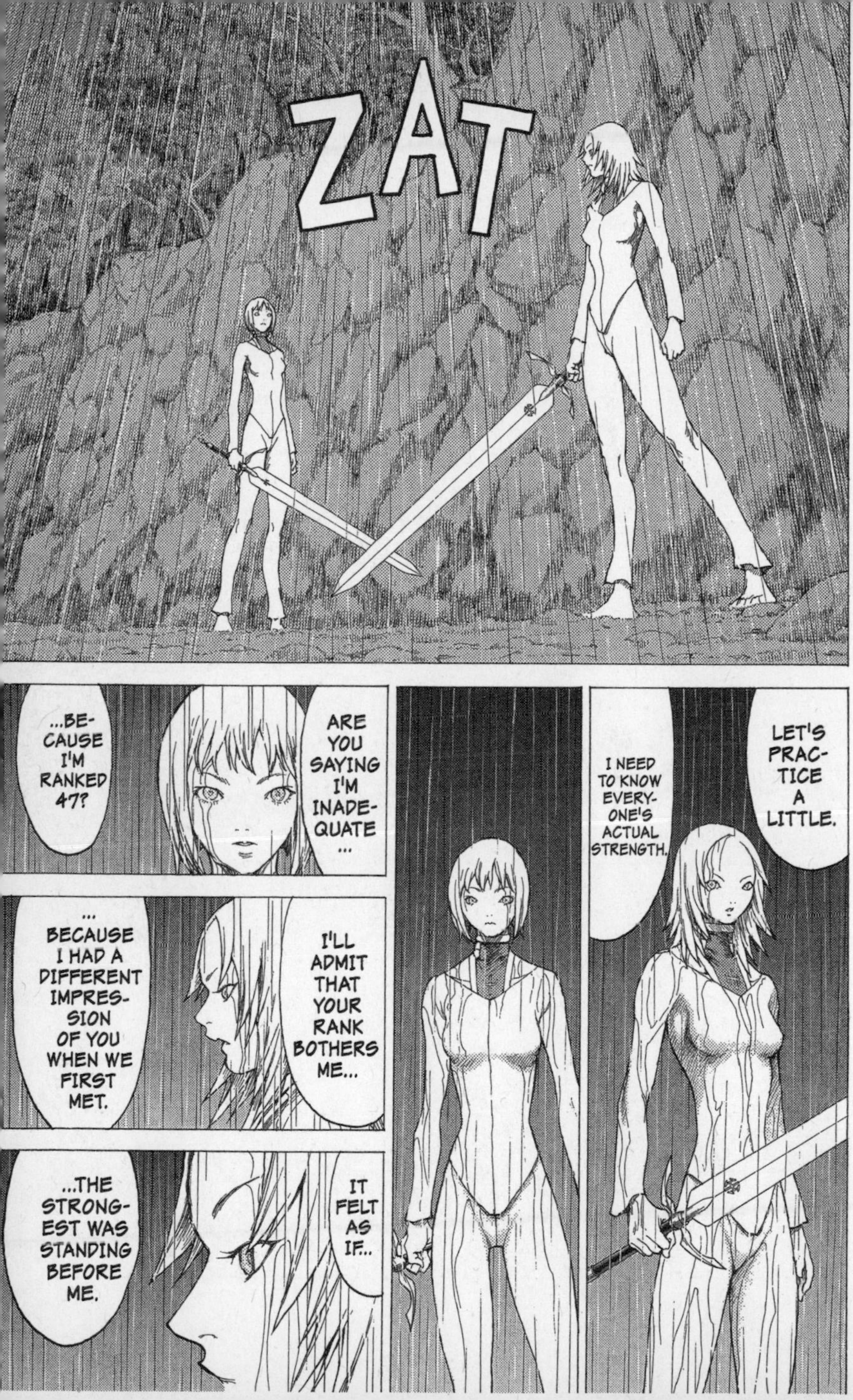
ZAT
LET'S PRACTICE A LITTLE.
I NEED TO KNOW EVERYONE'S ACTUAL STRENGTH.
ARE YOU SAYING I'M INADEQUATE...
...BECAUSE I'M RANKED 47?
I'LL ADMIT THAT YOUR RANK BOTHERS ME...
...BECAUSE I HAD A DIFFERENT IMPRESSION OF YOU WHEN WE FIRST MET.
IT FELT AS IF...
...THE STRONGEST WAS STANDING BEFORE ME.

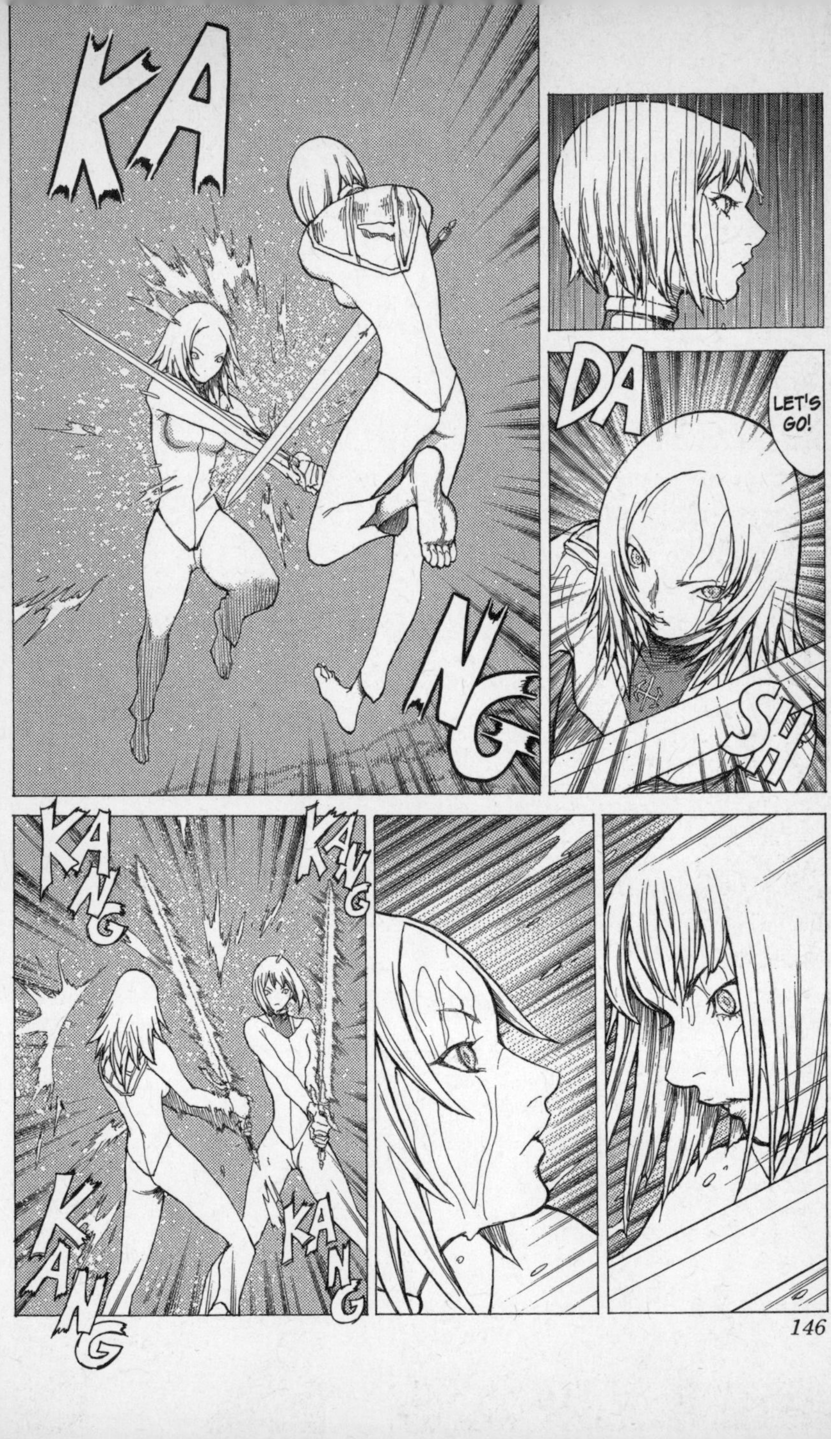
DA
LET'S GO!
SH
KA
NG
KANG
KANG
KANG
KANG

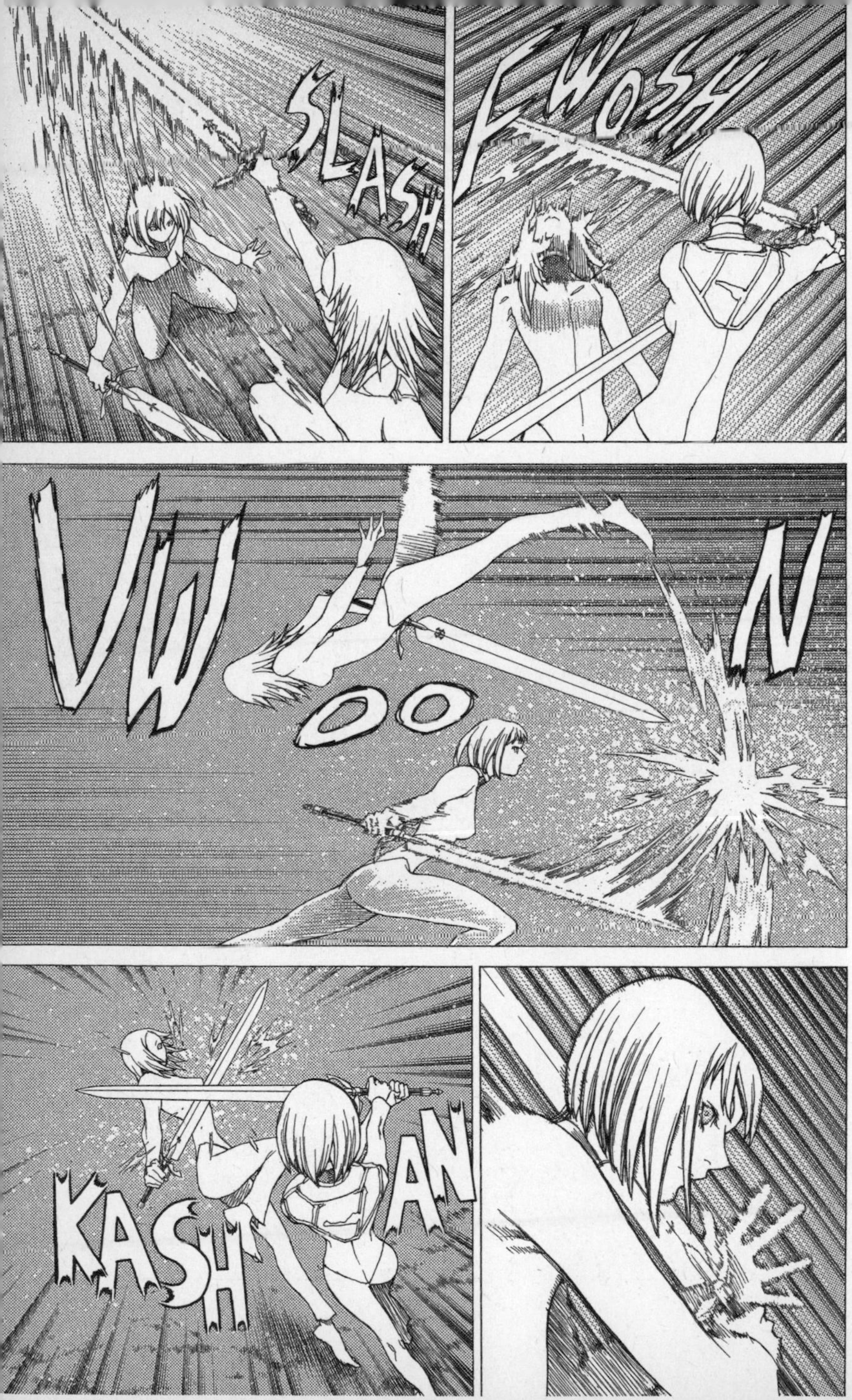
FWOSH
SLASH
VWOON
KASHAN

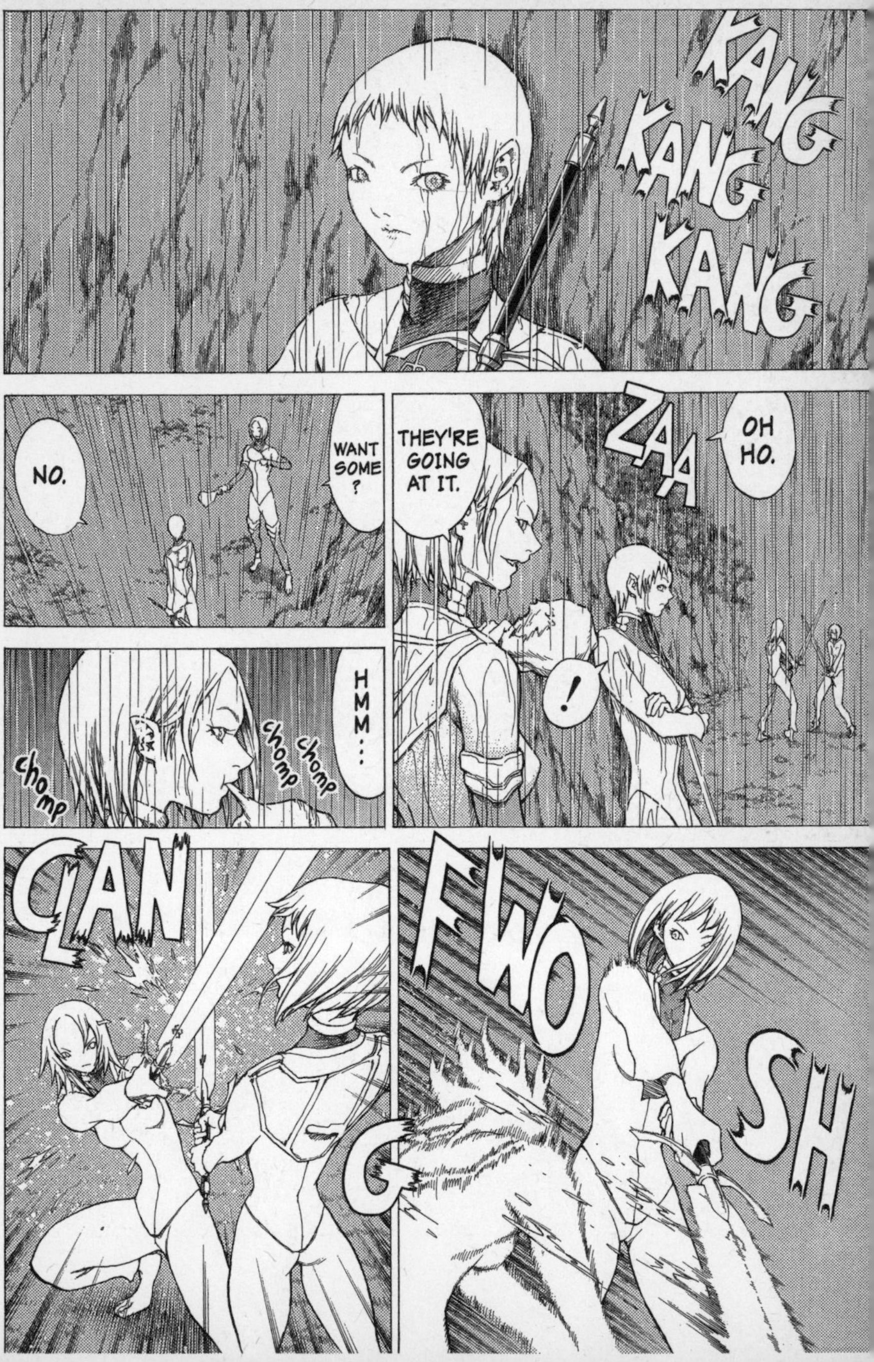
KANG
KANG
KANG
KANG
ZAA
OH HO.
THEY'RE GOING AT IT.
!
WANT SOME ?
NO.
HMM...
chomp
chomp
chomp
FWOSH
CLANG

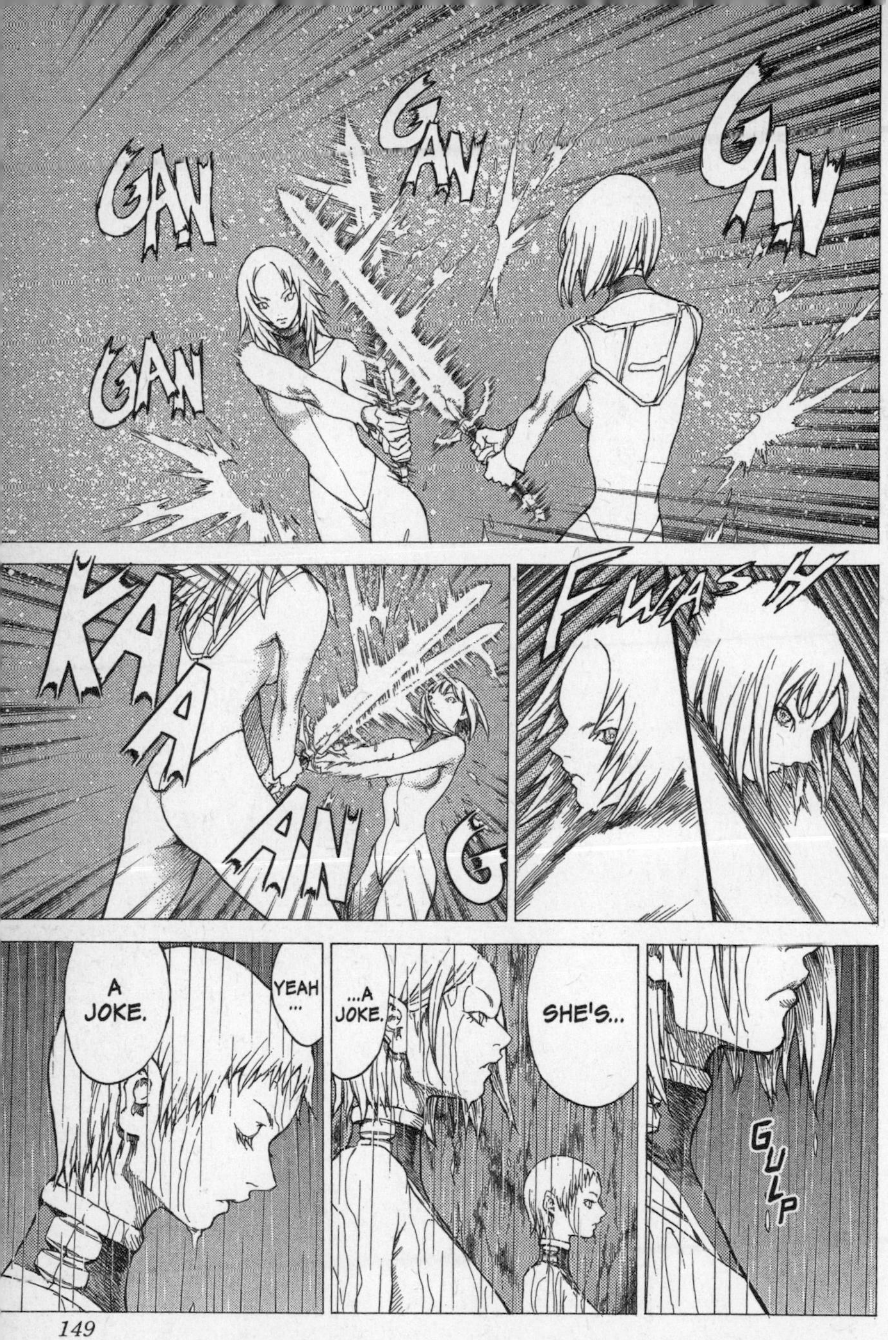
GAN
GAN
GAN
GAN
FWASH
KAAANG
GULP
SHE'S...
...A JOKE.
YEAH ...
A JOKE.

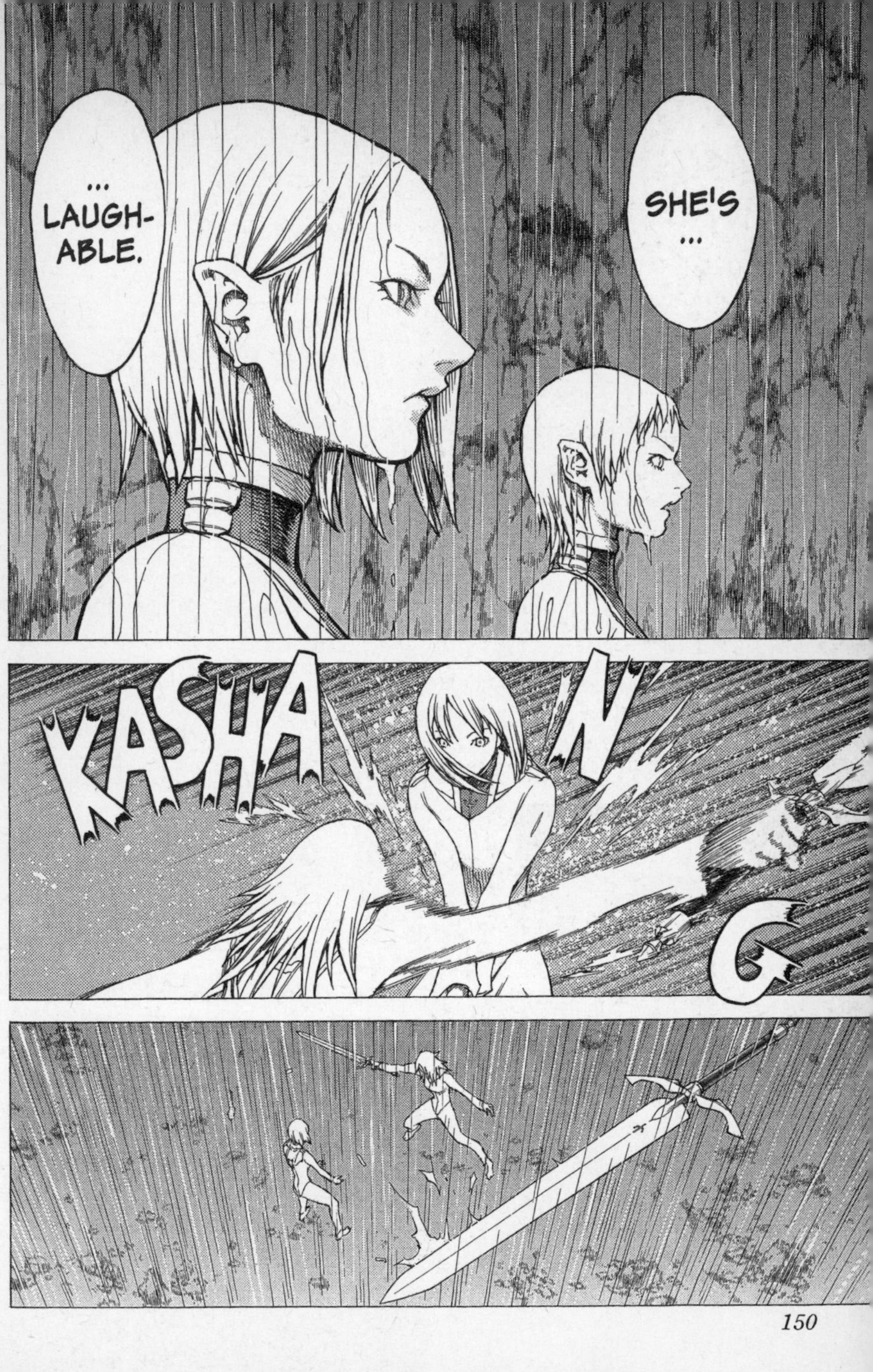
SHE'S ...
... LAUGH-ABLE.
KASHANG

ZAA AA

THUNK

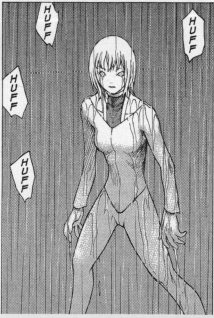

HUFF

HUFF

HUFF

HUFF

I SEE.

...

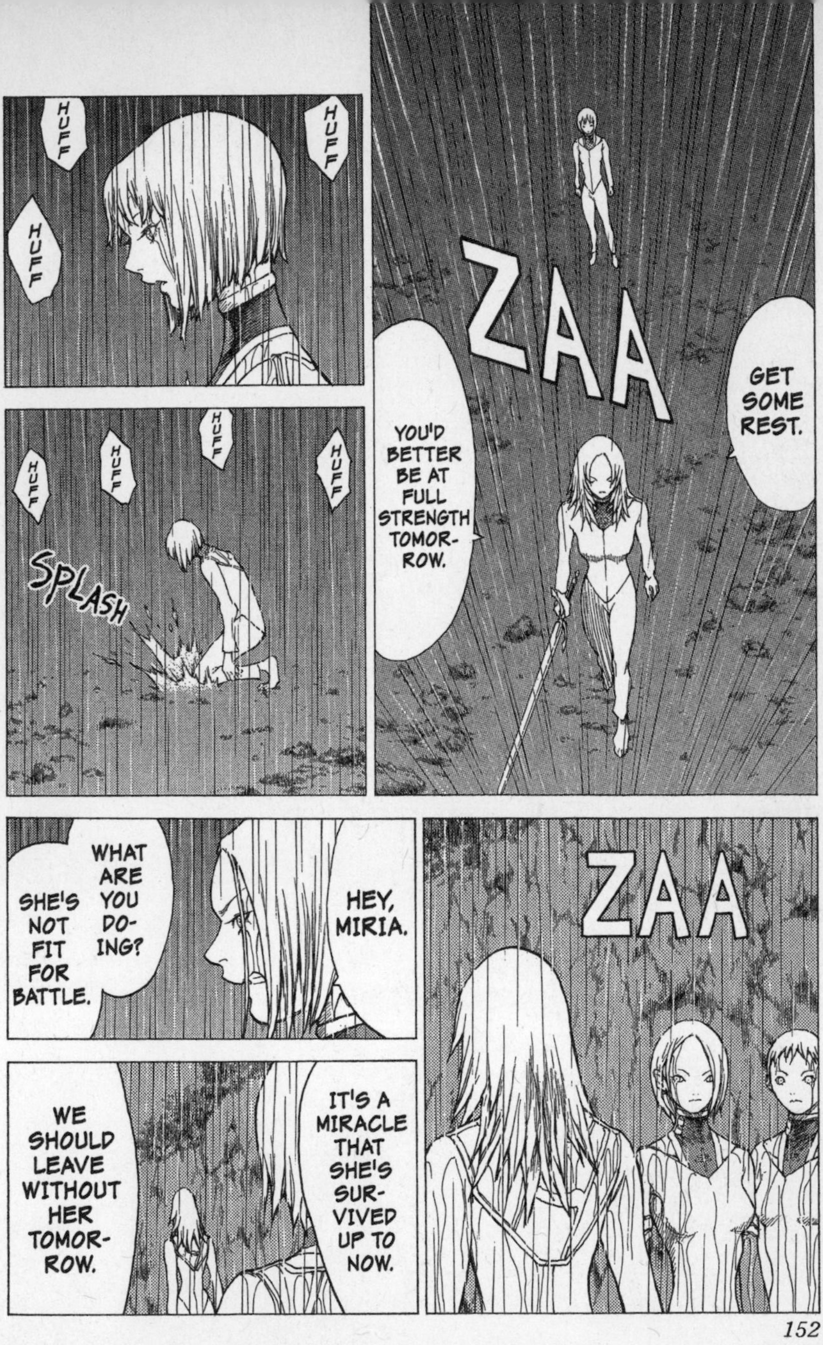
ZAA
GET SOME REST.
YOU'D BETTER BE AT FULL STRENGTH TOMORROW.
HUFF
HUFF
HUFF
HUFF
HUFF
HUFF
HUFF
SPLASH
ZAA
HEY, MIRIA.
WHAT ARE YOU DOING?
SHE'S NOT FIT FOR BATTLE.
IT'S A MIRACLE THAT SHE'S SURVIVED UP TO NOW.
WE SHOULD LEAVE WITHOUT HER TOMORROW.

READ THIS WAY

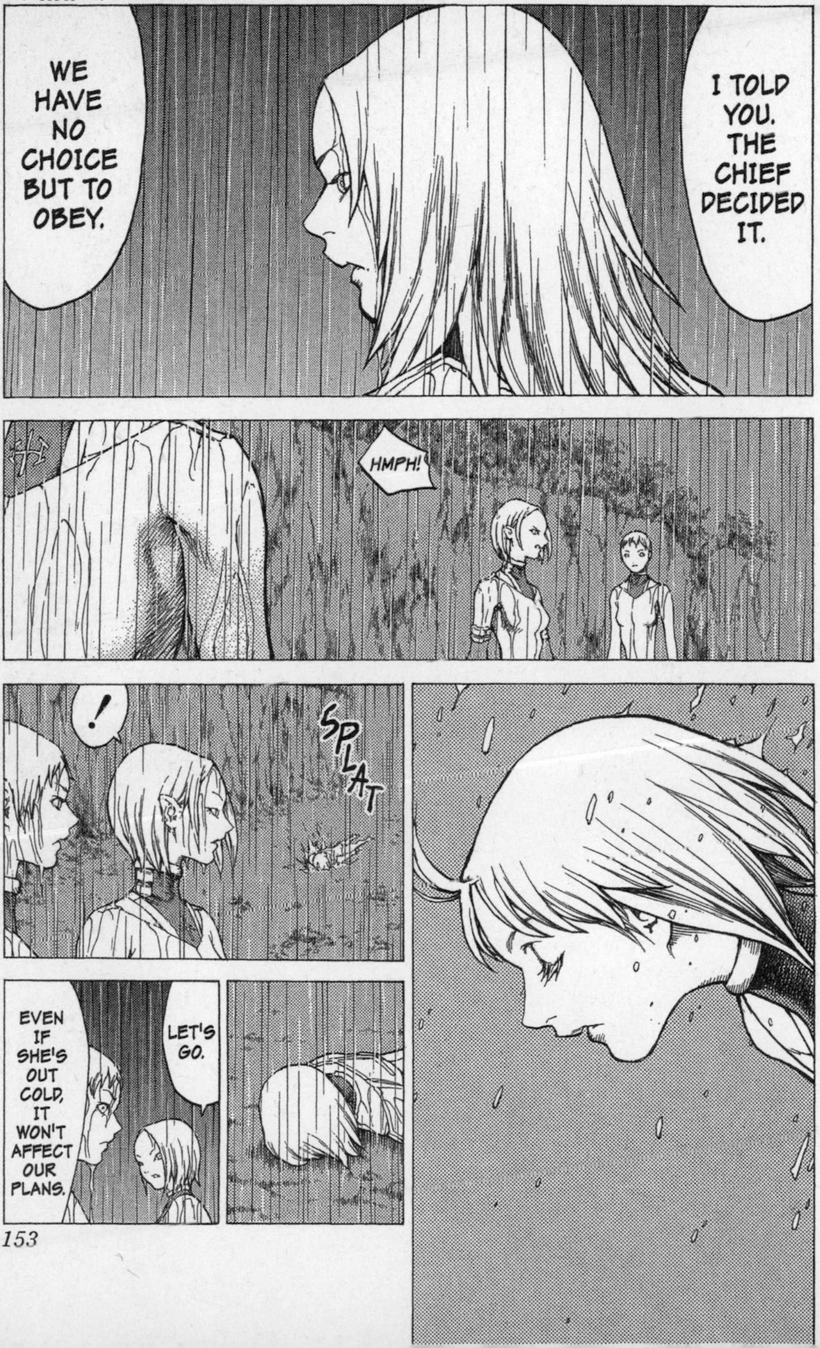
I TOLD YOU. THE CHIEF DECIDED IT.
WE HAVE NO CHOICE BUT TO OBEY.
HMPH!
!
SPLAT
LET'S GO.
EVEN IF SHE'S OUT COLD, IT WON'T AFFECT OUR PLANS.

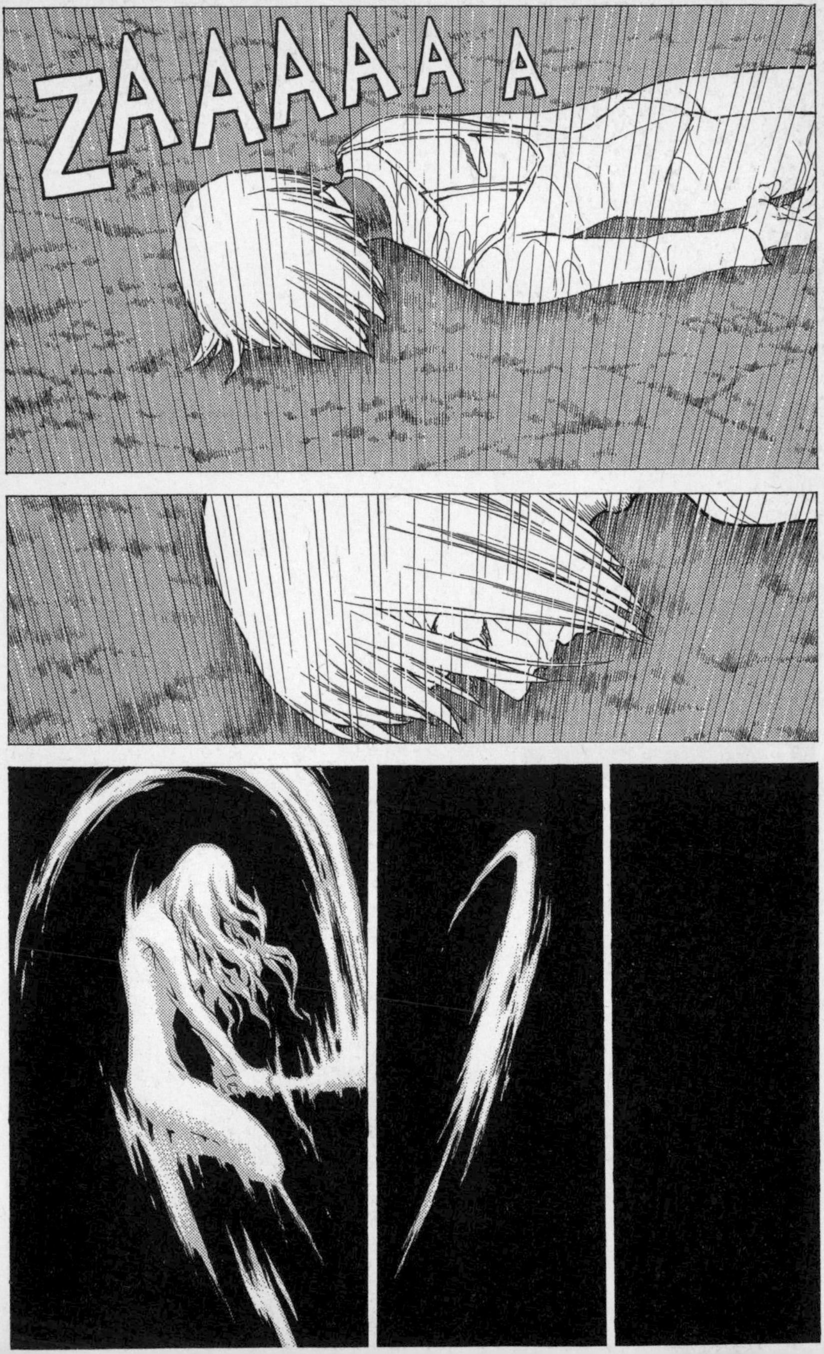
ZAAAAA A

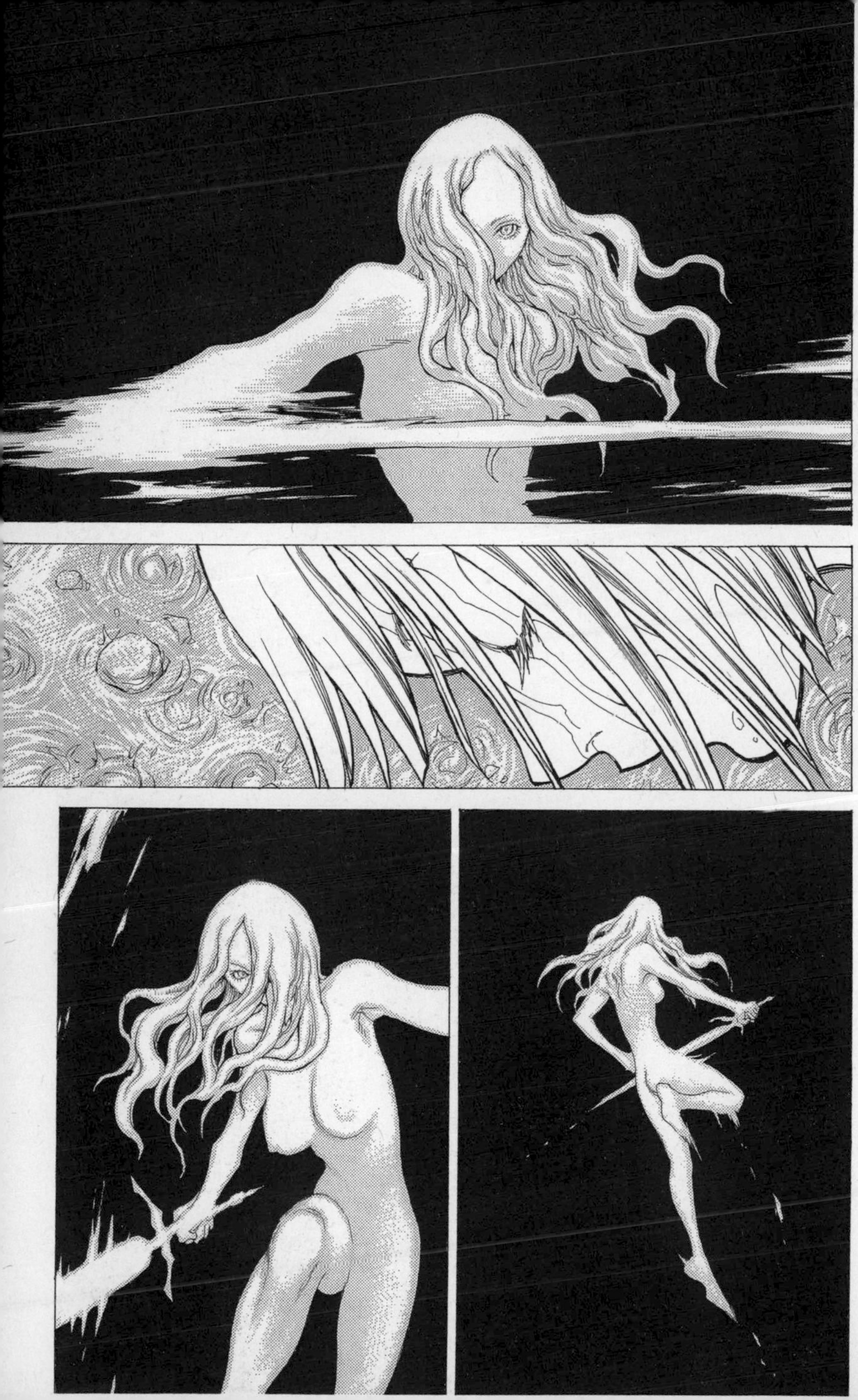

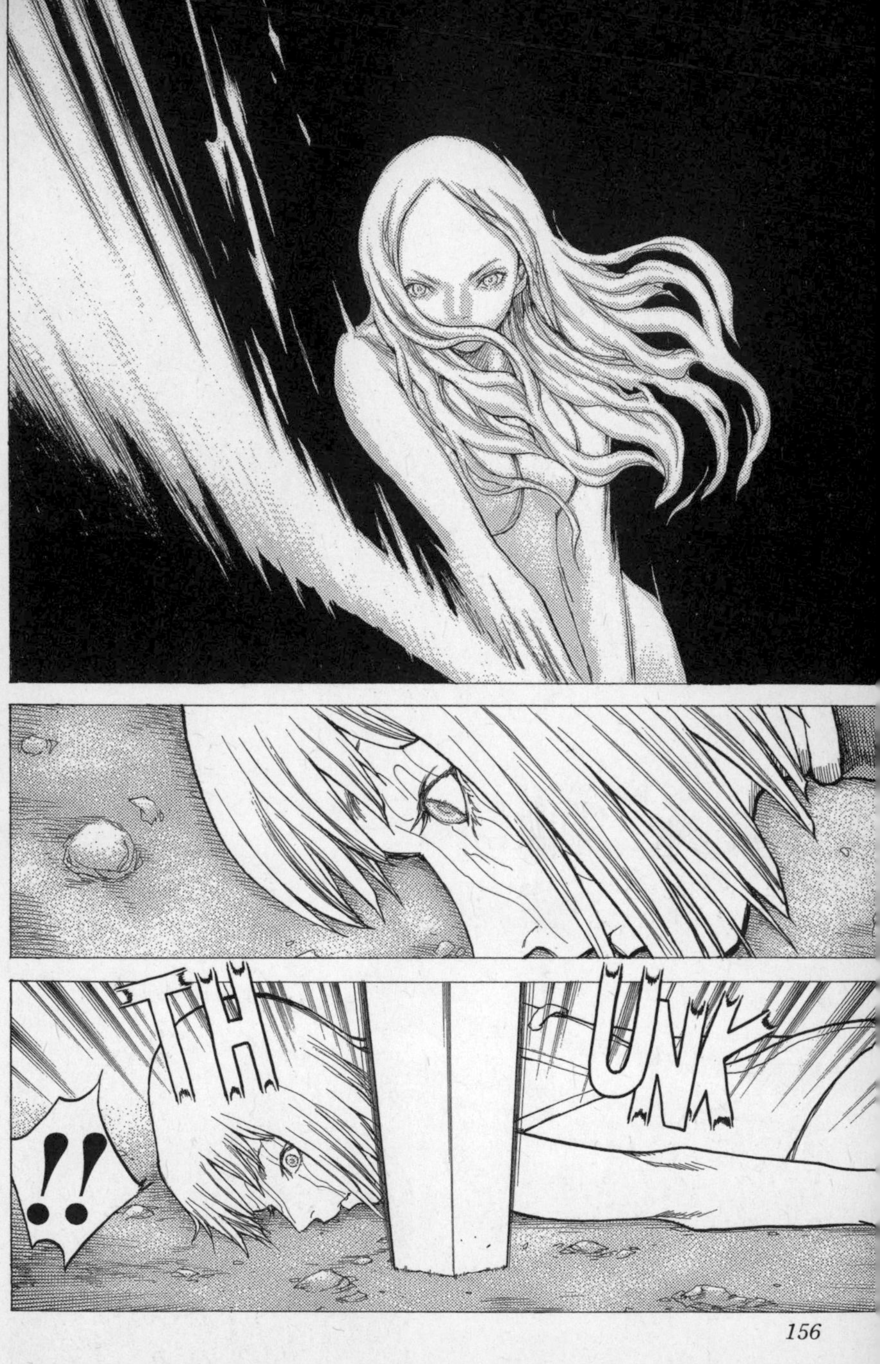
TH UNK
!!

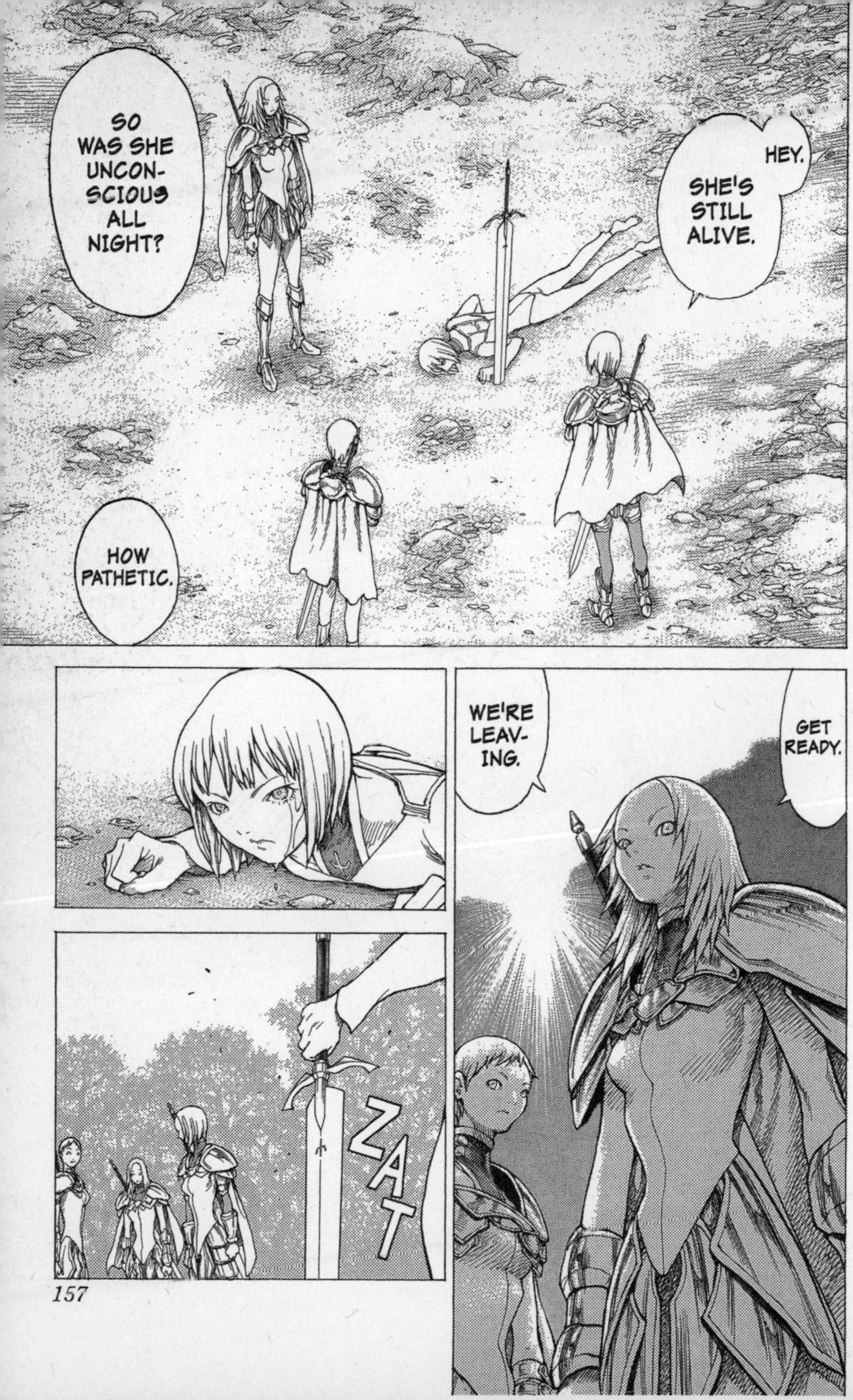
HEY.
SHE'S STILL ALIVE.
SO WAS SHE UNCON-SCIOUS ALL NIGHT?
HOW PATHETIC.
GET READY.
WE'RE LEAV-ING.
ZAT

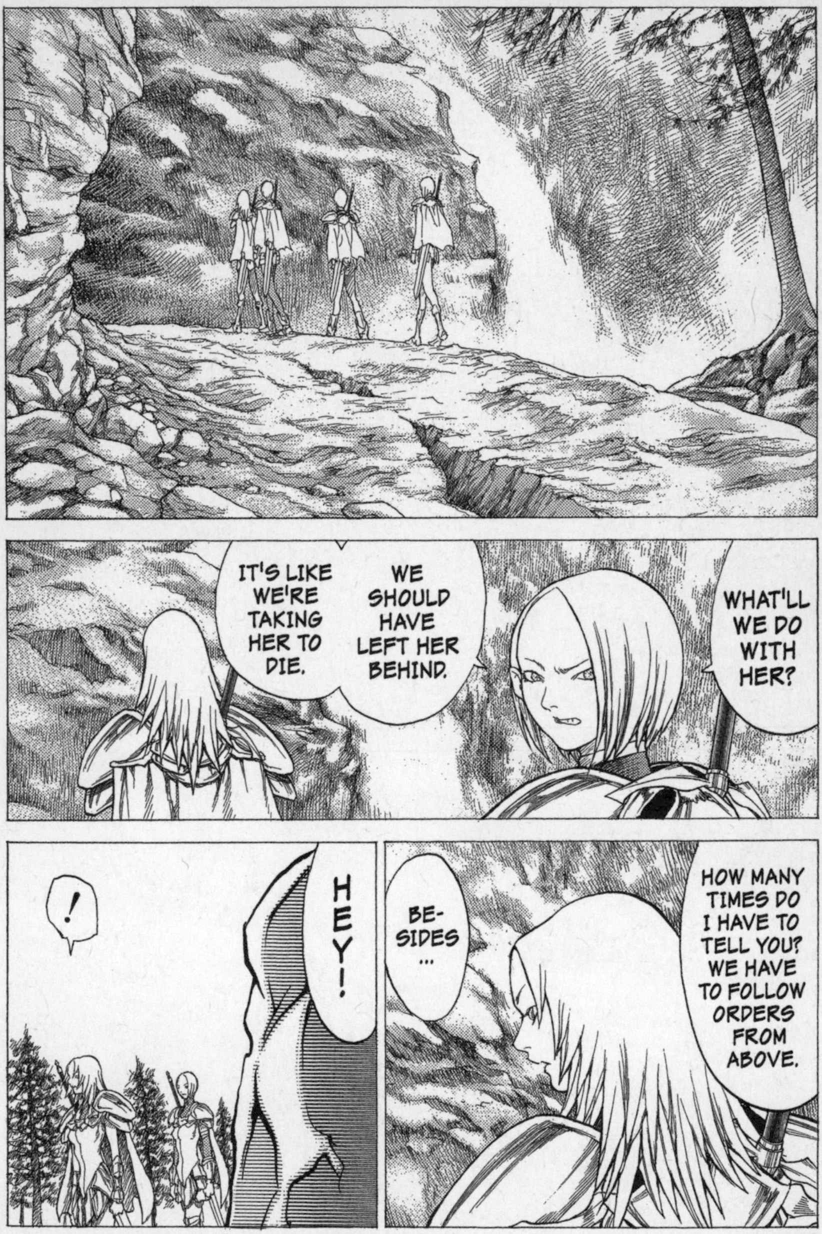
WHAT'LL WE DO WITH HER?
WE SHOULD HAVE LEFT HER BEHIND.
IT'S LIKE WE'RE TAKING HER TO DIE.
HOW MANY TIMES DO I HAVE TO TELL YOU? WE HAVE TO FOLLOW ORDERS FROM ABOVE.
BE-SIDES ...
HEY!
!

READ THIS WAY

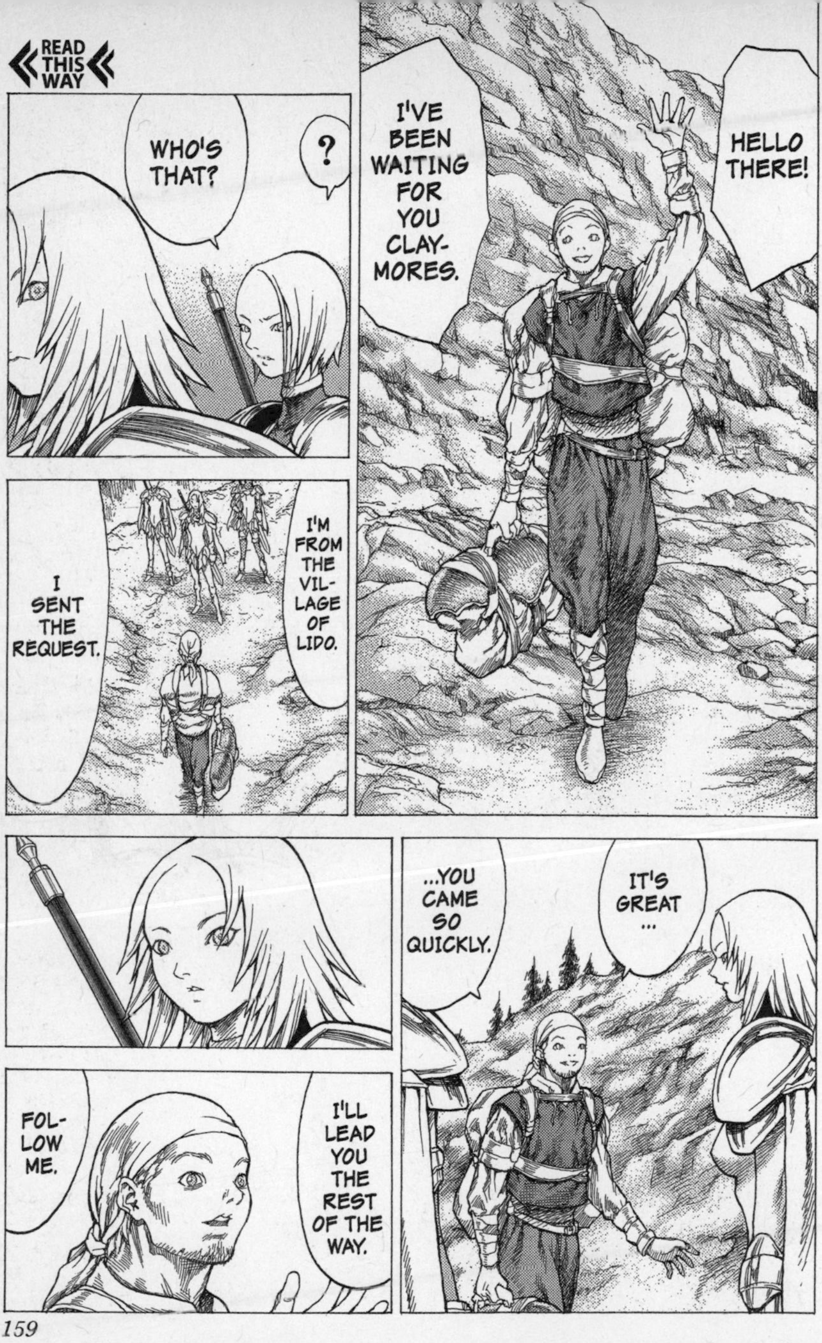
HELLO THERE!
I'VE BEEN WAITING FOR YOU CLAY-MORES.
?
WHO'S THAT?
I'M FROM THE VIL-LAGE OF LIDO.
I SENT THE REQUEST.
IT'S GREAT ...
...YOU CAME SO QUICKLY.
I'LL LEAD YOU THE REST OF THE WAY.
FOL-LOW ME.

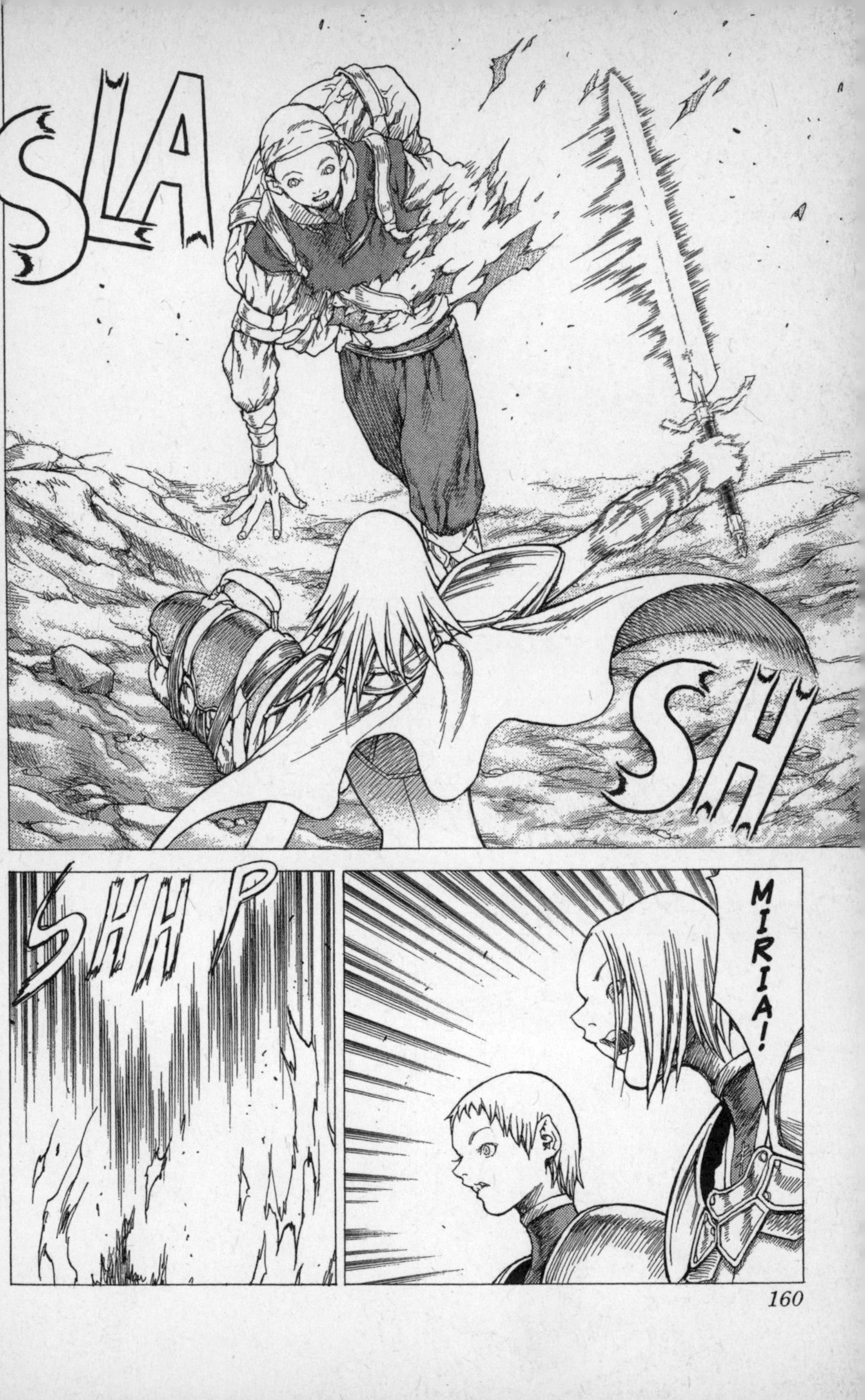
SLA
SH
MIRIA!
SHHP

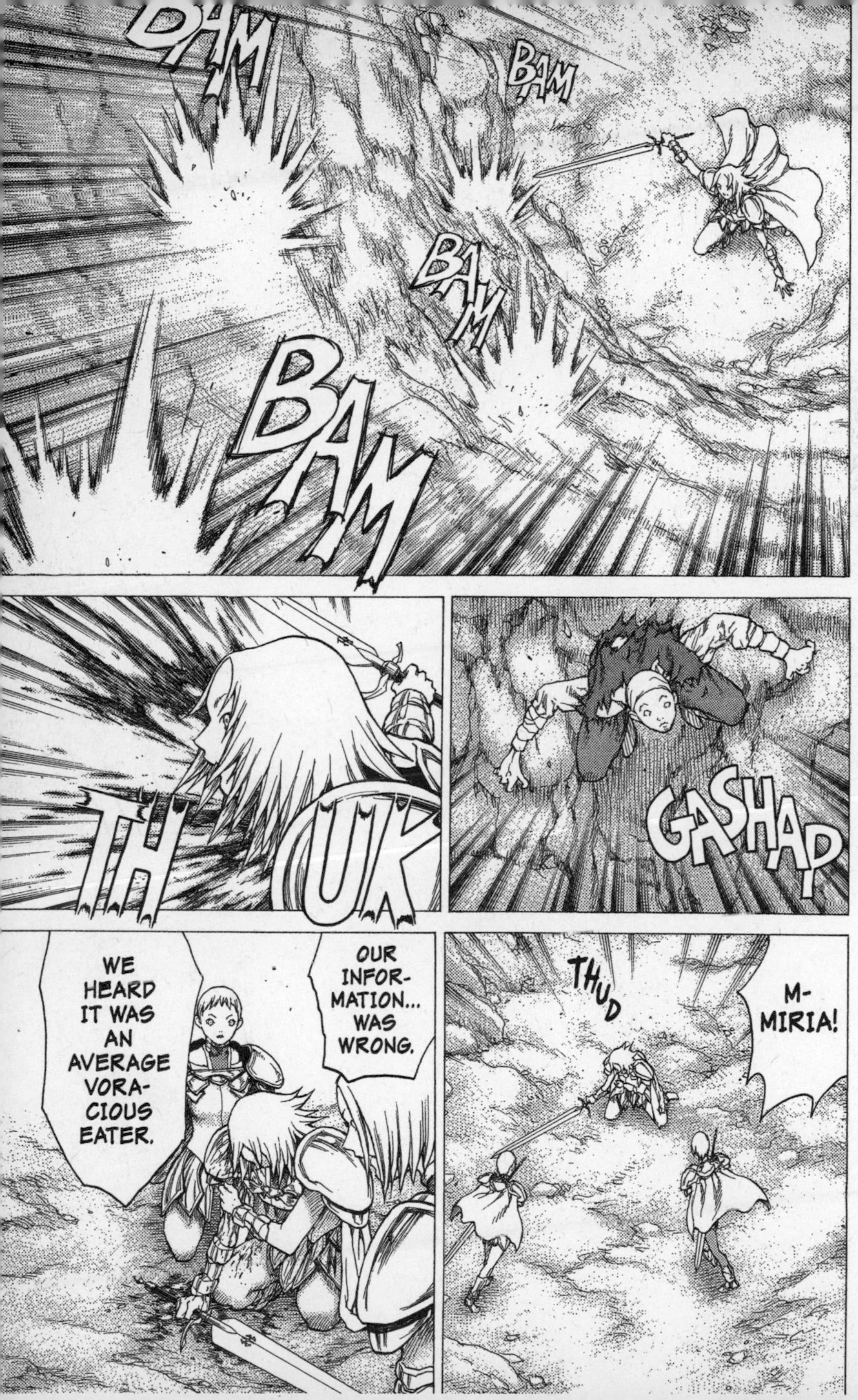
BAM
BAM
BAM
BAM
GASHAP
THUK
THUD
M-MIRIA!
OUR INFORMATION... WAS WRONG.
WE HEARD IT WAS AN AVERAGE VORACIOUS EATER.

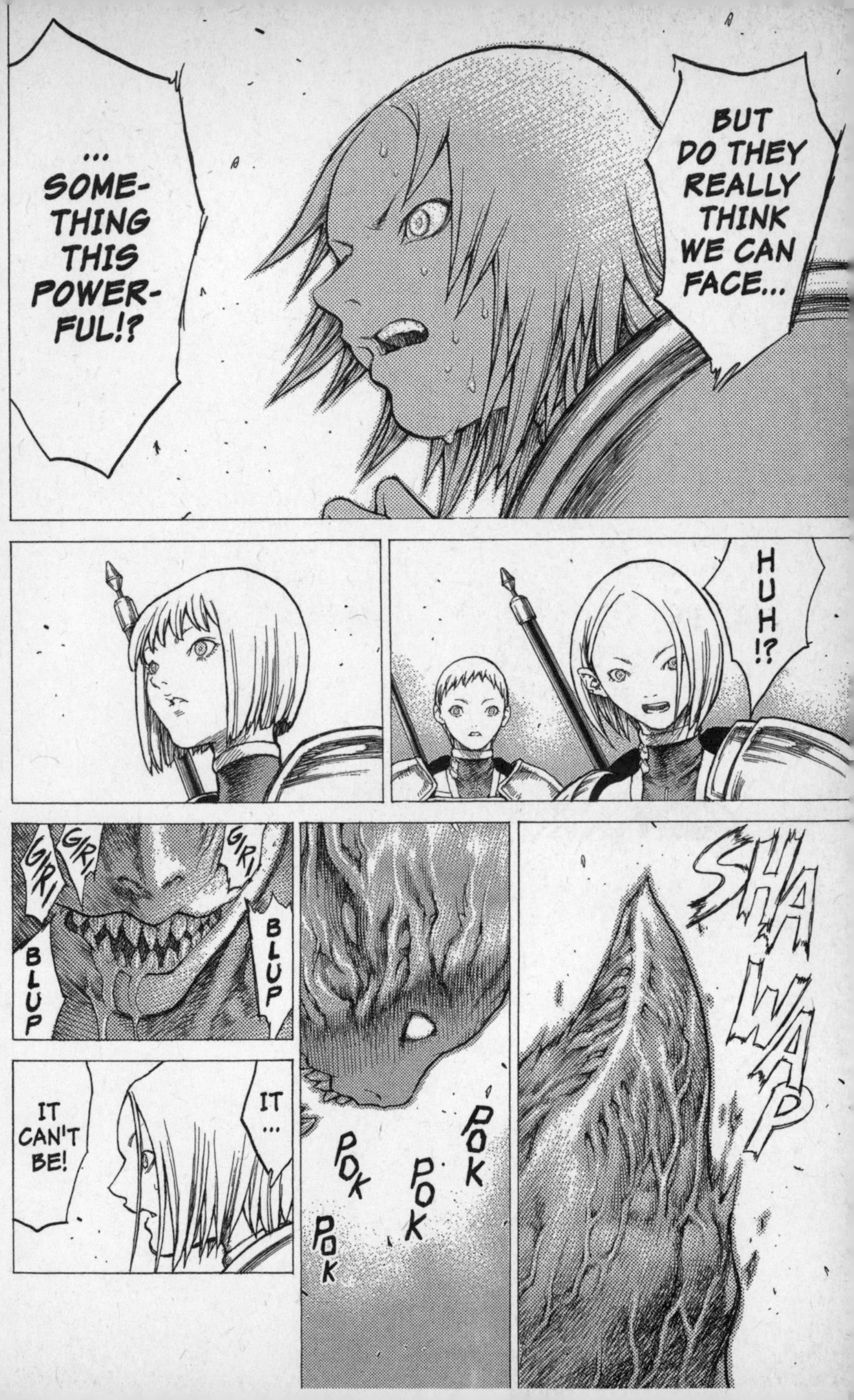
BUT DO THEY REALLY THINK WE CAN FACE...
... SOME-THING THIS POWER-FUL!?
HUH!?
SHA WAP
POK
POK
POK
POK
GIRI
GIRI
GIRI
BLUP
BLUP
IT ...
IT CAN'T BE!

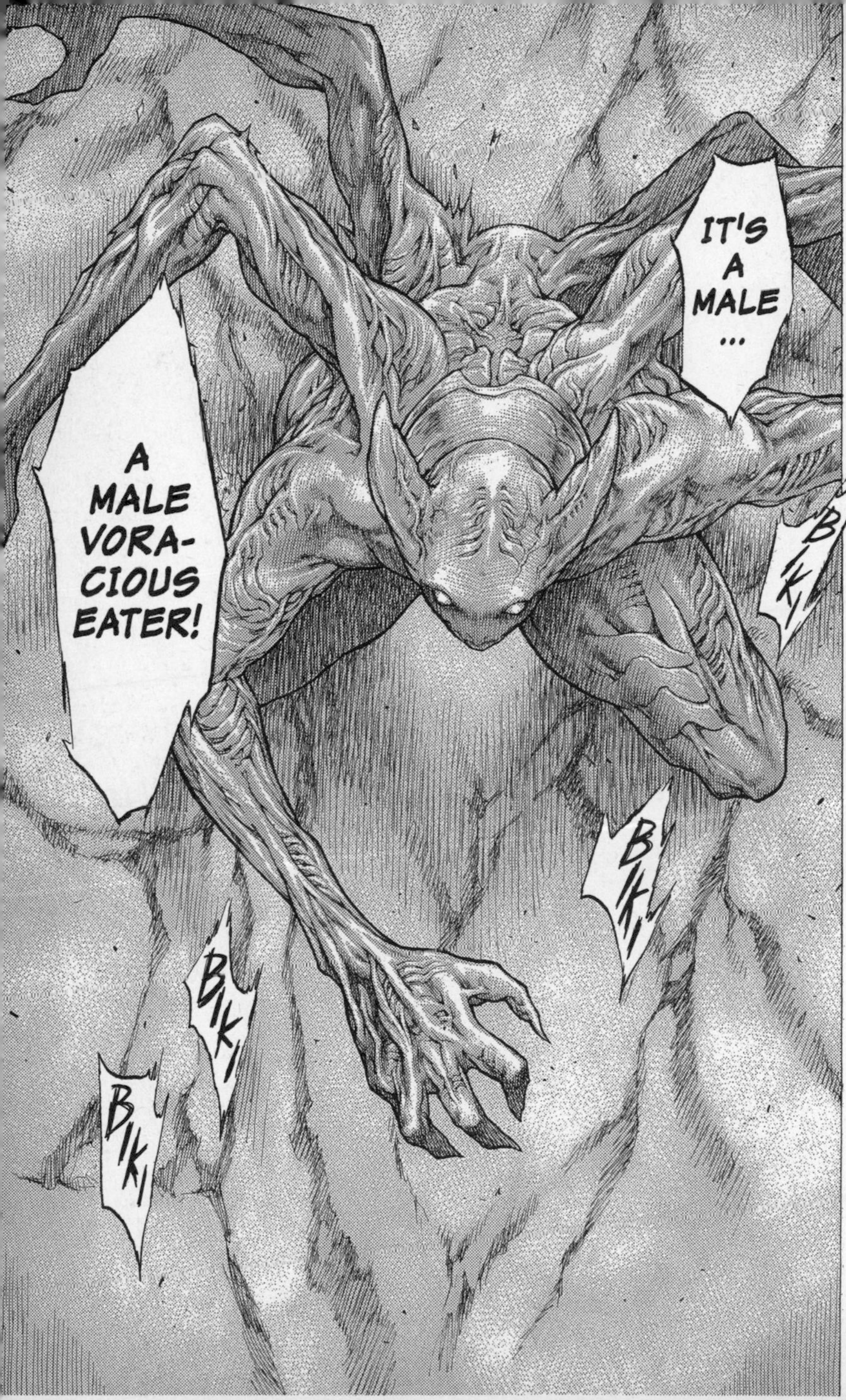
IT'S A MALE ...
A MALE VORACIOUS EATER!
BIKI
BIKI
BIKI
BIKI

クレイモア
Claymore™

Scene 27: The Slashers, Part 3

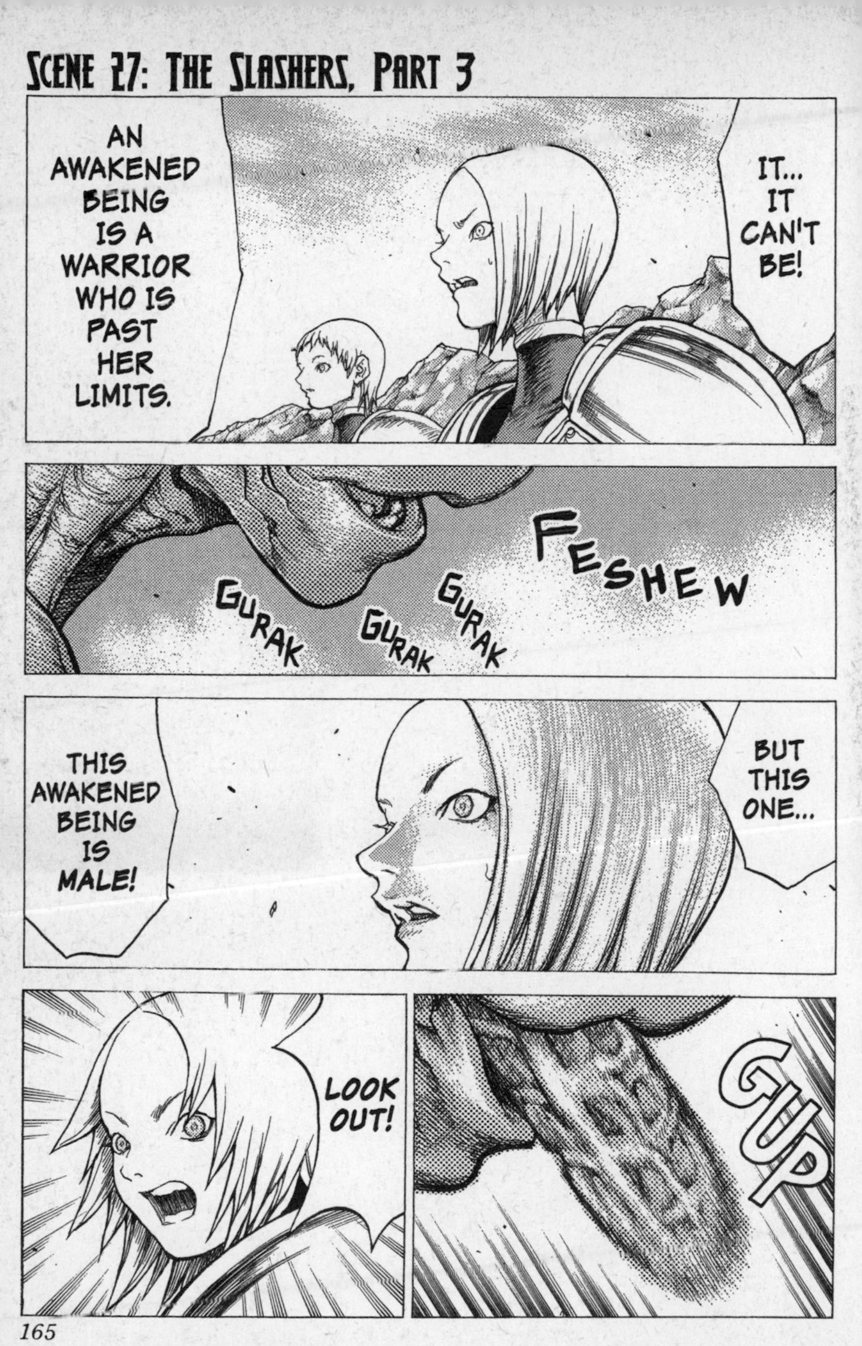
IT... IT CAN'T BE!
AN AWAKENED BEING IS A WARRIOR WHO IS PAST HER LIMITS.
FESHEW
GURAK
GURAK
GURAK
BUT THIS ONE...
THIS AWAKENED BEING IS MALE!
GUP
LOOK OUT!

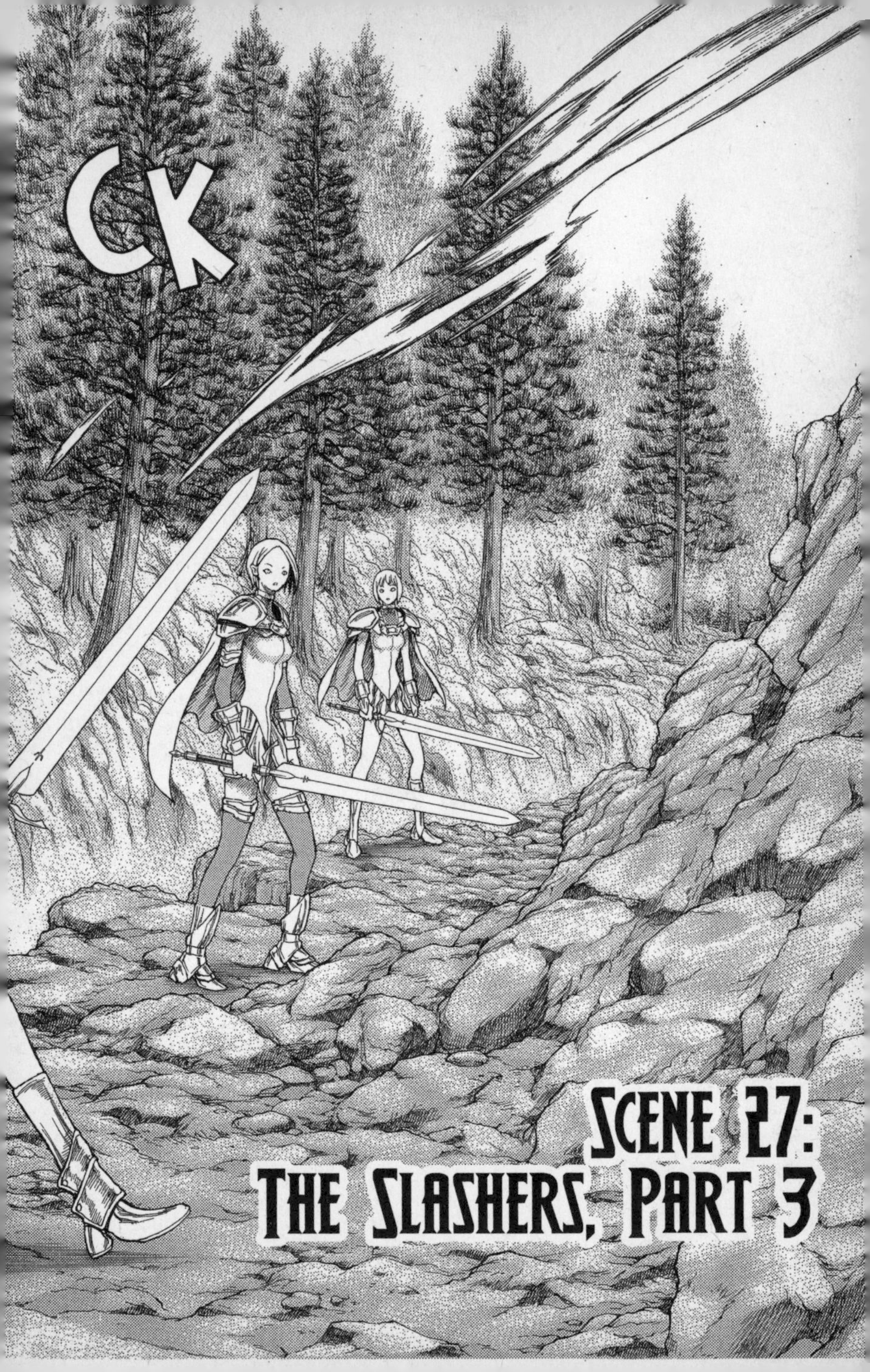
CK
SCENE 27:
THE SLASHERS, PART 3

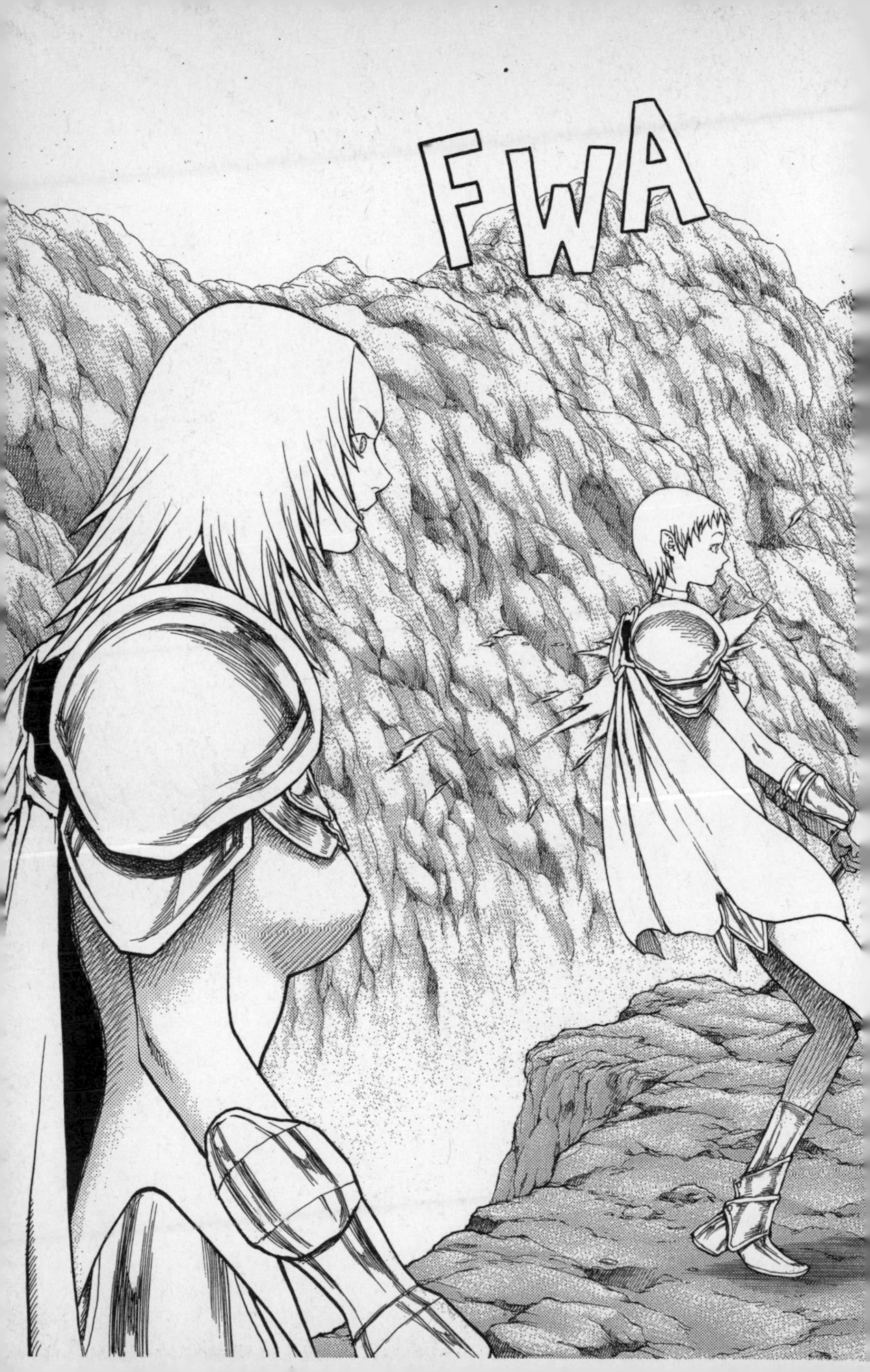
FWA

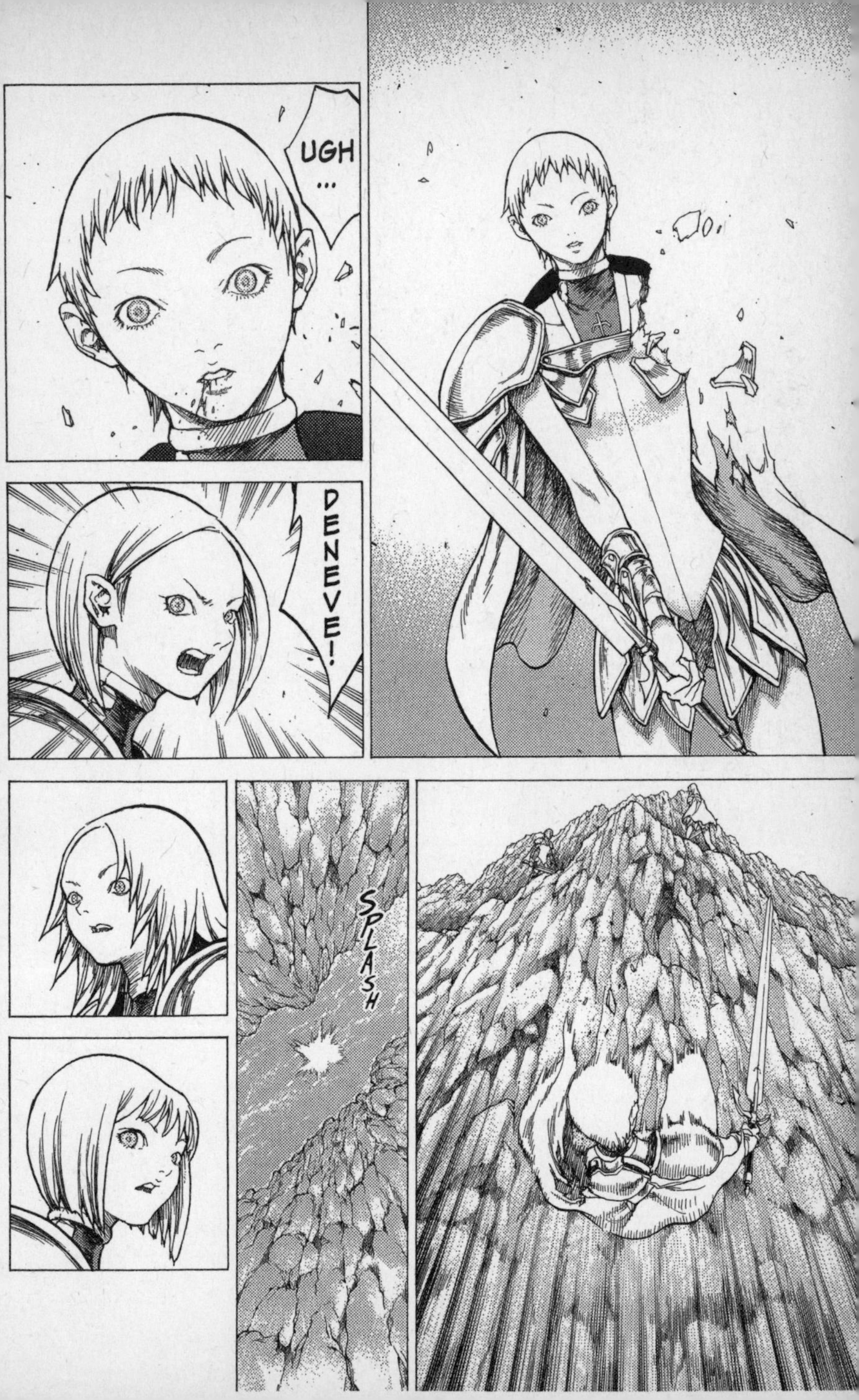
UGH...
DENEVE!
SPLASH

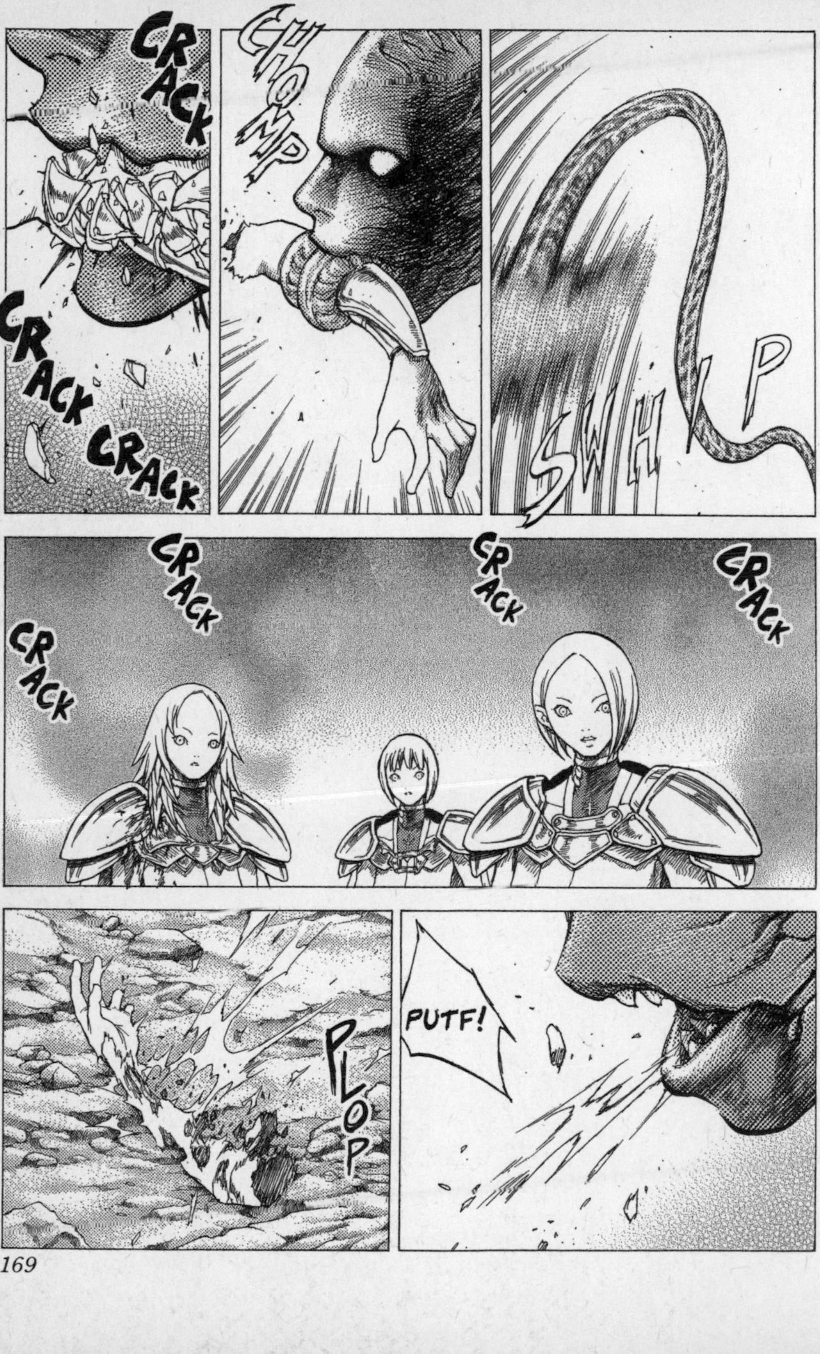
SWHIP
CHOMP
CRACK
CRACK
CRACK
CRACK
CRACK
CRACK
CRACK
PUTF!
PLOP

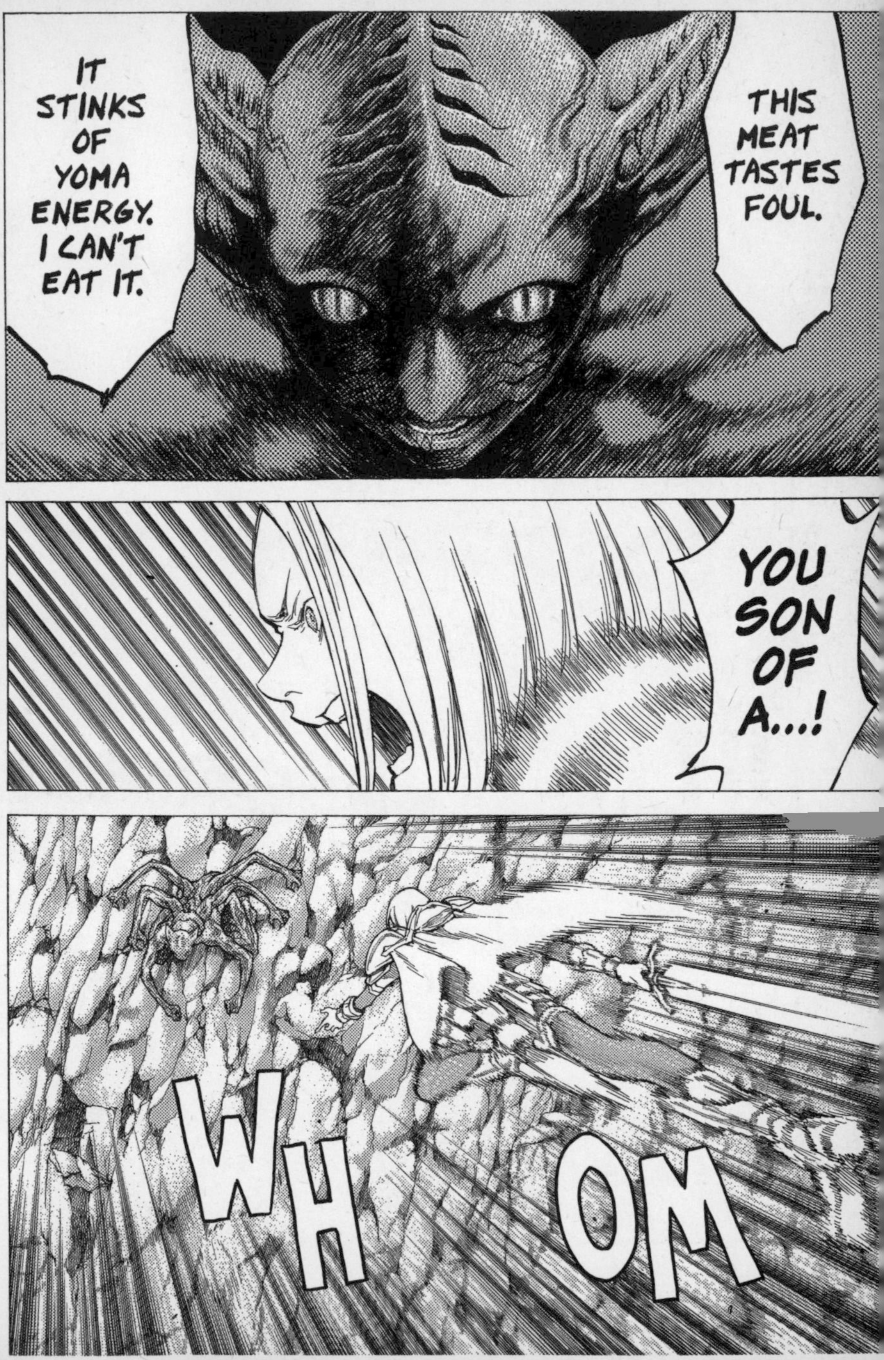
THIS MEAT TASTES FOUL.
IT STINKS OF YOMA ENERGY. I CAN'T EAT IT.
YOU SON OF A...!
WH OM

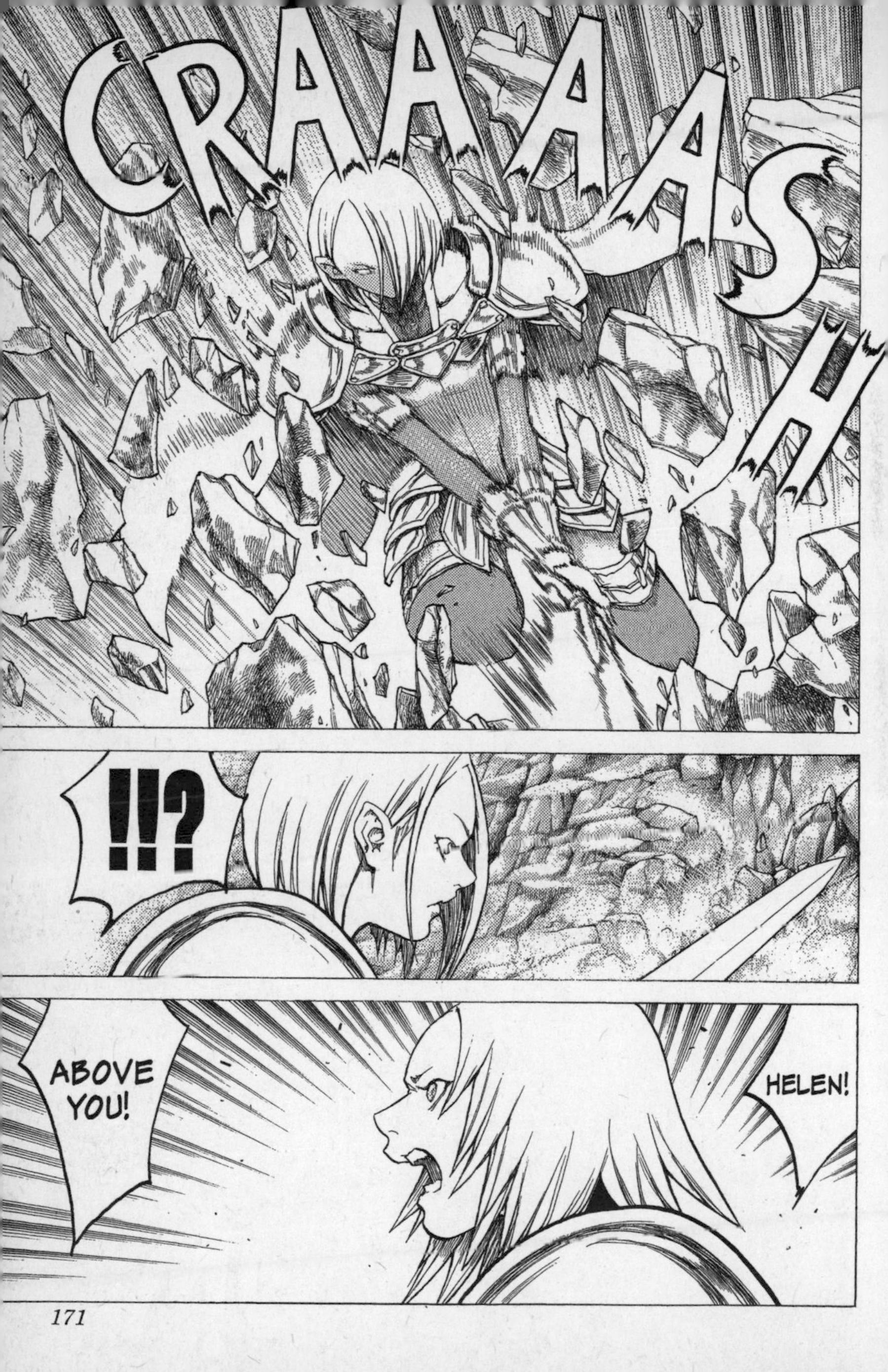
CRAAAASH
!!?
HELEN!
ABOVE YOU!

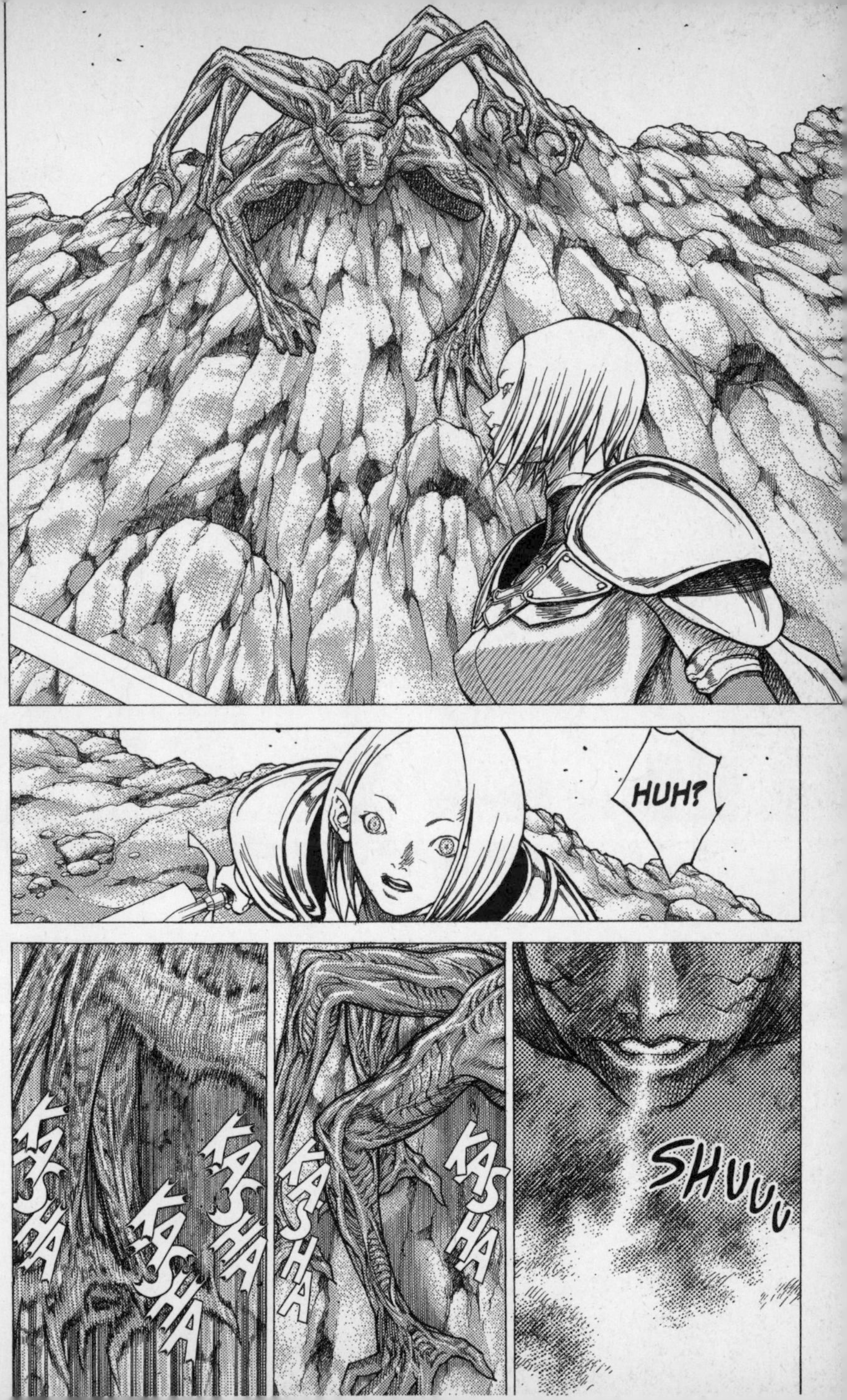
HUH?
SHUUU
KASHA
KASHA
KASHA
KASHA
KASHA

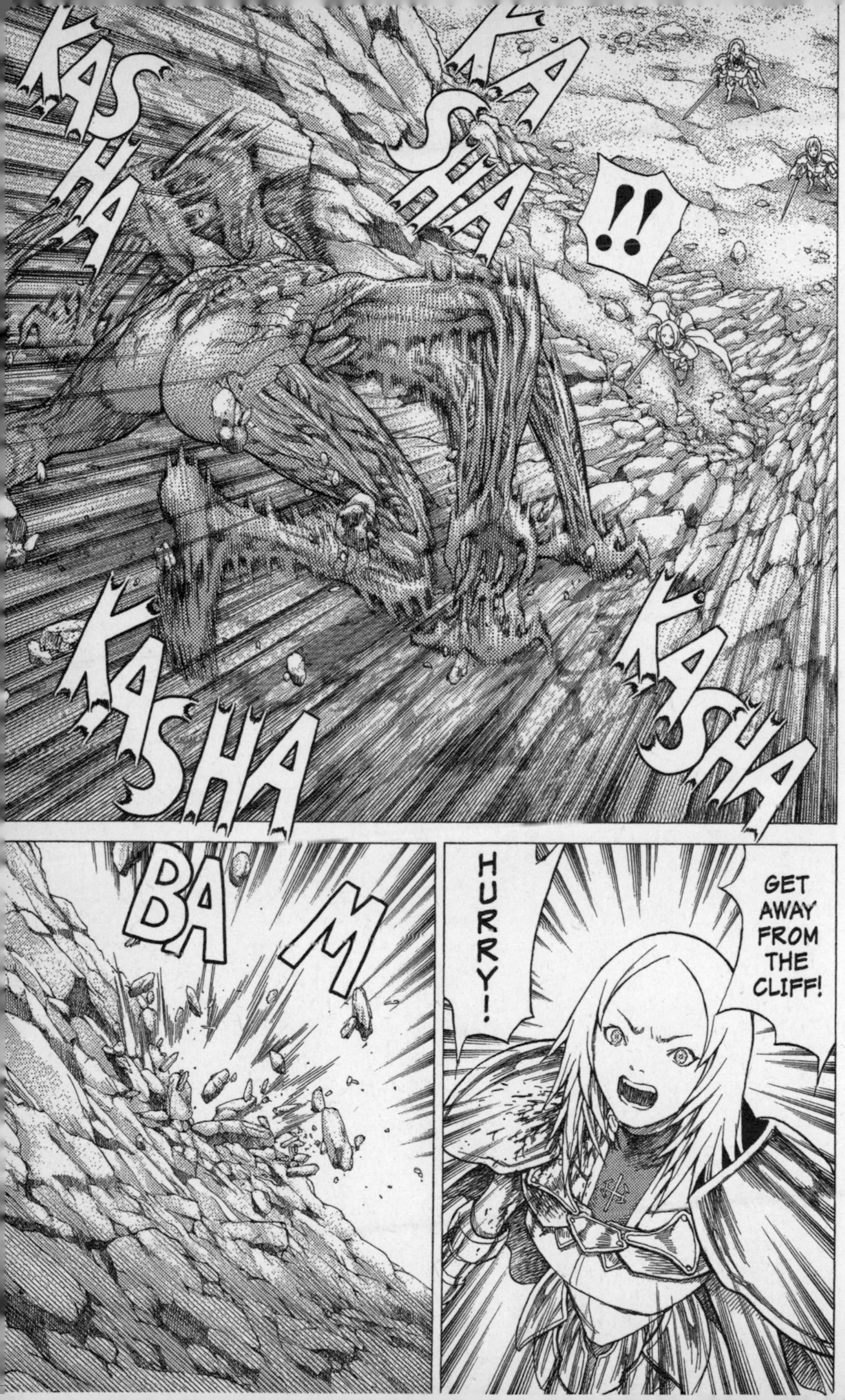
!!
KASHA
KASHA
KASHA
KASHA
GET AWAY FROM THE CLIFF!
HURRY!
BAM

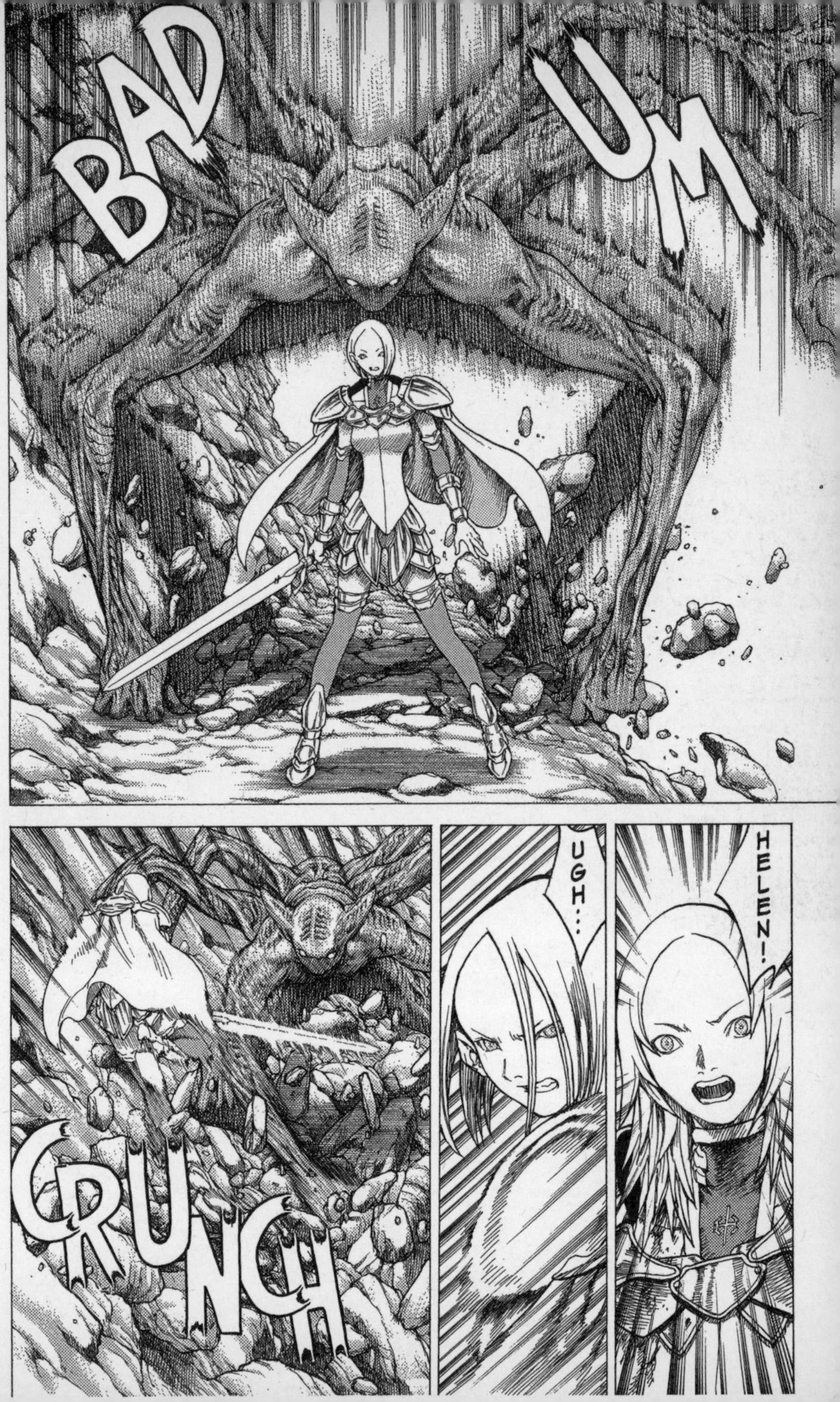
BADUM
HELEN!
UGH...
CRUNCH

READ THIS WAY

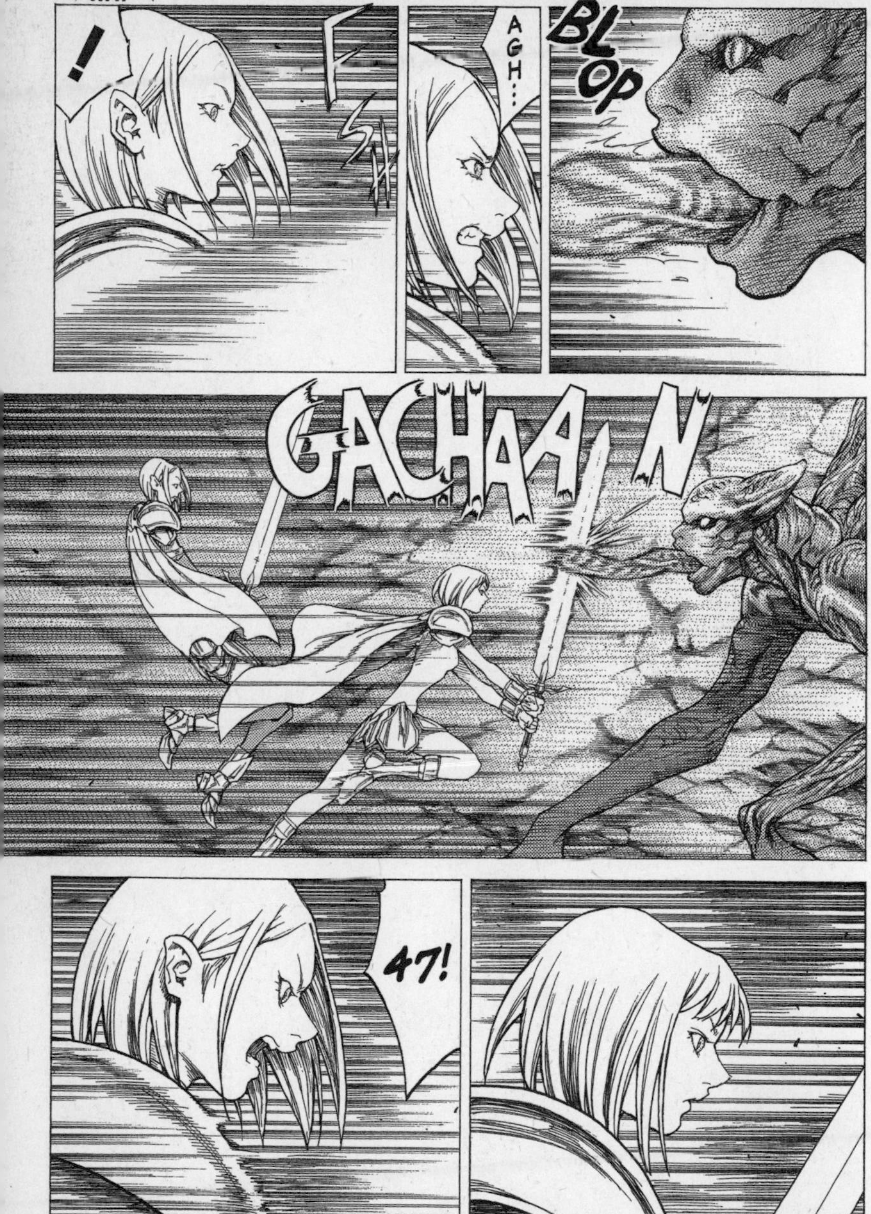
BLOP
AGH...
FSH
!
GACHAAN
47!

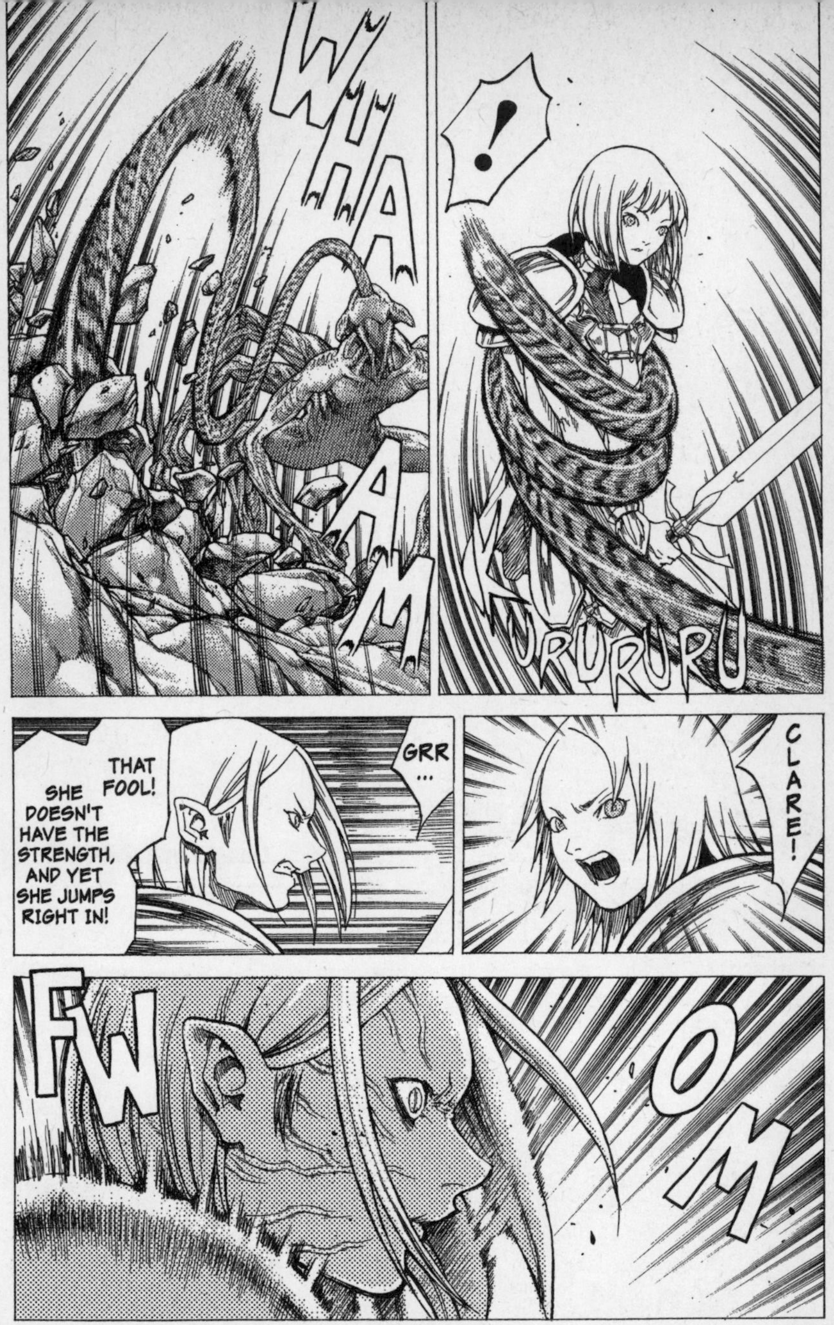
!
KURURURU
WHAM
CLARE!
GRR...
THAT FOOL! SHE DOESN'T HAVE THE STRENGTH, AND YET SHE JUMPS RIGHT IN!
FWOOM

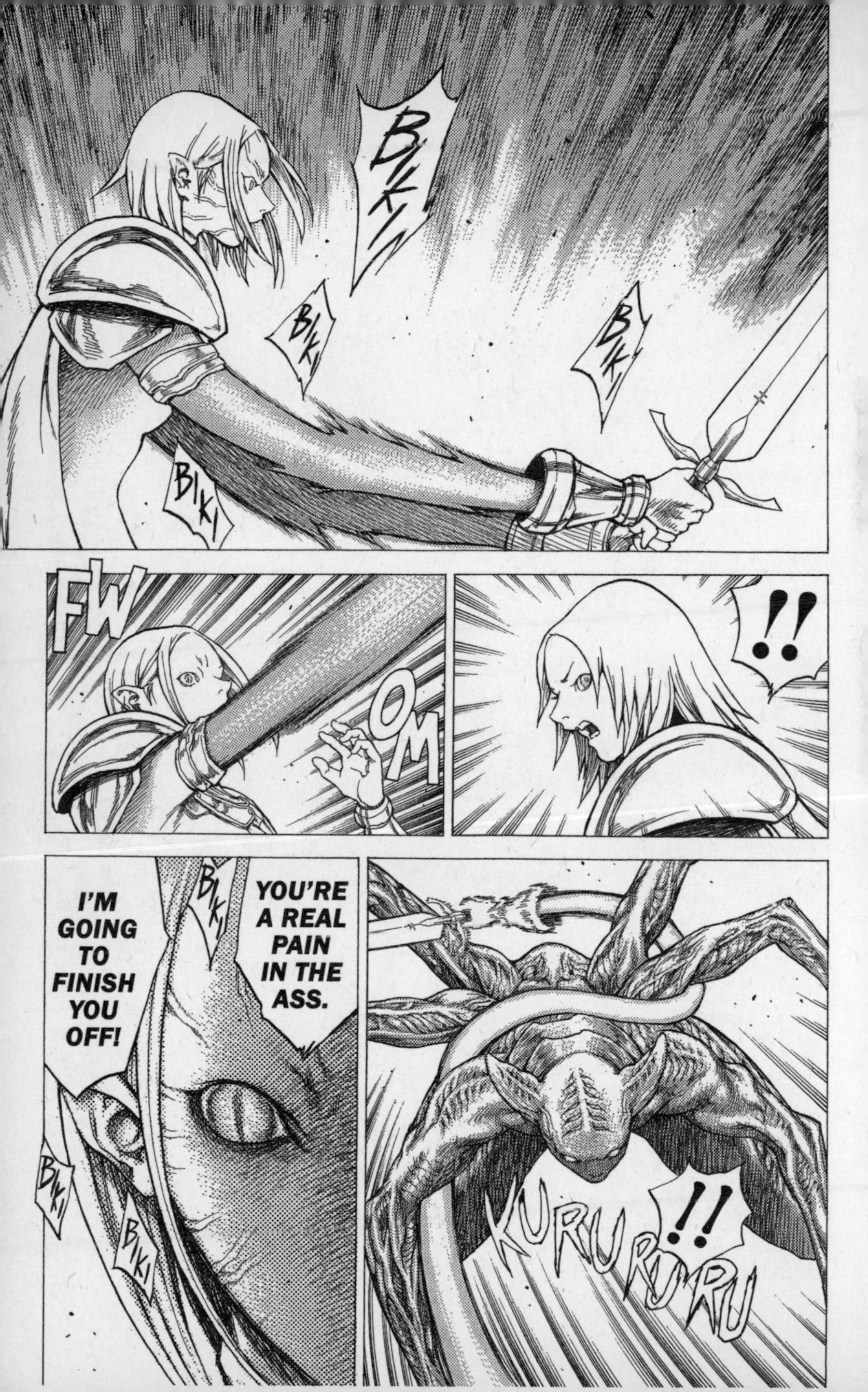
BIKI!
BIKI
BIKI
BIKI
!!
FWOM
!!
KURURURURU
YOU'RE A REAL PAIN IN THE ASS.
I'M GOING TO FINISH YOU OFF!
BIKI
BIKI
BIKI

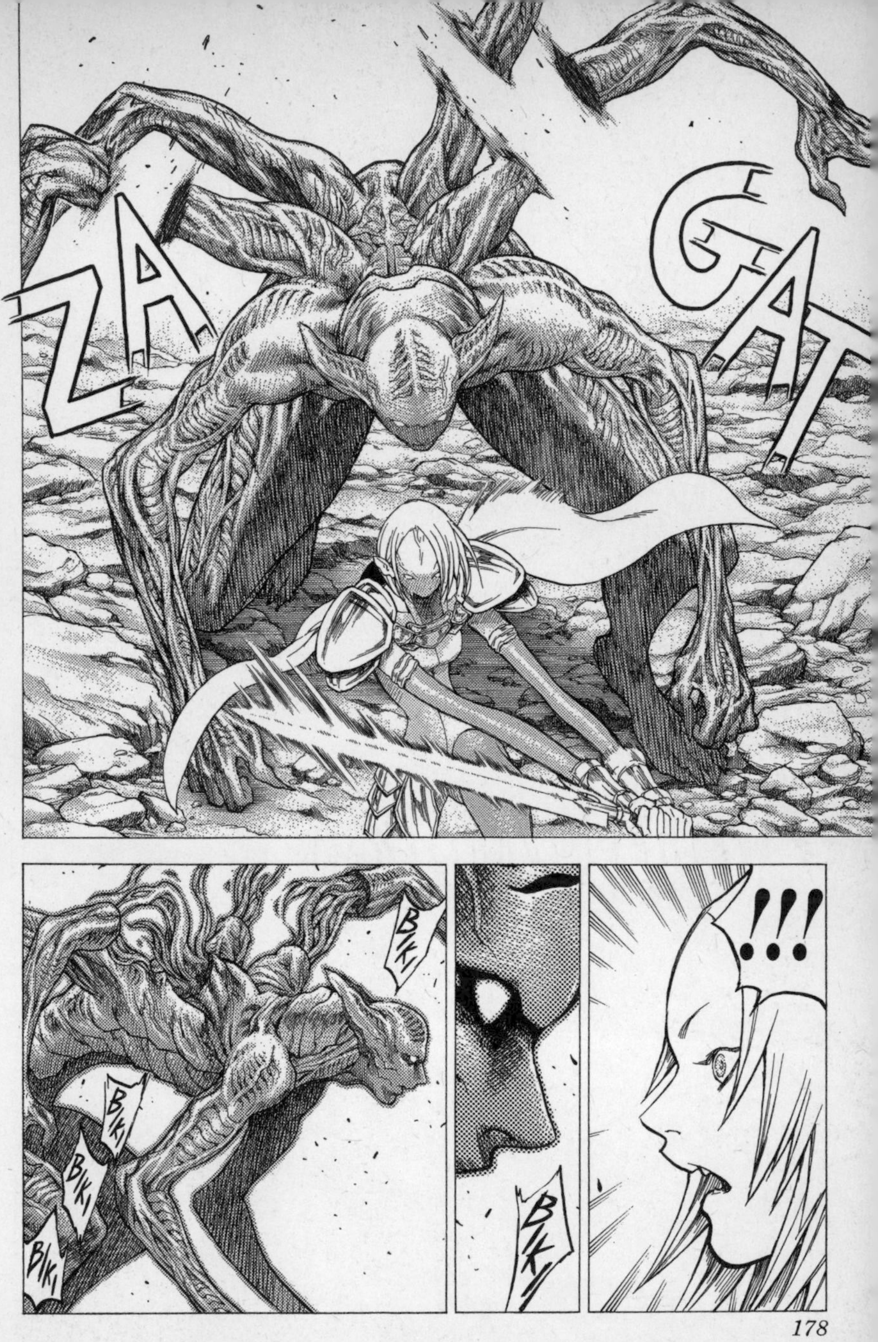
GAT
ZA
!!!
BIKI
BIKI
BIKI
BIKI
BIKI

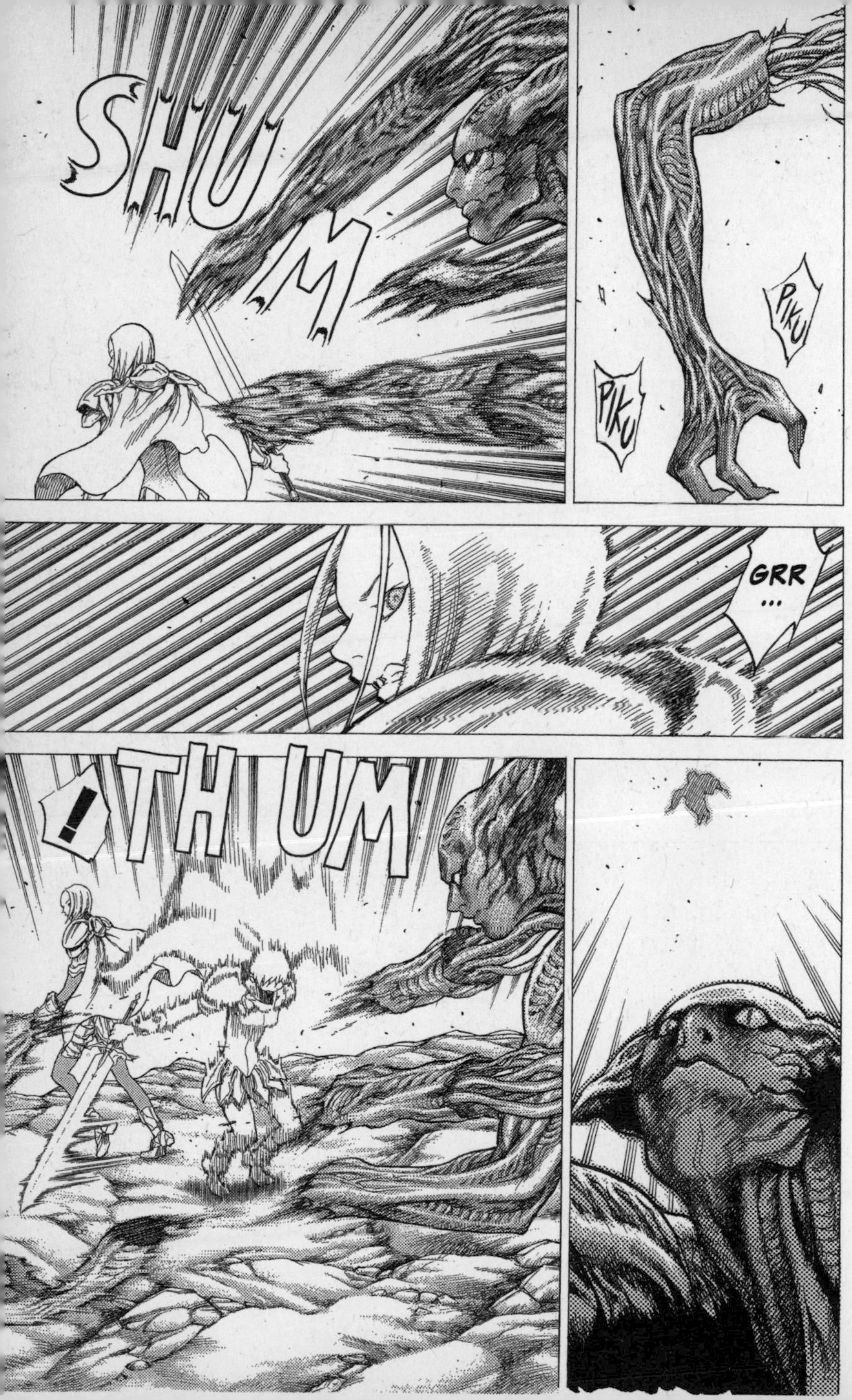
PIKU
PIKU
SHUM
GRR
...
THUM
!

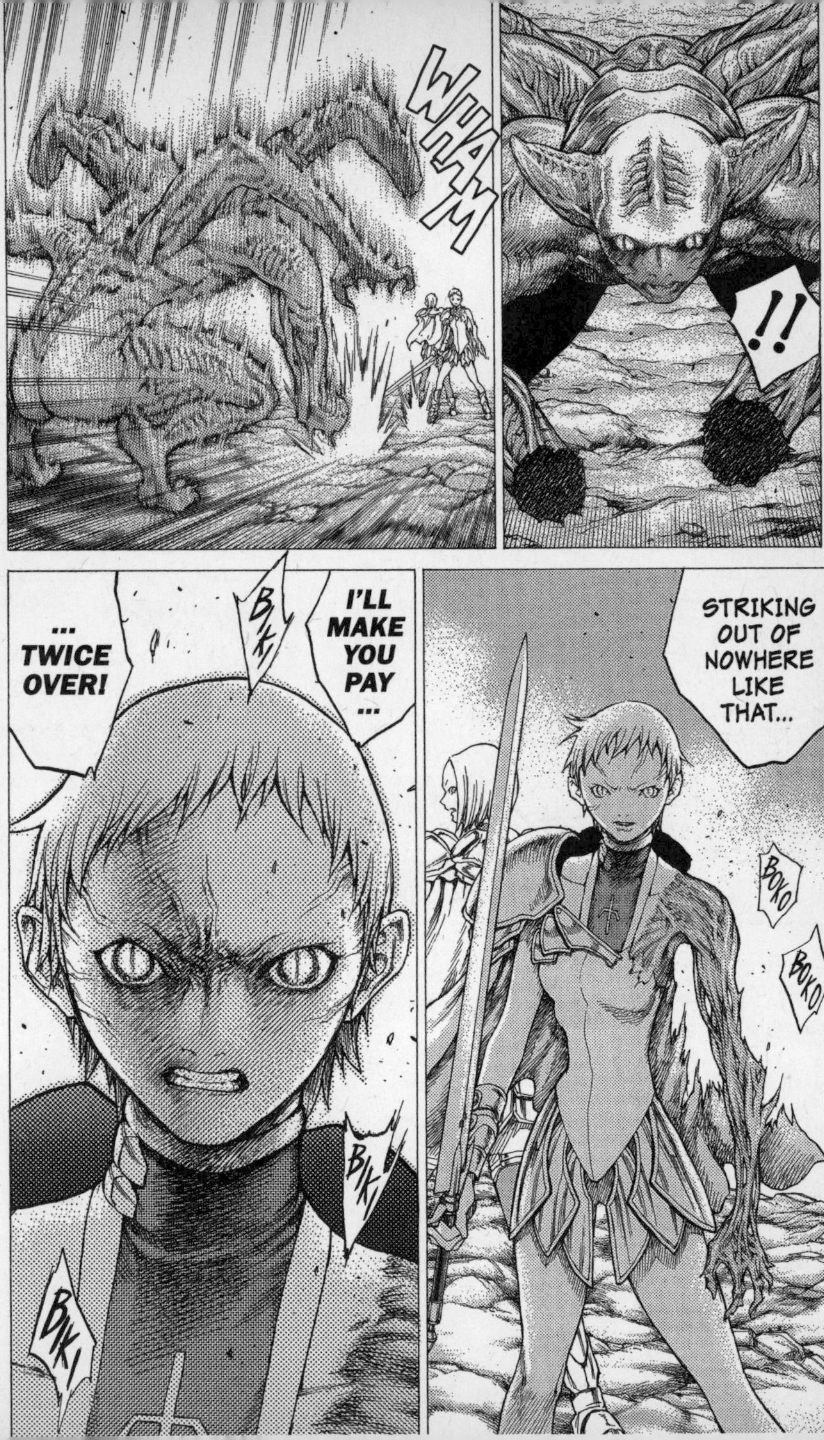
!!
WHAM
STRIKING OUT OF NOWHERE LIKE THAT...
BOKO
BOKO
I'LL MAKE YOU PAY ...
BIKI
... TWICE OVER!
BIKI
BIKI

READ THIS WAY

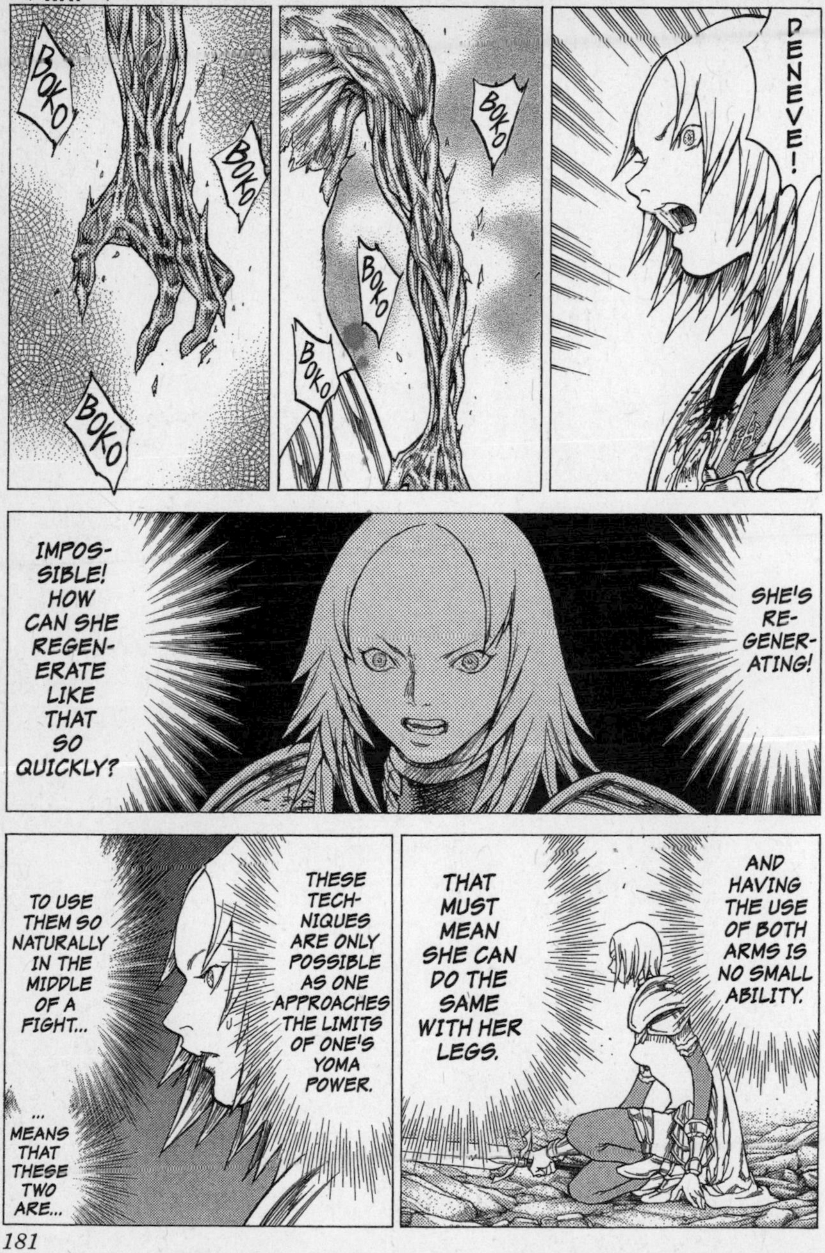

DENEVE!
BOKO
BOKO
BOKO
BOKO
BOKO
BOKO
SHE'S RE-GENER-ATING!
IMPOS-SIBLE! HOW CAN SHE REGEN-ERATE LIKE THAT SO QUICKLY?
AND HAVING THE USE OF BOTH ARMS IS NO SMALL ABILITY.
THAT MUST MEAN SHE CAN DO THE SAME WITH HER LEGS.
THESE TECH-NIQUES ARE ONLY POSSIBLE AS ONE APPROACHES THE LIMITS OF ONE'S YOMA POWER.
TO USE THEM SO NATURALLY IN THE MIDDLE OF A FIGHT...
...MEANS THAT THESE TWO ARE...

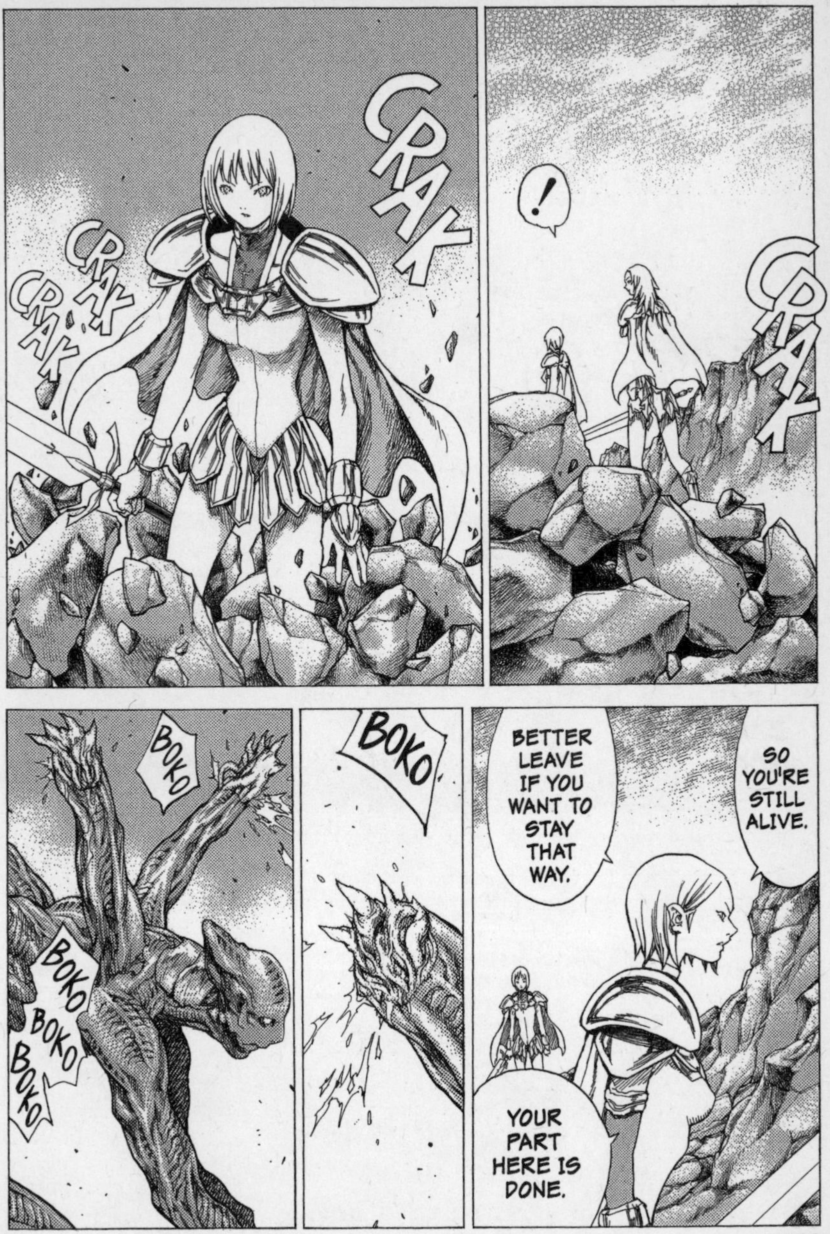
!
CRAK
CRAK
CRAK
CRAK
SO YOU'RE STILL ALIVE.
BETTER LEAVE IF YOU WANT TO STAY THAT WAY.
YOUR PART HERE IS DONE.
BOKO
BOKO
BOKO
BOKO
BOKO

READ THIS WAY

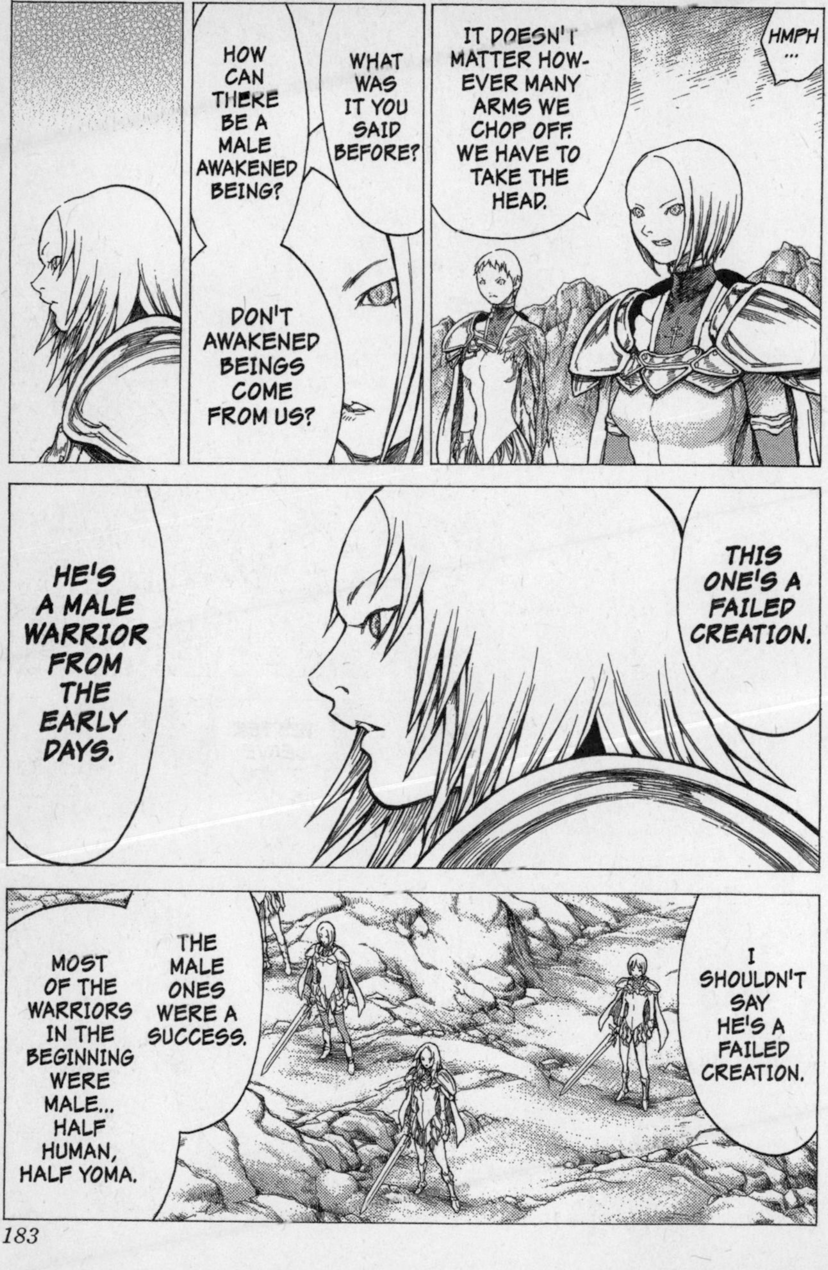
HMPH ...
IT DOESN'T MATTER HOW-EVER MANY ARMS WE CHOP OFF. WE HAVE TO TAKE THE HEAD.
WHAT WAS IT YOU SAID BEFORE?
HOW CAN THERE BE A MALE AWAKENED BEING?
DON'T AWAKENED BEINGS COME FROM US?
THIS ONE'S A FAILED CREATION.
HE'S A MALE WARRIOR FROM THE EARLY DAYS.
I SHOULDN'T SAY HE'S A FAILED CREATION.
THE MALE ONES WERE A SUCCESS.
MOST OF THE WARRIORS IN THE BEGINNING WERE MALE... HALF HUMAN, HALF YOMA.

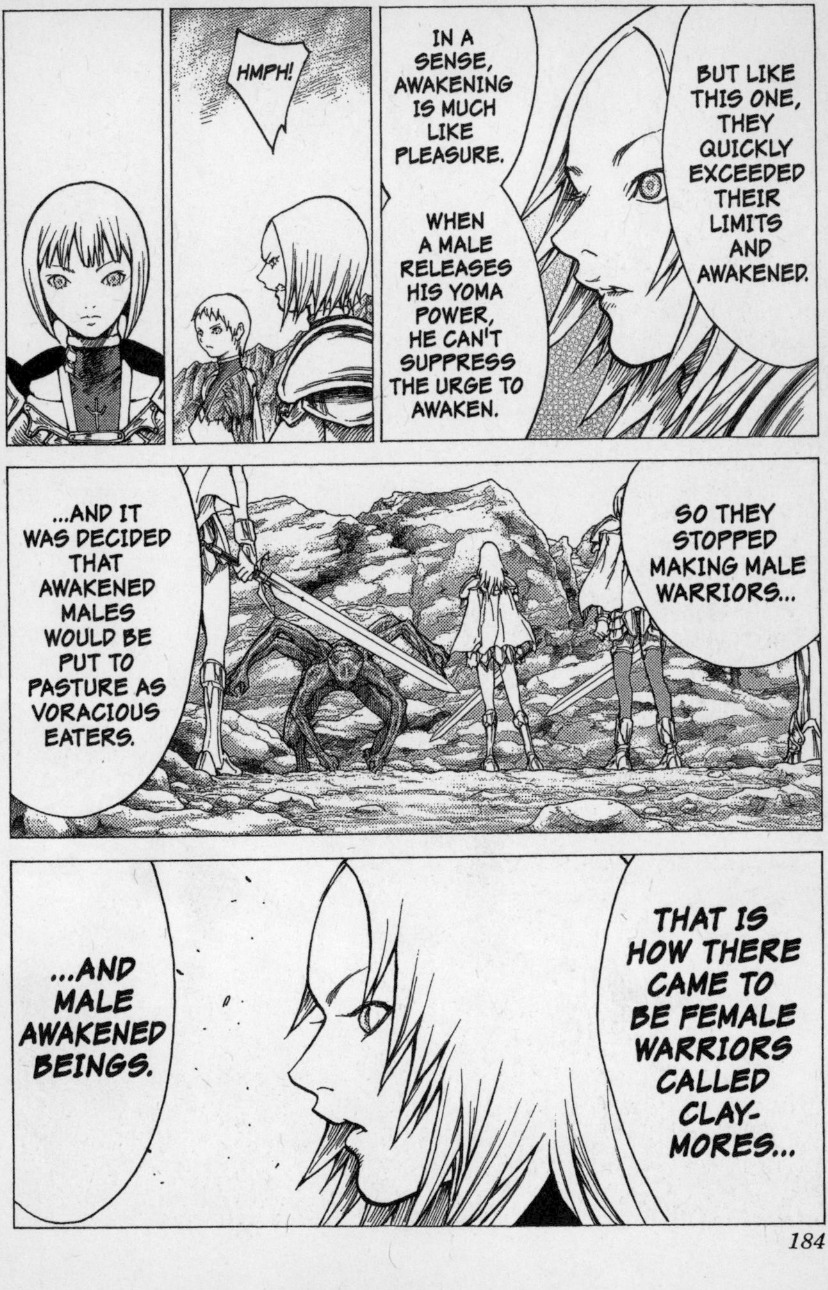
BUT LIKE THIS ONE, THEY QUICKLY EXCEEDED THEIR LIMITS AND AWAKENED.
IN A SENSE, AWAKENING IS MUCH LIKE PLEASURE.
WHEN A MALE RELEASES HIS YOMA POWER, HE CAN'T SUPPRESS THE URGE TO AWAKEN.
HMPH!
SO THEY STOPPED MAKING MALE WARRIORS...
...AND IT WAS DECIDED THAT AWAKENED MALES WOULD BE PUT TO PASTURE AS VORACIOUS EATERS.
THAT IS HOW THERE CAME TO BE FEMALE WARRIORS CALLED CLAY-MORES...
...AND MALE AWAKENED BEINGS.

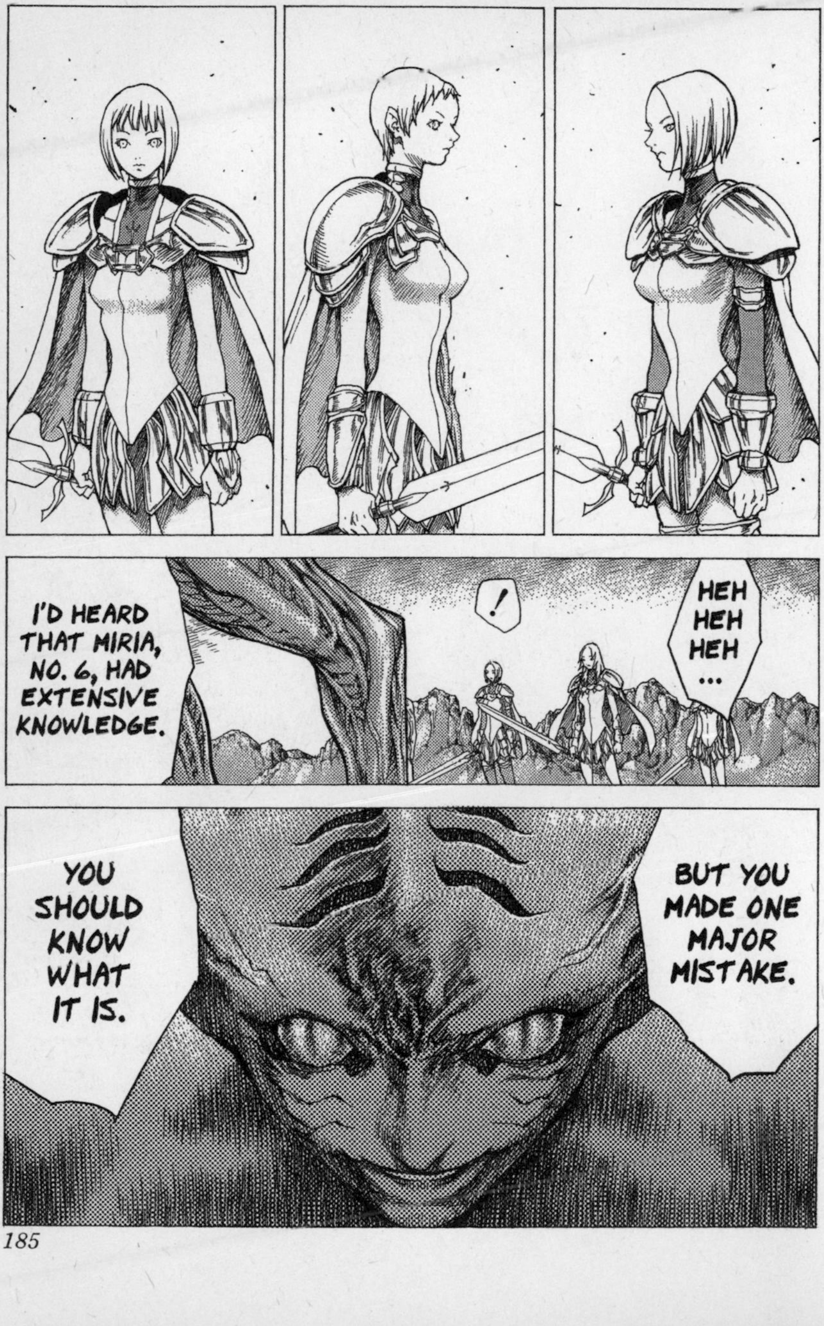
HEH HEH HEH ...
!
I'D HEARD THAT MIRIA, NO. 6, HAD EXTENSIVE KNOWLEDGE.
BUT YOU MADE ONE MAJOR MISTAKE.
YOU SHOULD KNOW WHAT IT IS.

HUH?

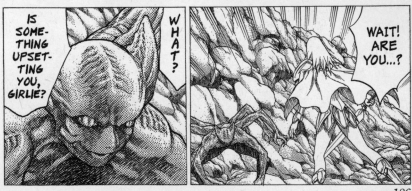

IS SOME-THING UPSET-TING YOU, GIRLIE?

WHAT?

WAIT! ARE YOU...?

THIS GROUP ...

THAT'S IT!

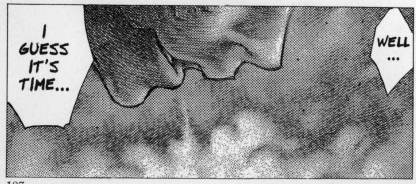

I GUESS IT'S TIME...

WELL ...

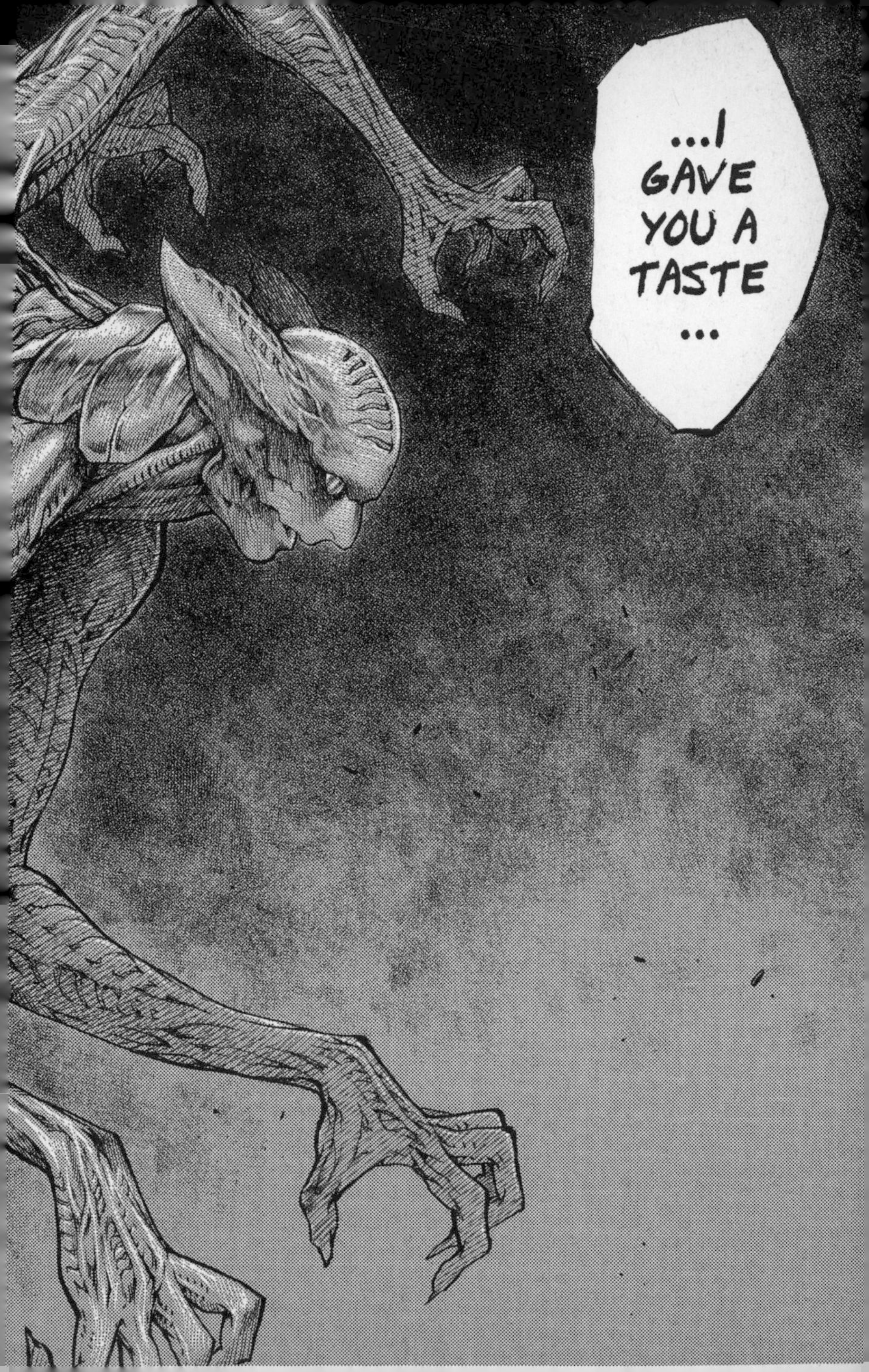
...I GAVE YOU A TASTE ...

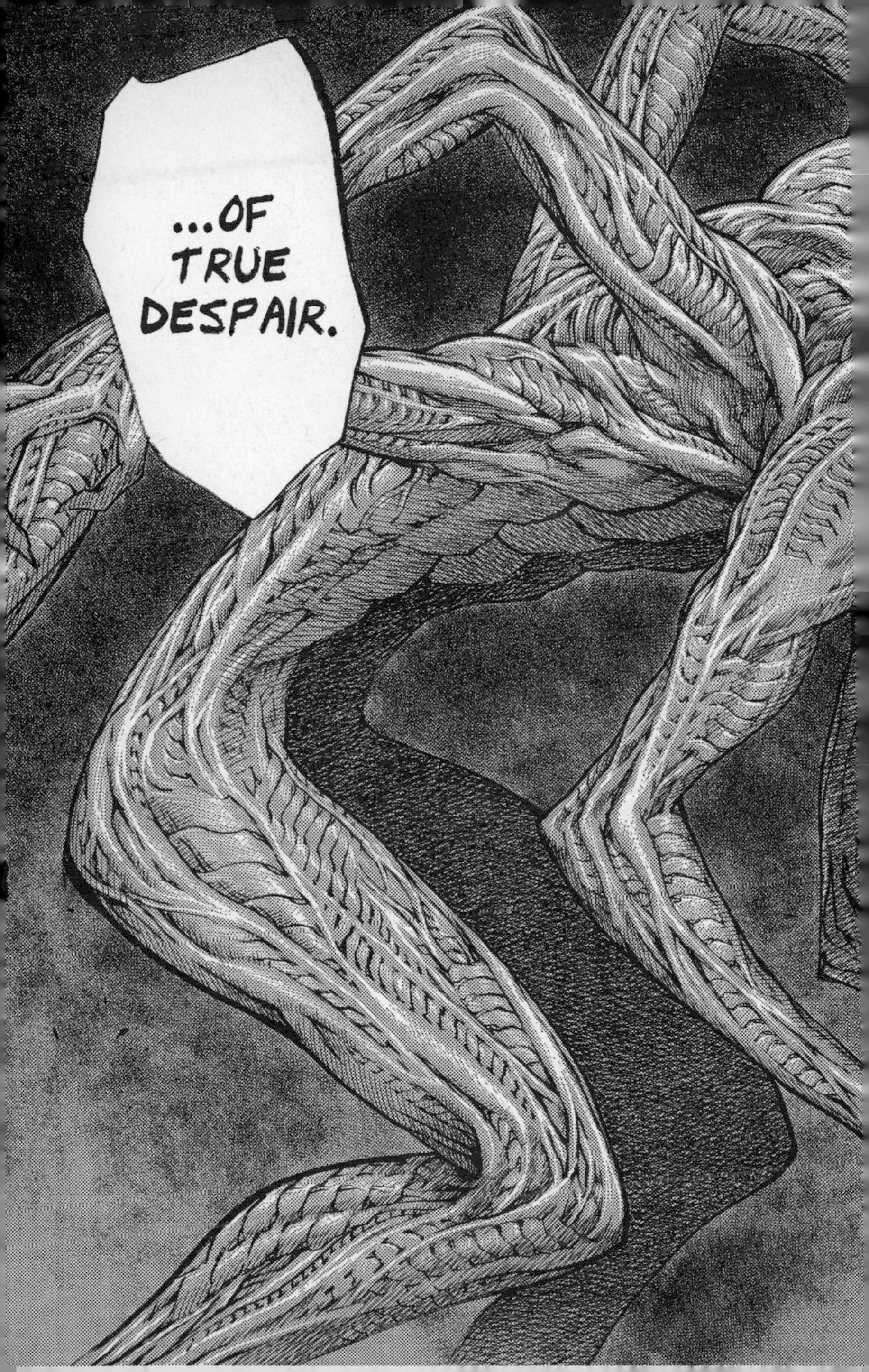
...OF TRUE DESPAIR.

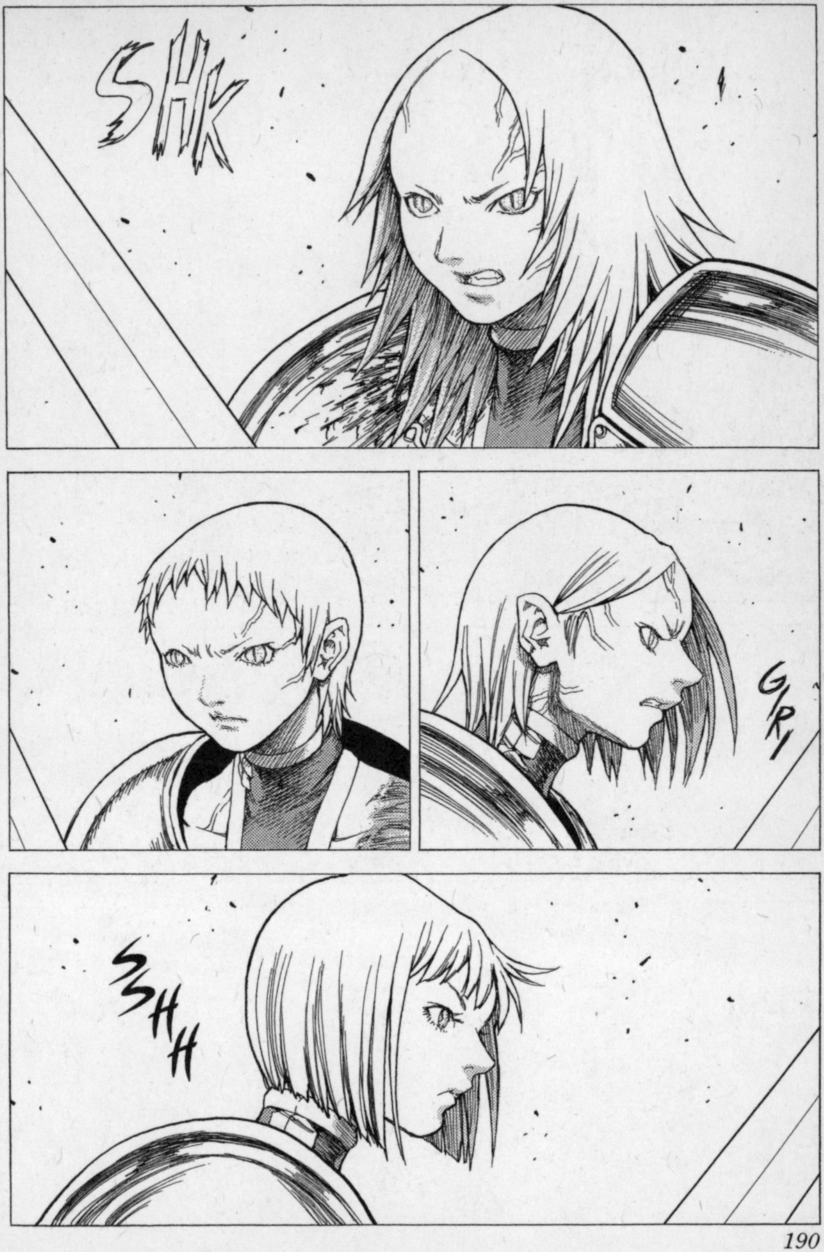
SHK
GRI
SHH

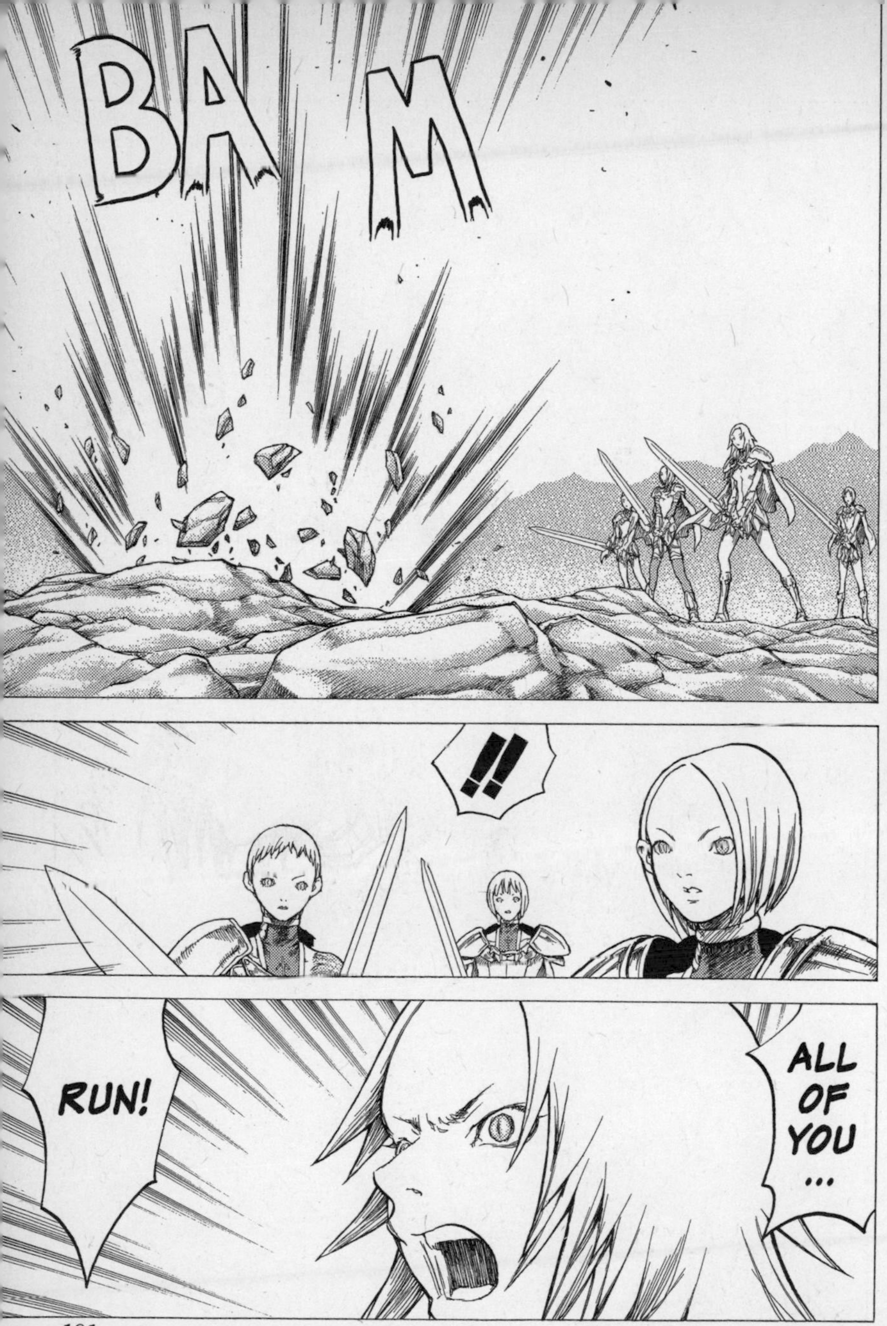
BAM
!!
ALL OF YOU ...
RUN!

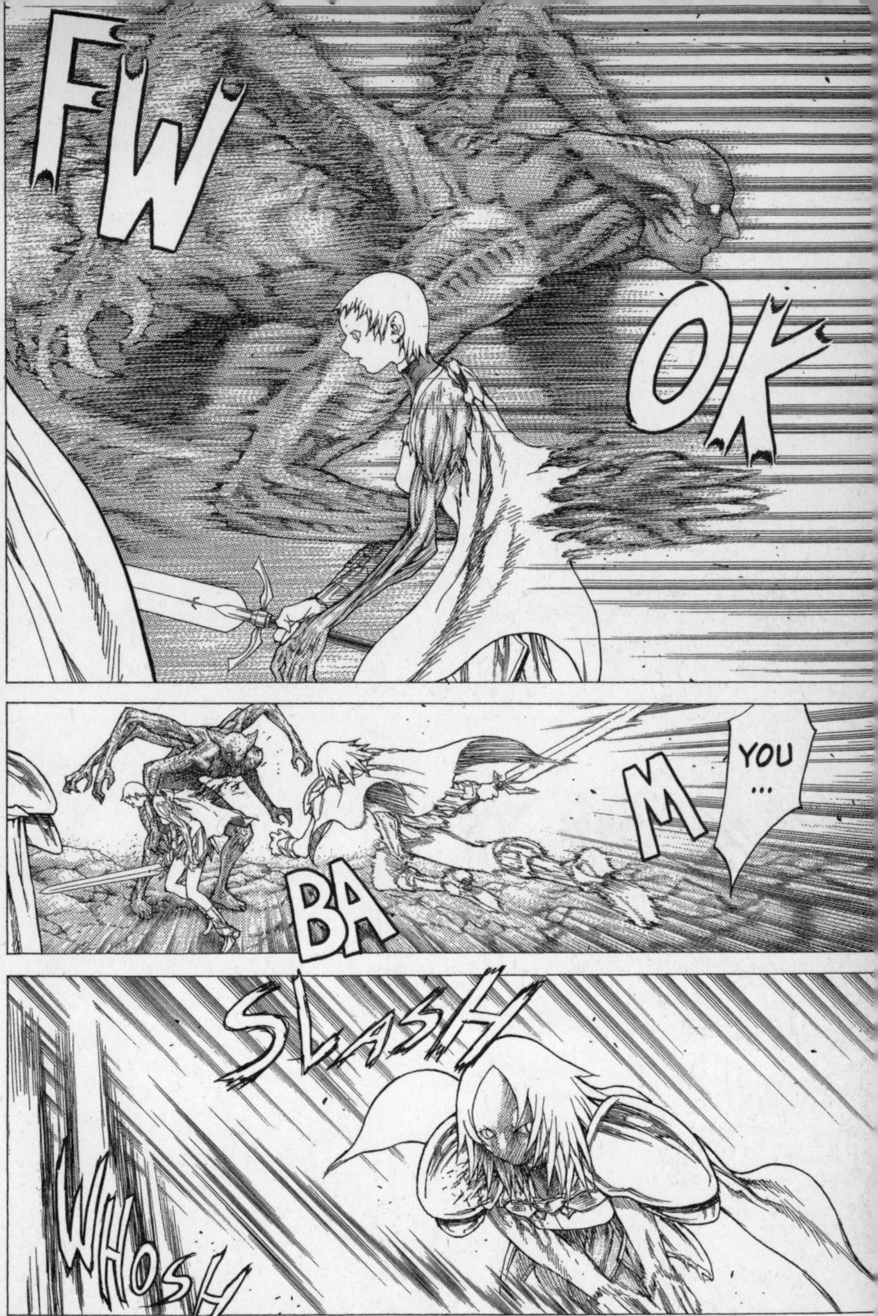
FW
OK
YOU ...
BA
M
SLASH
WHOSH

READ THIS WAY

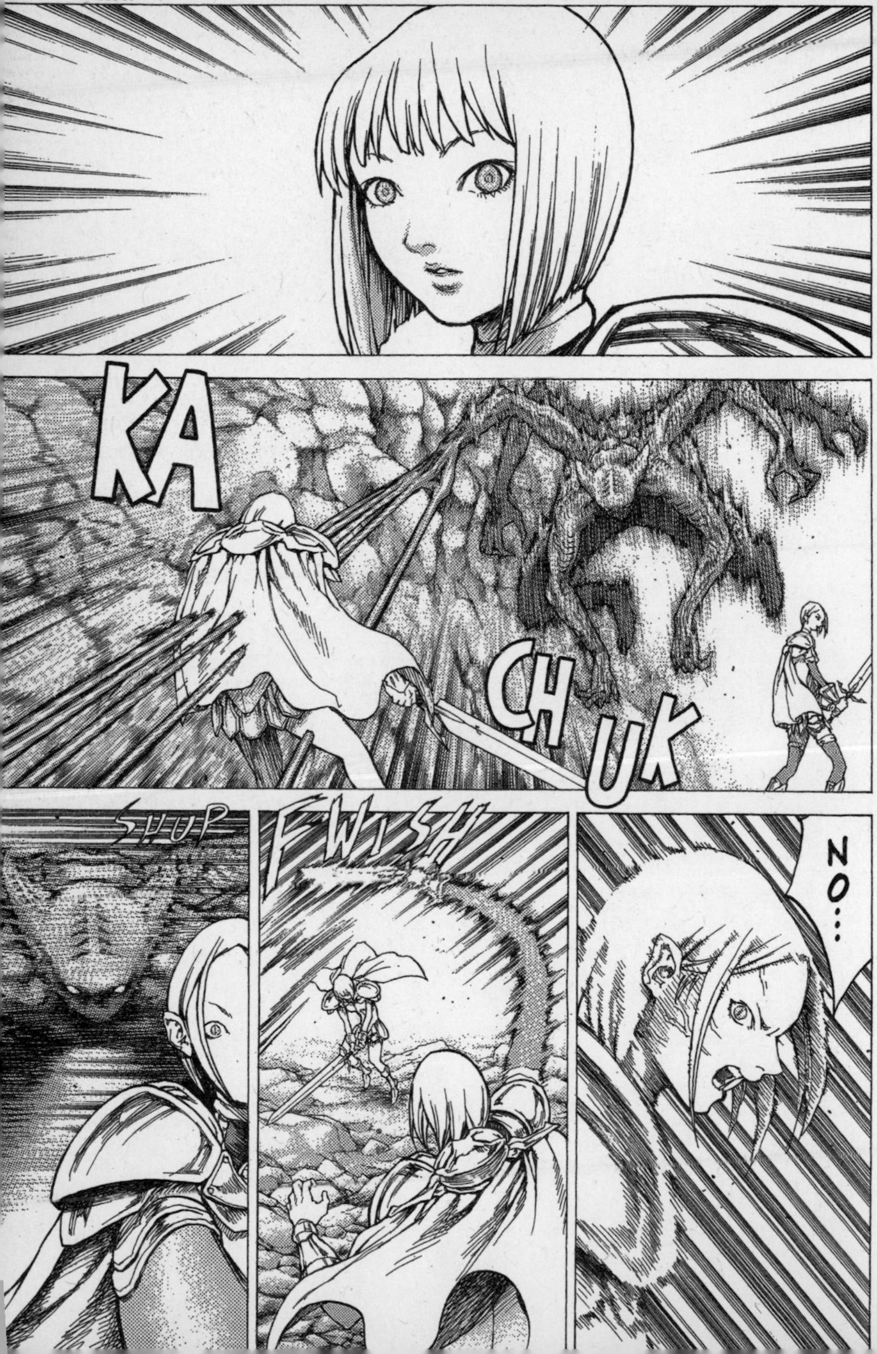
KA
CHUK
NO...
FWISH
SUUP

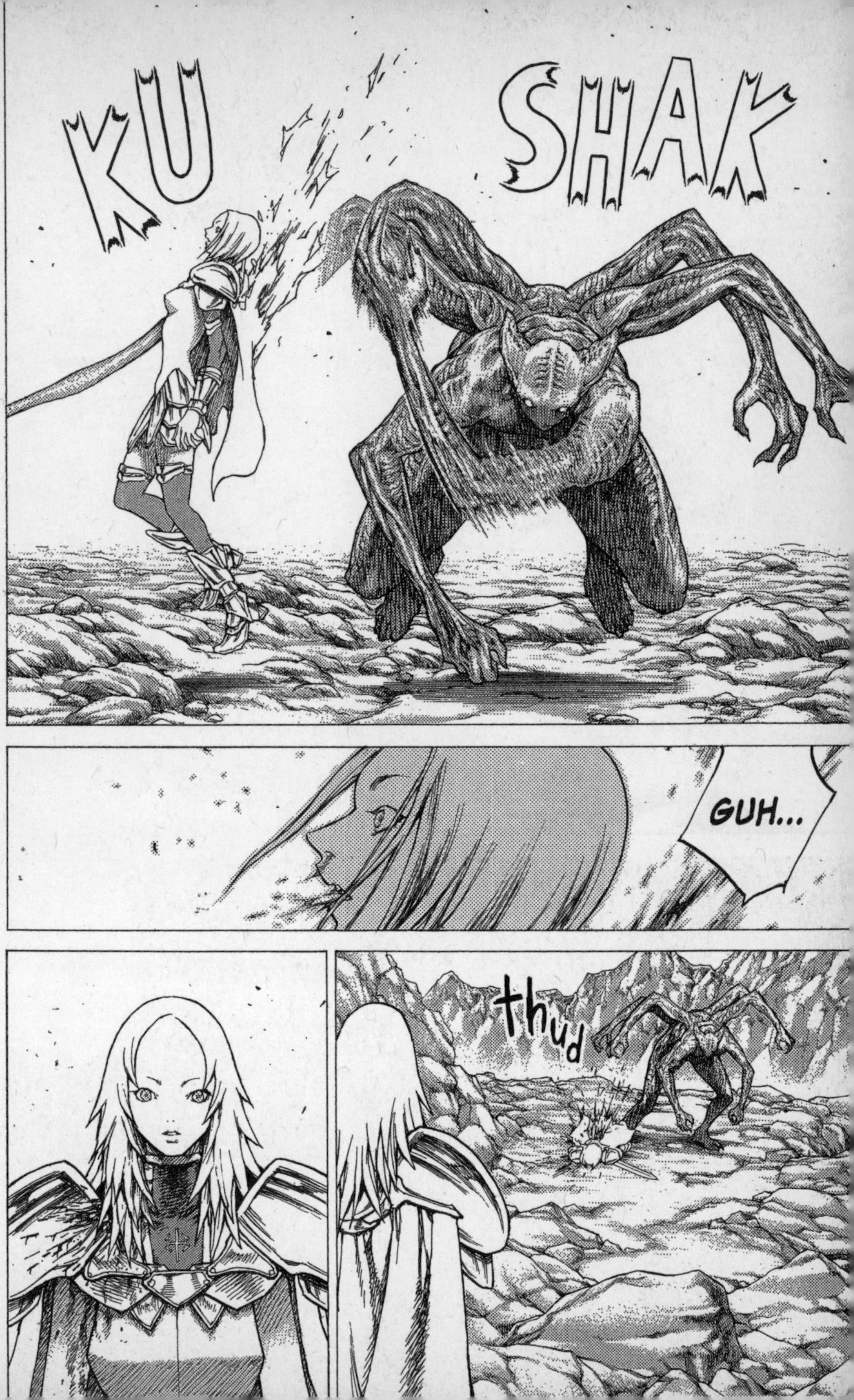
KU SHAK
GUH...
thud

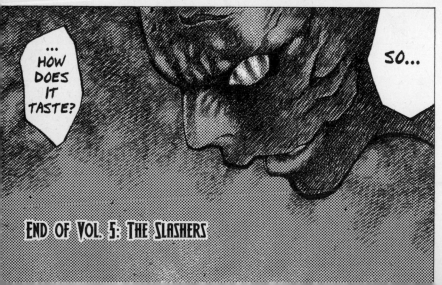

...HOW DOES IT TASTE?

SO...

END OF VOL. 5: THE SLASHERS

IN THE NEXT VOLUME

The battle with the male Awakened Being intensifies, forcing the Claymores to exhaust their strength in hopes of slaying the creature. The fate of the group ultimately rests with Clare, who is on the verge of becoming an Awakened Being herself.

Available in February 2007

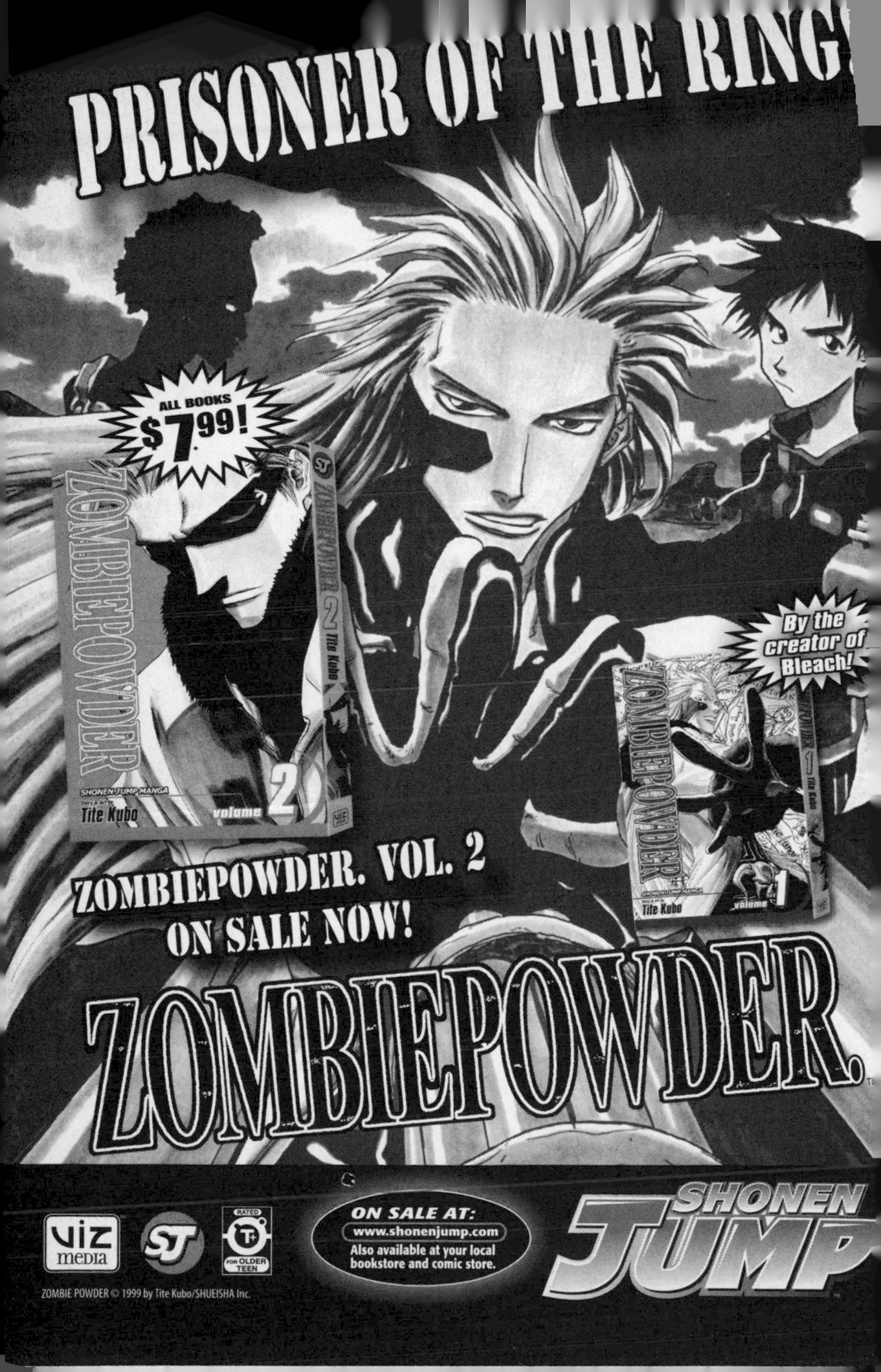
PRISONER OF THE RING
ALL BOOKS $7.99!
ZOMBIEPOWDER
SHONEN JUMP MANGA
Story & Art by Tite Kubo
volume 2
ZOMBIEPOWDER 2 Tite Kubo
By the creator of Bleach!
ZOMBIEPOWDER
SHONEN JUMP MANGA
Story & Art by Tite Kubo
volume 1
ZOMBIEPOWDER. VOL. 2
ON SALE NOW!
ZOMBIEPOWDER.
viz media
SJ
RATED T+ FOR OLDER TEEN
ON SALE AT:
www.shonenjump.com
Also available at your local bookstore and comic store.
SHONEN JUMP
ZOMBIE POWDER © 1999 by Tite Kubo/SHUEISHA Inc.

Tell us what you think about SHONEN JUMP manga!

Our survey is now available online.
Go to: *www.SHONENJUMP.com/mangasurvey*

Help us make our product offering better!

SHONEN JUMP
THE WORLD'S MOST POPULAR MANGA
www.shonenjump.com

SJ ADVANCED

SJ

VIZ media

BLEACH © 2001 by Tite Kubo/SHUEISHA Inc. NARUTO © 1999 by Masashi Kishimoto/SHUEISHA Inc.
DEATH NOTE © 2003 by Tsugumi Ohba, Takeshi Obata/SHUEISHA Inc. ONE PIECE © 1997 by Eiichiro Oda/SHUEISHA Inc.

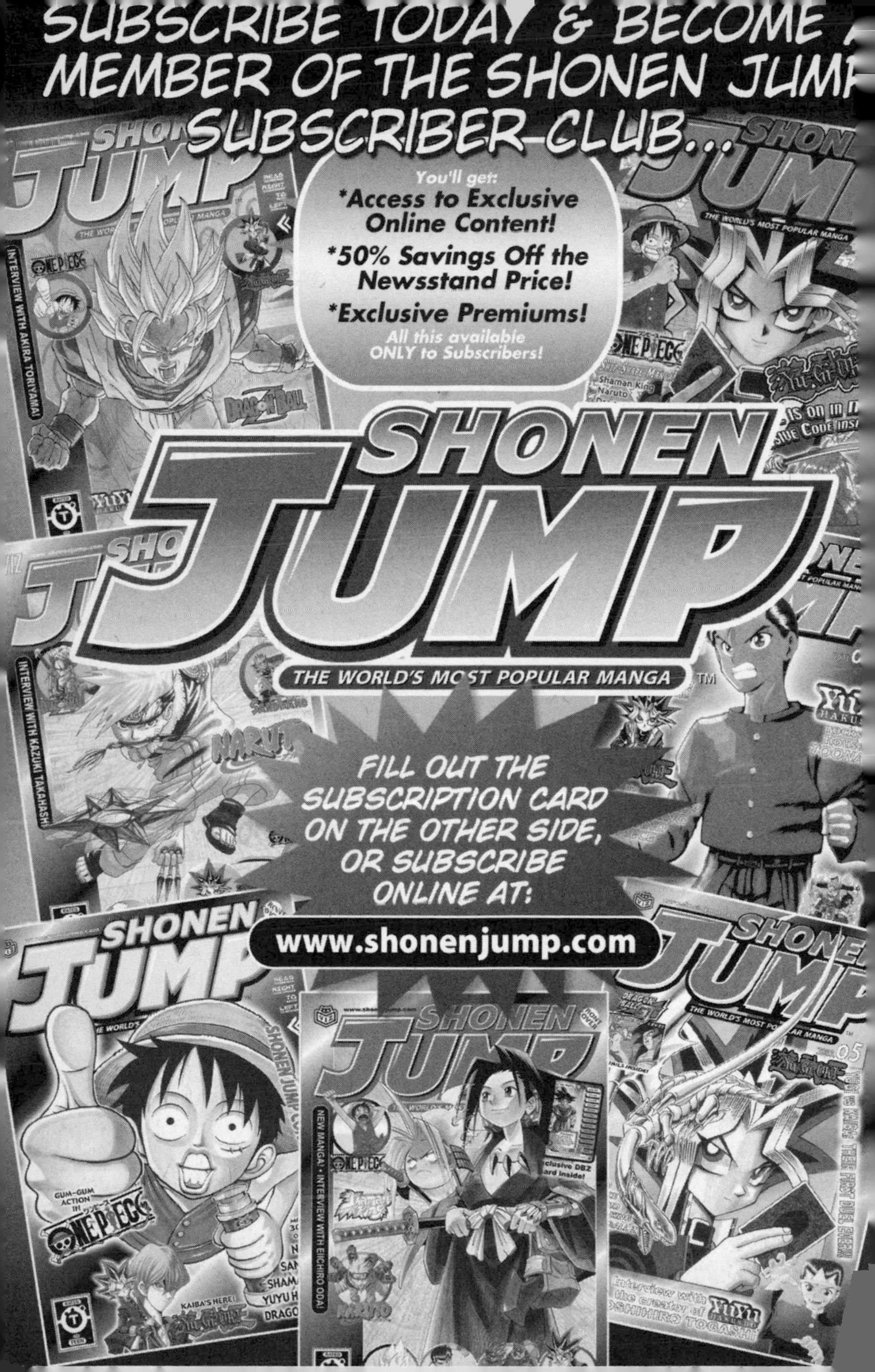
SUBSCRIBE TODAY & BECOME A MEMBER OF THE SHONEN JUMP SUBSCRIBER CLUB...
You'll get:
*Access to Exclusive Online Content!
*50% Savings Off the Newsstand Price!
*Exclusive Premiums!
All this available ONLY to Subscribers!
SHONEN JUMP
THE WORLD'S MOST POPULAR MANGA
FILL OUT THE SUBSCRIPTION CARD ON THE OTHER SIDE, OR SUBSCRIBE ONLINE AT:
www.shonenjump.com

Save 50% off the newsstand price!

THE WORLD'S MOST POPULAR MANGA

SUBSCRIBE TODAY and SAVE 50% OFF the cover price PLUS enjoy all the benefits of the SHONEN JUMP SUBSCRIBER CLUB, exclusive online content & special gifts ONLY AVAILABLE to SUBSCRIBERS!

☑ **YES!** Please enter my 1 year subscription (12 issues) to *SHONEN JUMP* at the INCREDIBLY LOW SUBSCRIPTION RATE of $29.95 and sign me up for the SHONEN JUMP Subscriber Club!

Only $29⁹⁵!

NAME

ADDRESS

CITY   STATE   ZIP

E-MAIL ADDRESS

☐ MY CHECK IS ENCLOSED   ☐ BILL ME LATER

CREDIT CARD: ☐ VISA   ☐ MASTERCARD

ACCOUNT #   EXP. DATE

SIGNATURE

CLIP AND MAIL TO ➤ SHONEN JUMP
Subscriptions Service Dept.
P.O. Box 515
Mount Morris, IL 61054-0515

Make checks payable to: **SHONEN JUMP.**
Canada add US $12. No foreign orders. Allow 6-8 weeks for delivery.

P6SJGN   YU-GI-OH! © 1996 by Kazuki Takahashi / SHUEISHA Inc.